KU-208-882

POLITICS, PRODUCTS, AND MARKETS

Exploring Political Consumerism Past and Present

edited by
Michele Micheletti
Andreas Follesdal
Dietlind Stolle

Transaction Publishers
New Brunswick (U.S.A.) and London (U.K.)

Third paperback printing 2009

Copyright © 2004 by Transaction Publishers, New Brunswick, New Jersey.

All rights reserved under International and Pan-American Copyright Conventions. No part of this book may be reproduced or transmitted in any form or by any means, electronic or mechanical, including photocopy, recording, or any information storage and retrieval system, without prior permission in writing from the publisher. All inquiries should be addressed to Transaction Publishers, Rutgers — The State University, New Brunswick, New Jersey 08903. www.transactionpub.com

This book is printed on acid-free paper that meets the American National Standard for Permanence of Paper for Printed Library Materials.

Library of Congress Number: 2003053135
ISBN: 978-0-7658-0200-2 (cloth); 978-1-4128-0552-0 (paper)
Printed in the United States of America

Library of Congress Cataloging-in-Publication Data

Politics. products, and markets : exploring political consumerism past and
    present I Michele Micheletti, Andreas Follesdal, and Dietlind Stolle, editors.
        p. cm.
    Includes bibliographical references and index.
    ISBN 978-1-4128-0552-0 (paper : alk. paper)
        1. Politics, Practical — Congresses. 2. Political ethics — Congresses. 3.
    Consumption (Economics) — Political aspects — Congresses. 4. Consumer
    behavior — Moral and ethical aspects — Congresses. I. Micheletti, Michele.
    II. Follesdal, Andreas. III. Stolle, Dietlind, 1967-

JF799.P6395 2003
324—dc21   2003053135

POLITICS, PRODUCTS, AND MARKETS

Contents

Foreword

The book that you are about to read is the first general study of the phenomenon of political consumerism, the use of market action as an arena for politics, and consumer choice as a political tool. Its basis is conference papers for the International Seminar on Political Consumerism hosted by The City University of Stockholm, Sweden, in May-June 2001. A variety of themes were announced in the call for papers for the international seminar, which encouraged scholars to focus on an emerging theme in the social sciences that concerns the use of market action by individuals and institutions to create trust, control uncertainty, and solve common problems. In particular, I sought papers that discussed the ethical and global components of political consumerism as well as its historical roots and role in politics. Scholars investigating the institutional design of labeling schemes were approached specifically. During the four intense days of seminar discussion we penetrated the phenomenon of political consumerism normatively, theoretically, empirically, and historically. All in all we were twenty-five scholars representing eleven disciplines (political science, sociology, history, social psychology, business studies, communication, information technology, culture studies, history of ideas, philosophy, and policy studies) and eight countries (Denmark, France, Germany, Great Britain, India, Norway, Sweden, and the United States).

The cross-disciplinary and multicultural setting of the International Seminar on Political Consumerism proved to be ideal for the exchange of ideas on a common area of research. The papers on different countries and time periods and from different academic disciplines showed the breadth and richness of the phenomenon for scholarly research. Our historian colleagues reminded us that political consumerism is not a new phenomenon. Their good command of history urged all of us to consider and identify eventual differences between older and newer forms of political consumerism. Interestingly enough, the participants agreed generally on how political consumerism should be interpreted. We could unite on basic criteria for evaluating the relationship of political consumerism and democracy.

This volume includes heavily edited versions of fourteen papers presented at the international seminar. All contributions represent original research by scholars who have studied political consumerism in depth. The authors investigate different cases from history and contemporary times as well as discuss their theoretical and philosophical significance. They explain aspects of political consumerism, test hypotheses, understand it as a phenomenon, argue its normative aspects, point to its ethical shortcomings, and tell stories of its use. As such, the chapters employ the variety of scholarly approaches that are available for the study of political, economic, and social phenomena.

For me, the International Seminar on Political Consumerism as well as the editorship of this anthology together with two very competent social scientists, Andreas Follesdal and Dietlind Stolle, have been highly rewarding intellectual experiences. A network of political consumerist scholars has been established and joint research projects have evolved from our seminar discussions. I want to thank everyone who participated in the seminar for making it successful and enjoyable. The City University of Stockholm deserves special thanks for hosting and organizing the seminar, which was part of a large research program led by Emil Uddhammar, entitled *Ethics, Virtues, and Social Capital in Sweden,* and financed by Axel and Margaret Ax:son Johnson's Foundation. Two people at The City University in particular helped make the first International Seminar on Political Consumerism a pleasurable experience for all involved. They are Per Dahl and Agnes Svensson. I want also to thank Nils Karlson, president of The City University, for his help in completing this anthology according to plans and Kristina von Unge for editorial assistance.

Michele Micheletti
Stockholm
October 2002

Introduction

Michele Micheletti, Andreas Follesdal, and Dietlind Stolle

The Market as a Site of Politics

Spectacular events such as the international boycott against South Africa, the campaign against Nestlé, the student protest against Nike as well as the violent demonstrations in connection with meetings of the World Trade Organization and G-8 summit call our attention to the role of the global market as a site for ethics and citizen action as well as the phenomenon of political consumerism. Together with the loud protests surrounding international meetings and the quiet institutionalization of eco-labeling and forest stewardship certification, these examples show how citizens and institutions voice concern about the present global role of business. What is striking is how neo-liberal capitalism has triggered an economic globalization that heightens the influence of transnational corporations over our lives and our common future. Political consumerism acknowledges this new power of corporations and uses the market as a powerful site for politics. Political consumers respond to corporate policies and products as reflecting, expressing, and promoting political, social, and normative values beyond those of consumer price, taste, and quality of goods. This volume examines closely the roots and contemporary forms of the phenomenon of political consumerism.

The United Nations, Amnesty International, and other international governmental and nongovernmental organizations claim openly that they must rely on market actors to accomplish their goals. UN Secretary-General Kofi Annan explains his decision to sign a global compact with business with the words, "let's choose to unite the powers of markets with the authority of universal ideals" (United Nations 2002). Amnesty International's *Human Rights Guidelines for Companies* urges businesses, citizens, and consumers to consider the direct responsibility that companies have for "the impact of their activities on their employees, on consumers of their products and on the communities within which they operate" (Amnesty International 2002).

Other transnational actors formulate their position less diplomatically. They confront transnational corporations directly in the global marketplace, accuse them of violating human rights, and criticize them for their lack of dedication to sustainable development. One of the most adamant critics is the global civil society movement for universal workers' rights. It uses the Internet, conventional political tools as well as market-based inventions like boycotts, buycotts, and culture jamming to publicize its claim, "Sweatshop labor is modern, global capitalism stripped bare." It calls on consumers to take action when they shop for themselves and their families and to build a common, united campaign action against economic globalization (No Sweat 2002).

Individual consumers also voice their views through their choices of products or producers. This is not a new development. Historically, consumers often preferred products for reasons other than classic economic calculations. They connected consumption with their religious, ethnic, racial, national, class, and other identities. In recent decades, consumers' product choice has been increasingly influenced by a growing concern for transnational and global issues of justice, care for the environment, and human rights. Global movements and networks help mobilize consumers to make political and ethical purchases (see Micheletti 2003).

Disembeddedness, Politics, and the Market

Why politicize the market? In some instances, the market becomes a site for politics when people are disassociated from political life. Earlier in history, people who were not part of the demos of political life often chose the market as an arena for politics. These people were without full citizenship rights and political voice. They were disembedded from politics. They fought against marginalization, colonization, and the repercussions of enslavement in one of the few arenas available for the oppressed and invisible: the market. Their aspirations for full citizenship and a good life for themselves, their community, and their nation urged them to partake in signing a new social contract based on civil, political, social, and economic rights of full citizenship that were embedded in democratically regulated structures of social, economic, and political life (cf. Granovetter 1985; Polanyi 1944; Swedberg 1997).

Without suffrage rights and the respect embedded in full citizenship, people resorted to the marketplace as a site for political action. They used their ability to make choices among consumer goods through boycotts and selective preference of goods (buycotts and labeling schemes) as their political voice. Market-based action called attention to political, social, and economic oppression. Most of this activity took place within the economic framework of colonial empires or single nation-states. Today the market arena continues to be an important site for action long after these first struggles for democratization were won. Newer groups seeking full citizenship rights and democratic respect currently turn to it to plead their cause.

Use of the market as a political tool is not, however, reserved for the oppressed. Empowered and embedded people use their purchasing choices to criticize the policies and practices of corporations in their own and other countries in situations where strong government regulation in domestic and export settings is absent. Political consumer activists use the market to communicate their disapproval with other countries. They boycott goods from countries that violate the human rights of their own citizens and call on their states to use the market-based tools at hand to sanction these countries economically. The export market has frequently been chosen as their site for international politics because no other arena is really open for them to affect these foreign causes. International governmental organizations have not had sufficient regulatory power to solve the problems at hand. In particular, boycotts have been international market-based pressure group politics. By viewing businesses as political actors and as new alternatives to political parties and interest groups, citizens articulate and promote their interests to society, businesses, and government through the market.

Problems of global governance may be among the roots of this politicization of the market, which is triggered by the globalization trends of technological innovation, information technology, and free trade that have developed after the Cold War. These trends are opening up new opportunities and space for political and especially economic life. Market actors readily exploit these new possibilities to establish their business projects globally. Multinational companies are expanding rapidly as are transnational trade, production, and financial transactions. Political actors like political parties, governments, and diplomats also seek to use the new opportunities and spaces to establish political systems regionally and globally. However, they have yet to show the same successes as market actors. A new balance of economic and political power has been struck that favors market thinking and action over politics. This new situation represents a great transformation that differs significantly from Adam Smith's and Karl Polanyi's observations on the supreme importance of statecraft in creating national mercantilist capitalism (Smith 1776; Polanyi 1944; Polanyi 1957).

The influence of markets is a central issue of politics in the twenty-first century. The asymmetrical balance between economics and politics, with market actors taking initiatives that formally belonged to the regulatory prerogative of the state, and the state as unable to develop itself more globally, has led to serious problems of political responsibility-taking nationally and worldwide. Consider how the United Nations and Amnesty International now turn to multinational corporations for help in performing their important global tasks. The call for politicians and governments to take responsibility nationally and worldwide has not yielded sufficient response. No wonder the market is once again politicized and a site of citizen action. Worried, conscientious people use the marketplace to vent their frustration, take responsibility concerning global injustices, and as a way of initiating discussions and standard-setting for global economic regulation. The transboundary character of certain problems in the world today can only be solved by transnational or global effort. Examples include the thinning out of the ozone layer, international migration flows, and global violations of human rights. These problems cannot be solved by single nation-states alone. Rather they require transnational or global collective action. However, as global political coordination has been much slower to develop than economic globalization, contemporary political systems are ill equipped to deal with these serious problems. Global ungovernability forces citizens to develop creatively more global political tools and to use these tools in new arenas for politics and ethics. As explored in this book, citizens sometimes mobilize into networks that target the most developed global institutions, namely the global market arena constituted by transnational market actors. The anti-sweatshop movement is an example of such citizen mobilization as are the use of many labeling schemes, which represent market-based global regulatory institutions.

A final important cause for the politicization of the market is the ever-increasing importance of consumer goods and consumption in the world today. This relationship of dependence triggers politicized market action in several ways. One view argues that the struggle between consumerism and citizenship, between market values of competition and political values of solidarity, politicizes the market and privatizes and commercializes politics (Klein 2000). The market must, therefore, be politicized to liberate people from the dominance of consumer society. It is argued that citizens lured by the babbles of logotypes become slaves of mass customized lifestyle fashion, some even willing to kill for high-status brand goods. Thus, consumer society's transformation of citizens into manipulated, passive buyers of goods must be checked through market-based political action as well as political regulation (Packard 1981; Friedan 1965; Marcuse 1964; Ewen 1988).

A second view of ever-increasing consumption acknowledges our dependence on market consumer goods but does not see it as necessarily detrimental to democracy. This dependence is really a relationship of power that can be changed through collective action. The market becomes politicized when it is used to change the power balance between producers and consumers. Many scholars see shopping as embodying this struggle for power and consider consumer choices as infused with citizenship characteristics (Scammell 2000, 351). Some scholars go so far as to consider consumers the primary agents of democracy in the world today (Beck 2000; Nava 1991; Miller 1995). They analyze how citizens, and particularly young people, attempt to balance promotion of their personal identity and lifestyle through consumer choice with their commitment to global ethical issues. Their interpersonal, private struggle has, in much the same way as earlier efforts, spilled over into a search for arenas for political action. Thus, the market becomes politicized as a site for action and ethics. It is this struggle of wanting affordable lifestyle material goods and of practicing public morals on an everyday basis that has sparked the politicization of the market and turned it into an arena for political contestation. It is here, with these ethically responsible consumers, that we see the "creativity, autonomy, rebelliousness and even the 'authority' of the consumer" (Slater 1997, 51).

A third view points to the shift from industrial society to postmodern society for politicizing the market. Among other things, this shift implies the increasing importance of consumption over production for the creation of political identity. Consumption as an organizing relation in its own right supplements and may even come to replace production, class position, and occupation as the hub of public identity, authority, and political controversy (Livingston 1998; Miles 1998; Inglehart 1997). Here the argument is that once consumption becomes a potentially powerful steering mechanism, the market becomes a site for politics and ethics.

Politics behind Products:
The Phenomenon of Political Consumerism

How can we recognize political consumerism? The fact that our languages now include such terms as citizen-consumer, ethical consumption, and socially responsible investing signifies that our consumer choices and money-making strategies are embedded in a political context that many hold cannot be avoided in shopping trips to the market or in discussions with our investment counselors. These terms imply that we have a responsibility to act as citizens when we make our consumer and investment choices. We cannot, therefore, simply pursue rational self-interest goals in our market transactions. The ideal-type Egoistic Economic Man must be modified to an ideal-type Responsibility-Taking Political Consumer, who applies values other than purely self-interested economic ones in consumer choice situations. Business has become such an influential force in our lives that it, somewhat surprisingly, is now becoming imbued with the concerns of state and civil society. Corporate success has inadvertently become embedded in a political context that requires of it a new form of responsibility-taking, involving values other than competition and profit-maximization. The terms "fair and ethical trade" mark the importance of equality in cooperation among all the stakeholders in global economic affairs.

How can we define political consumerism? For this volume, we define it as consumer choice of producers and products with the goal of changing objectionable institutional or market practices. It is based on attitudes and values regarding issues of justice, fairness, or noneconomic issues that concern personal and family well-being and ethical or political assessment of business and government practice.

Regardless of whether political consumers act individually or collectively, their market choices reflect an understanding of material products as embedded in a complex social and normative context which may be called the politics behind products.

How lasting and successful is political consumerism? Some scholars argue that consumerism is the political answer to our current problems with globalization, governance, and disembeddedness (Beck 2000). Consumers, according to them, generally have the necessary commitments, resources, and maneuverability to meet the democratic challenges of economic globalization. Others consider political consumerism a partial answer to the negative side effects of economic globalization. They argue that consumer choice must be bolstered institutionally and supported by government, international law, and civil society (Moberg 2001). A third group of scholars is skeptical about whether consumerism can successfully influence politics in a way consistent with democratic equality. They argue that political consumerism, like some other forms of political participation, is highly dependent on the financial resources of the people involved. For them, this form of political engagement can only attract the wealthiest and most established people and therefore reproduces patterns of marginalization, powerlessness, and disembeddedness nationally and globally (Basu 2001; Bauman n.d.). A final group is of the definitive opinion that political consumerism cannot be a solution to political problems of local, national, or global magnitude, viewing it instead as a problem in itself, because consumers as political agents are unreliable and capricious. This flexibility is implicit in consumer choice, which cannot bind consumers to any ideology other than free choice. Consumers, they argue, will drop their ethical concerns about the politics behind products when their private economy slumps, and when other preferences entice them in new directions (Levinson 2001).

Although they disagree, these scholars acknowledge the rise of political consumerism and the market as an important current arena for politics. They disagree about political consumerism's usefulness, success, and general implications for politics and society nationally and globally. At this point in time, it is impossible to determine which position best explains and assesses the various acts of political consumerism. We do not know whether political consumerism is a temporary feature of our world that will disappear once political globalization develops more completely, or whether it signals the gradual construction of a new world order based on market power rather than political accountability. For the present we can acknowledge that the phenomenon is a clear signal of the magnitude of the processes of globalization, individualization, governance, and postmodernization that are restructuring our lives.

Purpose and Structure of the Book

The overriding theme of this anthology on political consumerism is how actors and institutions appear to take and promote responsibility through market purchases. Its purpose is to give answers to a number of central questions regarding the phenomenon of political consumerism. Our authors investigate different cases from history and contemporary times as well as discuss their theoretical and philosophical significance. They explain aspects of political consumerism, test hypotheses, understand it as a phenomenon, argue its normative aspects, point to its ethical shortcomings, and tell stories of its use. As such, the chapters employ the variety of scholarly approaches that are available for the study of political, economic, and social phenomena.

The book contains four parts, which address the concerns discussed in this introduction. Part I, entitled "Making Money Morally," concerns why it may appear controversial to call upon market actors to act in a morally responsible way. As discussed above, political consumerism challenges the traditional division of private interest pursued by private actors in the market, and public interests pursued through political means. It crosses over this division in its attempts to compensate for ethical unfairness in a variety of ways. Yet the practices of political consumption also create new dilemmas often ignored by consumers. Andreas Follesdal explores philosophically why we need to concern ourselves with the moral responsibility of the market in the world today. He discusses how political consumerism takes on particular normative importance under conditions of economic globalization, and offers suggestions for a political theory of political consumerism. Among his concerns is the development of normative criteria for assessing the legitimacy of political consumer action in the global marketplace that aims at supplementing governmental regulation. He wonders how these citizen watchdogs can develop and maintain their credibility and integrity in the absence of global, institutionalized checks and balances. Paul Kennedy's chapter focuses on the impact of political consumers on business. He asks what happens to business as a market actor once it adapts itself to more ethical and political concerns. He addresses two different ways in which political consumers affect enterprises that have as their market niche green or ethical consumer goods. His study shows that company leaders may solicit business from political consumers for profit reasons or because company leaders intentionally want to use their business for political change and thereby seek the support of political consumers even at the cost of business growth. Interestingly, in either case, the companies may find themselves facilitating political consumer awareness and engaging in forming the preferences of their customers.

Part II, entitled "Consumer Choices and Setting the Agenda of Politics," focuses on three basic questions that are often asked about political consumerism: what is new about using the market as a site for politics, how effective is it, and does it always promote good causes? Answers are gathered from historical and current examples of how political consumerism sets the agenda of politics. The chapters illustrate how political consumerism channels the attention of the media and politicians toward citizens who are outraged over or mobilized through the politics behind products. These citizens utilize various forms of market-based actions such as boycotts, buycotts, demonstrations, investment decisions, and opinion formation to raise their concerns publicly.

Monroe Friedman discusses in his chapter three important criteria for evaluating consumer boycotts: their successfulness, effectiveness, and ethical quality. He makes an important distinction between successful boycotts, which mobilize large numbers of citizens into action, and effective boycotts, which change the policies or practices of the institutions targeted by the boycott. Not all successful boycotts are effective and not all effective boycotts require successful mobilization of consumer support. Effective but unsuccessful boycotts usually rely on the media to name and shame companies publicly. Today we see an increased use of media-oriented rather than marketplace-oriented boycotts. This change signals that threats to images and logotypes are becoming more important than immediate slumps of purchases, which have traditionally been the explicit goal of the boycott call. Changes in corporate character and the increased importance of the media as a force in economics and politics are the explanation. Thus, two important, distinguishing characteristics between old and new forms of political consumerism emerge in his chapter: the role of media and the character of business. A final important aspect addressed in Friedman's chapter is the importance of good organization for successful and effective boycott actions. Not only is it important for organizers to give careful thought to their choice of target. It is also necessary for them to be able to "call off their troops" once the boycott reaches its goals. The problem is that boycott organizers, unlike organizers of union strikes, seldom have this kind of control over their supporters, who often regard boycotting as part of their political identity and moral responsibility as citizens rather than a tool to be used in an instrumental fashion.

Cheryl Greenberg's chapter draws on American history to remind us that there is nothing inherent in political consumerism that guarantees the moral respectability of its pursued goals, and that good motives do not replace the need for strategic planning. Like Friedman, she underscores the need to consider the serious effects of boycotts on innocent third parties. The possibilities of misuse of political consumerist boycotts, as well as the difficulty that boycott leaders have in controlling their members, have led to efforts at institutionalizing such protests so as to make them more accountable and subject to public scrutiny, as discussed in Part III.

David Vogel's chapter also draws on the United States to show how Americans have expressed their concern over political injustices in the marketplace. Their goal has been to influence corporate hiring and investment practices that have large political consequences. He offers examples of the repertoire of market-based actions available for political consumers that have been used in the United States. Interestingly, he finds that the roots of contemporary political consumerism can be found in American political and economic entanglements in the Vietnam War. Citizens used their economic means to demonstrate their opposition to the war in the stock market. Their involvement marked the beginning of the American public-interest movement, which set out to narrow the boundaries of managerial discretion and embed corporations in a more democratic setting. This movement is the forerunner of contemporary, socially responsible investment, which encourages people to invest their money in companies with ethical profiles, by developing institutions for monitoring and encouraging business ethics and corporate citizenship. Although Vogel acknowledges the limits of the power of political consumerism, he also shows how citizens with clear political preferences can use their economic power to pressure corporations to consider ethical issues as part of their policy agenda.

Part II moves from historical cases to new developments that characterize political consumerism today. W. Lance Bennett's and Jonah Peretti's chapters make clear how the media play an important role in mobilizing support for large campaigns that criticize existing corporate practices. Bennett focuses on campaigns directed at large, globalized corporate enterprises. He discusses the role of consumer issues in transnational advocacy campaigns, and how these campaigns are setting a new agenda for public interest politics that give priority to global responsibility-taking. Bennett uses the Nike sweatshop labor campaign and the campaign against Microsoft to illustrate how permanent campaign networks are created to monitor large global corporations. Most importantly, he demonstrates how the Internet enhances the opportunity for effective political consumerism by facilitating communication among and mobilization of consumer activists. These activists utilize a horizontal decentralized network structure of communication and interaction, which is in stark contrast to the centralization in union structures through which corporate practices were criticized traditionally. A central case in point is the contemporary phenomenon of culture jamming as a way for young, high tech people to express their outrage against what they consider pervasive market advertisements in our common public space.

Jonah Peretti's chapter, together with Michele Micheletti, describes an excellent example of the importance of media for newer, global forms of political consumerism. Peretti's request to order a pair of customized Nike shoes with the name "sweatshop" on them turned him into a global celebrity. His emails—though unintended—reached an estimated 11.4 million people around the globe. His chapter tells the story of his experience with culture jamming as a tool of political consumerism. He used Nike's own marketing strategy to argue for his request: "Your web site advertises that the NIKE iD program is 'about freedom to choose and freedom to express who you are.' I share Nike's love of freedom and personal expression. The site also

xx   Politics, Products, and Markets

says that 'If you want it done right...build it yourself.' I was thrilled to be able to build my own shoes, and my personal iD was offered as a small token of appreciation for the sweatshop workers poised to help me realize my vision. I hope that you will value my freedom of expression and reconsider your decision to reject my order." The chapter puts the email exchange in a larger activist framework and illustrates a point stressed in Bennett's chapter concerning the importance of the Internet for global, social activist network building. It also shows how individualized lifestyle choices can dovetail with responsibility-taking for global social justice.

"Building Responsible Institutions in Multi-Risk Society" is the title of Part III, with the establishment of new political consumerist institutions as the central theme. The chapters address questions frequently asked about political consumerism that concern the difference between newer forms and older ones, the kinds of institutional arrangements that have developed as a reply for responsible actions of consumers and producers, and the relationship between globalization and political consumerism. An important difference between the historical and contemporary variants of political consumerism is the current proliferation of institutions for positive consumer choice, such as "buycott" institutions or labeling schemes that help consumers practice political consumerism. These institutions are watchdogs of global industries and supplement government regulation in crucial ways.

Franck Cochoy's chapter shows how the old and established institution of standardization, originally set up to make manufacturing more effective, has revamped itself into an institution for product certification that reflects consumers' concerns. Initially, standardization was production-oriented. The advent of consumer society encouraged standardizers to take responsibility for product certification by ensuring that products were safe for home use. Today standardization increasingly concerns such post-material values as environmental safety, gender equality, and corporate social accountability. Therefore, product transparency takes on a new meaning in the world of global free trade. In his study of France, Cochoy discusses how standardizers unintentionally set the agenda for global consumer responsibility-taking. This happened when they opened up the standardization process to consumers' interests in a move to promote their own professional interests in power relations with manufacturers. At first, consumers applauded the fact that standardizers made consumer interest an issue in the standardization process. They saw this as responsibility-taking on the part of standardizers. However, in the post-war period, the consumer's movement was involved in a struggle with standardizers over who best could represent consumer interests and assume responsibility in consumer society. The struggle illustrates how organized consumers develop into a countervailing force with the power of placing demands on both business and government.

The countervailing force of political consumers is also a theme taken up in the chapters on labeling schemes. Consumers have appealed to civil society associations and public agencies to develop transparent criteria to help them make responsible political consumerist choices. Over the last few decades and particularly in the 1990s, several labeling schemes have been established because of this. Some of them are considered both successful and effective. Many of them encourage multinational corporations to go beyond the call of law in their environmental and human rights practices. They differ from boycotts, which are contentious in nature, as they foster the institutionalization of consumer action and encourage cooperation with industry to solve problems. The aim is to arrive at a more satisfactory allocation of responsibility and accountability for the risks present in an increasingly complex global setting. The authors discuss fair trade labels, forest stewardship certification, and eco-labeling schemes, with eco-labeling as the most institutionalized political consumerist scheme in existence today.

The chapter co-authored by Andrew Jordan, Rüdiger Wurzel, Anthony R. Zito, and Lars Brückner offers a comparative assessment of the important national eco-labeling schemes now in operation in Europe. Different institutional designs characterize these schemes. The role played by consumers and consumer representatives varies, as does consumer response to their certified products. Of the four schemes that are investigated in this chapter, the authors find that only one, the German Blue Angel, can really be considered as successful. Two important ingredients of success are consumer support and market competition. Consumer support is crucial for the success of the labeling schemes because the level of consumer awareness, as well as public support of the eco-label, decides whether business finds eco-label schemes attractive or not. Market competition is important, because businesses make note of whether their competitors make use of the scheme or not. If they fear that a competitor's use of an eco-label will lead to a loss in market shares they seek eco-label certification of their products, which in turn helps raise public environmental consciousness and gives added support to the labeling scheme.

In the final chapter of Part III, Benjamin Cashore, Graeme Auld, and Deanna Newson discuss a labeling scheme of increasing importance: forest certification schemes. In many ways, this scheme is similar to standardization, because it is also a non-state market-driven policy instrument that addresses the concerns of producers. However, it also provides consumers with important information in the form of a label that concerns global green forestry practice and issues of fair trade. This chapter discusses the differences between forest stewardship certification (FSC) and industry-developed certification schemes that have developed as a response to its establishment. The authors show that, while forest stewardship certification attempts to restructure the power relations among all stakeholders (including consumers and forestry workers) over use and exploitation of the world's forest resources, the schemes developed by business and landowner associations attempt to reduce the number of stakeholders and maintain more traditional power relations. The chapter uses scholarship on institution-building to identify criteria for assessing the legitimacy and effectiveness of certification schemes. Many different factors explain whether forest stewardship or a business-developed certification scheme is able to establish itself successfully. The chapter confirms a result from the eco-label study that characteristics of the domestic and global market are important for assessing successfulness.

Part IV, "Politicizing Consumers and Change in Politics," demonstrates how political consumerism does not fit our conventional view of political participation, and it challenges central assumptions of social science. Traditionally, political participation has involved the relationship between citizens and their government, which in turn regulates the market. Political consumerism challenges this conception by showing how citizens turn directly to the market with a variety of political concerns. The phenomenon of political consumerism encourages scholars to rethink the function and meaning of political participation in society, since political consumerism involves citizens' willingness to defend, reform, improve, and even build institutions that have influence over our common well-being regardless of whether they are part of the political sphere, in the strict sense, or not. Political consumerism is thus an example of political action where citizens increasingly turn to tools other than voting and membership in established civil society associations to take responsibility for our common lives.

The chapters in Part IV address a number of issues of crucial importance for assessing the magnitude of the phenomenon of political consumerism. They consider the role of consumers in solving our current problems of globalization, governance, and disembeddedness in a variety of ways. In their chapter, Jørgen Goul Andersen and Mette Tobiasen present findings from the most comprehensive survey investigation of political consumers to date. They examine the social characteristics of political consumers and the extent to which political consumerism is truly a political phenomenon. They also address the question of whether demonstrating morality in the market is necessarily tied to economic resources. Interestingly, they find that income is not an important factor here. Rather, their Danish data show that political consumers are disproportionately highly educated and characterized as having slightly left political leanings, an increased awareness of political issues, and a global identity. The study also confirms that political consumerism is recognized as a tool of political participation and used by those who are already politically active. Yet the results also point to the fact that political consumerism can be seen more as an act of individualized political participation, in contrast to collective or group-oriented forms. An important conclusion from their research is that political consumerism is more constructive than its critics claim, because Danish political consumers are not just cynical bystanders. They also trust the political system.

Bente Halkier's chapter uses focus group interviews of green consumers to assess the extent to which political consumerism involves important dimensions of political participation. She distinguishes different groups of consumers in terms of how they handle risks in food consumption and examines whether they use political consumerism as a political tool or not. Her interviews cluster risk-handlers into different types. One type comprises those who view themselves as having sufficient autonomy to act in society; they follow the public debate on health and the environment closely. Another type characterizes consumers who experience discussion about risks related to food as a threat to their everyday lives; they have difficulty seeing themselves as societal actors in the process of consumption. A third group of consumers pushes aside completely the topic of risks in relation to food; these consumers spend greater energy on the satisfactory aspects in their lives than trying to influence society via the consumer role. Halkier's conclusion helps us to distinguish political consumers from conventional consumers: the former see themselves as active agents of society who are in charge of their lives and well-being; conventional consumers do not.

An important social dimension of political consumerism is gender, which is the topic of Michele Micheletti's chapter. Her study (based on historical examples, current attitudinal studies, and a case study of contemporary green political consumerism) shows that women were and still are more present as political consumers. We see interesting similarities in the historical examples that are also found in the contemporary case study. Women used political consumerism then, and still do today, as a way of working with issues either very close to the home or expressive of their general humanitarian care ethic. They utilize market-based political activity because conventional political venues have been less open and attractive to them as women. An important side effect of their involvement is empowerment, consciousness-raising, and identity formation. The chapter continues with a theoretical discussion of how characteristics of women or characteristics of the marketplace explain the gender gap in political consumerism. Micheletti concludes that political consumerism can be seen as an engendered form of political participation triggered both by an engendered ethic of care and an engendered dissatisfaction with conventional forms of political engagement. Women find the market an attractive site for politics because it is open for everyday, low-cost political involvement and individualized engagement. The characteristic of the market as unregulated political space explains the attractiveness of its nature to women and other groups that are marginalized politically.

Part IV concludes with a general assessment of political consumerism. Dietlind Stolle and Marc Hooghe's chapter focuses more directly on the controversial issue of whether political consumerism can be seen as a successful additional tool in political life that might substitute for the lack of traditional political involvements. This question has arisen in the context of a seeming decline in traditional political activity of citizens in Western democracies. The authors ask whether we can categorize political consumerism as politics and, if so, how political consumerism can strengthen democracy. The point of departure for their answer is the emerging body of theoretical and empirical work on political participation, social capital, and citizenship, which they use to assess the vitality, scope, and limits of political consumerism as a form of political participation. Finally, the chapter discusses how we can measure the phenomenon of political consumerism as a citizen activity. They argue that not every consumer, who is aware of labels and ethical distinctions between products, should be defined as a political consumer. Political consumerism for them requires the frequent purchase of products or services based on ethical motivations or an active political involvement in support of ethical and global consumer issues.

* * *

Political consumerism is the use of market purchases by individuals, groups, and institutions, who want to take responsibility for political, economic, and societal developments. The chapters in this volume address this phenomenon from several different countries and disciplines and from a variety of times and settings. Together the scholars offer a sample of the breadth and richness of the phenomenon for academic research. Contemporary political consumerism signals a number of developments that involve the processes of globalization, new forms of governance, individualization, global consumer society, and the role of human rights' norms. For the authors of this book, political consumerism represents an interesting form of collective action and responsibility-taking under shifting action opportunities and responsibilities. The possibilities and challenges of market purchases by individuals and institutions that thereby seek to take responsibility over political, economic, and societal developments, are indeed important and worthy topics of research.

References

Amnesty International Business Group. 2002. *Human Rights. Any of Your Business?* <amnesty.se/businessgroup.nsf>. Accessed June 11.

Basu, Kaushik. 2001. "A Better Mousetrap," in Archon Fung, Dara O'Rourke, & Charles Sabel, eds., *Can We Put an End to Sweatshops?* Boston: Beacon Press.

Bauman, Zygmunt. n.d. "The Self in a Consumer Society." *The Hedgehog Review.* <religionanddemocracy.lib.virginia.edu/hh/fall99/BauSelfVol1.html>. Accessed June 11, 2002.

Beck, Ulrich. 2000. *What is Globalization?* Oxford: Polity.

Ewen, Stuart. 1988. *All Consuming Images.* New York: Basic Books.

Friedan, Betty. 1965. *The Feminine Mystique.* Harmondsworth: Penguin.

Fung, Archon, Dara O'Rourke, & Charles Sabel, eds. 2001. *Can We Put An End to Sweatshops?* Boston: Beacon Press.

Granovetter, Mark. 1985. "Economic Action and Social Structure: The Problem of Embeddedness." *American Journal of Sociology* 91 (3): 481-510.

Inglehart, Ronald. 1997. *Modernization and Postmodernization. Cultural, Economic, and Political Change in 43 Societies.* Princeton, NJ: Princeton University Press.

Klein, Naomi. 2000. *No Logo.* London: Flamingo.

Levinson, Mark. 2001. "Wishful Thinking," in A. Fung, D. O'Rourke, & C. Sabel, eds., *Can We Put an End to Sweatshops?* Boston: Beacon Press.

Livingston, James. 1998. "Modern Subjectivity and Consumer Culture," in Strasser, McGovern, & Judt, eds., *Getting and Spending. European and American Consumer Societies in the 20th Century.* Cambridge: Cambridge University Press.

Marcuse, Herbert. 1964. *One Dimensional Man.* London: Sphere.

Micheletti, Michele. (2003). *Political Virtue and Shopping. Individuals, Consumerism, and Collective Action.* New York: Palgrave.

Miles, Steven. 1998. *Consumerism as a Way of Life.* London: Sage Publications.

Miller, Daniel. 1995. "Consumption as the Vanguard of History. A Polemic by Way of an Introduction," in Daniel Miller, ed., *Acknowledging Consumption. A Review of New Studies.* New York: Routledge.

Moberg, David. 2001. "Unions and the State," in A. Fung, D. O'Rourke, & C. Sabel, eds., *Can We Put an End to Sweatshops?* Boston: Beacon Press.

Nava, Mica. 1991. "Consumerism Reconsidered. Buying and Power." *Cultural Studies* 5 (2): 157-73.

No Sweat 2002. *Where Do We Stand?* <nosweat.org.uk sections.php?op=viewarticle&artid=3>. Accessed June 11.

Packard, Vance. 1981. *The Hidden Persuaders.* Harmondsworth: Penguin.

Polayni, Karl. 1944 [1957]. *The Great Transformation.* Boston: Beacon.

___, C. Arnesburg, & H. Pearson. 1957. *Trade and Market in the Early Empires.* New York: Free Press.

Scammell, Margareth. 2000. "The Internet and Civic Engagments: The Age of the Citizen-Consumer." *Political Communication* 17: 351-5.

Slater, Don. 1997. "Consumer Culture and the Politics of Need," in Mica Nava, Andrew Blake, Iain MacRury, & Barry Richards, eds., *Buy This Book. Studies in Advertising and Consumption.* London: Routledge.

Smith, Adam. 1776 [1954]. *An Inquiry into the Nature and Causes of the Wealth of Nations.* London: Dent.

Strasser, Susan, Charles McGovern, & Matthias Judt, eds. 1998. *Getting and Spending. European and American Consumer Societies in the 20th Century.* Cambridge: Cambridge University Press.

Swedberg, Richard. 1997. "New Economic Sociology: What Has Been Accomplished, What is Ahead?" *Acta Sociologica* 40, 2: 161-82.

United Nations. 2002. *The Global Compact.* <unglobalcompact.org/>. Accessed June 11.

Part I

Making Money Morally

Political Consumerism as Chance and Challenge

Andreas Follesdal

Introduction

Globalization affects the opportunity space, informational bases, and coordination capacities of states, multinational enterprises, non-governmental organizations (NGOs), and citizens. With such changing resources come changing allocation of power and responsibilities—or so argue international NGOs and other vocal contributors to public debates. They challenge existing expectations and institutions and use terms such as "corporate citizenship," "citizen-consumer," and "ethical trade" to emphasize their point. The topic of these reflections is the responsibility of consumers in a global marketplace, committing acts of "political consumerism." Traditionally, political participation has involved the relationship between citizens and their government, which in turn regulates the market. Political consumerism adds to this conception in that citizens turn directly to the market with a variety of political concerns. This phenomenon of political consumerism needs a political theory. We need a plausible account of consumer activism, which will allow us to identify and clarify its role within the political and economic global institutional order and provide criteria for its normative assessment.

The Need for Political Theory: Puzzles of Political Consumerism

Some scholars hail political consumerism as a practice within "civil society," indeed within "global civil society." Civil society steps up to global governance at a time when globalization threatens traditional structures of authority (Eide 1998, 631-32). The need for systematic reflection arises in part from what appears to be valid criticisms of political consumerism, especially as committed by individuals. Political consumer actions often seem counterproductive. Consider cases of objectionable company practices that worsen the

3

situation for a local population, or that exploit and violate workers' basic rights. Sometimes when political consumerism targets such a company, the action "works" in the sense that the company pulls out. But several unfortunate effects of company exit have been reported. Other, less sensitive, companies move in and continue the abuse. Sometimes, if no other employer moves in, the workers may be left even worse off, in unemployment or prostitution. Exploitation such as child labor, while an evil, may, thus, be the least foul alternative. Other critics denounce political consumerism as illegitimate insofar as the loose networks or organizations behind such protests should be democratic, transparent, and accountable, which some of them patently are not. Yet other criticisms charge that consumer action, on the basis of Western consumers' own values, amounts to blatant disregard for the local culture and values: Political consumerism is cultural imperialism through market means.

These criticisms fail against several plausible conceptions of political consumerism. This response does not amount to denying the empirical claims, but instead draws on what we may think of as the political theory of political consumerism. At first glance, this label may seem inappropriate. Political theory is typically concerned with questions such as by what authority, and within what limits, political power may impose laws and practices with threats of sanction. Acts of political consumerism are not exercises of political power in this strict sense. It does not appear to be a collectively enforced, social arrangement, and hence does not restrict the legally regulated opportunity space of others. Yet, insofar as political consumerism is widely followed, it can effectively restrict the feasible options of companies, employees, and other consumers for better or worse. As with a wide range of practices that affect others, we may require that such practices be *normatively justifiable*. Moreover, through political consumerism citizens sometimes seek to build, reform, or improve institutions that have influence over our common well-being, regardless of whether these acts are part of the political order in the strict sense. Therefore, the phenomenon of political consumerism encourages scholars to rethink the function and meaning of political participation and authority.

The effectiveness of political consumerism can only be assessed on the basis of a clear understanding of its ends. In the next section, I identify and discuss five different conceptions of political consumerism. Many of them are not affected by the criticisms discussed above. However, the criticisms do challenge political consumerism, regarded as a practice aimed at institutional reform. These worries merit close attention and assessment, particularly under globalization, which is the topic of the second section of the chapter. The third section sketches a normative framework of the market that takes its point of departure in Adam Smith's discourse on the subject for domestic markets. Then I explain why shifts in capacities among governments, business, and civil society may be thought to bolster the need for political consumerism or other non-traditional measures of political action. The fifth section identifies some of the challenges facing political consumerism as a mechanism for changing institutions and business practices towards international human rights standards.

Conceptions of Political Consumerism

At least five different conceptions of the role of political consumerism can be identified. They may not be exhaustive and are not mutually exclusive. I distinguish arguments based on consideration of what I call Agency, Expression of Self, Expression of Mutual Respect, Instruments for Reforming Wrong-doers, and Instruments for Reforming Business Practices.

Argument of Agency: Clean Hands

Boycott has long been regarded as a way to disassociate oneself from what are viewed as evil acts. The element of self-purification in Gandhian Satyagraha is an example. Boycott avoids complicity by seeking non-cooperation with evil, thus reducing the causal chain between one's own acts and the immoral outcomes by avoiding personal participation and responsibility. Of course, negative consequences are important, but what also matters is whether evil comes about through one's own agency. Such concerns have been defended and discussed among moral philosophers including Kant (Kant 1964), and more recently under the heading of "integrity" or "agent-relative reasons" (cf. Williams in Smart & Williams 1973; Hill 1979; Sen 1982; Mills 1996). Criticisms against such views include insistence that this is a case of moral self-indulgence, that considerations of responsibility matter little or as nothing as compared to the moral quality of outcomes in the world, and observations that it is impossible to extricate oneself completely from patterns of interaction anyway, which makes participation in corrupt trade practices unavoidable.

Such criticisms notwithstanding, political consumer actions on this basis avoid some of the problems. Firstly, while morally relevant, whether the suffering abates is not decisive. Secondly, the grounds for action may arise from one's personal moral view with no claim to be properly part of the common normative basis of society. Thirdly, such political consumerism need not be considered as an institutionalized practice, needing organizations, publicly defendable criteria, and the like.

Arguments of Identity: Expressing Self

Other conceptions of political consumerism regard it as a more active expression of one's values. Such self-expressive conceptions may typically be part of what is often termed post-materialist values (Inglehart 2000). In societies where economic survival is taken for granted, younger generations give more priority to non-material values, such as making autonomous choices, spontaneous participation in political life, and environmental and gender issues, as discussed by Stolle and Hooghe in this book (see also Putnam 2000). Consider lifestyle preferences in general or Expressions of Self, where participants do not claim that all other citizens should so react, or that businesses should change their policies—except insofar as others happen to share these morally neutral values. An example may be political consumerism on the basis of aesthetic considerations, for instance, avoiding chain stores whose storefront ruins the small-town neighborhood image. For our purposes, we may note that such reactions need not be institutionalized, especially since they are volatile in several senses. Individuals' values may shift rapidly, and post-materialists are also said to be wary of hierarchy and long-term organizations, preferring fluent networks.

Arguments of Identity: Expression of Mutual Respect

Other self-expressive actions may best be regarded as Expressions of Mutual Respect. They are undertaken on the basis of beliefs that certain companies violate fundamental normative constraints. In these cases, the values are thought to be not only optional preferences but legitimate standards for company behavior. Such cases may well arise for post-materialists, for even although their values tend to favor individualistic responses rather than collective, they are not egoistic or unduly self-interested. The high value given autonomy for oneself is often combined with respecting the autonomy of others, prizing individual liberties and social tolerance, and fostering civic participation—but in new social movements rather than in established organizations (Welzel, Inglehart, & Klingeman 2002). Spontaneous political consumerism may thus be a natural response to perceived abuse of workers or environmental degradation. Kant seems to have held such a view regarding disentangling oneself from immoral actors (Kant 1964; Hill 1979, 1991; Mills 1996). Political consumerism may express and foster a shared public understanding of what it means to be a responsible and fully human person (cf. Galston 1991).

Some features of these views may be noted. The central aim is not to change a practice or even to stop a particular case of abuse; "merely symbolic" action with no impact on the abuse may still serve the expressive purpose. Coordination dilemmas for the kind, "even if our company stops, the suffering will not stop," do not affect expressive arguments. One's self-image and values are important, but the general trustworthiness of any coordinating organization is not an issue, as long as the protester has trust in them. While detrimental effects by other companies may play a role in the decision, such effects are not part of the agent's responsibility or expressive of identity in the same sense. Still, for Expressions of Mutual Respect, some such considerations of effects on the suffering may matter, for instance, insofar as the values include what John Rawls calls the natural duty of justice to "support and to comply with just institutions that exist and apply to us. It also constrains us to further just arrangements not yet established, at least when this can be done without too much cost to ourselves" (Rawls 1971, 115).

Instrumental Arguments: Re-Socializing Wrong-Doers

Some actions aim to re-socialize those who do wrong by shunning them, thus impressing on them the need to change their values. With such a change of heart, the unacceptable behavior should cease—for moral, rather than economic reasons, as pointed out in Friedman's chapter. While such protests may often work, they can also backfire, causing hostility and suspicion rather than transformation, as Gandhi was well aware (Gandhi 1918).

Instrumental Arguments: Changing Business Practices

Other acts of political consumerism seek to reform business practices. Such social action at the domestic level has been somewhat successful in the case of labor, civil rights, and women's rights. Again, a variety of ends can be distinguished. Political consumerism may be part of a concern to replace parliaments and national governments as sites of political power. This may draw on a radical denial of the need for centralized power for maintaining the political order (cf. Burnheim 1986; cf. Held & McGrew 2000, 412; Goodin 1992). Or actions can be regarded as supplementary to government action in several ways, as a permanent supplement to government's coercive power or using extra-parliamentary means to get stricter government and intergovernmental regulation of business. Political consumerism can also be a stopgap measure until global structures are in place with sufficient enforcement power. The aim would be changes in domestic and global regulation, which should be restricted to such issues, properly regulated by state power rather than more contested issues. Among proper aims would then be fair trade, human rights, and human security. Protests may be directed against governments or against companies, that may pressure host governments to implement human rights and monitor compliance to avoid future boycotts (Spar 1998). Several features of these instrumental arguments are important. Their effect on desired change is highly relevant, although single cases of success or failure are not decisive when assessing the *practice* of political consumerism. The central issue is instead whether the practice of boycotting secures stable shifts in the values or expectations of businesses, and hence affects practices—recognizing that mishaps will still occur. Dilemmas may arise due to the need to reward good behavior by lifting the boycott, even if the business' values may remain unchanged (Mills 1996). When political consumerism aims to change governments' regulations or the practices of businesses, a number of issues of institutional design and assessment must be addressed. The most important of these are accountability of the organizations involved and their value basis. The remainder of this chapter addresses these institutional issues.

Of particular concern is political consumerism, interpreted narrowly as a practice involving consumers as a collective agent participating in *the global governance of markets,* supplementing states, intergovernmental bodies as the UN, NGOs, and multinational enterprises. One central aim of such political consumerism is to provide added incentives for compliance with, and the creation of, legitimate conditions on global trade, in circumstances of globalization with weak enforcement mechanisms. On this view, political consumerism is also a collective expression of mutual respect, of our individual and collective responsibility to protect the interests of those whom we can affect, and particularly of those who are dependent on our actions through international trade. Important issues concern "whose standards" to use, when assessing business behavior. For reasons of space, I must here simply suggest that some vital human needs may be regarded as such common factors, and that they are best secured by domestic legal orders that respect *human rights*—including political, civil, social, and economic rights. Such a normative basis for human rights is compatible with a broad range of religious and philosophical traditions, and these rights are part of international law, subscribed by a large majority of states and endorsed in documents as The European Monitoring Platform, OECD guidelines, and the UN Committee on Transnational Corporations under the UN Economic and Social Council (ECOSOC). Such norms can be defended across a broad range of normative theories. While these premises are contested and contestable, I take them for granted for our purposes. Among the issues targeted are workers' rights, the human rights' violations of their sub-contractors, the plight of local communities affected by corporations, and the lax enforcement of human rights by host governments.

In the absence of global instruments of formal governance, citizens have come to use political consumerism to demand enforcement of existing international human rights norms. In this view, appropriate political consumerism must actually improve the plight of those suffering from the injustice, if not in this particular case, then at least by improving the practice in general, for instance by securing agreement among companies or if the host government enforces stricter standards or better options for workers.

In summary, this account of political consumerism would appear to fall clearly within the *métier* of normative political theory. Political consumerism forms part of *governance*—arrangements by which agents regulate some issue area by means of extra-institutional authority, involving non-public actors and without secure enforcement (Rosenau 1992; Commission on Global Governance 1995; Banchoff & Smith 1999, 15). We must ask similar questions of such forms of governance as of governments' use of power: What are the grounds of such authority, what should be its institutionally circumscribed limits, and how should it be exercised within such limits when we seek to treat all affected individuals as moral equals? A legitimate conception of political consumerism must be consistent with—or may even be required by—the proper role of individuals in the market in a globalized world order. We turn first to consider why globalization matters for these normative arguments.

Globalization of Market Actors: Citizens of No Country, Cosmopolitan Consumers

The effects of globalization have important normative aspects for any normative theory insisting that practices should be defensible towards all affected parties. Insofar as globalization means that actions have global implications, the impact on foreigners must also be included in the normative justification of practices, such as global trade regimes. We are often said to be living in the era of globalization. As with most slogans, such claims are vague, perhaps essentially contested, and often dubitable as general statements. In a historical vein, global perspectives on economic affairs are not new. Cosmopolitan perspectives led Diogenes (412-323 BC) to declare, "I am a citizen of the world," in defense of his refusal to pay local taxes. Later cross-border mobility rendered such claims more plausible. Writing more than two hundred years ago, Adam Smith observed, "A merchant, it has been said very properly, is not necessarily the citizen of any particular country. It is in a great measure indifferent to him from what place he carries on his trade, and a very trifling disgust will make him remove his capital, and together with it all the industry which it supports, from one country to another" (Smith 1776, 3, 4).

Both globalization and cosmopolitan ethics have changed since Diogenes and Adam Smith. For our purposes, globalization is the fact that actions and practices systematically affect others across territorial borders. Among the results are increased living standards for many and increased access to goods and services. Unfortunately, globalization also has some highly problematic consequences. The digital economy is a contributing cause of shifting control from domestic governments to globally integrated financial markets and multinational enterprises (Strange 1986), which impacts on governments' perceived policy options. Some of the traditional instruments of the state acting singly and sovereign—taxation, final adjudication, and regulation—have withered, leading sometimes to increased international regulations, for example, within the European Union.

Other times, governments are led to compete for mobile capital and multinationals leading, some fear, to a race to the bottom regarding wages, health, and safety standards. The acceptable limits to such variations must be addressed and enforced, for example, concerning bribery, human rights, and wage levels (Donaldson & Dunfee 1999). International business ethics has become an important topic, because transnational enterprises have effects on vulnerable individuals, both inside and outside the marketplace, who do not have decent protection (e.g., Donaldson 1989). Existing constraints are insufficiently enforced, due to lack of international regulations and bodies. There is nothing in the way of a "global government."

Globalization affects the capacities, roles, and responsibilities of governments, business, and civil society. The increased territorial impact of international business, combined with the reduced capacities of governments and civil society, help explain why international business may stand in need of justification in ways that domestic business need not. We must rethink the distribution of responsibilities that traditionally have justified business and consumer practices in the domestic setting. To explain how globalization changes the normative assessment of the responsibilities of businesses and of consumers, we can draw on Adam Smith's defense of the market within state borders.

Moral Framework of the Market

Many have been struck by the apparent differences in behavior between citizens in society in general and the behavior of business people. Among ordinary individuals, equality, sympathy, honesty, and concern for the common good are maintained as high ideals. In contrast, many business practices appear to distribute benefits according to the bargaining power and the starting positions of players acting on the basis of self-interested choice. Behavior, elsewhere condemned, might well be rewarded in business. So the role and rules of business seem different than for other parts of society. This raises the fundamental question of whether they can be reconciled.

Business' reliance on immoral motives was a topic of central concern to Adam Smith (Muller 1992; Werhane 1991). In *Wealth of Nations*, the great economist and moral philosopher argued most famously that, under certain conditions, even self-motivated market agents will freely exchange goods in such ways that some will be better off without rendering anyone else worse off. Thus, market behavior serves the common good in the utilitarian way he defined it, at least when embedded in an elaborate distribution of social responsibility between what we may re-label business, government, NGOs, and civil society. Markets can be morally legitimate, but preferably when the state maintains just rules of the game, only as long as it ensures a "fair" distribution of the benefits over time. Bargaining power must not be skewed inappropriately but leave all parties with acceptable ranges of options. Proponents of free markets have hailed Adam Smith, while critics say that the preconditions he assumed are seldom found in real life, indeed that those with nothing to sell may be left worse off. Proponents of market freedom often forget that Smith argued for severe constraints on the market, and critics often ignore that Smith himself insisted that governments must not only regulate the market and correct market failures, but that they must be supplemented. Markets do not ensure that all individuals develop their talents and a benevolent moral character required in society. And Smith recognized that the market does not secure distribution of goods to those without money, thus the need for private benevolence and re-distributive luxury tax to subsidize basic goods to the poor.

Elaborating on this defense, we may say that businesses are permitted to focus on value creation within constraints set by governments and as long as other agents secure other important societal functions such as redistribution, socialization to concern for others, and scrutiny of governments and business. Problems arise when this distribution of responsibilities fails: when third parties are affected, when re-distributive tasks are not performed, or when some firms abuse the rules. In such cases, business—and consumers—may have to take on responsibilities beyond value creation, or exercise more self-restraint.

The Role of Political Consumers in a Just Global Market

Globalization has caused a mismatch between global economic effects and global political regulation. States may have their formal sovereignty intact, but they lose options and face eroding general trust in their ability or willingness to regulate markets domestically and beyond their borders. In particular, they appear unable or unwilling to secure a high economic floor and safe working environments for workers in the global economy. While such claims are often excuses, globalization does appear to affect governments who have been accustomed to being policymakers rather than policy-takers. The changes in options and capacities of business and domestic governments weaken Adam Smith's justification of business' license to pursue profits. There is no global government in the sense of an institutional body with enforcement and re-distributive authority, and there is little in the way of a global civil society ensuring inculcation of mutual respect across borders. So the constraints on business must be rethought. If global markets are to be normatively justified, the responsibilities for re-distribution and prevention of harm must be borne by agents other than the state—namely corporations and consumers. I submit that political consumerism may be interpreted in this light.

Corporations are not only accountable to shareholders but are also subject to domestic and international law, and they are dependent on consumers. Political consumerism may bolster shifts in corporate responsibilities by providing incentives for some firms to engage in more fair business practices. The minimum requirements of business under globalization merits careful attention. I here lay out only a few considerations. What may be required of business need not be charitable work in general. It is not obvious that corporations can be trusted to plan and act for the common good rather than for the good of their shareholders. Yet businesses may be required to avoid wage slavery and certain forms of child labor and—not least—comply with legislation enacted by host governments and not block proposed human rights legislation. Constraints may include respecting ILO regulations, refraining from bribing government officials, and the requirements of the UN's Global Compact.

Some argue that multinational corporations should abide by further moral considerations. Thomas Donaldson (1991) proposes ten human rights, said to protect interests of extreme importance without imposing undue burdens on business. These rights include freedom of physical movement, ownership of property, freedom from torture, fair trial, non-discrimination, physical security, freedom of speech and association, minimal education, political participation, and subsistence. A fundamental objection to such lists must be addressed. There are situations where unilateral self-constraint by one company does no good. For example, consider that many violations of human rights and basic needs are perpetrated with the express or tacit permission of domestic governments to serve business interest. Firms may face hard dilemmas where self-constraint on their part may do no good. One upright corporation cannot prevent others corporations from abusing workers. Thus, oppression may happen regardless of what one single corporation does. Unless all competing corporations are regulated and all governments agree to high standards, oppressed workers of the world cannot avoid being mistreated. While such coordination traps no doubt exist, firms should not be allowed to excuse themselves from all compliance with such norms as Donaldson's by such arguments. Instead, work must be done—or at least not prevented—on three fronts by businesses and others. Realistic rules must be available that would allow companies to make a profit and secure basic needs. For this, international standard setting, even without sanctions, plays a crucial role. Secondly, in certain cases industry-wide agreements are required. Thirdly, partial compliance by some companies is often better than none, but this can be difficult to achieve. Political consumerism may contribute to all three tasks.

Political consumerism may contribute to convergence between good ethics and a healthy bottom line by shifting companies' payoffs. Organized consumers can stimulate the creation of norms, foster compliance by industry sectors, and promote compliance by individual companies, all of which are more difficult under globalization. Consumer pressure may counteract coordination problems by creating a market for companies that can credibly claim to honor good standards in areas such as child labor, sustainable forest harvesting, or animal rights. If consumers succeed, they create a demand among companies for sufficiently clear rules. One response by some firms is to develop or subscribe to voluntary, industry-wide standards such as Social Accountability 8000, the principles of the Caux Round Table, the UN's Global Compact, or the work of Amnesty International's Business Group. While voluntary standards may not always be enough, political consumerism can add pressure for compliance, supervision, and global regulation—sometimes even enticing companies to lobby host governments into establishing, monitoring, and sanctioning industry-wide standards to block less scrupulous competitors and avoid consumer actions (Spar 1998).

Globalization may increase the need for political consumerism but may also facilitate it for two reasons. Firstly, information gathering is eased by information technology, for instance between activ-

ists in Southern NGOs about labor problems or environmental issues and consumers in other countries. Secondly, globalization low-
ers the cost of political consumerism when the market offers alternative, nearly equivalent products at only slightly higher prices. Then
normative considerations become less costly.

I have explored an institutional role of political consumerism,
understood as the coordinated use of purchasing power that serves
the role of promoting certain changes in global business practices—
including business behavior in particular cases as well as business
regulation. As an instrument aimed at stricter governmental regulation, political consumerism exerts leverage on business and indirectly on governments. It may boost the formulation of voluntary
and legal codes, pressure companies to sign voluntary codes, and
sanction businesses, all of which take on particular urgency under
globalization.

Challenges for Political Consumerism:
Earning and Keeping Trust

Political consumerism promises to alleviate some of the problems
created by globalization. With such influence come responsibility
and the need for scrutiny of organizations that coordinate political
consumerism. I suggest that at least five issues must be addressed, if
political consumerism is to establish and maintain legitimacy and
trustworthiness.

Effectiveness

While identity arguments need not be concerned about effectiveness, it is a central question for political consumerism regarded as
an instrument for reforming business practices. It is not at all clear
that political consumerism always improves the plight of the worst
off, as shown in Friedman's chapter in this volume. Nor is it clear
that such protests are more effective than "constructive engagement"
by companies remaining in problem areas (Risse, Ropp, & Sikkink
1999). Thus, Unocal claims that by remaining in Burma it has a
more positive effect than isolating the country (Greenhouse 2000).
The examples presented in Part II of this volume suggest that political consumerist actions are more likely to be effective if they combine credible threats and promises by addressing a target with clear
and achievable demands. Research is needed to render such actions

more effective. For instance, we need to know whether actions against child labor typically improve their plight or rather force the children into prostitution. Do environmental boycotts tend to improve the environment or merely scare away those companies most vulnerable to bad press, leaving the field open to less scrupulous players? As discussed in the chapter by Cashore et al., important issues include how to set standards that are realistic yet do not "sell out."

Whose Values? What Standards?

The goals of political consumerist organizations must be assessed carefully. *The Economist* asks rhetorically, "Are citizens' groups, as many of their supporters claim, the first steps towards an 'international civil society' (whatever that might be)? Or do they represent a dangerous shift of power to unelected and unaccountable special-interest groups?" (*Economist* 1999). I think it a mistake to regard these two options as mutually exclusive. There is no guarantee that civil society is particularly civil. Unfortunately, we have no guarantee that "transnational civil society networks—the emerging third force in global politics—tend to aim for broader goals based on their conceptions of what constitutes the public good. They are bound together more by shared values than by self-interest" (Florini 2000, 7). Indeed, the history of political consumerism includes illegitimate shared values (Halliday 2000): in the 1930s against goods produced by Jews (Encyclopædia Judaica Jerusalem 1971), by blacks in New York against Italian-Americans as shown in Greenberg's chapter in Part II.

The public should be able to determine whether the organizations want to improve global business practices or whether they would rather see global business abolished, whether the anti-globalization movement is against globalization in general or whether it is just against globalization on the present terms. We can also expect more conflict regarding the content of standards. Even good faith NGOs may lay down incompatible standards for determining unacceptable business practices (see Cashore et al., Jordan et al. in this volume for details). We can also expect a market for lax standards by businesses eager to avoid criticism, as has been a worry concerning the UN Global Compact that allegedly requires little in the way of real action by the signatories. Much work is done, but more remains concerning how standards should accommodate the very different powers and roles of governments and businesses. Within a system of coordinated, yet largely sovereign states, the international community can hold governments responsible for fulfilling the range of political, civil, economic, and social rights. However, even if one company respects all such rights of individuals, other agents may violate them if enforcement is lax. Thus, the satisfaction of individuals' vital interests seems clearly beyond the reach of any single company. The relevant standards for companies must therefore be specially drafted, as indeed is the case.

Whose "Facts"?

Political consumers must rely for fact-finding on NGOs such as Amnesty International, Transparency International, and Consumers International. Quality control is a perennial challenge even for well-intentioned NGOs. NGO credibility is obviously even more important, when high ethical standards become a comparative advantage and competitor companies may criticize "findings" for less than honorable reasons, (cf. Cahore et al. this volume). Trustworthiness is even more problematic when organizations are established, or used intentionally, to slant information, as when multinationals use the international lobby group "The Coalition for the Right for Truth in Environmental Marketing" to influence governments and WTO in their favor (Micheletti 1999). The Internet also creates new pitfalls, since it lacks quality control and hence leaves it to users to distinguish well-founded cyber activism from unfounded "cyberterrorism." The trustworthiness of standard setting and fact-finding must be secured through a variety of institutionalized means: governmental expertise or, to the contrary, independence of government (Micheletti 1999), auditors such as Price Waterhouse Coopers, Ernst & Young, and Deloitte, or by cooperating with academics.

Who Guards These Guardians?—Is Democratic Accountability Required?

A fourth challenge is to maintain public confidence that the organizations for political consumerism reliably fulfill their role professionally and effectively. This would seem to require public scrutiny and accountability, though perhaps not that the organizations are internally democratic. Neither the Identity nor Instrumental arguments require that the organizations for political consumerism are internally democratic. Democratic accountability may not be equally important for such agents of civil society. It may suffice that organizations of political consumerism are subject to media scrutiny within civil society. Individual consumers may then choose to use these organizations and their information and possibly decide to exercise "market accountability" against the firms violating standards.

The Appropriate Roles of Governments

On the Instrumental account, political consumerism must find its role alongside governmental action. In addition to providing quality control of standards and information and scrutiny, we should recall the limits to effective political consumerism where government action alone seems useful. There are several ills that political consumerism is unlikely to combat due to the limited range of goods under consumer control, lack of sanctions of voluntary codes, and coordination problems. At best, political consumerism may prevent human rights' violations by particular firms such as child labor, environmental damage, etc. Consumers cannot affect companies that do not sell products to individual consumers. Many requirements of social justice seem to be beyond what can be asked of individual companies—for instance, massive redistribution, public education, etc. Governments thus have several important tasks, even when political consumerism is effective. It is an important task to find and implement the institutional solutions that best divide up or share these responsibilities.

Conclusion: Consumerism with a Vengeance?

Political philosophers have long lamented the shift in public perception towards regarding the citizen as a consumer (MacIntyre 1978, 245). Citizens' concern for the general good was replaced by concern for satisfying consumption preferences (cf. Sandel 1996, 224). The point of democracy became to secure "the widest range of economic satisfaction" more fairly distributed rather than the formation of republican citizens (Weyl 1912 in Sandel 1996, 225). The practice of political citizenship transcends this conflict.

Political consumerism is strikingly different from consumerism as an ideological basis for politics that developed in the United States in the 1920s (cf. Strasser, McGovern, & Judt 1998). Indeed it inverts the relationship between means and ends. Political consumerism does not regard poor consumer quality of goods as cause for political action but considers the poor political quality of goods as cause for consumer action. It insists that a working market does not assume that consumers only seek self-oriented satisfaction. Consumers are also citizens and can be strongly committed to distributive justice and the decent and respectful treatment of those they affect. This commitment can find expression through purchases. Political consumerism allows individuals, living under conditions of globalization beyond control of accountable governments, to express their sense of justice as citizens of the world. A defensible role as consumer and citizen under globalization requires them to exercise their economic power responsibly when seeking to promote a legitimate global economic order that treats all as equals.

References

Banchoff, Thomas, & Mitchell P. Smith. 1999. "Introduction: Conceptualizing Legitimacy in a Contested Polity," in Thomas Banchoff & Mitchell P. Smith, eds., *Legitimacy and the European Union*. London: Routledge.

Burnheim, J. 1986. "Democracy, Nation-States, and the World System," in D. Held & C. Pollitt, eds., *New Forms of Democracy*. London: Sage.

Caney, Simon. 1992. "Liberalism and Communitarianism: A Misconceived Debate." *Political Studies* 40: 273-89.

Commission on Global Governance. 1995. *Our Global Neighbourhood*. Oxford: Oxford University Press.

Donaldson, Thomas. 1989. *The Ethics of International Business*. New York: Oxford University Press.

___. "Rights in the Global Market," in R. Edward Freeman, *Business Ethics. The State of the Art*. New York: Oxford University Press.

___, & Thomas W. Dunfee. 1999. "When Ethics Travel: The Promise and Peril of Global Business Ethics." *California Management Review* 41: 4.

Economist. 1999. "The Non-Governmental Order: Will NGOs Democratise, or merely Disrupt, Global Governance?" *The Economist*, 11 December.

Eide, Asbjorn. 1998. "Article 28," in Gudmundur Alfredsson & Asbjørn Eide, eds., *The Universal Declaration of Human Rights: A Common Standard of Achievement*. The Hague: Martinus Nijhoff.

Encyclopædia Judaica Jerusalem 1971. "Boycott, Anti-Jewish." Band 4. Jerusalem: Keter Publishing House.

Florini, Ann. 2000. *The Third Force: The Rise of Transnational Civil Society*. Washington, DC: Carnegie Endowment for Peace.

Galston, William. 1991. *Liberal Purposes: Goods, Virtues, and Duties in the Liberal State*. Cambridge: Cambridge University Press.

Gandhi, Mahatma. 1918. *The Collected Works of Mahatma Gandhi*. Vol. 15. New Delhi: Publications Division, Ministry of Information and Broadcasting.

Goodin, Robert E. 1992. *Green Political Theory*. Cambridge: Polity/Blackwell.

Greenhouse, Steven. 2000. "The Boycott Returns," *New York Times*, 27 March.

Halliday, Fred. 2000. "Global Governance: Prospects and Problems." *Citizenship Studies* 4, 1: 19-23.

Held, David, & Anthony McGrew, eds. 2000. *The Global Transformations Reader: An Introduction to the Globalization Debate*. Oxford: Polity Press.

Hill, Thomas E. 1979. "Symbolic Protest and Calculated Silence." *Philosophy and Public Affairs* 9, 1: 83-102.

___. 1991. "The Importance of Autonomy," in Thomas E. Hill, *Autonomy and Self-Respect*. Cambridge: Cambridge University Press.

Inglehart, Ronald. 2000. "Globalization and Postmodern Values." *Washington Quarterly* 23, 1: 215-28.

Kant, Immanuel. 1964. *The Metaphysical Principles of Virtue*. James Ellington, transl. Indianapolis: Bobbs-Merrill.

MacIntyre, Alasdair. 1978. *Against the Self-Images of the Age: Essays on Ideology and Philosophy*. Notre Dame, IN: University of Notre Dame Press.

Micheletti, Michele. 1999. "Put Your Money Where Your Mouth Is! Political Consumerism as Political Participation." Paper for Workshop No. 6 of *Nye politiske identiter og institutioner i hverdagens politiske praksis*, Nordic Political Science Association Meeting, August.

Mills, Cynthia. 1996. "Should We Boycott Boycotts?" *Journal of Social Philosophy* 27: 136-48.

Muller, Jerry Z. 1992. *Adam Smith in His Time and Ours*. New York: Free Press.

Putnam, Robert D. 2000. *Bowling Alone: The Collapse and Revival of American Community*. New York: Simon & Schuster.

Rawls, John. 1971. *A Theory of Justice*. Cambridge, MA: Harvard University Press.

Risse, Thomas, Steven C. Ropp, & Kathryn Sikkink, eds. 1999. *The Power of Human Rights: International Norms and Domestic Change*. Cambridge: Cambridge University Press (Cambridge Studies in International Relations no. 66).

Rosenau, James N. 1992. "Governance, Order, and Change in World Politics," in James N. Rosenau & Ernst Otto Czempiel, eds., *Governance Without Government: Order and Change in World Politics*. Cambridge: Cambridge University Press.

Sandel, Michael. 1996. *Democracy's Discontent: America in Search of a Public Philosophy*. Cambridge, MA: Harvard University Press.

Sen, Amartya K. 1982. "Rights and Agency." *Philosophy and Public Affairs* 11, 1: 3-39.

___. 1997. "Human Rights and Asian Values: What Lee Kuan Yew and Li Peng Don't Understand About Asia." *The New Republic* (July 14): 33-40.

Smart, J.J.C., & Bernard Williams. 1973. *Utilitarianism for and Against*. Cambridge: Cambridge University Press.

Smith, Adam. 1776 [1954.] *An Inquiry into the Nature and Causes of the Wealth of Nations*. London: Dent.

Spar, Debora L. 1998. "The Spotlight and the Bottom Line: How Multinationals Export Human Rights" *Foreign Affairs* 77, 2: 7-12.

Strange, Susan. 1986. *Casino Capitalism*. Oxford: Blackwell.

Strasser, Susan, Charles McGovern, & Matthias Judt, eds. 1998. *Getting and Spending: European and American Consumer Societies in the 20th Century*. Cambridge: Cambridge University Press.

Welzel, Chris, Ronald Inglehart, & Hans-Dieter Klingeman. 2002. "The Theory of Human Development: A Cross-Cultural Analysis" *European Journal of Political Research*. 41.

Werhane, Patricia H. 1991. *Adam Smith and His Legacy for Modern Capitalism*. Oxford: Oxford University Press.

Selling Virtue: The Political and Economic Contradictions of Green/Ethical Marketing in the United Kingdom

Paul Kennedy

Introduction

Some capitalist enterprises have always been prepared to demonstrate social responsibility by supporting charities, founding educational trusts, sponsoring artistic endeavors and so on. Such actions legitimized the quest for profit and enhanced their public profile. However, in recent years the rise of green/ethical businesses has revealed not just a willingness to become involved in non-economic, even political, activity to a much greater extent than before, but a tendency for some businesses to become key agents of cultural and political change in their own right. The discussion in this chapter explores this general theme.

It is largely informed by the results of a small study of green/ethical businesses conducted in northwest Britain in 1994, but especially in the Manchester conurbation and in West Yorkshire (Kennedy 1996). The research included various kinds of enterprises—worker's and other cooperatives, sole proprietorships, partnerships and limited liability companies—whose managers and owners were involved in providing green/ethical goods or services for final consumers, whether as contributors to a supply chain or as immediate providers in direct contact with the consuming public. The goods and services provided by these enterprises varied a great deal and included the following: recycled plastics, clothes, wood and paper products; cruelty-free, non-animal-based body products (cosmetics and soaps); biodegradable chemicals and cleaning agents; organic, vegetarian "wholefoods" and beverages; the printing, publishing and retailing of radical or alternative materials; services such as ethical finance, investments and accountancy; and general-purpose retailing of a range

21

of green/ethical goods, educational materials and fair-trade Third World craft products.

The sample was in no sense a random or representative one, because at that time there was no available data base for such enterprises and a dearth of resources dictated that the study had to be conducted in northwest Britain. Thus, the sample was obtained partly by consulting national magazines and directories or by visiting exhibitions, which specialized in informing individuals and businesses about green/ethical affairs, and partly by employing a "snowball" approach—following up the leads obtained from an initial sample of self-styled enterprises operating in this area of activity concerning their suppliers, market outlets, and other business connections. Apart from a few intrinsically interesting cases the study avoided contacting very large international companies and national chains, including supermarkets, because these were only very marginally involved in green/ethical enterprise, and their head offices were usually located outside the region.

The research did not directly attempt to investigate the attitudes and actions of consumers per se. Nevertheless, the evidence strongly suggests that the growing phenomenon of political consumerism affected these enterprises in one of the following ways. First, business survival and market expansion depended on their ability to foster the awareness and commitment of new consumers to green/ethical lifestyles while retaining the confidence of those who were already converted to the "cause." Second, some of these entrepreneurs went considerably further and deliberately organized their enterprises as campaigning vehicles designed to support the concerns of political/ethical consumers. But giving equal or even greater priority to such normative considerations as against the "normal" goal of profit, risked jeopardizing business growth and even survival. Surprisingly, even the more commercially driven businesses also found themselves drawn towards adopting some of the features of political campaigns.

The chapter will examine the differences and the similarities between two types of enterprise—radical and mainstream—and the contradictions they both face, by exploring the logic of green/ethical market capitalism. First, however, I outline briefly some of the main transformations currently re-shaping contemporary society and which appear to underpin the rise of political consumerism, and then I offer a typology of the consumers who were regarded by the respondents in this study as crucial in shaping their business decisions.

Socio-Cultural Change and Political Consumerism

Political consumerism is not new, but it does seem to be assuming a much more central role in civic life as consumption becomes increasingly "suffused with citizenship characteristics" (Scammell 2000, 351)—giving rise to the activist, concerned citizen-consumer— and as issues of personal identity and lifestyle associated with life-politics (Giddens 1991) assume greater importance along with the possibilities for massively extended interpersonal interaction brought by electronic communication including cyber-protest. Whether all this adds up to a "new" politics, which is replacing the conventional forms of protest and engagement we associate with party competition, democratic voting, class-based interests, and nation-state citizenship, or whether, instead, we are simply dealing with a significant and necessary broadening of the "old" politics, remains unclear. Nevertheless, many contemporary social observers argue that several linked changes are currently transforming our lives and these underpin a relative shift in the dominant modes of political engagement. Included among these changes are the following: continuous technological development, especially the rise of the "informational economy" (Castells 1996); the geo-politics of the post-Cold War era including the advent, even before 1989, of neo-liberal economics and the disappearance of a realistic alternative to capitalism; the rise of postmodern sensibilities; the growing impact on socio-political life of knowledgeable, self-monitoring individuals in what Beck (2000a) calls the second or reflexive era of modernity along with strong pressures for self-realization or individualization; and the intensifying processes of globalization. The discussion will now briefly explore three of these changes, namely, postmodernity, reflexivity/ individualization, and globalization, and will then indicate how these inform the research findings discussed in this chapter.

Postmodern Sensibilities

Many social scientists have argued that the last thirty years or so, have seen a collapse of once familiar boundaries: between "high" and "low" cultures, different fields of artistic endeavor and the worlds of art and non-art; and between the various social spheres of home and production, leisure and work and class identity. Alongside this a radical deconstruction has taken place of previously unquestioned categories in the areas of gender and sexuality. There has also been a celebration of the creative and empowering possibilities provided by material consumption, the pursuit of hedonism, and the increased importance of style—the aestheticization of everyday life—in the quest for personalized meaning and identity (Lash 1994; Lash & Urry 1994), including in the sphere of politics. It is also argued that the affective and aesthetic qualities of commodities have become much more important than their functionality or social status, and alongside this has gone the increased importance of a signifying culture rooted in a media-dominated world of swirling, unstable signs, images, and symbols. Culture is said to have become autonomous from the spheres of production and economy leading to its greater dominance in social life (Bradley & Fenton 1999, 112). Simultaneously there has been a growing preference for non-judgmental and more emotional evaluations of culture and social life giving rise to a relativism, which gives more credence to personalized and subjective interpretations of everyday experience (Sayer 1999, 53-57). This "de-moralization of culture" (Ray & Sayer 1999, 12) has also affected politics. Thus, the issues of poverty, inequality, and social justice that once dominated political agendas—the "politics of distribution"—have been largely displaced by the "(cultural) politics of recognition" (Sayer 1999, 54) involving a concern with previously neglected issues of gender, sexuality, and the environment.

Reflexivity, Individualization and Self-Realization

Much recent sociological thinking has pointed to the growing impact of self-monitoring individuals on late modern life, whether this reflexivity is conceptualized as primarily cognitive (based on lay expertise and knowledge), moral *and* cognitive, as Beck (1992) seems to think, or as expressive and aesthetic as Lash (1994) suggests. Moreover, it is argued that the era of reflexive modernity requires individuals to confront new phenomena. These include the information revolution with all its repercussions (Castells 1996), a revolution in gender relations, the rise of widespread environmental threats, the reconfiguration of state sovereignty, and the final dissolution of those remnants of tradition on which people could still depend during the long era of the first modernity—class, unambiguous gender divisions, family, and the nation-state. Beck (1992, 1994, 2000a) observes that these multiple changes, especially the sheer enormity of environmental risks, gives us no choice but to demand safer economic and political systems and to take greater responsibility for our own protection. Meanwhile, declining traditional support systems leave us largely alone to construct our own life course (see also, Castells 1997). However, we now enjoy the freedom to pursue a path of individualization with few social constraints, and even though this could result, in extreme cases, in the collapse of normative control in social life (Touraine 1998, 130f) or the loss of society's "collective self-consciousness and therefore its capacity for political action" (Beck 2000b, 8).

Globalization

There is general agreement that the processes of globalization have intensified and accelerated in recent years (Cohen & Kennedy 2000; Held et al. 1999; Scholte 2000) and may also have assumed entirely new and distinctive forms (Robertson 1992; Albrow 1996; Beck 2000b). For one thing there is our exposure to ever greater cultural flows, especially though not only through the media, so that it becomes more difficult to inhabit purely localized worlds, while even the poorest people are offered the possibility of alternative lives through the imaginings stirred by their awareness of numerous "others" (Appadurai 1991). Similarly, cultures have become de-localized from particular and familiar places assisted by the revolution in information technology and communications (Featherstone & Lash 1999), and are giving rise to effective transnational communities, networks, and organizations including many which operate entirely or partly through cyberspace (Hannerz 1996; Kennedy & Roudometof 2002). Some of these transnational relations involve the renewal and strengthening of traditional, ethnic or diasporic ties, while others are concerned with the founding of new communities or the pursuit of global political and ethical goals. Then there is the growing interdependence of world economic life through commodity chains and the spatial optimization (Dicken 1992) of production systems between nations and regions—made possible by an increasingly dominant and footloose capitalism supported by a neo-liberal regime of deregulation, casualization, and insecurity across the entire world— but also a huge increase in people's understanding of how this globalized economy works and a determination to resist or reform its inherent disadvantages. Linked to the latter has been the rapid rise of a multifaceted anti-globalization movement formed out of a transnational collaboration between trade unions, churches, non-governmental organizations (NGOs), various anarchist and socialist groups, and celebrities from the world of popular culture, among others.

Contemporary Social Changes and Their Effects on Consumers

All three of the changes we have outlined have some bearing upon the rise of green/ethical consumerism and its political ramifications as a possible force for wider change. They also have explanatory usefulness in trying to unravel the opportunities, the problems, and the contradictions experienced by businesses working in this field.

1. The "bads" and "goods" of postmodern consumer practices. Postmodern consumerism is notable for the sheer scale of production engendered by the search for symbolic values, in the attempt to construct personal lifestyles by assembling a mass of inherently unstable images. The increasingly symbolic nature of consumption, however, cannot conceal the underlying materiality of the products to which such meanings are attached, nor the relentless pressure on resources and the generation of wastes that accompanies these lifestyle practices; postmodern society enhances creativity, but it incurs enormous environmental and perhaps social costs. Yet, the very power of symbolic consumption also contains the potential to counteract such environmental dangers, because for some people goods and services can assume meanings containing connotations of green or ethical/political virtue as against the "evils" of environmental destruction and injustice. Given that the moralization of consumer practices involves the deliberate attempt to combine lifestyle preferences with "goodness" and /or political correctness—both essentially symbolic qualities—some forms of commercialized signifying culture can be made to work for the environment and social justice rather than against them.

2. Reflexivity and the pressures of self-realization. Whether or not the actual market for green/ethical goods has increased, it seems that levels of concern and awareness have risen markedly in recent years. A series of food scares have certainly contributed to this, particularly Bovine Spongiform Encephalopathy (BSE), but also the growing fear of skin cancer from ozone depletion and the suspicion that climatic irregularities associated with global warming are in-

creasing rapidly and are manifest everywhere. Indeed, the very concerns of all postmodern citizens with issues of narcissistic self-
realization—including issues such as how to reach a healthy old
age and to remain sexually active and desirable as long as possible—
must compel them to worry increasingly about a whole range of
problems or relinquish any possibility of pursuing such goals mean-
ingfully. Thus, obsessively trying to preserve a beautiful body is
pointless if poisons and toxins are being ingested with every action
we take, or if economic insecurities and the consequences of social
collapse threaten human activity at every turn. Among such universal problems are, of course, environmental pollution and degradation, food production and contamination, traffic congestion, unequal
capital flows and escalating inequality, climatic change, the dangers
of rising crime, drug abuse and social disintegration, and much else
besides. Of course, increasing individualization—not just the need
to become more autonomous and self-directed, but also the un-
ashamed preoccupation with issues of personal self-realization and
hedonistic satisfaction—does not necessarily preclude a parallel lean-
ing towards moral concerns involving a willingness to respond to
societal needs. Indeed, the significance of the moral dimension of
reflexive action has probably not been given the emphasis it deserves. Certainly, the evidence from the present study suggests it
can sometimes be a very powerful force and this has been borne out
by recent protests in the global arena. Thus, a growing number of
mostly educated citizen/consumers are not only increasingly concerning themselves with the complexities and minutia of economic
organization and how these affect their personal lives, they are also
seeking to exercise a moral influence, whether through overt political actions or indirectly by exercising informed consumer choices,
over the institutions shaping everyday life.

3. The effects of globalization. As we have seen, economic globalization, and therefore the growing interconnectedness and market interdependence engendered by transnational corporations, vast
financial flows, E-technology, and the now worldwide sway of capitalist markets, has generated a massive anti-globalization movement
since the late 1990s. But these anti-globalization protests demonstrate the extent to which moral and political concerns have been
extended to a rising number of issues: not just environmental degradation, continuing gender inequality and human rights, but also to
concerns about child labor, sex tourism, Third World debt and pov-

erty, the need for fair trade and so on. Moreover, protest is being mounted against a widening spread of targets far beyond what were once the "usual suspects": governments, oil, pharmaceutical, chemical, and building companies or banks. Instead, hardly any interest believed to be complicit in North-South trade, the exploitation of cheap labor, the perpetuation of poverty or the destruction of the environment in a very broad sense, can expect any longer to remain immune from campaigning activities. Indeed, the very interdependent nature of the global economy manifest, for example, in the linkages between transnational corporations (TNCs) and their Third World subcontractors, is compelling many of the former to impose codes of ethical and labor conduct on the latter because of the intensifying risk of adverse media coverage and a consequent loss of market share and asset value. In effect, globalization is leading some TNCS to "export human rights" (Spar 1998, 7). Intergovernmental organizations such as the World Trade Organization, universities, scientific research organizations, local authorities and other public institutions have also become prime targets. Thus, the scope for exercising consumer power through transnational boycotts, selective buying by individuals on a growing scale (Nava 1991), as well as demonstrations, petitions, lobbying, picketing, and other attempts to shape public-opinion, grows all the time.

The Crucial Role of Consumers

The respondents in this study pointed to a range of stakeholders who were influential in shaping their business choices including NGOs, the media, citizen's networks, professional/scientific advisors and sympathetic help agencies such as local councils or specialist advisory organizations. Nevertheless, they were also strongly convinced that consumers were the key driving force to be reckoned with. Drawing upon the information offered by the respondents, roughly six types of consumers emerged as particularly crucial in influencing the dilemmas they faced and their growth prospects.

Professionals. This group of relatively wealthy, ethically aware, and highly informed consumers, was composed mostly of people living in "two career" families and with professional occupations. They could afford, and were often willing, to pay premium prices for certain commodities rather than buy cheaper alternatives from large companies or stores, even if the evidence suggested that the green/ethical claims made for the latters' goods were trustworthy. Partly, this group was engaged in legitimizing their privileged position while seeking credentials to validate their moral and political priorities.

Lower "professionals." A second group was equally well-informed, demanding and critically self-monitoring concerning their own actions and lifestyles, but received much lower incomes: students, those working in one of the arts, young educated individuals who were not yet established in a permanent career structure, or those in the so-called caring professions—nursing, social work, teaching, or the voluntary sector. Despite their strong leanings toward green/ethical lifestyles, their modest incomes prevented them from expressing these preferences on a regular and wide basis.

Vegetarians and vegans. Their primary concern—whether for reasons of personal health, the aesthetics of taste or because of their commitment to animal rights causes—led them to seek cruelty-free household and body products as well as foodstuffs containing no animal products. Like group two, many lived on modest incomes.

Alternative lifestylers and "drop-outs." These consumers had deliberately rejected the careerist and materialistic lifestyle preoccupations of the citizen majority. Indeed, they identified these as the chief cause of the environmental and social malaises of contemporary society. Consequently, many were unemployed and dependent on social benefits or engaged in insecure, casualized part-time work probably by choice. Their alternative lifestyles rendered them highly sympathetic to green/ethical products and to the radical political leanings demonstrated by the businesses we studied. However, their low incomes severely restricted their ability to purchase these products.

According to the enterprise managers, many individuals belonging to these four categories shared two further orientations. One was an antagonism towards supermarkets, retail chains, and other corporate giants—whom they regarded as the cynical and exploitative "great devils" of capitalism, guilty of a multiplicity of worldwide unethical and environmental unfriendly activities. The other was a contempt for the glitzy arcades and the postmodern signifying culture of narcissistic self-realization and celebrity imitation available on the shelves of the glamorous city center superstores. On the other hand, the respondents also feared that, despite such moral/political leanings, these consumers were not always able to resist such temptations.

Those with special health needs. A small but important source of market demand emanated from an assortment of people across the class and ethnic spectrum suffering from a variety of persistent maladies that conventional medicine seemed unable to cure completely. Included here were the old, disabled people, children, or adults with allergies, diabetics, people with skin diseases or those who believed that additives in conventional foods, beverages, and cosmetics were causing them permanent harm. Very often health was their sole or main preoccupation.

Ordinary mass consumers. By far the largest consumer group identified by our respondents was also that for which they had little or no personal experience since "ordinary mass consumers" rarely if ever purchased ethical/green goods and services, or did so only through a chance encounter or as a last resort. As such they were unlikely to be repeat customers. This was the unconquered market, whose members were largely indifferent to and/or ignorant of the virtues of green/ethical products. It was this group, above all, whose *absence* rendered business life so inherently precarious. Although generally ignorant concerning this majority, some respondents suggested reasons why one particular strand of this large group, namely, working class males, might be repelled by what these enterprises had to offer. Thus, supposedly, they perceived green/ethical products and those who supplied and bought them as faddish and effeminate. They also resented the atmosphere of political correctness and the middle class "do-gooders" or the hippie new age lifestyles they associated with these products. Clearly, a major problem faced by green/ethical businesses is how to extend their market reach to these majority groups by overcoming their resistance to such goods. Overcoming this obstacle would ensure long-term business expansion and reduce current economic insecurities, especially if this could be achieved without alienating committed repeat customers.

These very different types of consumer obviously create particular challenges and opportunities for businesses that choose to operate in this field of enterprise. Thus, group one, the "professionals" provides a ready-made core market, because they are both wealthy and strongly committed, but they are also very demanding and are likely to be opposed to any compromises. Groups two, three, and four provide the basis for a more extensive market and one that has a potential to be expanded further. However, their meager incomes mean that most can only purchase a limited range of green/ethical goods; they cannot usually build an entire lifestyle around green/ethical products. This, in turn, may mean that at certain times such consumers are unreliable or even fickle: on occasion they might be attracted by the attentions of the large chains or supermarkets, if the latter can convincingly demonstrate that their promises of lower prices without jeopardizing green/ethical standards are creditable. Group five is also likely to be rather problematical in terms of market security, since it is likely that its members will be interested in a rather narrow range of health products and, again, larger and less ethically committed businesses may be able to offer equally attractive prospects at lower prices. Finally, group six—though made up of an enormously variable range of groups and individuals—clearly presents the most severe challenge both to green/ethical businesses as such, and to prospects for political consumerism as a phenomenon shaping contemporary political and social life. Yet, no one living on this planet, and certainly not those we have designated as "ordinary mass consumers," can escape from the tensions and problems created by the underlying socioeconomic divisions and conflicts—along with environmental and other threats—that are endemic to late capitalism and globalization. Thus, the possibilities for mobilizing political consumerism as a much greater force for change in the years ahead would appear to be considerable.

The Dilemmas of Green/Ethical Marketing:
Marrying Profit and Principle

Approximately thirty of the enterprises included in the study were "mainstream" enterprises: they were privately owned, with professional and hierarchical management structures, highly unequal systems of remuneration, and a specialized organizational structure. Their involvement in green/ethical business formed only a part of their overall operation. Their motivation for marketing such products was primarily driven by profit considerations, though this was beginning to change. A second group of around thirty-three "radical" enterprises displayed most of the following characteristics. First, political and moral considerations in business received nearly equal or even higher priority than purely profit considerations, so that it often seemed as if a business existed more as a vehicle for conducting a moral/political campaign than as a means of achieving a livelihood. Second, the radical firms leaned strongly toward democratic and equalitarian work practices, both internally—job rotation, employee consultation, reduced pay differentials and so on—and with respect to serving the wider community, for example, by donating food or the use of premises free of charge to local causes, employing disabled people, or subsidizing tiny satellite enterprises. Lastly, the radical proprietors and their employees revealed a preference for alternative, relatively non-materialistic lifestyles outside work.

Ostensibly, these two types of enterprise not only seemed to be worlds apart, but in many respects they were. However, both types were compelled to cope with similar pressures and problems arising from their decision to operate in this particular market niche. Consequently—and paradoxically—while starting with completely opposite goals and orientations they ended up evolving towards a rather similar situation, though this was more evident in the case of the mainstream firms than the radical ones, because of the latters' reluctance to give full reign to the pursuit of economic growth. In order to explain this paradox I now outline the business parameters, which confront any firm—mainstream or radical—that chooses to operate in this field, and then discuss these in more detail:

- the need to participate in converting more consumers to green/ethical causes as a necessary ploy for business expansion;

- the commodification of ethicality as a profitable market strategy;

- the need to cultivate an interactive relationship with reflexive, informed consumers;

- increased exposure to, and dependency upon, a range of external pressure groups and specialized agencies whose agendas are non-commercial; and

- the parallel need to enjoy the close interpersonal confidence of other businesses working in related fields.

The Market Pressure to Convert Unbelievers

In a capitalist system, all of these firms were compelled to maintain or increase profits, to cover costs, and to retain their market share or risk market extinction. Consequently, it is in the immediate economic interest of those engaged in this sphere of business activity—radical and mainstream alike—to seek expansion by actively participating in the process of converting unbelievers to the correctness of green/ethical causes while striving to retain the political or moral enthusiasm of existing converts.

Selling Virtue

Given the nature of the market niche in which they operate, all these firms were directly or indirectly providing goods and services perceived by their customers as embodying some elements of moral or political credibility in addition to the utility functions and other symbolic values they contained. These enterprises were *commodifying ethicality* or selling the proofs of moral virtue. This, in turn, generates additional consequences and presupposes certain preconditions.

Consumer–Seller Interaction

Thus, it must be possible for green/ethical businesses to meet with, and connect to, certain types of consumers in the market arena—people who were engaged in *moralizing their own consumer practices*. Such individuals tended to be informed, demanding, ethically caring, and politically aware. The class and political struggles over working conditions, employment opportunities, wages, and the distribution of wealth that were once so commonplace, rarely involved a parallel concern on the part of workers or citizens to question the whole morality of economic growth, the harnessing of science to industrial aims, or the minute basis for the organization of production. Moreover, most postmodern consumers today choose passively from a predetermined array of market signifiers and demand little or no say in, or knowledge of, the circumstances in which goods are produced, packaged, transported, distributed, or displayed—though this may now be changing. In sharp contrast, most green/ethical consumers are trying to acquire some knowledge of, and the ability to exercise a degree of influence over, all the stages and processes involved in the decision-making process associated with the supply of goods and services, including the disposal of wastes. Achieving this goal, even to a small degree, requires that such consumers demand a highly interactive relationship with all those involved in supplying their needs.

Exposure to and Dependence upon External Agents

The commodification of ethicality as a market strategy necessarily invites the scrutiny of others—who will wish to investigate the authenticity of such claims—and calls for proof. As we have seen, this inevitably increases business exposure to the demands of discerning and scrupulous consumers who require accountability and concrete evidence of their own virtues and those of the enterprises whose products they acquire. However, making claims of ethicality simultaneously exposes these enterprises to the scrutiny of a host of additional interests. Among these will be social movements, NGOs, voluntary and community groups, informed citizen networks, schools and colleges, the media, specialized research groups with relevant knowledge, professional associations, and so on. The point about such groups is that their rationale is likely to be primarily moral, political, or cultural rather than technical or economic; their agendas are not commercial ones. In addition, not only is it likely that green/ethical enterprises will be exposed to such external scrutiny, but they may also become dependent upon such groups in a number of ways, in addition to the latters' ability to confer proper credentialization on business claims. Thus, enterprises may be able to obtain specialized knowledge concerning the continuous changes with respect to standards of environmental safety for different products or processes. Alternatively, these agencies may be a primary source of certain inputs needed in production, for example: recycled materials—raised by schools, neighborhood groups, local councils, private charities, churches, or workplace collections schemes; sympathetic media coverage and advertising; technical advice; help in obtaining loans; or even market opportunities, as in the case of the trading sections of powerful NGOs such as Greenpeace or Oxfam.

The Needs of Businesses in the Demand or Supply Chain

A further source of external pressure came from other businesses operating in the same arena of green/ethical marketing and who formed part of a firm's supply or demand chain. Clearly, it was not in any firm's interest to knowingly act in such a way as to alienate its own final consumers. However, nor was it sensible to do so with respect to those upon whom a client enterprise depended, since a supplier-company's *own market ultimately depended* on the degree to which final customers were satisfied with buyer-companies. In addition, no enterprise will want to risk contravening the growing volume of environmental and other legislation pertaining to business by dealing with an unreliable company. What these backward and forward market linkages between different green/ethical enterprises required was a bank of sympathetic support agencies and like-minded businesses held together by trust. This trust was based not only on the dis-embedded, impersonal professional orientations typical of social life under modernity (Giddens 1990), but also upon a re-embedding of such highly personalized relationships, based on close friendships and genuine mutual liking, into business exchanges. Such friendship networks were especially likely in the case of the radical enterprises. One likely consequence of such networks among the radical firms was that they tended to pay their invoices in full and promptly—something that is much rarer in the "mainstream" economy—and this had apparently helped many such enterprises to survive the steep recession that hit the British economy in the early 1990s. Personal friendship can therefore operate as a key business resource in more ways than one.

The Contradictions and Constraints Faced by Green/Ethical Businesses

The marriage of profit with principle is an uneasy one. A likely consequence is that to different degrees enterprises are driven to adopt a political and moral campaigning profile—something we do not normally associate with capitalist businesses. To this extent such enterprises become agents of cultural and political change in their own right. The willingness to assume this role is not surprising in regard to the radical enterprises, because their founders and current members were already committed to using their businesses as vehicles for expressing political, moral, and green ideas, as well as a means of earning a livelihood, before they established or joined the firm in question. This internalized, shared, moral and political intentionality simply worked in tandem with all those pressures towards adopting a campaigning profile that stemmed from the types of consumer they dealt with and the external attention they attracted from pressure groups. However, the evidence that some mainstream companies, too, were combining cultural, "political" and educational functions—the features of a campaign—with narrow economic ones, albeit driven almost entirely by profit considerations and the need to expand the market for their products, seemed rather surprising. Moreover, to the extent that they were moving in this direction, this placed them in the same cultural and political frame as the radical firms. What was the evidence for such unlikely mainstream business leanings?

Towards the "Campaigning" Mainstream Company?

The thirty mainstream enterprises were involved in such economic sectors as textiles, paper products, plastics, chemicals, paints, food, financial services, and waste recycling. Around one-third, provided clear information concerning the authenticity of their green/ethical products and strove to create images of simplicity and naturalness with respect to their business operations. They were also keenly aware of their market dependence upon cultural change in the wider society. However, they showed little or no actual involvement in public debates on such issues nor did they attempt to demonstrate a commitment to them by overtly wooing public concern. In short, they revealed no campaigning features despite their dependence on the political and cultural activities of others. This minimalist response was either linked to the fact that green/ethical marketing formed only a small part of their business, or their tendency to rely on supplying "own brand goods" to supermarkets or other chains. This protected them from "front-line" exposure to final consumers, so that they did not need to justify or legitimize their involvement in this area, but it also meant that they could not directly influence overall market demand for such goods but had to rely on their larger business customers.

In contrast, approximately two-thirds of the mainstream firms (twenty) were either directly dependent upon sympathetic green/ethical customers and other agents in the wider society as sources for some of their raw materials, information, technical assistance, or networking opportunities and/or they (fifteen firms) were simultaneously engaged in developing a pro-active stance on their own account with respect to raising public awareness. This pro-activity assumed various and sometimes overlapping forms. Eight firms had adopted an educational profile with respect to schools, colleges, and the general public. This usually involved one or more of the following activities: producing highly professional films, videos, and brochures demonstrating the roles their firms—and industry—were playing in adopting improved systems for public environmental management; holding and attending exhibitions, craft fairs, or industry events that were designed to inform consumers and the general public about green/ethical issues; hosting regular school and college visits to their premises; and making company facilities and their environmental expertise available to student placement schemes and to local educational programs. Six enterprises were engaged in targeting and gaining the support of different interest groups, for example, by participating in voluntary schemes designed to promote environmental awareness in cooperation with green pressure groups. Alternatively or additionally, they had joined in local or central government initiatives or had provided financial sponsorship, active organizational support, or free advertising and communication facilities to one or more NGOs. Nine companies had employed a core of professional managers or technicians, who combined environmental training and a degree of personal commitment to these issues. These employees were then given considerable scope, in terms of investment and company facilities, to develop and enhance the firm's environmental activities and public profile. Finally, at least three enterprises had been involved in sponsoring local community activities of a voluntary and ethical nature such as helping to finance a nature reserve.

Clearly, these moves in the direction of campaigning activity by mainstream firms were motivated originally by commercial considerations. Yet, as in the case of some TNCs who find it necessary to impose social codes on overseas subcontractors (Spar 1998), it could be argued that this field of business endeavor—with its exposure to community groups, NGOs, highly demanding consumers and their like—inevitably draws enterprises into a web of obligations, loyalties, and interpersonal as well educational pressures that generate their own logic. One kind of commitment presupposes and engenders others, while exposing companies to ever more compelling demands from outsiders (and insiders) for detailed investigation. Indeed, this trend has become much more marked during the last few years and is clearly demonstrated, for example, by Shell's dramatic "conversion" to good causes in 1998 after prolonged exposure to adverse publicity, consumer boycotts, and a threatened shareholders' revolt. Should the cultural changes that underpin the rise of green/ethical awareness deepen further, an increasing number of firms may find themselves crossing a threshold between business motivated solely by profit and that which begins to be propelled partly by non-economic orientations. In this event, the campaigning characteristics manifested by such enterprises may intensify, and they might resemble the radical firms rather more closely.

Radical Enterprises: The Dilemmas of Business Growth.

Although the radical firms were bound by commercial considerations, they were also dedicated to non-economic goals because of
the personal values held by their staff. As two informants said, this is
a "profit-plus business" and "this is so much more than just a business." Partly because of their personal values, but also in order to
continue attracting their core of repeat customers—many of whom
were just as involved in green/ethical causes as the radical members
themselves—the latter pursued their commitments to radicality to a
very marked degree. For example, they operated very strict criteria
of what constituted the proper standards of "purity" required with
regard to the ingredients used in production, what they were and
were not prepared to sell, how they organized their day-to-day operations, their degree of engagement in community causes and in
recycling of waste materials, and so on. Compromises with these
high purity standards were normally rare, had to be justified, and
might provoke bitter disputes among the business members.

Also strongly evident was their open commitment to a high campaigning profile. Indeed, this was precisely what helped them to
retain the loyalty of their main customers and to give them a much-
needed market edge over their larger and cheaper rivals as well as
the glitzy shopping malls located in prime city sites with car parking
facilities and other attractions. Thus, what the radical enterprises—
especially the retailers—could offer, which their large, powerful rivals could not, was an all-encompassing aura and experience of
alternativeness, evidence of personal and business commitment to
the importance of the campaign and the "proofs" of moral and/or
political responsibility.

This took many forms: the simplicity of the packaging resonant
with images of naturalness; the wholesome, informal, exciting atmosphere; the emphasis on the availability of sophisticated knowledge shared between client and proprietors concerning a wide range
of issues; the opportunities to pursue personal networking with and
through like-minded groups and individuals; an abundant supply of
information concerning radical causes, petitions, forthcoming protests and invitations to attend alternative health schemes, ethnic music
or arts festivals, to support local charities, housing co-operatives or
Third World awareness activities; and the cultivation of an ambi-
ence of friendliness and personal attention, where everyone's ethi-

cal commitments were acknowledged, validated, and valued. In fact, the radical enterprises often had no choice but to foster and promote such a total cultural package. Many of their clients expected nothing less; a milieu offering social warmth and personal attention, the enjoyment of community feeling, links to quasi-political groups and activities and a venue for displaying moral/political activism, and the affirmation of private credentials. The ability of the radical enterprises to act in this capacity—as cultural intermediaries—rested on the complicity of their customers and clients.

Fostering this cultural milieu bestowed immediate competitive advantages on the radical enterprises. Nevertheless, they also faced considerable constraints and, in part, it was their commitment to maintain this very high campaigning profile that reinforced these constraints. Like all businesses operating in a market economy, survival depended on their ability to retain their market share. But it was also important for them to expand, since firms that avoid growth and which stand still run the risk of being ousted from business altogether by more ruthless competitors who do not share their modest aims. The most likely prospect for widening their market appeal probably required the attempt to achieve a break-through into mass marketing. This might involve one or more of the following: winning contracts with supermarkets and so moving towards the manufacture of "own brand" products using the client's name; stocking a wider range of products of more dubious ethical content, but which are cheaper or that have a greater chance of catering to the needs of poorer customers; relaxing the strictness of their purity criteria in production, sales, business organization, and other areas; or playing down their current alternative and quasi-political image so as to bring in those consumers hostile to political correctness. But any or all of these possibilities incurred severe risks and dangers. Thus, several manufacturers of organic, cruelty-free and environmentally friendly body products, household cleaning goods and foodstuffs observed that a move towards manufacturing such goods for supermarkets and other chains would inevitably lead to a progressive tightening of control over their operations, employment practices, and choice of ingredients, so that the commitment to ethicality would be compromised. There would also be demands for cost-cutting. Eventually, the radical enterprise involved would have to agree to produce "own brand" products and lose their identity. Meanwhile previous loyal outlets might be lost. Secondly, business expansion might require the introduction of more hierarchic, technically specialized forms of management and organization, a highly unequal distribution of power and remuneration and the adoption of other conventional forms of business behavior. This would provoke serious disputes among the present members even to the point of breaking up the enterprise altogether.

Lastly, diluting standards in order to appeal to mass markets might very well alienate the radical enterprises' original, and most ethically committed, core clientele, especially those who are willing to pay premium prices. Of course, supplying a larger market might reduce unit costs and so bring down prices. This might compensate radical clients and consumers for any diminution in the expression of radicality. On the other hand, once these former attributes are lost, earlier customers might feel that there is no longer sufficient reason why they should not purchase their goods directly from the large companies or the retailing chains. Moreover, the willingness of more affluent consumers to pay premium prices as evidence of their own moral responsibility may lose its former rationale.

Faced with these dilemmas concerning business growth—and the related difficulties associated with seeking joint ventures as a way of gaining investment capital and increasing market share—most of the radical enterprises chose to continue prioritizing the campaign as their key objective, while forgoing the chance to achieve business growth beyond a certain limited point. Of course, from their perspective, these self-imposed restraints did not constitute business "failure." Nevertheless, this unwillingness to compromise principles not only jeopardizes long run expansion; it also threatens the very survival of the business itself, since businesses that avoid expansion run the risk of stagnation or eventual decline. Here, *prioritizing the campaign becomes self-defeating, because marginality in the market or economic failure may cripple or remove the very vehicle for conducting the campaign in the first place.* In addition, by choosing to confine their activities mostly to catering for the limited niche markets provided by the most ethically and politically conscious consumers, the radical enterprises are caught between either mainly preaching to the already converted or risking business collapse because of their reluctance to seek the paths that offer possible expansion. But the disappearance of the radical enterprises would leave the uninformed citizen majority fully exposed to powerful corporate interests whose willingness to assume responsibility for green and ethical issues remains largely untested, and whose resolve to do so may be weakened if their more radical rivals are driven from the scene.

Conclusion

The implications of this particular study are that political consumerism, at least in the United Kingdom, currently has some way to go before it becomes a major political phenomenon. This is simply because, at the present time, the market niches for green/ethical products are rather limited. Moreover, from the perspective of businesses working in this field, the wide spectrum of social groups with which they need to cope presents different kinds of opportunities and constraints. Yet, achieving real solutions to environmental problems and overcoming social injustices worldwide depends on converting *the majority* of citizen-consumers to levels of ethicality and greenness approaching those already displayed by the more reflexive minorities. This is the challenge for the future faced by all those individuals, social movements, NGOs, businesses and others who are currently engaged in the various activities included under the general heading of political consumerism. The evidence from this study is that flourishing, radical enterprises can play a leading role in helping to bring about this wider transformation. But this may depend upon their willingness to follow more closely in the unashamedly commercial yet also, in part, socially and environmentally responsible footsteps of the mainstream firms working in this field—paradoxical and perhaps undesirable though this may seem.

References

Albrow, M. 1996. *The Global Age.* Cambridge: Polity.
Appadurai, A. 1991. "Global Ethnoscapes: Notes and Queries for a Transnational Anthropology," in R. G. Fox, ed., *Recapturing Anthropology: Working in the Present.* Santa Fe, NM: School of American Research Press.
Beck, U. 1992. *The Risk Society.* London: Sage.
___. 1994. "The Reinvention of Politics: Towards a Reflexive Theory of Modernization," in U. Beck, A. Giddens, & S. Lash, *Reflexive Modernization; Politics, Tradition and Aesthetics in the Modern Social Order.* Cambridge: Polity.
___. 2000a. *The Brave New World of Work.* Malden, MA: Polity.
___. 2000b. *What is Globalization?* Cambridge: Polity.
Bradley, H., & S. Fenton. 1999. "Reconciling Culture and Economy: Ways Forward in the Analysis of Ethnicity and Gender," in L. and A. Sayer, eds., *Culture and Economy After the Cultural Turn.* London: Sage.
Castells, M. 1996. *The Rise of the Network Society.* Oxford: Blackwell.

___. 1997. *The Power of Identity*. Oxford: Blackwell.

Cohen, R., & P. Kennedy. 2000. *Global Sociology*. Basingstoke: Macmillan.

Dicken, P. 1992. *Global Shift; The Internationalization of Economic Activity*. London: Paul Chapman.

Featherstone, M., & S. Lash, eds. 1999. *Spaces of Culture: City-Nation-World*. London: Sage.

Giddens, A. 1990. *The Consequences of Modernity*. Cambridge: Polity.

___. 1991. *Modernity and Self Identity*. Cambridge: Polity.

Hannerz, U. 1996. *Transnational Connections: Culture, People, Places*. London: Routledge.

Held, D., A. McGrew, D. Goldblatt, & J. Perraton. 1999. *Global Transformations: Politics, Economics and Culture*. Cambridge: Polity.

Kennedy, P. 1996. "Capitalist Enterprise as a Moral or Political Crusade: Opportunities, Constraints and Contradictions," in J. O'Connor & D. Wynne, eds., *From the Margins to the Centre: Cultural Production and Consumption in the Post-Industrial City*. Aldershot: Ashgate.

___, & V. Roudometof, eds. 2002. *Communities Across Borders: New Immigrants and Transnational Cultures*. London: Routledge.

Lash, S. 1994. "Reflexivity and Its Doubles: Structure, Aesthetics, Community," in U. Beck, A. Giddens, & S. Lash, *Reflexive Modernization; Politics, Tradition and Aesthetics in the Modern Social Order*. Cambridge: Polity.

___, & J. Urry. 1994. *Economies of Signs and Spaces*. London: Sage.

Nava, M. 1991. "Consumerism Reconsidered: Buying and Power." *Cultural Studies* 5 (2): 157-73.

Ray, L., & A. Sayer. 1999. "Introduction," in L. Ray, & A. Sayer, eds., *Culture and Economy After the Cultural Turn*. London: Sage.

Robertson, R. 1992. *Globalization: Social Theory and Global Culture*. London: Sage.

Sayer, A. 1999. "Valuing Culture and Economy," in L. Ray, & A. Sayer, eds., *Culture and Economy After the Cultural Turn*. London. Sage.

Scammell, M. 2000. "The Internet and Civic Engagements: The Age of the Citizen-Consumer." *Political Communication* 17: 351-5.

Scholte, J. A. 2000. *Globalization: An Introduction*. Basingstoke: Macmillan.

Spar, D. L. 1998. "The Spotlight and the Bottom Line: How Multinationals Export Human Rights." *Foreign Affairs* 77, 2: 7-12.

Touraine, A. 1998. "Sociology Without Society." *Current Sociology* 46, 2: 119-43.

Part II

Consumer Choices and Setting of the Agenda of Politics

Using Consumer Boycotts to Stimulate Corporate Policy Changes: Marketplace, Media, and Moral Considerations

Monroe Friedman

Introduction

Consumer boycotts have long been a popular form of protest against perceived wrongdoing in the private sector. In fact, the term was first used more than a century ago to characterize the actions of Irish peasants to protest the inhumane treatment they had received from Charles Cunningham Boycott, a notorious land agent of the British ruling class, whom the peasants sought to ostracize for his actions (Redpath 1881). A consumer boycott can be defined as "an attempt by one or more parties to achieve certain objectives by urging individual consumers to refrain from making selected purchases in the marketplace" (Friedman 1999, 4).

This chapter focuses on contemporary consumer boycotts and their role in stimulating changes in corporate policy and procedures. It discusses boycotts as a special type of activity and shows that they take on a variety of forms. We look first at marketplace-oriented boycotts, which are one such form; they are defined and analyzed in terms of their role in corporate change. For this analysis, criteria of successfulness and effectiveness are developed and applied. Next, media-oriented boycotts, a newer form, are introduced and explained, and their characteristics are specified and analyzed. The final important chapter topic is boycott ethics. Here the concern is with the ethical and moral implications of initiating and terminating boycotts as well as the impact of boycotts on innocent third parties.

Before getting into the three major sections of the chapter, we start by reviewing types and sequential components of boycott actions. An examination of news accounts of boycott actions reveals that many of them follow a path of escalating militancy, a path that begins with an announcement that a boycott action is under consideration. Some boycotts do not go beyond this point, and we refer to them as *action-considered boycotts*. However, those that do go further usually take the same next step, namely, to announce that a boycott is being called, and that participation in the action is requested. Many boycotts go no further; these are called *action-requested boycotts*. Those that go beyond this stage often issue an announcement indicating that the boycott is being organized and noting what preparations are underway. We refer to boycotts that stop at this juncture as *action-organized boycotts*. Finally, the boycotts that go beyond organization and preparation to take such concrete actions as initiating demonstrations and/or picket lines to publicize and stimulate the boycott activity are referred to as *action-taken boycotts*.

Many protest groups apparently do nothing more than engage in an action-considered or action-requested boycott (Friedman 1985). Since some of these efforts seem more concerned with publicity in the news media than with action in the marketplace, we refer to them as *media-oriented boycotts*. The focus on the news media often reflects the fact that the organizations calling for the boycotts lack the necessary resources or appropriate circumstances to implement a full-scale marketplace boycott. So they decide instead to attack the image of the target by generating press releases that depict the target in an unfavorable light, and endeavoring to have these releases carried by the various news media. Sometimes media-oriented boycotts escalate into action-organized boycotts and action-taken boycotts. If these initiatives focus primarily on boycott activities in the marketplace (e.g., frequent picketing or demonstrations at retail stores), we refer to them as *marketplace-oriented boycotts*. It should be clear, however, that these boycotts, like virtually all organized protest actions, are media-oriented as well. But their use of the news media to attack the image of the target is secondary to their use of the boycott in the marketplace to damage the target economically by depriving it of sales.

It is important to note, too, that some media-oriented boycotts that escalate into action-organized boycotts and action-taken boycotts remain primarily media-oriented. Thus, a boycott group may decide to organize and stage a series of dramatic demonstrations to capture the attention of television news cameras or newspaper reporters. These demonstrations may occur far away from the retail marketplace—at, for example, the headquarters building of the target being boycotted.

Developing and Applying Criteria for Successful Marketplace-Oriented Boycotts

Having identified marketplace-oriented boycotts and distinguished them from media-oriented boycotts, we look next at their likelihood of success in affecting corporate policy. At the outset, it is necessary to consider "the criterion problem." Criteria for the success of marketplace-oriented boycotts are often not easy to identify, because boycott leaders are reluctant to pin themselves down. Consumer boycotts are, after all, political actions, and few political leaders are willing to issue statements listing their objectives with sufficient specificity to permit empirical tests of success or failure. A second criterion problem considers the need to draw a distinction between the *short-term* and *long-term* effects of marketplace-oriented boycotts. While the dividing line between the two is often not clear, short-term success has been claimed by many boycotts, but long-term success has apparently proved more elusive. A third criterion problem concerns the distinction between *execution criteria* and *consequence criteria*. The former asks whether the marketplace-oriented boycott was *successful*, that is whether it was implemented as planned in that the consumer commodities to be boycotted were indeed not purchased. The latter asks whether the boycott was *effective* in that the larger organizational objectives of the boycott activity were realized (e.g., lower prices, union recognition, or corporate divestiture from South Africa).

For a given boycott activity, it should be clear that performance on one type of criterion is not necessarily related to performance on the other. For example, even a hint or suggestion of a boycott by a powerful group may be enough to achieve its goals (the consequence criterion) without having to actually engage in a boycott (the execution criterion). Conversely, a boycott group may be successful in persuading consumers not to buy a specified commodity only to find that the target refuses to yield to the group's demands. While the consequence criterion is clearly important to boycott groups and their targets, the execution criterion is also important to the targets, because boycott success here means a loss of retail sales.

Even if agreement could be reached on criteria for judging the success of a boycott, analysts would still encounter problems in applying them. As already indicated, the consequence criteria are often vaguely stated and, indeed, may change over the course of a boycott. Furthermore, reliable hard data on the execution criterion may be difficult to secure since both sides have a vested interest in presenting evidence favorable to their positions. And finally, even if a reliable change in criterion data could be identified, it may be unclear whether the change is due to the boycott action. (Time-series analysis may be helpful here in ascertaining the cause; this was the statistical approach taken by Pruitt and Friedman (1986) in a study of the impact of boycott announcements on stock market prices for target companies.)

The last-mentioned point is particularly relevant to consumer economic boycotts, called to lower prices for products whose prices have recently risen sharply. When fewer consumers buy the products after a boycott has been called, it is sometimes not clear how much the decrease in demand is due to the boycott and how much is due to the products' rapid rise in price (i.e., the products may have become prohibitively expensive for many consumers). Moreover, if the price rise is anticipated by consumers, matters become more complicated and cause-and-effect analysis more uncertain. As Jones (1977) has indicated in a discussion of the rather abrupt increase in retail prices that triggered the 1977 nationwide coffee boycott, much of the decreased demand apparently derived from the fact that shoppers, upon realizing that prices were about to rise rapidly, had stocked up.

To sum up, this analysis has identified several factors that make it difficult, if not impossible, to determine how effective marketplace-oriented boycotts have been in reducing consumer purchases of targeted products and services. And without clear evidence of such purchase reductions together with a clear cause-and-effect linkage to a boycott campaign (the execution criterion), many companies are unlikely to yield to boycotters' demands (the consequence criterion). Yet despite this seemingly pessimistic appraisal of marketplace-oriented boycotts, some circumstances seem more likely than others to lead to boycott successes.

Characteristics of Successfully Executed
Marketplace-Oriented Boycotts

Research shows that successful marketplace boycotts often have several characteristics in common. This section identifies five such characteristics and offers short illustrations to explain the importance of each. The first two characteristics focus on the kind of services or products targeted by boycotts. First, successful boycotts often focus on items easily identified by consumers. Fresh produce is an example of a product that is problematic in this regard. For example, consumers found it difficult to implement the boycott on lettuce, called by the United Farm Workers in the United States a few decades ago, because it was difficult for them to differentiate between boycott-targeted lettuce, harvested by their nonunion counterparts, and lettuce picked by unionized farm laborers. Second, successful boycotts often target as few brand names as possible with one being the ideal. It is a cognitively simple task for consumers to keep one brand name in mind in their efforts to cooperate with a marketplace boycott, but as the number increases, so does the difficulty of the task. A good example here is the boycott of Nestlé discussed later in this section.

A third characteristic of successful boycotts concerns strategic planning. Successful boycotts are often planned for a time when there are few, if any, competing boycotts on related issues. The reason here is quite simple. Competition among boycotts confuses consumers and makes it difficult for them to shop in a political consumerist fashion. Fourth, successful boycotts are often called only when there are acceptable substitutes readily available for the boycotted products or services. There are at least three elements involved here: accessibility, price, and taste. Substitutable goods that are difficult to find, more expensive, and unattractive to consumers are likely to constitute a recipe for boycott failure.

Finally, successful boycotts often select publicly visible boycott targets to facilitate identification of consumer violations. This characteristic focuses not on the ease of complying with a boycott but rather on the social stigma that may be associated with not complying with it. The stigma is, of course, likely to be particularly strong for highly publicized and polarized local actions against retail stores. This happened in 1971 in a small town in the southern part of the United States, where local African Americans called a boycott of the town's white retail merchants for failing to assume leadership in combating "police brutality" against local African Americans. Boycott leaders were in place to observe whether the boycott was adhered to by the town's African American residents. They approached violators and informed them about their protest action. Most of the violators responded by honoring the boycott (Brockway 1975).

Characteristics of Effective Consequential
Marketplace-Oriented Boycotts

Research shows that several characteristics of marketplace boycotts are often associated with achievement of their goals, that is,
the consequence considerations. First, boycotts engaged in by many
consumers are likely to encourage a targeted firm to consider yielding to the boycotters' demands. The effect of the mass support of a
boycott on a company can, of course, be measured in various ways,
including decreases in total purchasers, total units purchased, sales
volume, and estimated profits. The point is that a boycott that has a
major deleterious economic effect can be expected to make the target give serious thought to meeting the boycotters' demands. For
instance, in 1976, Mexico's decision to vote in the UN General As-
sembly for a resolution equating Zionism with racism and racial
discrimination stimulated American Jews to organize a grassroots
tourism boycott, which according to the Mexico Hotel Association
resulted in 30,000 cancellations in one week. The magnitude and
swiftness of the boycott led the Mexican president to state publicly
that Mexico should not have voted the way it did. His apologetic
statement ended the boycott (Wells 1976). Second, the larger the
general adverse impact on the company in terms of drops in sales
due to the boycott, the more likely that the company will yield to
the demands of the boycotters. Large companies with many product lines and subsidiaries may be in a position to weather even
successful boycotts. However, small producers and especially those
with few product lines are often more vulnerable to a sales downturn and thus may be more likely to yield to boycott pressures.
The example above on the tourist boycott against Mexico shows
how even a relatively poor developing country could ill-afford to
suffer such a blow to its economy. Third, the more distant the perceived time horizons for a boycott, the more likely the target will
yield to the demands of the boycotters. Time horizons are easier to
project for seasonal businesses. To illustrate, a successful marketplace boycott of a professional sports team is likely to be especially worrisome to management, if it occurs at the beginning of
the season rather than near the end. Over the course of the off-
season months passions may well cool, causing fan interest in the
boycott to wane.

Media-Oriented Boycotts

The last few decades have witnessed a far greater use of media-oriented boycotts by political consumer advocates of policy changes, who in earlier years had opted for marketplace-oriented boycotts. Why the change in strategy? Several reasons suggest themselves. The first concerns the lack of foot soldiers to staff the boycott picket lines at the entrances to retail stores. Except for labor strikes, with their usually predominantly male participation, these foot soldiers, as discussed in the chapter by Michele Micheletti, have for years been middle-class female homemakers, and many of their current counterparts have jobs outside the home. A second reason stems from the new cognitive burdens on marketplace-oriented boycotters. More and more of today's boycotts are directed at large national and transnational corporations with many subsidiaries marketing their own goods under a variety of brand names. A case in point was the consumer boycott of the Nestlé Company, a major Swiss multinational corporation that sells a vast array of consumer products (including wines, cheeses, cosmetics, canned food, candy, coffee, and frozen foods) and operates large chains of restaurants and hotels. Since many of these items are not sold under the Nestlé name, the cognitive demands on consumers wishing to honor the boycott become extremely onerous, therefore making it difficult for boycott organizers to execute a truly successful boycott (Friedman 1985). A third reason concerns the practical difficulties in turning consumers away from many boycotted products in today's more branded world (Klein 2000). With huge increases in recent years in advertising expenditures, many consumer products have now acquired strong customer loyalties that are not easy to break, and have, as shown in Lance Bennett's chapter, become part of an individualized lifestyle. To illustrate, it appears that many young African Americans did not honor the Operation PUSH boycott of Nike athletic shoes, even though they were sympathetic with the boycott's objectives (one of which was placing more African Americans in executive positions at Nike). Evidently honoring the boycott meant not buying and wearing articles of clothing representing a strong expression of their personalized lifestyles, which are associated with the media images of such celebrated corporate spokespersons as superstar athlete Michael Jordan.

Characteristics of Media-Oriented Boycotts

Rather than simply choose a particular product or service to target, as was the case with many marketplace-oriented boycotts, organizers of media-oriented boycotts often consider a large variety of considerations. These include the choice of corporate target and the steps to be taken to persuade the target to meet the boycott objectives. These factors are discussed in this section.

In choosing corporate targets for media-oriented campaigns, boycott leaders have typically looked to exploit image-related weaknesses. Researchers have identified numerous characteristics of corporations that have been used successfully by boycotters to weaken a corporation's image. Six of them are discussed here. The first is corporate visibility. The preferred target of a media-oriented boycott is often well known, with a highly recognized brand, which is a leader, if not the leader, in its field. Second, the preferred target often has a reputation for social responsibility and trust, a reputation that might well be threatened by refusing to yield to the demands of a conscience-oriented boycott. Examples of the importance of sympathetic market targets for political consumerism are discussed in the chapters by Paul Kennedy and Cheryl Greenberg. The third characteristic concerns the economic status of the corporation. A corporation may well be a preferred target for a media-oriented boycott if it has had a recent downturn in sales and/or profits that might make it willing to accede to a boycott group's demands if this is what the corporation believes it takes to get back to profitability expeditiously. Fourth, corporations new in the area of concern to the boycotters may be more amenable to change than are competitors with long-established positions in the field. Benetton experienced this in 1988 when it became a boycott target for an animal rights group fighting against cosmetic companies that tested their products on animals. Benetton was chosen because it had just started to sell its own brand of cosmetics, and its policies regarding animal testing of these products were newly formed (Friedman 1999). Finally, the preferred target has both the producer and retailer under the same name, as in the case of Mitsubishi, Benetton, and Nike. This allows political consumer activists to focus on the corporation's headquarters and logo as part of their media-oriented boycott, as well as its retail stores in their marketplace-oriented boycott.

Because the primary focus of the newer boycotts is media image rather than marketplace sales, boycott leaders need to make skillful use of dramatic devices and techniques to secure media attention. Some of the most important tactical actions identified in research are noted here. Culture jamming, or using creative parodies of corporate names and slogans to advance the boycott cause, is increasingly common. For example, an animal rights boycott group claims that more than a million copies of its version of the familiar Avon door hanger were left on residential front-door knobs. Normally they say "Avon calling," to indicate a sales representative of the cosmetics firm recently dropped by. The boycott group's version said "Avon killing," and went on to make a claim that Avon was killing animals in the process of testing its new cosmetics for safety. The impact of this tactic, as discussed in Peretti's chapter, can be quite significant. Boycotters may even call for a national or international day of protest against the boycott target and plan demonstrations in many cities, an activity facilitated by the development of informational technology. Boycott groups have gained publicity for their causes with such dramatic measures. A good case in point in the late 1980s was the call for an international day of protest against Gillette for refusing to stop testing its cosmetic products on animals (Friedman 1999). A third action identified by researchers is the involvement of children as activists. Environmental groups have been particularly successful doing this in support of the tuna boycott and the tropical timber boycott. The human-interest value of these stories of activist schoolchildren was clear to the news media, which gave the stories wide coverage. Fourth, committing acts of civil disobedience is commonly used by boycott groups to force corporate targets to call in the police to arrest individual demonstrators. The presence of police exercising power over the demonstrators at the behest of large corporations is thought by activist groups to engender feelings of sympathy for the demonstrators and their cause. Moreover, it may well attract the attention of the media. A fifth tactic is advertising in the mass media. What better way to embarrass a boycott target than to use the same venue it uses to launch an attack upon it? Several animal rights and environmental boycott groups have used this technique. Finally, boycotters use graphic pictures to convey the boycott message. Pictures, it turns out, may well be worth a thousand words or even more, when it comes to dramatizing boycott issues. Animal rights groups have recognized this for years by their frequent depictions of pet-like furry animals in painful circumstances (e.g., rabbits and monkeys) to convey the need to stop animal testing.

Effectiveness of Media-Oriented Boycotts

Earlier we identified several criterion problems related to market-place-oriented boycotts, and the reader should not be surprised to learn that similar problems exist for media-oriented boycotts. As a result it is usually not possible to claim that an actual change in corporate policy occurred as a result of a media-oriented boycott. The change may have happened for a host of other reasons, with the boycott assuming a minor, causative role. An exception to this circumstance is one that finds the affected corporation identifying the largely media-oriented boycott as a key factor in its decision process. The tuna boycott of Heinz and the animal rights boycott of Benetton are two recent examples of such a connection, in that both corporations made the policy changes sought by the boycotters, and both corporations attributed their actions, at least in part, to the media-oriented boycott campaigns (Friedman 1999). However, such clear cause-and-effect connections are the exception rather than the rule.

Ethics of Consumer Boycotts

It is somewhat surprising, given the extensive use of boycotts as a tool for political and corporate change, that scholars have not given much serious consideration to ethical issues surrounding them. What little has been published has dealt primarily with the decision to initiate a boycott.

Far less has been reported on the ethics of ending a boycott, even though boycott termination decisions often raise significant ethical problems. A scholar who has considered this issue is the philosopher Claudia Mills (1996), who in a stimulating and provocative essay "Should We Boycott Boycotts?" raises a number of important ethical issues relating to decisions to start and end consumer boycotts. Mills distinguishes between two justifications that boycott groups offer for their actions, a "strategic justification" and an "integrity-based justification." The first focuses on the instrumental value of the boycott to various activists, who often pursue such practical objectives as getting corporation A or nation B to stop engaging in practice C, since it is offensive to the activists. This justification implies that the boycott is called off once the boycott target ends its objectionable practices. The second, the integrity-based justification for boycotts, comes in several forms, but Mills' essay focuses primarily on one variant, the "shunning justification." Boycotters, who engage in shunning, do so not simply because a particular business or political practice is offensive, but because those engaging in the practice have become offensive through their association with it. Boycotters and boycott supporters, who justify their involvement this way, may find it difficult to determine if and when to terminate a boycott.

When one examines the Mills essay in the real-world context of consumer boycotts, a significantly different picture emerges of activist initiatives. In particular, boycott groups rarely employ the shunning justification, which is especially ironic when one considers the "shunning" origins of the boycott term (Redpath 1881). Why have modern consumer boycotters shunned the shunning justification? While the question is easier to pose than to answer, it would seem that the pragmatic nature of activist agendas is an important contributing factor. News media representatives as well as prospective boycott campaign participants all have the same question of boycott organizers: What specifically are the boycott goals? The results-oriented character of boycott initiatives usually yields answers, which deal with getting the bad guys to stop their bad behavior (the strategic justification), rather than getting them to transform themselves into good guys so that they no longer have to be ostracized (the shunning justification). Here we see a possible difference in motivation between boycotts and labeling schemes, as discussed in the chapters included in Part III of this book.

This is not to say that a shunning justification plays no role in consumer boycotts. Indeed, an example provided by Mills (as well as ordinary experience) suggests that shunning may sometimes have an influence on the decision to end a boycott and especially at the individual rather than the group level. As Mills (1996, 146f) notes in a personal observation:

> ...To this day I don't feel right buying Gallo wine or Nestlé bars. I think this is because I feel myself caught between a strategic and shunning justification for the boycott. If the boycott was a strategic one, then it should end when the offending behavior ceases; one then feels some imperative to "reward" the company in question by making good on the implied offer to continue business with them if they mend their offending ways. But if the boycott was a shunning one, then merely ceasing to sin may not be enough to warrant renewed fellowship with the sinner. One expects some public acknowledgment of wrongdoing, some public display of repentance, some public plea for forgiveness.

Some individual boycotters apparently feel even more strongly about the shunning option, in that they believe the corporation's actions may be so deplorable that it deserves to be boycotted forever—a form of economic capital punishment for an egregious offense. To illustrate, in a letter published in the *Boycott Quarterly*, reader Will Ettinger asks, "...if a company being boycotted for its actions that cause *murder, misery and pain* finally ends its nasty ways and cleans up its act, *why* does it automatically become OK [the strategic justification] to buy their products again?!?" He goes on to express his justification for deciding to shun a particular company: "In my mind, Nestlé, a company run by butchers, should never be listed as 'OK to buy from.' Never. I have a long memory, and if I remember all the pain and misery Nestlé has been responsible for (and still is) I would not be able to go into a shop and buy a product of theirs even though they ended their evil" (Ettinger 1996, 4).

While many individual boycotters may agree with Mills and/or Ettinger, at the group level it is remedial action rather than a public apology, which is typically sought by veteran boycott leaders. This means that reaching a well-defined operational objective (e.g., a union contract for the grape pickers, or an infant formula marketing practice for developing nations that is in accordance with United Nations guidelines) is sufficient reason for calling off a boycott. But Mills' point still has validity in that a boycott publicly called off by its leaders may be quietly pursued by some of its grassroots participants, who remain offended by the past practices of the boycott target. Indeed, a case can be made that the key ethical question concerning consumer boycotts with a shunning justification is not under what circumstances they should be initiated, but under what circumstances they should be terminated. To illustrate, in light of new evidence emerging with regard to the marketing of cigarettes to minors by major tobacco interests in the 1970s (e.g., Meier 1998), some tobacco company boycotters have privately communicated to this writer that they do not now see how in good conscience they can ever urge consumers to resume buying any products manufactured by these firms.

Here the important point is that use of the shunning justification by individuals can be ethically problematic for boycott organizers, who have difficulty calling off their troops once corporate leaders concede to the boycotters' demands. Potentially this jeopardizes the effectiveness of the boycott action, because targeted corporations will not know whether boycott leaders will be able to call off their boycott, once the corporations acquiesce to their demands. For corporations, use of the shunning justification may mean that they are damned if they do acquiesce to the boycotters' demands, because unforgiving political consumers are likely to continue to focus on them, and damned if they don't, because the boycott is not likely to be terminated by its leaders for strategic justifications.

Obviously ending a boycott can pose a problem that jeopardizes the trustworthiness of the boycott action. Yet for many observers the more salient ethical issue concerns the act of starting a consumer boycott. For them the key question is whether the ends sought by boycotters justify using a boycott as a tool for political and corporate change. In their efforts to deal with this question some analysts have focused on the problems of boycott goals while others have concentrated on problems with the means or scope of boycotts.

To illustrate how analysts have viewed *boycott goals*, Neier (1982) has proposed a simple model based on the nature of the offensive behavior, which the boycott seeks to end. He is most sympathetic to "boycotts against *practices* that are deemed objectionable," such as sweatshop conditions in the garment industry and the exploitation of farm workers (Neier 1982, 642). He is least sympathetic to "black list" type boycotts, which attempt to punish individuals or groups (often performing artists) simply because they hold points of view which are offensive to the boycotters. It was such a threatened boycott of the Boston Symphony Orchestra that is believed to have led it to cancel a scheduled appearance in 1982 with actress Vanessa Redgrave, a performer known for her outspoken views on controversial political issues. Neier's position on such boycotts was echoed by Mills (1996), who cites philosopher Michael Bayles' statement: "Social pressure as opposed to persuasion for political beliefs must cease at some point, or a society fails to respect freedom of political beliefs"(Bayles 1980, 5). With the Boston Symphony Orchestra example the case is even stronger, since it combined economic pressure with social pressure, and the two together threatened not only Redgrave but the many others in the orchestra whether or not they shared her political views.

To illustrate how analysts have viewed *boycott scope* in ethical terms, Garrett (1986) has identified three parties who could be unfairly injured by injudicious use of the boycott strategy. One, of course, is the corporate target, and the ethical questions loom large if it finds itself falsely accused, or if it is incapable of responding to the boy-cotters' demands. A second group identified by Garrett consists of the customers of the boycotted firm whom, he believes, should not be forced by intimidating tactics to honor the boycott against their will. Finally, Garrett's third group consists of secondary parties (typi-cally non-principals in the boycott struggle, who find themselves caught in the cross-fire, e.g., workers, suppliers, and distributors), whose economic fortunes could well be affected by the boycott and its outcome. Potentially these groups can be harmed by three kinds of boycotts: obstructionist, secondary, and surrogate boycotts.

Obstructionist boycotts raise important ethical issues, because they place obstacles in the way of consumers who are attempting to pur-chase a boycotted product or service. Perhaps the best-known vari-ety is the *sit-in*, a technique used by African Americans at segre-gated lunch counters in Southern communities in the United States in the 1950s and 1960s. By "sitting in," the protesters occupied lunch counter seats for hours at a time, thus preventing other customers from being served.

Secondary boycotts focus on an economic entity, usually a re-tailer, who buys the wares of the primary boycott target for the pur-pose of reselling them to consumers. Needless to say, the planners of a secondary boycott would like to see all the retailer's wares boy-cotted, either as a punishment for dealing with the boycotted prod-ucts of the primary target, or as an incentive for discontinuing this practice. This could mean, for example, boycotting a supermarket chain (a secondary boycott), which carries the breads and rolls made by an offending bakery, which is already being boycotted (a pri-mary boycott). Since the targeted supermarket chain may sell many thousands of products, it seems highly questionable ethically to threaten its economic viability and the livelihood of its workers sim-ply because it carries a few products sold by the offending bakery. This point has been recognized in the law, which has often banned secondary boycotts but allowed picketers to inform the customers of a retail store that it is selling certain goods, which are the focus of a consumer boycott, a boycott undertaken because the goods are being made by a firm whose actions are considered offensive by the boycotters (Minda 1999). If the presence of informational pick-eters is intimidating to some customers, they may decide to shop elsewhere rather than cross the picket line. If this occurs, the pick-eting action has, in effect, become an obstructionist boycott, and the affected retailer may decide to yield to the pressure by no longer carrying the products provided by the primary boycott target.

Ethical issues relating to the scope of boycotts are especially important in light of the growing popularity of *surrogate boycotts*. These boycotts can be characterized as indirect actions by protest groups, which express their dissatisfaction with the public policies of local, regional, national, or foreign governments by calling a boycott of surrogate institutions (the business firms operating in the affected geographic area). Needless to say, there are many non-principals in such boycott struggles who may be adversely affected by their outcomes. One of the most publicized examples of this problem surfaced in the late 1970s, with the boycott called in the United States by the National Organization for Women (NOW) to limit tourist and conventioneer travel to states whose legislatures had not ratified the proposed Equal Rights Amendment (ERA). NOW was hoping that the affected tourism industries in the targeted states would successfully lobby their state legislators to pass the ERA. An ethical concern noted at the time was that the owners and employees of restaurants and hotels in major cities in the boycotted states (e.g., Chicago, Miami, and St. Louis, since the Illinois, Florida, and Missouri legislatures had not ratified the ERA), might well be "innocent victims" of a successfully executed boycott, in that it was not their behavior that was deemed objectionable by the boycotters, but the behavior of the state legislatures (Friedman 1999). A more recent example, that involved the same general problematic conditions, is the international 1995 boycott of French wine and other food products as a way of expressing dissatisfaction with the French government's decision to test nuclear weapons in the South Pacific Ocean.

Consumer Boycott Ethics in Perspective

This section on the ethics of boycotts makes two observations relating to the problems involved with using the boycott as a tool for corporate and political change. A first observation considers the possibility of different concerns being expressed on the part of boycott group leaders as compared to group members. As we have seen, boycott groups have typically concerned themselves with strategic considerations, which often means trying to get a boycott target to take actions which are consistent with the boycott group's agenda. And while individuals participating in a boycott usually have the

same strategic goals as the group of which they are members, sometimes they are more concerned with such non-strategic matters as
the morality of the actions taken by the boycott target. As suggested
by the personal statements of Mills and Ettinger, some boycott participants may feel so personally put off by what they see as the
unacceptable actions of a boycott target, that they simply refuse to
ever again have any marketplace contact with the target or its consumer products or services. These participants may maintain this
position despite the efforts of boycott group leaders to have them
"reward" the target with consumer purchases for taking the strategically correct actions demanded by the boycott group. Under such
highly divisive circumstances, boycott leaders may find that they
are simply unable to deliver the "consumer vote" as a quid pro
quo for a cooperating corporate response to group boycott pressure. Should such circumstances become more frequent in the future, questions may well arise about the likelihood of group boycotts fulfilling their strategic goals.

Despite this possibility we note as our second observation that
our analysis reveals that consumer boycotts have the potential to
harm many innocent parties, including rank-and-file workers and
the various economic entities dependent upon the boycotted firms
that employ these workers. And, of course, certain variations on
the boycott theme can damage even more neutral parties, as became evident in the discussion of obstructionist boycotts, secondary boycotts, and surrogate boycotts. Taken together, this discussion gives one reason to ask if instances ever arise in which a
boycott's ends can be said to justify its means. Before answering,
however, it is well to remember that the potential for harm to neutral parties is unlikely to be realized with many contemporary boycotts, because many of them are not really boycotts but rather
threats or calls for boycotts with no demonstrable effect on any
group, and today's boycotts are likely to be media- rather than
marketplace-oriented, which means that they emphasize tarnish-
ing corporate image rather than decreasing corporate sales.

Consumer Boycotts as Political Action: Some Concluding Comments

This chapter shows that consumer boycotts have had a mixed
record in effecting corporate and political change. The chapter also
underscores the different dynamics underlying media-oriented and

marketplace-oriented boycotts. Behind successful marketplace-oriented boycotts are often found talented political consumer leaders, who have been able to mobilize and focus public sentiment on boycott targets and then re-channel it once the boycott goals have been met by corporate executives. The high levels of talent and resources needed to mount effective marketplace-oriented boycotts explain in part why we are seeing a shift towards media-oriented boycotts, the effectiveness of which demands far less on the part of consumer participants. Supporters of marketplace-oriented boycotts need to understand the logic of market-based political action for their boycotts to be successful and effective. They also need to understand the proper scope of a boycott for it to have a chance of initiating political or corporate change. Moreover, they need to confront the ethical and pragmatic dilemmas often associated with terminating a marketplace-oriented boycott once it has achieved its goals.

Moving next to media-oriented boycotts, we find that their leaders need to possess the requisite skills and resources to bring their boycott issues to the attention of the news media. This means selecting issues that people will readily understand and find emotionally arousing. Issues that do not meet these two psychological conditions are unlikely to be the subject of news media reports, especially television news reports. And, as we have seen, organizers of media-oriented boycotts need to be master stagers of media events, to generate the necessary drama to attract reporters to attend and to craft sympathetic stories in support of the boycott activity. In the current era of microelectronics and globalization we find that media-oriented boycott efforts are increasingly led by a younger generation of activists, with a sophisticated understanding of modern communications technology and the news media that uses it, as well as a sympathetic interest in larger issues that cross national borders, issues such as animal rights and environmental protection.

In conclusion, the chapter emphasizes the problematic nature of boycotts in two significant ways. It shows that boycotts are often contentious in orientation, a characteristic that can preclude cooperative solutions and constructive dialogue between consumers and producers. Also, it highlights the ethical responsibilities of consumers who organize and participate in boycotts. How individual political consumers use the boycott initiative is an increasingly important concern today, especially since, as the editors of this volume have noted herein, the relationship between politics and economics is becoming more complex, due to the influence of such processes as globalization, individualization, and postmodernization.

References

Bayles, M. 1980. "Political Process and Constitutional Amendments." *Southern Journal of Philosophy* 18: 5.

Brockway, G. 1975. "The Effects of an Economic Boycott on Retail Strategic and Tactical Decision-making." Ann Arbor, MI: University Microfilms International.

Ettinger, W. 1996. "Headline Sickens." *Boycott Quarterly*, 3 (4): 4.

Friedman, M. 1985. "Consumer Boycotts in the United States 1970-1980: Contemporary Events in Historical Perspective." *Journal of Consumer Affairs* 12: 96-117.

___ 1991. "Consumer Boycotts: A Conceptual Framework and Research Agenda." *Journal of Social Issues* 47: 149-68.

___ 1996. "Grassroots Groups Confront the Corporation: Contemporary Strategies in a Historical Perspective." *Journal of Social Issues* 52: 153-67.

___. 1999. *Consumer Boycotts*. New York: Routledge.

Garrett, D. E. 1986. "Consumer Boycotts: Are Targets Always the Bad Guy?" *Business and Society Review* 58: 17-21.

___. 1987. "The Effectiveness of Marketing Policy Boycotts: Environmental Opposition to Marketing." *Journal of Marketing* 51: 46-57.

Jones, B. 1977. "Consumers Find Coffee only as Good as Next Price Drop." *New York Times*, 17 August, 29-30.

Klein, Naomi. 2000. *No Logo*. London: Flamingo.

Meier, B. 1998. "Files of R. J. Reynolds Tobacco Show Effort on Youths." *New York Times*, 15 January, A10.

Mills, C. 1996. "Should We Boycott Boycotts?" *Journal of Social Philosophy*, 27, 136-48.

Minda, G. 1999. *Boycott in America*. Carbondale: Southern Illinois University Press.

Neier, A. 1982. "On boycotts." *The Nation* (May 29): 642-643.

Pruitt, S., & M. Friedman. 1986. "Determining the Effectiveness of Consumer Boycotts: A Stock Price Analysis of Their Impact on Corporate Targets." *Journal of Consumer Policy* 9: 375-87.

Redpath, J. 1881. "Talks of Ireland." *Magazine of Western History* 5: 214-5.

Smith, N. C. 1990. *Morality and the Market*. London: Routledge.

Wells, B. 1976. "Travel Power: The Story behind the Mexico Boycott." *New York Times*, 27 June, section 10, 1.

Political Consumer Action: Some Cautionary Notes from African American History

Cheryl Greenberg

Introduction

Politically weak populations with focused goals have historically found boycotts and other consumer protests immensely useful. In the United States, a national grape boycott called by Cesar Chavez helped build the United Farm Workers Union. When southern civil rights groups picketed and boycotted businesses that would not serve them, such actions helped end segregation. Here, tightly focused actions linked to explicit and concrete goals performed by a group of people large enough to disrupt business, provided the necessary ingredients for success.

Other consumer protests have been far less successful. Following the Italian invasion of Ethiopia, black nationalists attempted to drive Italian ice peddlers from their neighborhoods by calling for a boycott. It failed because the organizers could not attract enough participants. The community rejected both the goal of economic nationalism and the organizers' racist tactic of linking American individuals and the actions of a nation from which they had emigrated. Furthermore, Italian ice peddlers provided a necessary product that others offered at higher prices or not at all. Without an alternative source of inexpensive ice, the boycott could not be sustained.

Any examination of consumer protests must consider their potential pitfalls as well as their potential for social change. Historically, boycotts and other consumer campaigns have offered multiple and often conflicting messages, which attracted participants with very different perspectives and agendas. Sometimes the breadth of participation proved a consumer movement's strength: there was a role and a place for everyone. In other cases, this produced sharp internal divisions that weakened or diverted the effort or alienated potential supporters. Here I consider several consumer protests involving American black communities from the 1930s through the 1950s to identify which elements of protests seem necessary conditions for success. Certainly among those are that goals and means are clearly articulated and consonant with the political and civic views of the community, that the action has a specificity of purpose, and that the threatened actions are feasible. Friedman's chapter elaborates on criteria required for success.

But first we must confront the fact that there is a political dimension to our scholarly work. We cannot refrain from making judgments about the moral worth of a campaign's aims; indeed, as global citizens, we ought to do so. As scholars of political consumer action, however, we must always keep in mind that whether it succeeds (is the goal achieved?) and whether we want it to succeed (is the goal desirable?) are two distinct questions that must be kept separate. In other words, the same tactics, the same support, the same rhetoric will cause us to rejoice in one instance of mass action and despair in another. But a campaign's success does not depend on the moral rightness of its goals but rather with (among other, more tactical questions) how well those goals motivate the community to act.

I begin with a "good" protest, a jobs campaign in Harlem, New York that both succeeded and rooted itself in democratic values. I turn then to an examination of more problematic protests: WWII and postwar campaigns in black communities against racist business practices that became anti-Semitic, and white resistance to housing and neighborhood integration in the 1940s and 1950s that turned violent. These campaigns, whose successes were more mixed, raise questions about the role of ideology in consumer action and the efficacy of protest in challenging structural inequities.

Don't Buy Where You Can't Work

Black activists in depression-era Harlem waged a "Don't Buy Where You Can't Work" campaign to obtain white-collar jobs in local stores for African American residents.[1] It began in 1930 as a protest led primarily by women's and church groups against stores without black clerks. After a dramatic but ineffective petition campaign by shoppers pledging to patronize stores with black employees, tactics shifted to picketing and boycotts. The now-expanded coalition was driven by two factions with often conflicting agendas.

A nationalist "Buy Black" campaign enjoyed some community support but occasionally employed racist rhetoric. Alongside them worked integration-minded advocates of white-collar job opportunities for black residents. While some black businesses employed no help, and some white businesses did employ African Americans, the campaign targeted stores that were white-owned with no black staff. Both factions, then, could comfortably promote their agenda from within the coalition, called the Citizens' League for Fair Play (CLFP). Hundreds from all political and economic backgrounds participated in its demonstrations. "Don't Buy Where You Can't Work," pleaded picket signs. However, when the CLFP brokered a deal with several merchants to place black workers, nationalist groups broke away from the coalition claiming color and class discrimination because, they asserted, only light-skinned women with education received employment.

The more confrontational and sometimes explicitly anti-white and anti-Semitic rhetoric of these nationalist organizations brought condemnation by the more integrationist and moderate faction. "Renegade 'Boycott Committee' Runs Wild, Assaults Shoppers," lamented the pro-jobs campaign *New York Age*. Allegations that group leaders "used the[ir] platform to vilify the Jewish race" were made not only by the Jewish press but the black press as well.[2] The jobs effort had attracted divergent and often antagonistic partners; their infighting disrupted the campaign's progress and provoked a legal backlash. Merchants complained about the increasingly confrontational and bitter protests, police arrested protest leaders for disorderly conduct, and in 1934 the state Supreme Court ruled that picketing was illegal because the dispute was a racial rather than a labor issue. Without a picket line in place, and with erstwhile supporters turned critics, the campaign lost its focus and did not seek other means to promote the boycotts. As a result the agreed-upon hirings did not occur and the effort collapsed.

Only after a 1938 Supreme Court case restored the right to picket for racial grievances did the jobs campaign revive. Ultimately, it succeeded not only in placing black clerks, but also in expanding the effort beyond the confines of Harlem to compel hiring changes in the public utilities, bus companies, and the World's Fair. What made this consumer protest more effective? This time, the coalition was both broader and more focused. It now included a wide range of political, social, fraternal, religious, and civic groups, but explicitly excluded nationalist groups. Furthermore, it offered a role for everyone concerned about the issue: to aspiring politicians, a soapbox; to activists, a picket line; to the law-abiding, legal sanction; to those unwilling to protest publicly, a boycott. Finally, the coalition's explicitly integrationist goal: to hire African Americans without firing white workers; and its tactics: court-approved picketing, boycotts, threats to slow service, and negotiations, proved both morally and economically compelling enough to achieve a critical mass.

Also crucial for the boycott's success, the products provided by those boycotted could be replaced. As black car pools in Montgomery, Alabama, during the 1955 bus boycott demonstrated, this element of replaceability often determines the success or failure of consumer action. Black-owned stores and those that did hire black clerks could be patronized while boycotting stores facing picket lines. Indeed, this was precisely the merchants' motivation for settling. Where replacement services did not exist, such as with the telephone company (which refused to hire black operators or repairmen), or gas and electric companies (which hired African Americans only for menial jobs) protesters threatened not to boycott the service but to slow it at critical moments. They threatened to pay gas bills in pennies and to tie up phone lines at stock closing times. Consumer action succeeded when its efforts were clearly focused, its goals resonated with the community, and its tactics proved both politically and pragmatically acceptable to consumers.

The Don't Buy campaign's goals were consonant with U.S. civil rights efforts generally. They were integrationist rather than nationalist, advancing the cause of economic justice without challenging America's entrepreneurial individualism. Happily, we historians conclude that such protests reflect the desire of otherwise powerless people to embrace ideals of justice and equality too long denied them, and we applaud consumer action as advancing those democratic ideals. That, however, is not always the case.

Sometimes racism or bigotry motivates protest action, as indeed it had motivated the anti-Semitism of some in the nationalist groups. The 1935 riot that rocked Harlem when the campaign stalled also revealed anti-white and anti-Semitic feeling (as well as class-based resentment at exploitation).[3] Indeed, community advancement and bigotry against outsiders are often difficult to disentangle in American society, where ethnic and racial groups segregate (not always voluntarily) and class and race so often overlap. When segregation defines communities and opportunities by race, resistance is often race-based as well. Since racial solutions by definition exclude other groups, the border between nationalism and bigotry is often a fine one. As historian Winston McDowell observed, "these tensions were the historical liabilities inherent in all race-based strategies advocated and employed in a community such as Harlem with strong Jewish origins." Nationalist leaders "reveal these significant liabilities even as [they] exploited them."[4]

Anti-Jewish Boycotts

A 1958 Harlem handbill illustrates the link between economic nationalism and racial or religious bigotry.[5]

HIT NOW   **HIT HARD**

Oust the Jews from Harlem
Negro Ministers, Straighten up or Go

Buy Black   **Buy Black**

BUY BLACK COMMITTEE
MEETING EVERY TUESDAY AND FRIDAY NIGHT

Direct calls for boycotts of Jewish-owned stores on the basis of unfair and discriminatory business practices were common in black urban neighborhoods during and after World War II, and they often enjoyed some success. Anti-Semitism proved a compelling tactic in many ways. It tapped into deeply felt sentiment in the black community,[6] and targeted a highly visible outsider group. Jews, who often lived in the very communities into which African Americans settled, who were both poor enough and non-racist enough to run businesses in black areas, often worked there as rental agents, store owners, social workers, and landlords. Equally important, anti-Semitism was effective because many in the organized Jewish community perceived it as a significant threat. Thus, Jews were both the most visible targets for black protest and the most likely to respond, a point Kennedy's chapter raises as well.

Nationalists intended their campaigns both to run Jewish stores out and to bolster black unity. "There is trouble out there," the Chicago newspaper *Dynamite* explained, "trouble started principally by JEWISH merchants....Inferior merchandise, short changing and weights, goods sold on time payments, trick contracts...and various other schemes too numerous to mention are practiced by JEWS on COLORED people."[7]

Such calls for ethnically based boycotts rarely succeeded directly. Like the "Don't Buy" nationalists, they did not generate enough community support to close down Jewish businesses. Perhaps few could accept such sweeping and toxic generalizations. More likely, Jewish stores served black clientele when other white stores did not, provided low-cost goods, and offered ready credit. There were few replacements available to a poor, under-served community.

Yet while few were willing to so aggressively pursue economic separatism, more shared nationalists' goal of ending economic exploitation. These protesters, too, targeted Jewish stores in their campaigns, for much the same reasons: Jews, with their substantial entrepreneurial presence in black communities, were visible, already objects of resentment, and likely to respond. Black community challenges to unfair business practices escalated after the war, and whether nationalist or not, tended to single out Jews for committing abuses more widely practiced. In newspaper articles, soapbox speeches, and the like, protesters highlighted Jewish-owned stores' maltreatment of black customers or refusal to hire black workers, and made the owner's religion explicit in the critique. In North Carolina, for example, although all white shoe stores refused fitting services to black patrons, a black newspaper insisted, "Jews...Must Stop Practices of Discriminating [Against] Negroes in Stores." The *Chicago Defender* ran the 1956 headline, "Grossman's Fights Negro Grocer; Jews, Realtor, Conspire to Oust Businessman."[8]

Walter White, head of the National Association for the Advancement of Colored People (NAACP), focused on religion in negotiations with Baltimore department stores over better treatment of African American patrons. "One of the leading Jewish department store heads even became offended because I very mildly pointed out the parallel between what Hitler was doing to Jews in Germany and what Jewish and Gentile merchants were doing to another minority group right here in the United States."[9] In part, then, targeting Jews was for these activists a strategic choice. Unlike the nationalists, their goal was not to rid their community of Jews or whites. Rather, they sought to reach those most likely to improve. Jews had faced oppression at the hands of others. They might come to understand more readily than other whites the dangers of discrimination.

Anti-Semitism?

Was this singling out of Jews anti-Semitic, as most Jews believed, or legitimate criticism, as most African Americans insisted? The answer depends on one's standpoint. While most black leaders publicly criticized overt expressions of black anti-Semitism, they also blamed Jews for bringing it upon themselves with their exploitative behavior. "Anti-Semitism is regrettable," asserted a 1938 *Amsterdam News* editorial, "but the Jew himself is its author, insofar as it concerns the American Negro." The NAACP's Charles Houston acknowledged, "Yes there is anti-Semitism among a large part of the Negro population, largely because of some covetous and greedy Jewish landlords and merchants." The Chicago Urban League reported that it "has stated publicly its opposition to any campaign that is...an attack against a whole race of people, but at the same time has expressed its recognition of the fact that there might be certain unfair and over-reaching practices carried on by Jewish merchants in the Southside community which give cause to criticism and indignation." Walter White noted that "prominent Jewish leaders" were "very much disturbed by what they conceive to be a growth of 'anti-Semitism' among Negroes in some of the larger cities of the country. In these contacts I have stressed as have others that much of what is considered to be anti-Semitism is not that at all but instead it is a legitimate and understandable feeling against acts by a certain type of Jewish merchant and landlord which Negroes would resent no matter what the race or religion of the offending group."[10]

Jewish agencies, on the other hand, organized for the protection of Jews, insisted that such singling out of Jews for behaviors common to many whites was anti-Semitic. They defended these businessmen as simply rational operators, acting no differently from other businesses around them.

When discrimination occurred in the South, for example, agencies noted that Jim Crow was standard practice there. Several black papers published a 1941 story about discrimination at Kaplowitz's, a Jewish-owned department store in Washington, D.C. Kaplowitz's had issued the following notice to its employees:

> During busy periods and on sale days we wish to avoid waiting on COLORED
> TRADE.... If you know these people it is good business to give them service and when
> you do it must be given unobtrusively and in such a manner that it will not look like a
> colored convention.
>   ...All others...in some way, without offending them, get them out as quickly as
> possible.

An Anti-Defamation League (ADL) memorandum noted, "Actually, the Kaplowitz store was by no means the only offender, nor were the Jewish stores the only ones guilty." Another pointed out the difficulty in violating local mores. "Washington...practices the same discrimination as in the South, but it is definitely due to the pressure of non-Jews.... The fact that other people are guilty of similar things does not excuse the Jewish store, but it does throw a different light upon the assertions." A third argued that if only Jews "individually alter their present policy, it would affect their business, and would be opposed by the majority of residents of the community."[11]

This was precisely the argument Jewish merchants themselves made. In 1938, Walter White had complained that in Baltimore, "Out of nine large department stores...seven...are operated by Jews....[A]ll nine...bar Negroes.... They all...justify it on the ground that they might lose some white trade if they stopped discriminating against Negroes." The American Jewish Committee (AJC) commented, defensively but accurately, "Objectively, there are Jewish-owned stores that accept Negro customers and Christian-owned stores that do not. However, there can be no doubt that most of the blame for the situation is placed on the Jews."[12]

Jewish groups responded similarly in the North. The AJC investigated Jewish business practices in Harlem. Given "the entirely reasonable principle of economics as well as the course of New York City history applying to the present housing situation in Harlem," the report pointed out that "high costs went far beyond any question of Jewish management or ownership, or abuses by any particular group of landlords." The high rate of black ownership of Harlem real estate demonstrated that rental patterns were not based on race or religion. The AJC thus countered critics that "identical conditions apply whether the property is owned or managed by Jews, or banks, or Negroes themselves."[13] Such responses were neither incorrect nor unfair. Indeed, the AJC's analysis suggests one weakness of these consumer protests: they do not address underlying, structural problems, an issue we shall return to in a moment. Nevertheless, from the perspective of many African Americans, the AJC's response did beg the question of whether or not landlords and business owners, among them Jews, were indeed exploiting black people.

Why It Succeeded

Nevertheless, whether one considers this tactic of singling Jews out anti-Semitic or not, it worked. After their initial defensiveness, Jewish organizations became militant about what they recognized as unethical behavior by some Jewish storeowners, particularly as their own involvement with civil rights efforts intensified. "I am in no mood to protect any slumlord who is a Jew," S. Andhil Fineberg of the AJC wrote. "All people have a right to hate them. My only concern is that their activity be not catalogued as Jews."[14]

Certainly, Jewish leaders recognized the validity of many of the allegations. The ADL investigated the "anti-Semitic propaganda and sentiment among Harlem Negroes" in 1939. The report concluded: "Jewish merchants in Harlem are continuing to subsidize anti-Semitism in Harlem...by their short-sighted relationship with the community...The Negro['s]...'rent-hogging' Jewish landlord, his 'short weighting' Jewish merchant, and the Jewish housewife who feels the muscles of a servant-applicant make him feel that the Jew more than anybody is trying to keep him enslaved." That same year the *Jewish Morning Journal* evaluated grievances Harlemites voiced against Jewish businesses there and reported: "the dissatisfaction of the Negroes and their resulting anti-Semitism—which is not anti-Semitism in the ordinary sense of the word but which is a manifestation of social economic tension—have their roots in concrete situations."[15]

Jewish groups also recognized that many of these protests used Jews to represent all whites. They understood that at least in part this reflected the ubiquity of Jewish merchants in black neighborhoods. The ADL's Abel Berland argued, "[W]hile the Jewish merchant conducts his business no differently than a non-Jew," given the virtual Jewish monopoly in black areas "the anti-white sentiment of many Negroes is translated into anti-Semitism." The ADL's study reinforced this view. "The exploitation which the Negro suffers from the whites he therefore experiences from the hands of Jews.... The present antagonism grows out of the fact that whenever the Negro comes in contact with white discrimination he can find a Jew to blame."[16]

Behind these facts were political considerations motivating a Jewish response. The longstanding fear of anti-Semitism, given the history of Jewish oppression, and its intensification, given the results of the Nazis' transformation of anti-Semitic sentiment into action, made Jewish community leaders deeply fearful. They viewed improving Jewish behavior as one way of stemming anti-Semitism. During a 1941 ADL discussion of exploitation of domestic workers in New York, the ADL director expressed his concern that "negro [*sic*] women might still feel they were being exploited" and reminded those present that in determining what to do, "our primary interest was to prevent anti-Semitism." The Chicago ADL responded to the *Dynamite* articles not only by enlisting the support of black groups, but also by working to improve the behaviors of Jewish merchants. As the League explained, "This local situation is dangerous inasmuch as, should disorders break out, the Negro-Jewish question would appear in an intensified form in other cities which at the present are experiencing no trouble."[17]

Beyond fear of anti-Semitism lay ethical concerns. By the late 1940s, Jewish agencies had plunged into the struggle for black civil rights. Self-interested in the sense that they hoped religion as well as race would cease to be cause for discrimination, Jews' involvement expanded far beyond issues of explicit Jewish concern to embrace a more universal conception of equality. While Jewish engagement in civil rights is a topic beyond the scope of our discussion, it was more extensive than that of any other white group, and involved strong working relationships between black and Jewish leaders and activists.[18] Racist Jewish business practices jeopardized these relationships and were increasingly insupportable in the face of emerging Jewish political commitments. As the ADL director commented, because of these economic tensions, "As is obvious, the problem of Jewish-Negro relationships is becoming more delicate and strained...and we have to tackle it from both ends."[19] Jewish organizations increasingly intervened with Jewish businessmen. While black-led consumer protests were rarely successful enough to convince businesses to change their practices on their own, the threat of escalating anti-Semitism they represented and the intensifying moral commitment among Jewish leaders to racial justice, compelled the organized Jewish community to act. Three factors, then, help explain the success of the protest tactic of singling out Jews: the depth of black anti-Jewish sentiment that made the black community susceptible to calls for anti-Semitic action, the sensitivity of the Jewish community to that threat, and the growing contradiction between civil rights commitments and racist practice. Rabbi Simon Kramer nicely combined these concerns in a 1940 letter to his congregants regarding accusations that Jewish women exploited black domestic workers. While such claims were "terribly exaggerated," he wrote, nor could he "conceive of any Jewish housewife being guilty of such practices," nevertheless, "I am asking you to be very careful in your treatment of these part time colored houseworkers...be...considerate of the reputation of the Jewish community and the rights of human beings to fair and honorable treatment."[20]

Organized Jewish interventions with Jewish merchants became increasingly commonplace. The Cincinnati AJC sought to "foster maximal ethical standards in Jewish business...to help answer accusations in antisemitic [sic] literature." The ADL included business ethics in its "Internal Jewish Education Program." In Chicago and New York, it pressed Jewish merchants operating in black neighborhoods to improve behavior and open hiring practices. Beginning in 1938, New York black and Jewish journalists, business owners, community and political leaders collaborated to address a range of issues from the treatment of domestic workers to the establishment of a consumer complaint office. In Chicago, after some struggle with local Jewish business owners, the South Central Association (SCA) was launched in 1944. The Association announced as its mandate, "To improve the living conditions of the Negro.... To...appeal...to all employers to eliminat[e] policies of racial discrimination.... To improve the standard of business ethics in the Community."[21] A 1948 letter suggested the magnitude of the improvement. Harry Englestein, owner of a department store there and a founder of the SCA, 99 percent of whose clerical staff was black, received an award from the Mayor's Commission on Human Relations for improving intergroup relations. "It has not always been so," noted the ADL. "In total candor it must be said that in the past the gentleman's practices and views are alleged to have been responsible for engendering a certain amount of friction and misunderstanding."[22]

In Washington, D.C., the Jewish umbrella organization National Jewish Community Relations Advisory Council (NJCRAC) publicly pressed a Jewish-owned theater to integrate its audience. "That democracy should be made a mockery of in the national capital of this the world's greatest democracy, that the equal rights of men should be flouted within the very shadow of this nation's governmental buildings, seems to us monstrous and intolerable," it scolded. The Jewish Community Relations Council of Indianapolis negotiated between the NAACP and a Jewish theater operator there who "discouraged" black attendance, convincing the theater to change its policy. This success not only prevented "very bad working relations between the Negro and Jewish Community because of the adverse publicity in the Negro Press on a Jew discriminating," it also provided "the first break in the neighborhood theater segregation policy." Furthermore, "the mediation by the Jewish Community Relations Council has developed a fine esprit de corp and will make for much better working relations between Negroes and Jews in our own community."[23] In Baltimore and New Jersey, Jewish leaders met with Jewish department store owners to press them on racist hiring and promotion policies. As Walter White observed, regarding Baltimore, those efforts "resulted in a considerable change of policy by a majority of the Jewish stores, while the two gentile stores are as adamant in their prejudice as they have ever been."[24] Jewish leaders intervened to protect Jewish interests, to advance black-Jewish cooperation, and to follow through on their moral commitment to justice.

Lessons Learned

While we might hope that when protest against exploitative practices turns into attacks on a group, the effort collapses, this seems not to be true. In the case of calls for boycotts of all Jewish stores, blatant appeals to anti-Semitism failed, as nationalists discovered. The community did not accept the legitimacy or morality of such a blanket indictment. But their appeals did find an audience steeped in both anti-Semitism and class-based resentment; by running up the cost of doing business in black communities they convinced Jewish storeowners to leave once they could. "Get the hell out of Harlem. Leave Harlem to Harlem," one Jewish business owner declared in disgust.[25] By the late 1950s, few Jewish businesses remained in black neighborhoods; in that sense one could argue these protests ultimately succeeded.

In the case of protests that targeted specific Jewish stores for unfair business practices, whether one viewed them as anti-Semitic or morally justified, they certainly enjoyed success. Jewish organizations, largely motivated by their desire to diminish anti-Semitism, did intervene to ameliorate some of the most troubling practices of these businesses. Clearly, non-Jewish white merchants did not demonstrate the same willingness to change. Whether guilt or pressure proved more effective in improving Jewish business behaviors, the fact remains that black campaigns made greater inroads among Jewish than non-Jewish whites.

Whether targeting Jews was a tactic (to convince Jewish businesses to change practices) or a goal (to rid the community of Jews), the call had resonance in both communities. It was an expression of resentment for African Americans, for Jews a fear of its consequences. Without preexisting black anti-Semitism, which legitimized the strategy in the black community and made protesters' claims compelling, the effort had less of a chance, as the failure of the Harlem ice vendor boycott suggests. And without vulnerability on the part of Jews, who both heard the call to racial justice and remembered the genocidal danger of unaddressed anti-Semitism, the effort was similarly hopeless, as the refusal of Christian-owned Baltimore stores to desegregate demonstrates. Scapegoating may not seem morally defensible, but it can be effective.

In another sense, however, these efforts solved little. They all sought to end exploitation; nationalist protest also sought to keep control of neighborhood institutions within the black community. Ultimately, protests that targeted Jewish stores accomplished neither. The paucity of black-owned stores had more to do with broader forces of institutional racism and limits on economic opportunity and education than on Jewish competition. Jews, while clearly charging high prices, did not do so because they were Jewish. They did so because they were near-poor themselves, and because the price of doing business in poor communities was in fact higher. This is not to justify exploitation, but to suggest that the problems were structural and the consequences the same for owners of any race or religion. The protests did nothing to address those issues. While the alteration of Jewish business practices achieved by direct intervention did end certain forms of economic exploitation, no small victory, even this could do little to alter the deeper problems faced by poor black communities.

This raises a further issue: Can consumer protests, which require clear targets and specific demands, be effective against the broader challenges of institutional or structural oppression? The shift in tactics by civil rights activists in the late 1960s occurred in large measure because of the ineffectiveness of earlier protest strategies against structural inequality. To challenge segregation one can picket or boycott a segregated facility. This strategy works less well against inequitable school funding or a racially biased criminal justice system. Targeting Jewish stores is a concrete strategy, and buying black a specific goal. It is less clear how consumer action can tackle larger problems of undercapitalization, insurance redlining, poverty which necessitates buying on credit, and other forces that operate to maintain economic exploitation in poor minority communities.

Certainly neither the anti-Semitic boycotts nor the targeted public protests addressed those larger problems. Nor did they establish local all-black economies, the second goal of the nationalists. While Jews generally left black neighborhoods, they were often replaced in later years by Koreans, who ended up facing much the same antagonism. The moral ambiguities of consumer struggles to sustain neighborhood businesses are thus no clearer today. By selecting a vulnerable target, and employing rhetoric that resonated with both the protesters and perpetrators, the consumer actions we have been looking at succeeded. Where they failed, they did so not because the community rejected the immorality of targeting Jews (or Koreans) as a group, but because driving them from the community did not resolve the real problem.

Restrictive Housing Covenants

The fact is group hatred has time and time again proved an effective motivation for consumer action. Sometimes a racist goal was precisely the one the community desired, and action was highly successful because all the necessary ingredients were present. Restrictive housing covenants, a complex form of political consumer action in which individuals used the market to achieve political aims, rested on the principle that discrimination was a legitimate and desirable goal for a community. They were so effective that it took a Supreme Court case to outlaw their enforcement. Even then, the practice continued illicitly. In a restrictive housing covenant, white Christian homeowners on a particular block or in a particular neighborhood sign an agreement not to sell their property to a specified group or groups. The precise makeup of the excluded groups varied, but almost always included African Americans, Jews, and Asians (or as they were then called, Orientals). A long-standing practice for maintaining the racial, ethnic, and religious purity of neighborhoods, it took repeated legal and legislative efforts by black and Jewish organizations to challenge the practice. In 1948, the Supreme Court ruled that such covenants could not be legally enforced (although it did not outlaw the covenants themselves).[26] Nevertheless, in 1952, attorney and housing expert Charles Abrams noted that the ruling "has not helped very much…. Other devices are being used for excluding Negroes" including mortgage and insurance redlining, and Federal Housing Authority (FHA) loan guidelines protecting the integrity of existing neighborhoods and perceived property values.[27] (Again the question arises: Can consumer protest be effective against these more diffuse, more entrenched, more structural issues?)

As housing integration efforts intensified after World War II and into the 1950s, white citizens continued to take matters into their own hands to keep their neighborhoods segregated. In Chicago alone there were six housing riots between 1940 and 1952 in which thousands took to the streets to prevent black tenants or homeowners from moving in. They marched and shouted, threw bricks and firebombs, battled police and attacked black passers-by. Although these actions did not employ the market directly, they certainly operated in much the same way as other consumer protests, and saw the same sorts of mixed results. Where police and officials refused to protect black renters, or when judges defended the protesters and blamed the violence on the integrating black families, protesters won the day. Where police and public officials held firm, the rioters were disarmed and black families moved in. Yet even in these cases, protesters could still savor their successes. In one case, the building housing the black family was razed. In another, the family left. And in every case, their larger point was heard by prospective black tenants—move in at your peril. Most chose not to face the hostility and danger, and communities as a result integrated far more slowly than the law and the need for housing warranted.[28]

In these cases, community support for protest was strong because residents agreed with its racist goal and were motivated to act because there was no good substitute available. Existing neighborhoods could not be easily moved or duplicated elsewhere, so staying and fighting seemed to offer the best choice. Meanwhile, the availability of choices worked in reverse for the black community. While housing needs were acute, most found other alternatives rather than move to antagonistic neighborhoods. In later years, when resistance proved less likely to succeed (although it was certainly attempted for many more decades—consider the violence in south Boston in the 1970s and 1980s), when faced with the undesirable reality of black neighbors, many whites exercised their consumer options by what we call white flight.

The Past is Prologue?

If these historical examples give us pause in our haste to praise consumer protest as the best democratic voice of the people, so, too, might the fact that, much to the distress of progressives, in the United States today the consumer protest tactics of the left have largely been taken over by the right. Now religious conservatives boycott Disney for supporting gays and lesbians, and white supremacists refuse to pay taxes or recognize the legal rights of a nation they believe has been hijacked by minority groups and internationalists. The mechanisms of protest are the same; the agenda has shifted. That they have generally failed has less to do with the ethics of their goals than with the fact that secular consumer culture is so relentless that one cannot avoid, say, Disney products and still live in the world (at least with children).

In short, consumer boycotts and other forms of civil rights protest we so admire are not always either as benign or as effective as we have assumed or hoped. They are fraught with political tensions, require sometimes problematic or essentialist forms of identity politics, and can be divisive or have repercussions unforeseen by organizers. As a mobilization strategy for community building, boycotts can fail as easily as they can succeed. They are limited in their goals to those that can be clearly articulated, lend themselves to specific targets, can be implemented by straightforward actions, and are broad and compelling enough to attract a large number of supporters. And while the goals must be attractive enough to effectively mobilize a potent bloc of protesters, they need not be either virtuous or democratic in order to succeed.

Consumer protests in the black community have been remarkably effective both in winning more opportunity and in building a stronger sense of community. The Montgomery Bus Boycott and the sit-in movement embody all that is good and valuable about consumer protest—a disenfranchised community acts in the only sphere in which it has power to challenge gross inequality, and builds a broad coalition for action in which there is room for all who believe in justice. It succeeded in changing a nation. But not all boycotts were this successful or this ennobling. As Follesdal's chapter reminds us, the aims of consumer protest are not always honorable. When evaluating the success of such protests we must consider whether the goals are explicit and the action focused, whether the actions and goals are actually linked in a persuasive way, whether the grounds for the boycott are politically and ethically defensible in the community, and whether the participants are unified in their understanding of their goals and acceptance of the tactics. Boycotts, in other words, succeed when there is a strong level of community support, concrete goals, straightforward tactics easily implemented by the community and that do not overly inconvenience them, specific and vulnerable targets, and surmountable external barriers.

Their success does not, however, require democratic goals. Housing riots by white residents when black neighbors moved in were often successful: their goal was explicit, their tactics focused, the actions linked clearly to the goal, the grounds for protest defensible within their community, and the participants understood those goals and accepted those tactics. Hatred has great potential for mobilizing effective action.

These protest examples also point up another important lesson: even well-intentioned grassroots action can be redirected by a dedicated group with a different agenda. In both the case of Harlem's "Don't Buy" campaign and the consumer protest campaigns that targeted Jewish merchants, nationalism both energized and undermined the struggle by defining it in terms that were meaningful to the community, but that ultimately did not address the problem. In other cases, benign-sounding goals can cover for self-interested action. Political consumerism provides an important vehicle for community expression when blocked from operating within traditional political frameworks. It gives voice to the voiceless. But precisely because it operates outside traditional politics, it can be dangerous in that it lacks the buffers against bias, ill-considered action, and vigilantism that such frameworks provide.

Notes

1.   This campaign explored in Greenberg 1991, chap. 5. Also see McDowell in Franklin, Grant et al. 1998, 208-36 (who is somewhat critical of my view).
2.   Quotations from Greenberg 1991, 122, 124, 126. For more on alleged anti-Semitism, see McDowell 1998, especially 226-30.

3.   For more on the riot, see Greenberg 1992, 395-441; for claims of anti-Semitism, see Friedman 1995, 94; Diner (1977) 1995, 238.
4.   McDowell 1998, 213.
5.   Handbill from 1958 in AJC library, inactive Vertical Files (VF): Negro-Jewish Relations (NJR): NYC. Sponsors' names and addresses appeared at the bottom of the handbill.
6.   For two views on the extent and nature of black anti-Semitism, see Greenberg forthcoming; Dinnerstein 1994.
7.   "A Word to Dr. Preston Bradley," in *Dynamite* (21 May 1938), 1, in AJC VF: NJR. Other examples: Friedman 1995, 97; Dinnerstein 1994, 203-04.
8.   Dan Gardner, *Carolina* [NC] *Times,* 28 May 1943, 4; *Chicago Defender,* 25 August 1956. Similar: "The Heighth [*sic*] of Something," in *Pittsburgh Courier,* 27 August 1938; "Negroes and Jews," in *Amsterdam News,* 22 August 1942; "Southern Exposure," in *Chicago Defender,* 15 December 1956.
9.   Walter White to Victor Ridder, 29 November 1938, NAACP papers, box I C 208.
10.   Editorial, *Amsterdam News,* 27 August 1938, cited in Ford 1939, 4. Houston to Ovrum Tapper, 5 December 1938, NAACP I C 208. Chicago: Earl Dickerson to Walter White, 5 July 1938, NAACP I C 208. White to Ted Poston, 15 September 1939, NAACP I C 277. These conflicts were about class, not just racism or anti-Semitism: see, for example, Isadore Zack (ADL) to Sidney Sayles, 10 December 1952, ADL microfilm: "Yellows" (hereafter Y): 1949-52 Negro Race Problems (hereafter NRP).
11.   The complaint appeared in Roy Wilkins's syndicated "Watchtower" column in 1941. Responses: Abel Berland to Finder ("individually"), Memorandum re "Article by RW,"12 September 1941; Finder to Nathan Kaufman, 30 October, 1942, ADL Y 1942 NRP; David Sullivan, in *NY Amsterdam Star News* to Louis Fabricant, 25 August 1941; Reply, 2 September [?] 1941 (contains store memo); Finder to Fabricant, 9 September 1941; Irving Maxon, NYC attorney, to ADL, 1 November 1941; reply by Finder ("offender"): 7 November 1941, all ADL Y 1941 NRP. Similar defensiveness: AJC, "Jewish Contributions to Negro Welfare," 14 May 1942, ADL Y 1942 NRP; J. Harold Saks to Nissen Gross, 6 September 1945, ADL Y 1945 NRP.
12.   White to Ridder, 29 November 1938. AJC, "The Truth About Baltimore." Report, January 1939, 36-38, 37, AJC Library.
13.   Aubrey Mallach, "Factors Contributing to Anti-Semitism in Harlem." Report, 11 June 1941, 1, AJC VF NJR: NYC.
14.   Quoted in Isaiah Terman, AJC, Memorandum, "With Respect to Jews and Race Relations," 20 August 1963, 2, AJC VF: NJR: AJC 1938-69.
15.   Maurice Rosenblatt to B.R.E. (Benjamin Epstein], Memorandum, "Re: Harlem Situation, Report to A.D.L. from M. R., April 23, 1939," 3, NAACP I C 277. "Complaints of the Negroes and Anti-Semitism in Harlem," in *Morning Journal* (30 October 1939), in AJC, "The Jewish Press and the Jewish-Negro Problem," 1939 (compilation of articles), 12, AJC VF: NJR.
16.   Rosenblatt, "Re: Harlem Situation." AEB [Berland] to REG [Richard Gutstadt], 1 September 1943, Memorandum re "Jewish Merchants in Chicago's Negro community," ADL Y1943 NRP.
17.   Chicago: ADL, "Bulletin," 15 November 1938, 2. NY: ADL, Minutes of Executive Finance Committee, 3 March 1941, 1, ADL warehouse box 178.
18.   There are dozens of books newly available on the subject of Jews and the civil rights movement, including Dollinger 2000; West & Salzman, eds. 1997; Friedman 1995; Franklin, Grant et al. 1998; Bauman & Kalin, eds. 1997; Svonkin 1997; Kaufman 1988; Adams & Bracey, eds. 1999; Berman, ed. 1994; Greenberg, 2004.

19. Leonard Finder to Nathan Kaufman, 30 October 1942, ADL Y 1942 NRP.
20. Rabbi Simon Kramer, Hebrew Institute of University Heights, to "Friends," 6 July 1940, ADL Y1941 NRP.
21. Cincinnati: A.N. Franzblau, "Objectives," n.d. [193?], 2, AJC VF: "Anti-Semitism." Chicago: Berland to Harry Lyons, Memorandum re "South Central Association," 9 November 1944; "Regarding South Central Association," Pamphlet, n.d. [1944?], ADL Y 1944 NRP; "Industrial Program of South Central Association," Report fragment, n.d. [1946] ADL Y 1946 NRP; Berland to Epstein, 12 November 1947; AEB [Berland] to Trager, 18 March 1948. New York: Transcript, ADL Committee on Inter-Racial Relations, 9 December, 1943; Minutes of Committee on Inter-Racial Relations, 22 November 1943, ADL Y 1943 NRP; Lionel Bernstein to Trager, 3 June 1948, ADL Y 1948 NRP; Uptown Chamber of Commerce, "Tentative Program of the Committee for the Improvement of Race Relations," and "Proposed Program of the Expansion of the Activities of the UCC," n.d.; Harry Lyons to Martin Frank, 12 July 1944; Sachs to Lyons, 18 November 1944, all ADL Y 1944 NRP; J. Harold Saks to Sachs, 4 February 1948, ADL Y 1948 NRP. Business ethics: Minutes, ADL National Commission meeting, 21-26 September 1946, 19, ADL warehouse box 176.
22. Stella Counselbaum to Frank Trager, 18 March 1948, Memorandum re "Harry Englestein," ADL Y 1948 NRP.
23. Indianapolis: "Near Morningside Theater Drops Jim Crow Policy," in *Indianapolis Recorder,* 17 July 1948; Indianapolis Jewish Community Relations Council, "Report on Segregation in Neighborhood Theaters, Indianapolis, Indiana," n.d. [1948] (source of quotations), both ADL Y 1948 NRP. D. C. theater: NCRAC to Actors Equity, "Re National Theater, Washington," n.d. [28 May 1947]. Also see Paul Richman (ADL) to Trager, 9 December 1946; Richman to Saks, Memorandum re "National Theater, Washington, D.C," 7 May 1947, all ADL Y 1947 NRP; "[American Jewish Congress] Joins Tolerance Fight," in *Chicago Times*, 27 August 1947; "Tallulah Raps D.C. Prejudice," in *Chicago Defender*, 6 September 1947, both in AJCongress clippings file.
24. Walter White to Gloster Current, 2 September 1947, Memorandum, NAACP II C 78. NJ: Sol Rabkin to Arnold Forster, ADL, 27 June 1947, Memorandum re "Essex County New Jersey JCRC Action Against Orbach's"; Rabkin to Forster, 10 July 1947, both ADL Y 1947 NRP.
25. Transcript, ADL Committee on Inter-Racial Relations, 9 December 1943, 3.
26. Known as *Shelley v. Kraemer*, and brought by the NAACP, it was actually three cases: *Shelley v. Kraemer* 334 US 1 (1948), *Sipes v. McGhee* 334 US 1 (1948), *Hurd v. Hodge* 334 US 24 (1948).
27. "Summary of Informal Dinner Meeting to Consider the Subject 'Discrimination in Housing,'" 30 April 1952, 2-4, ADL Y 1949-52.
28. For a fuller discussion of Chicago's housing disturbances, see reports and memoranda in ADL Y 1947 NRP and ADL Y 1949-52 NRP; *The Facts* 6:9 and 10 (September-October 1951): 1-4; *The Facts* 8:9 (November 1953): 3-4; Greenberg, 2004, chap. 4.

References

Adams, Maurianne, & John Bracey, eds. 1999. *Strangers and Neighbors*. Amherst: University of Massachusetts Press.

American Jewish Committee (AJC), Papers and Vertical Files (VF). AJC Library. New York: AJC Library. Used with permission.

American Jewish Congress (AJ Congress) papers. AJ Congress library. New York: AJC Library. Used with permission.

Amsterdam News (Harlem, NY), 27 August 1938; 22 August 1942.

Anti-Defamation League of B'nai B'rith (ADL) Papers and Microfilm. ADL Library. New York. Used with permission.

ADL Bulletin. Newsletter. New York: ADL Library.

Bauman, Mark, & Berkley Kalin, eds. 1997. *The Quiet Voices: Southern Rabbis and Black Civil Rights: 1880s to 1990s.* Tuscaloosa: University of Alabama Press.

Berman, Paul, ed. 1994. *Blacks and Jews.* New York: Delacorte Press.

Carolina Times (NC), 28 May 1943.

Chicago Defender (Chicago, IL), 25 August 1956; 15 December 1956.

Diner, Hasia R. (1977) 1995. *In the Almost Promised Land.* Westport, CT: Greenwood Press.

Dinnerstein, Leonard. 1994. *Antisemitism in America.* New York: Oxford University Press.

Dollinger, Marc. 2000. *Quest for Inclusion.* Princeton, NJ: Princeton University Press.

The Facts. Monthly report. ADL Library.

Ford, James. 1939. *Anti-Semitism and the Struggle for Equality.* Pamphlet. New York: National Council of Jewish Communists.

Franklin, V. P., Nancy Grant, Harold Kletnick, & Genna Rae McNeil, eds. 1998. *African Americans and Jews in the Twentieth Century.* Columbia: University of Missouri Press.

Friedman, Murray. 1995. *What Went Wrong? The Creation and Collapse of the Black-Jewish Alliance.* New York: Free Press.

Greenberg, Cheryl Lynn. 1991. *"Or Does It Explode?" Black Harlem in the Great Depression.* New York: Oxford University Press.

___. 1992. "The Politics of Disorder: Re-examining Harlem's Riots of 1935 and 1943." *Journal of Urban History* (August): 395-441.

___. (2004). *Troubling the Waters.* Princeton, NJ: Princeton University Press.

Kaufman, Jonathan. 1988. *Broken Alliance: The Turbulent Times Between Blacks and Jews in America.* New York: Scribner.

National Association for the Advancement of Colored People (NAACP) papers. Library of Congress Manuscripts Division. Washington, DC.

Pittsburgh Courier (Pittsburgh, PA).

Svonkin, Stuart. 1997. *Jews Against Prejudice: American Jews and the Fight for Civil Liberties.* New York: Columbia University Press.

West, Cornel, & Jack Salzman, eds. 1997. *Struggles in the Promised Land.* New York: Oxford University Press.

Tracing the American Roots of the Political Consumerism Movement

David Vogel

Introduction

This chapter traces the historical roots of the contemporary political consumption movement. It specifically explores the emergence of political consumerism in the United States during the 1960s and 1970s. During this period, activists targeted corporations around three broad sets of issues: civil rights, American participation in the war in Vietnam, and business investment in white-dominated Africa. The three cases represent milestones in the history of political consumerism in the United States. Not only were they politically visible, but the techniques they employed and in some cases pioneered, namely consumer boycotts, shareholder resolutions, demonstrations, and selective investments and disinvestment, have since become an important component of political consumerism in both the United States and Europe. The final section critically examines the scope and impact of the politicization of consumer and investor roles.

Market-based Activism in the Civil Rights Movement

The origins of contemporary political consumerism in the United States are linked to the civil rights movement. Both of the two critical events that sparked the American civil rights movement involved the efforts of black consumers to pressure businesses—one public and one privately owned—to end their policy of providing separate facilities for black and white consumers. On December 1, 1955, Rosa Parks was arrested for refusing to give up her seat on a Montgomery City Line bus to a white passenger. Following her arrest a friend casually suggested, "every Negro in town should stay off the buses for one day in protest" (Brisbane 1974, 21; Meier & Rudwick 1975, 101-24). The subsequent boycott lasted a year, costing the bus company more than $7,000 a day in lost revenue and severely undermining the economy of the downtown business district. It also mobilized the black community of Alabama's capital city, and within six months "had become the most popular cause in the United States" (Brisbane 1974, 38). More importantly, it marked the national debut of the civil rights movement's most influential national leader, the Reverend Martin Luther King, Jr., and his strategy of nonviolent resistance.

Five years later, an investor-owned corporation provided the setting for a political activity that ignited a second major wave of protest throughout the South. The spontaneous decision of four black college students to sit in the "whites only" section of a Woolworth lunch counter in Greensboro, North Carolina, sparked a nationwide protest movement. Within two months, sit-ins had taken place in seventy-eight southern communities, resulting in 2,000 arrests. Within twenty months, approximately 70,000 people in both the North and the South had either marched, sat-in, or picketed various business establishments. As a result, public accommodations in 110 cities and towns in southern and border-states were desegregated. "The movement managed to shake the foundations of Southern white society as it had not been shaken since Reconstruction..." (Brisbane 1974, 43). When executives of two chains of drugstores, namely Woolworth's and Kress, after meeting with Congress of Racial Equality (CORE) officials in New York, refused to desegregate their southern lunch counters, the recently revived civil rights group called for a nationwide boycott of both firms. Support rallies and picketing took place in a number of northern cities, including Chicago, San Francisco, Philadelphia, and New York. In New York City picket lines were established at thirty-five stores; three Saturdays later, sixty-nine stores were picketed. The picketing had an economic impact: Woolworth's officially reported an 8.9 percent decline in sales during March of 1960 from that of the previous year, for which CORE claimed credit.

In spite of the vulnerability of national retail enterprises to the consumer boycott and widespread public pressure generated in the North, the stores' central management refused to interfere with the policies of their regional managers. In time, public support in the North began to wane without the drama of the southern sit-ins to sustain them. As a CORE official acknowledged, "After all, it is difficult to expect the same people to picket week in and week out for a very long period of time" (Meir & Rudwick 1975, 122). The actual degree of integration of lunch counters was largely a function of local political pressures and social conditions. Accordingly, nearly all of the 140 cities in which dime store lunch counters were desegregated were located on the periphery of the South. In the Deep South, on the other hand, where white attitudes were more intransigent, most public accommodations remained firmly segregated until the passage of the Civil Rights Act of 1964. Even the Freedom Rides were unable to desegregate railway and bus terminals, although the Supreme Court had earlier held segregation of these facilities to be illegal. De facto segregation did not end until 1962, after three years of persistent direct pressures.

As the setting of civil rights conflicts moved north in the early sixties, attention shifted to the increasing employment opportunities of blacks. Between 1960 and 1964, hundreds of businesses in the North were pressured to increase their number of black employees. In addition to picketing, demonstrations, and selective boycotts, more disruptive tactics were also used. These included "shop-ins," many individuals filling their shopping carts with groceries then leaving the groceries at the cash register without paying; "cross filing," taking products from one part of a store and placing them on other shelves; and "phone-ins," tying up telephone lines by frequent calls.

Because of their vulnerability to boycotts, activists decided to concentrate on consumer goods manufacturers and retail establishments. In St. Louis, a successful attempt was made to mobilize the enthusiasm generated by the dime store sympathy boycotts to pressure the same stores' local employment policies. In Detroit, 300 ministers asked their congregations to refuse to buy Tip Top bread and Borden's milk; pamphlets were distributed that read, "Lock the Gate. Elsie Won't Cooperate." In Seattle, a boycott of the Bon Marche department stores resulted in the hiring of forty blacks. In Berkeley, fourteen local retail businesses signed employment agreements with CORE; under pressure from Berkeley CORE, Montgomery Ward agreed to hire a total of eighty-five minority members. In New York, National CORE, along with support from local chapters of NAACP, CORE, and Puerto Rican groups, won a preferential agreement from A&P: the supermarket chain agreed to employ 400 blacks and Puerto Ricans within two years without even forcing civil rights activists to resort to direct action. After a "TV Image Campaign" threatened several major companies with a consumer boycott unless they sponsored integrated commercials, more than a dozen companies began to use blacks in their commercials. In San Francisco, following a very bitter campaign, the Bank of America agreed to hire more minority employees, but the number was considerably less than that demanded by CORE.

In July of 1964, race riots occurred in Rochester, New York, a city whose economy was dominated by high technology corporations with relatively liberal and enlightened positions in race relations (Sethi 1970a). Following the riots, a group of local black and white church organizations decided that the city's minorities needed a political organization capable of articulating and representing the needs of the black poor. They invited Saul Alinsky, the "middle-aged deus ex machina of American slum agitation" (Sheridan 1973, 2), to come to Rochester to organize the city's black community. In the spring of 1965, 134 local black organizations joined together to form FIGHT (Freedom-Integration-God-Honor-Today). At its June 1966 convention, FIGHT resolved that "Eastman Kodak be singled out for special investigation this year" (Sethi 1970a, 113). Kodak's economic importance made it an ideal example for Alinsky to use in expanding the boundaries of a corporation's responsibility for the welfare of the community in which it was located. One of Alinsky's major objectives, in the words of Ed Chambers, his chief organizer, was "to force corporate America to live up to its previous statements about corporate social responsibilities. The idea was to create a domino effect: "We knew that if we could get Kodak in line every other business would follow" (Sethi 1970a, 21). At a meeting of FIGHT officials with Kodak's top executives, the organization demanded that Kodak hire and train 600 minority group members—to be selected and referred by FIGHT—over an eighteen-month period. After extended negotiations, an agreement was signed between Reverend Florence and a company assistant vice president.

However, Louis Eilers, the company's president, was outraged when he learned of the agreement, and the next day the company's executive committee repudiated it. Kodak apologized for the misunderstanding, but stated that it could not "discriminate by having an exclusive recruiting arrangement with any organization" (Sheridan 1973, 9). Kodak's decision totally transformed the nature of the conflict: its arena shifted from the local to the national level, and its debate shifted from the nature of Kodak's social responsibilities to a discussion of its integrity. Alinsky decided to confront Kodak at its annual shareholders' meeting, which was to be held in April in

Flemington, New Jersey. FIGHT bought ten shares of Kodak stock and sent 700 letters to clergymen and civil rights groups asking them to encourage their members who owned Kodak stock to attend.

FIGHT asked its supporters to withhold their proxies from management—an act that was unprecedented in the absence of a contest for financial control. In response, various church organizations and a score of investors announced that the power to vote a total of approximately 40,000 shares would not be surrendered to management, but would instead be used to protest symbolically Kodak's treatment of FIGHT. This marked the origin of a tactic that would subsequently evolve into one of the most important nongovernmental mechanisms to protest corporate policies, namely the filing of shareholder resolutions to challenge various corporate policies and practices. Two months later, the dispute was settled through the mediation efforts of Daniel P. Moynihan. Both sides claimed victory: Kodak recognized that FIGHT "speaks on behalf of the basic needs and aspirations of the Black poor in the Rochester area" (as quoted in Sheridan 1973, 11) and agreed to send interviewers into the city's slums, accompanied by representatives of FIGHT.

Shareholder Activism and Consumer Boycotts Challenge Business Investments in Southern Africa

The same year that FIGHT began organizing, market-based pressures on business emerged from another direction. Earlier, in 1960, a massacre of unarmed blacks by the South African police at Sharpsville focused world attention on that nation's apartheid system. An international conference was held in London to organize a worldwide boycott of South African products, but it was not until the mid-sixties that the issue began to generate momentum in the United States. It would emerge as a central focus of political consumerism over the next decade, as activists employed a wide array of tactics to pressure firms to withdraw from southern Africa, on the grounds that their investments supported racial and colonial oppression.

In 1966, public attention focused on the ten American banks that had, six years earlier, arranged a revolving loan to the South African government. The purpose of the loan was to provide a cushion for the government's foreign exchange reserves, which had become sharply reduced by international reaction to the massacre at Sharpsville. Citizen pressures centered on the two banks with the largest loan commitments: Chase Manhattan and the First National City Bank. A broad cross section of the civil rights movement was mobilized, inspired by the parallels between the treatment of blacks in South Africa and in the United States. The controversy over the loan decisions of the two New York banks also marked the debut of the New Left as a pressure group on business. One of Students for Democratic Society's (SDS) first major demonstrations took place at Chase Manhattan Plaza in the spring of 1966. Recruiters on several college campuses were confronted, and Princeton and Cornell were successfully pressured into selling their stocks in the two companies. In 1968, the United Methodist Church Board of Missions withdrew its $10 million investment portfolio from the First National City Bank. In addition, representatives of the American Committee Church groups attended the annual meetings of Morgan Guaranty Trust, Chase Manhattan Bank, and First National City Bank in 1967 and 1968, in order to publicize their disagreements with the decisions of the banks' management; the meetings were also picketed. All told, a total of $23 million was withdrawn from Chase, First National City Bank, and other banks by more than 200 groups and individuals, to protest their financial support for the South African government— considerably more than the banks' exposure in the loan itself.

In 1969, a subsidiary of the Gulf Oil Corporation began producing oil in the Cabinda province of the Portuguese colony of Angola. By 1974, Gulf had invested approximately $215 million in Angola, accounting for more than two-thirds of all American investment in Portuguese Africa. Between 1970 and 1974, Gulf's Cabinda operation was the focus of more intensive citizen pressure than any other aspect of the overseas operations of an American-owned corporation. A wide variety of political organizations, including New Left and radical black student groups, civil rights organizations, and several Protestant denominations, attempted to pressure Gulf to withdraw from Angola, on the grounds that the royalties it provided to the government of Portugal helped finance its continued occupation of the colony. Their tactics spanned virtually the entire repertoire of citizen pressures, involving participation and disruption of Gulf's shareholders meetings, shareholder resolutions, pressure on institutional investors, and an attempted boycott.

In the spring of 1972, the setting for the debate over Gulf's overseas investments switched to the campuses. Black students at Columbia, Cornell, Harvard, Princeton, and Oberlin demanded that these universities sell their shares of stock in Gulf. Both Columbia and Cornell agreed—Cornell after the occupation of campus halls. The most important confrontation took place at Harvard. A year before, a group of black students—members of the Pan-African Liberation Committee (PALC) had requested Harvard to sell its 683,000 shares of Gulf Oil. Shortly before Gulf's annual meeting, PALC took over Massachusetts Hall and the office of the president for one week.

After their demonstration at Harvard, PALC attempted to organize a boycott of Gulf products in the black community. They reasoned, "Gulf is very vulnerable to attack by the masses of black people, because Gulf presents their major products directly to the public as consumer items, and adequate substitutes can be found" (Righter & Roach n.d., 48). Based upon their analysis of the geographic distribution of blacks and the percentages of black car ownership, they picked ten target states. A full-page ad was placed in Ebony listing fifty-six prominent black Americans who supported the boycott. PALC's effort supplemented that of the church-based Gulf Boycott Coalition, which, headquartered in Dayton, Ohio, had been undertaking a similar effort in the white community since 1971. A Gulf Boycott Committee was also established in London.

Although the extensive distribution of posters, bumper stickers, and leaflets that accompanied the boycott campaign marginally increased the public's awareness of Gulf's presence in Angola, the economic impact of the two boycott efforts was minimal. A handful of cities agreed to stop purchasing Gulf products, but within the black community the boycott was almost totally ineffectual. Not only did the high point of PALC's effort coincide with the gasoline shortage, but those most immediately injured by the boycott turned out to be the black owners of Gulf service stations.

In 1976, several days of riots and demonstrations by black students in Soweto reduced the rate of foreign and domestic investment, again causing the South African government to substantially increase its foreign borrowing. In the spring of 1977, resolutions were submitted to the shareholders of First National City Bank, one of the principal organizers of the new loans, as well as to Continental Illinois, First Chicago, Manufacturers Hanover, and Morgan Guaranty Trust, asking them to establish a policy prohibiting further loans to the South African government. Several other banks, including the Central National Bank of Chicago and the First Pennsylvania Bank of Philadelphia, stated that they would no longer participate in any loans to the South African Republic. The First National City Bank also announced that it would no longer make loans to the South African government or to government-owned enterprises.

In 1997, faced with increasing racial unrest and reduced prospects for economic growth in South Africa, a number of corporations began to reconsider their financial involvement. General Motors, Control Data, and Ford announced that their future investment plans would be heavily influenced by prospects for the resolution of South Africa's racial tensions. Chrysler sold two-thirds of its South African subsidiary, and Weyerhauser withdrew completely. In addition, ITT sold its subsidiary to a local company, but retained a financial interest in it. These decisions were primarily motivated by an economic self-interest, but were nonetheless welcomed by the church groups. On the other hand, Union Carbide, Caltex (jointly owned by Texaco and Standard Oil of California), and Phelps Dodge announced major expansions of their South Africa operations.

The Anti-war Movement's Challenge to Business Defense Contracting

From its inception, the New Left was explicitly critical of business and the corporate system. Not surprisingly, during the 1960s and 1970s anti-corporate campaigns became a major focus of the anti-war movement, as activists employed the techniques of political consumerism as a vehicle of anti-war activism. A disproportionate amount of these protests were directed against the Dow Chemical Corporation, which enjoys the distinction of being directly challenged by more people using a greater variety of tactics than any other firm in the postwar period (Sethi 1970b; Lasser 1968; Friedman 1972, 128-53; Brandt 1968, 12-15). Between October 1966 and October 1969, a period that encompasses all but the last two years of popular anti-war pressures, the degree of visibility and attention that Dow experienced not only overshadowed that of any other nongovernmental institution; on many dimensions it rivaled that of any public one. Between 1966 and 1968, the chemical manufacturer was the object of 183 major campus demonstrations; in the fall of 1967, over one-third of all campus demonstrations protested Dow's presence on campus. In addition, a consumer boycott of two of Dow's better-known products, Saran Wrap and Handi Wrap, was organized. In New York City leaflets were distributed listing Dow's consumer products and informing shoppers: "If you buy Dow products, you help kill. Do not buy Dow products—buy substitutes as long as Dow makes napalm" (Sethi 1970b, 18). In some parts of the country, physicians ceased using drugs produced by Dow Chemical, and an effort was also made to encourage investors to sell their stock in the company.

The boycott does not appear to have been successful. According to a representative of the corporation's consumer marketing division, sales of Saran Wrap, the product most frequently singled out for attempted boycott, in 1967, ran 6.5 percent ahead of plan. Indeed, there is some evidence that it might have proved counterproductive, as some individuals showed their disapproval of the protests and their support of the war and Dow's contribution to it by increasing their purchases of Saran Wrap. While the napalm issue had no observable effect on Dow's stock price, in the first half of 1968, the number of shareholders did decline from 95,000 to 90,000—a development "the company feels...may in part be ascribed to the napalm situation" (Brandt 1968, 15). The Union Theological Seminary of New York, for example, sold its 6,000 shares of Dow Chemical stock as a "symbolic act" to protest the company's involvement in the war" (Sethi 1970b, 20).

However, Dow's executives were more troubled by the long-range impact on the company's image from the publicity it received. The company's treasurer noted, "Whether our stock will develop a defense image or a defense stock orientation as a result of our close association with napalm is definitely a problem" (Sethi 1970b, 20). Dow's chairman, Doan, described the whole controversy as "a stinking, lousy, goddam mess. None of us likes war. None of us likes to be called murderer" (Sethi 1970b, 25, "The Garbage Burner 1969). The company's board of directors, which included both "hawks" and "doves," spent two full days discussing the issue of napalm production. After a reportedly troubled night's sleep, they unanimously concluded that the company should continue its current policy. Doan's successor, Carl Gerstacker, later admitted, "We've been hurt by these demonstrations and there's no question that we've been hurt. The only question is how badly" (Brandt 1970, 14, as quoted in Vogel 1978, ch. 2). The company's concerned management was less upset by the immediate day-to-day difficulties of running a corporation practically under siege than by the long-range impact of the controversy on Dow's corporate image.

In 1970, Dow's contract to produce napalm was awarded to another, much less visible firm. An official from Dow remarked: "To deny that the protests had any impact on our bid would be to deny the facts. We were getting awfully tired of the protests and the people who prepared the bid were hoping that we wouldn't get it." He added, however, that the corporation "did make an honest effort to continue our business of producing napalm" and did not intentionally seek to submit an uncompetitive bid. This version is disputed by some of Dow's critics, who believe their role was more influential (quoted in Vogel 1978, 48). Dow, however, was not the only target of the anti-war movement. In 1970, angry confrontations or disruptions occurred at the meetings of approximately one dozen corporations; over seven firms were the objects of assorted acts of violence.

The most disruptive and bitter confrontation between anti-war activists and business occurred at Honeywell's annual meeting, held on April 28 in Minneapolis. The previous evening, 3,000 people had attended a rally at Macalester College to protest the company's manufacture of anti-personnel weapons. The next day, 2,000 demonstrators met at a Minneapolis city park and conducted an orderly march to the site of the stockholders' meeting. Approximately 1,000 were legally entitled to attend the meeting by virtue of their ownership of shares or control of proxies. However, once the meeting began, the tension both inside and outside the hall made its continuation impossible. Binger declared that he possessed enough proxies (87.7 percent of the outstanding shares) to be reelected by the corporation's directors, and amid shouts of "Sieg Heil," he immediately adjourned the meeting—only fourteen minutes after it began. The meeting represented the most dramatic moment of six years of continuous challenge to the corporation's production of anti-personnel weapons. The campaign against Honeywell was the longest lasting of any counter-corporate effort; its goal was "to bring world-wide pressure to bear upon Honeywell to stop not only the immoral production of anti-personnel fragmentation bombs, being used in a campaign of genocide in Vietnam, but also to persuade Honeywell to cease all aspects of defense production (Christmas & White n.d., 1).

Subsequently, an organization called Clergy and Laity Concerned About the War in Vietnam targeted four corporations for a nationwide campaign: General Electric, Honeywell, Standard Oil of New Jersey (now Exxon), and International Telegraph and Telephone (ITT). For CALC these campaigns represented a way to mobilize its own constituency. It would provide a mechanism through which members of churches and church-related groups all around the nation could oppose the war. A research unit of the National Council of Churches revealed that three of its member churches owned almost 40,000 shares of Honeywell stock worth about $5 million.

Shareholder resolutions were proposed and boycotts organized against each of the four firms. For example, the Women's Strike for Peace picketed ITT's international headquarters in New York City and attempted to encourage supporters of the peace movement to refuse to buy two consumer products made by ITT, Hostess Twinkies and Wonder Bread. The War Resistance League, as well as several other peace groups, also engaged in civil disobedience activities outside ITT's New York offices; they passed out leaflets in the form of anti-personnel weapons. However, CALC's campaign against Honeywell was the most important of the four. Their national steering committee reasoned: "We believe that Honeywell, Inc. symbolizes the heinousness of the entire South East Asia war, because it produces 70 percent of all anti-personnel weapons used in the war"(Usher 1972, 8).

Stocks Without Sin: The Emergence of Ethical Investing

The anti-war movement also witnessed the emergence of socially responsible investing as a political tactic. In late 1969, Alice Tepper Marlin, a financial analyst for a Boston investment firm, was asked by a local synagogue to prepare a list of companies that were not involved in the production of war materials. The resulting "peace portfolio" was advertised in the New York Times, and over 600 individuals and organizations requested additional information. The Wall Street Journal and the Associated Press picked up the story and, according to Marlin, "the idea just snowballed from there." Marlin subsequently founded the Council on Economic Priorities, an organization, which sought to politicize the investor role by providing detailed information on corporate social performance. The amount of information available about the behavior of specific corporations as well as the sudden increase of popular interest in corporate performance raised the possibility that ethical investing could become much more than a symbolic act: it could be generalized into a principle of corporate reform. The expectation underlay the initial conception of the Council on Economic Priorities. In an interview conducted soon after CEP was founded, Marlin remarked:

> ...there can be little doubt that advising and informing these institutions of the opportunities for socially conscious investments can bring financial pressure to bear on corporations....The Council is trying to foment a new market psychology which will provide corporate management with a rationale for their social responsibility...a corporation [should be]...aware that socially responsible behavior will attract the attention of investors. ("Social Dividends" 1970, 2)

The existence of socially oriented investors would, in turn, make it in the self-interest of the corporation to behave more responsibly. Investor "social responsibility" would thus inexorably lead to corporate "social responsibility," even if—or to be more precise, because—managers remained exclusively oriented to the bottom line. The investor, however, like the voter, would not necessarily be maximizing his economic self-interest, as he or she might have to be prepared to sacrifice some financial return. But what if "socially responsible" conduct turned out to be in the firm's self-interest as well? The steady increases in government regulation, along with growing public scrutiny of corporate decisions, appeared to be narrowing the boundaries of managerial discretion. If the preferences of socially oriented investors were to eventually be enacted into law, and/or if consumers increasingly favored more responsible companies, then the trade-off between profits and responsible behavior on the part of the corporation would be minimized. These investors could then have the best of all possible worlds: they could simultaneously appease their consciences, use their capital to improve society, and earn a high rate of return on their investments.

The stage was now set for the effort to place "corporate social responsibility" on a sound commercial basis (cf. Goodman 1971; Gapay 1973; Shaprio 1974-5; "The Funds" 1971; "Doing Well" 1975, "The Dreyfus Fund" 1976). The concept of "ethical investing," or "stocks without sin," as one writer termed it, convincingly demonstrated the viability of the American business instinct; even public criticisms of corporate performance could become marketable. In 1971, at least six mutual funds were established with social objectives. Their introduction was widely reported in the financial press and generally greeted with considerable enthusiasm; now individual investors would become part of the effort to transform the behavior of American business. As the prospectus of one fund put it, "Private investment can be a positive force to enhance and encourage further social progress in America" ("The Funds" 1971, 55).

The largest of the funds was established by the Dreyfus Corporation in the spring of 1972 with $26 million in assets—rather modest by Wall Street standards. It planned to invest at least two-thirds of its assets according to criteria quite similar to that of the council's studies. It would pick those firms, which, by comparison with their counterparts, had acceptable records in four areas of social concern: pollution control, occupational health and safety, product purity and safety, and equal employment opportunities. Up to one-third of its assets would be invested in companies "that are doing breakthrough work in ways that will affect the quality of life in this country in the decade ahead" (Gapay 1973; "Mutual Funds" 1973, 42). Of the first 300 companies it studied, 103 made it to the eligible list; investments in those companies were then made according to traditional criteria.

Other mutual funds were more oriented to individual investors. The Pax World Fund was established by two Methodist ministers in order to "contribute to world peace." It restricted its investments to those corporations less than 5 percent of whose sales derived from contracts with the Defense Department. The First Spectrum Fund was organized around the principle of avoiding any investment in corporations that the fund's managers had reason to believe were not in full compliance with existing laws and regulations governing protection of the environment, civil rights, and consumer protection. However, most funds initially attracted relatively few investors.

The Impact and Limitations of Political Consumerism

Over the last forty years, political consumerism has grown considerably in scope and sophistication. Literally hundreds of corporations have been subject to consumer boycotts or have been the target of demonstrations or other forms of protest activities, not only in the United States but increasingly in Europe as well. The issues addressed by these pressures have expanded considerably, ranging from corporate environmental and consumer practices in both the developed and the developing world to the treatment of workers and human rights. Negative political consumerism, namely avoiding a company's products to show disapproval of a firm's policies or practices, has been complemented by positive political consumerism, namely the decision to purchase a company's products as a way of showing approval of its social or environmental practices.

Ethical investment has grown considerably in the United States and expanded to Europe as well; literally billions of dollars are now managed according to various social, ethical, or environmental criteria, and there are now scores of socially or environmentally oriented mutual funds (Johnson 2001). Ethical funds and advisory services employ both positive screens, which promote investments in firms that meet various ethical or social criteria, and negative screens, which preclude investments in categories of firms, such as weapons producers or cigarette companies. Finally, the use of shareholder resolutions as a political tool has become routine: each year approximately one hundred public interest proxy resolutions are submitted by activist shareholders and included in proxy statements.

However, the politicization of consumer and investor roles has had a relatively modest impact on the behavior of firms in the United States. The civil rights, anti-war movements and campaigns against the political systems of Angola and the Republic of South Africa all were successful: American firms can no longer discriminate on racial grounds, American military forces have left Vietnam, Angola is independent, and South Africa is democratic. But while market-based pressures helped place these issues on the public agenda and provided an important vehicle for political activity, they did not play a central role in any of these outcomes. What was decisive were changes in public policy, and these occurred as a result of pressures on government itself. Political consumerism has and can complement political activity, but it cannot substitute for it.

While there have been numerous organized efforts to boycott a company's products, only a handful of these campaigns have had a measurable effect on either sales or financial performance (Koku, Akhibe, & Springer 1997). In the United States, it has proven very difficult to mobilize large numbers of consumers to avoid the products of particular companies for social or political reasons. Moreover, companies have often been able to counter threatened boycotts with more effective marketing. In addition, only firms, which make highly visible and easily identified consumer products, which are frequently purchased, are vulnerable to boycotts in the first place. In short, negative political consumerism in America is ad hoc and sporadic; it has proven difficult to sustain as an effective source of long-run pressure on business, though it certainly can embarrass firms in the short-run.

Positive political consumerism has sometimes proven more effective, in part because the costs on informing consumers are often borne by the companies, which hope to benefit from the politicization of the consumer role. But its role has proven far more effective in Europe, where there exists quasi-public labeling schemes, than in the United States, where there are fewer institutional supports for positive political consumerism.

However, even in Europe positive political consumerism has been confined primarily to the environmental performance of products, though there have been some efforts to employ labels that certify the working conditions under which a product is made. The most common form of positive political consumerism, namely eco-labels, has been applied to only a limited number of products and typically covers only a few dimensions of corporate environmental impact. Consequently, most corporate environmental practices remain relatively immune to consumer scrutiny. How many consumers, for example, know or care about the environmental practices of the factories in which their automobiles or cell phones are made? In addition, relatively few consumers are willing to pay more for a product due to its green characteristics, which severely limits the incentives of firms to design and market eco-friendly products (Reinhardt 1999: chap. 3).

The consumer marketplace is not, as many of its critics have suggested, either amoral or immoral: it promotes the values of diversity, innovation, liberty, and efficiency. But it is not capable of promoting a wide range of social and ethical values, for the simple reason that relatively few consumers take such values into account when making their purchasing decisions. There will always be some companies and some products that some consumers will be more or less likely to purchase for reasons unrelated to the value of the product itself. But the portion of consumer decisions, which falls into this category, remains extremely limited—and usually involves products that also provide some benefit to consumers, such as organic food. Accordingly, the consumer market is neither an effective vehicle for advancing or expressing social goals.

The politicization of the investor role has been far more extensive than that of the consumer role. According to a recent study by the American Social Investment Forum, one of every eight dollars under management in the United States is invested in companies considered socially responsible (Sinton 2001). This is clearly orders of a magnitude greater than the portion of consumer spending that is informed by social or ethical criteria. Large numbers of profit-oriented firms have developed products to meet what is clearly a substantial market demand for the social or ethical screening of investment portfolios, and a growing number of organizations provide research on corporate social and environmental policies, that, in turn, make ethical investment or screening possible. The demand for these ethical investments comes not only from individual investors, but from a number of institutional investors as well.

Much of the appeal of ethical investment is based on the widely publicized claim that investors need not sacrifice their profits for their principles, since more socially responsible firms will also have better financial performance. Whether socially screened investments actually outperform non-screened investments remains the focus of considerable debate. Much depends on how both social and financial performances are measured, and over what time frame: some years social investment funds outperform the market and other years they do not (Margolis & Walsh 2001, Ullman 1985).

But paradoxically, the growth of ethical investment has had even less impact on corporate behavior than the politicization of the consumer role. There are very few cases of firms that have changed their policies or strategy in order to either avoid having their shares proscribed by ethical funds or advisory services, or to become eligible for inclusion by them. Indeed, even advocates of such investment funds and strategies have been hard pressed to come up with specific examples of how the politicization of the investor role has actually changed corporate behavior. The share prices of a typical firm remain far less affected by its social or ethical performance than by conventional criteria of financial performance. However, according to Simon Zadek, a highly respected scholar and consultant, "the financial markets respond in a manner that suggests that they are far less concerned about [the impact of] ethical behavior...on the bottom line" (Zadek 2001, 62).

Nevertheless, the impact of both political consumerism and ethical investment should be measured not only by its impact on corporate behavior. For the politicization of both the consumer and shareholder roles has provided large numbers of individuals with the opportunity to express their political and social values through their consumption and investment decisions. Providing alternative vehicles for political expression represents an important contribution in itself. Indeed, it shows the market system at its best: it is flexible enough to respond to both those consumers and investors who are concerned about the social impact of their economic transactions, as well as the far larger number who are not.

Thus, those who care about improving the behavior of American corporations should not rely primarily upon consumer and investor pressures to accomplish this objective. Over the last half century, many American firms have changed their conduct, especially in the developed world. But this change has come about primarily not through consumer or investor pressures on firms to behave more responsibly, but as a result of government regulation. The politicization of the consumer and investor roles has contributed to this process, often by placing issues of corporate behavior on the political agenda, but it has not been central to it. Without changes in public policy, improvements in corporate behavior would have remained uneven and sporadic. Only the government has the legal and financial resources to define and enforce standards of corporate conduct. Political consumerism represents an important complement to conventional politics, but it should not be seen as a substitute for it.

Note

The historical material in this essay is drawn from David Vogel, *Lobbying the Corporation*, New York: Basic Books, 1978, especially chapters 2, 4, and 5.

References

Brandt, Ellis N. 1968. "NAPALM—Public Relations Storm Center." *Public Relations Journal* (July): 12-15.

Brisbane, Robert H. 1974. *Black Activism*. Valley Forge, PA: Judson Press.

Christmas, Jesse E., & Hugh C. White, Jr. n.d. "Honeywell, Inc. and the Bomb." Information distributed by the Institute of the Church in Urban-Industrial Society, no. 1045, 1.

"Doing Well by Doing Good: What's Happened to Ethical Investing." *Harper's Weekly* (May 23, 1975): 6.

Friedman, Saul. 1972. "This Napalm Business," in Robert Heilbroner et al., eds., *In the Name of Profit*. New York: Doubleday & Co.

Gapay, Les. 1973. "Mutual Funds and Social Conscience." *Progressive* 37 (March): 40-3.

Goodman, Walter. 1971. "Stocks Without Sin." *Harper's* (August): 61-7.

Johnson, Philip. 2001. "Social Investing Turns 30." *Business Ethics* (January/February): 12-16.

Koku, Paul, Aigbe Akhibe, & Thomas Springer. 1997. "The Financial Impact of Boycotts and Threats of Boycotts." *Journal of Business Research* 41: 15-20.

Lasser, Lawrence J. 1968. "Dow Chemical Company Case." Case under the supervision of Professor George Albert Smith Jr., 1968, revised 1971 by Barbara Prendergast and

George C. Lodge, no. 9-312-029. Case distributed by the Inter-Collegiate Case Clear-inghouse, Boston.

Margolis, Joshua Daniel, & James Patrick Walsh. 2001. *People and Profits? The Search for a Link between a Company's Social and Financial Performance*. Mahwah, NJ: Lawrence Erlbaum Associates.

Meier, August, & Elliot Rudwick. 1975. *CORE: A Study in the Civil Rights Movement*. Urbana: University of Illinois Press.

Reinhardt, Forest L. 1999. *Down to Earth. Applying Business Principles to Environmental Management*. Boston: Harvard Business School Press.

Righter, Richard, & Patricia Roach. n.d. "A Response to Exploitation." Pamphlet, p. 48. No publication information.

Sethi, S. Prakash. 1970a. *Business Corporations and the Black Man: An Analysis of Social Conflict: The Kodak-FIGHT Controversy*. Scranton, PA: Chandler Publishing Company.

___. 1970b. "Dow Shalt Not Kill. Case distributed by the Inter-Collegiate Case Clearing-house," Boston, no. 9-414-030.

Shapiro, Harry. 1974-5. "Social Responsibility Mutual Funds: Down the Down Stair-case." *Business and Society Review* 12 (Winter): 90-3.

Sheridan, Frances. 1973. "FIGHT and Eastman Kodak," a case prepared by Francis Sheridan under the direction of Professor Howard F. Bennett incorporating new material pre-pared by Linda Waters under the direction of Professor George C. Lodge. Boston: Inter-Collegiate Case Clearinghouse, no. 9-373-207, p. 2.

Sinton, Peter. 2001. "Crisis of Conscience." *San Francisco Chronicle*, 22 November, B3.

"Social Dividends—A New Corporate Responsibility." *Trends in Management/Investor Relations* (October 1970): 2.

"The Dreyfus Fund: Experience with Investing in the Public Interest." *Business and Society Review* (Spring 1976): 57-61.

"The Funds." *Forbes* (July 1, 1971): 55-62.

"The Garbage Burner." *The New Republic* (July 1969) 26: 7-8.

Ullman, Arieh. 1985. "Data in Search of a Theory." *Academy of Management Review* 10, 3: 540-557.

Usher, Dick. 1972. "Honeywell Campaign Meets the Press." *American Report* (May 5): 8.

Vogel, David. 1978. *Lobbying the Corporation. Citizen Challenges to Business Authority*. New York: Basic Books.

Zadek, Simon. 2001. *The Civil Corporation*. London: Earthscan.

Branded Political Communication: Lifestyle Politics, Logo Campaigns, and the Rise of Global Citizenship

W. Lance Bennett

Introduction

The scope of political consumerism has expanded greatly in recent years beyond the well-established forms of boycotts, buycotts, and socially responsible investing. Some observers argue that a clear distinction between citizen and consumer roles in public life is increasingly difficult to establish (Scammell 2000; Bennett & Entman 2001). Consumerism in the sense of more personalized, less collective public policy choices is becoming the core of the relationships between citizens, representatives, and governments in the electoral politics of a number of nations (Scammell 1995; Blumler & Kavanagh 1999). Outside the electoral arena, the expanding uses of consumer campaigns are transforming public interest politics by applying direct public pressure on government officials and corporations to adopt higher environmental, human rights, and labor standards. And beyond the nation state, the globalization of economic and communication systems has motivated and enabled citizen consumers to make political claims in international arenas.

This chapter explores the rise of what might be called *global citizenship* as characterized by broad coalitions of groups using campaigns against corporations, along with other tactics, to press for greater public accountability in trade regimes, labor practices, human rights, environmental quality, and other areas of corporate social responsibility. The focus of the analysis is on how these campaigns work, beginning with a brief introduction to ways in which globalization has affected both citizen identities and meaningful political action. Stated briefly, the argument goes like this. Public (citizen) identities change as global economies create new personal challenges for managing careers, social relationships, and family life. Cosmopolitan citizens in global societies process their political choices increasingly in terms of how those choices affect their own lifestyles. As lifestyles become more diverse, they are poorly articulated with old political categories such as class, party, or religion. As a result, ideological messages—particularly about global justice issues—are less likely to be received positively by typical citizens. In this context, effective activist political communication increasingly adopts a lifestyle vocabulary anchored in consumer choice, self-image, and personal displays of social responsibility. In particular, attaching political messages to corporate brands becomes a useful way to carry often radical ideas into diverse personal life spaces, as well as across national borders and cultural divides.

The core of the analysis in this chapter explores four general properties of a new global activism that is centered on these networked, lifestyle-oriented political communication campaigns. These defining properties of global activist communication are illustrated with examples from two logo campaigns: the consumer advocacy campaign against Microsoft and the sweatshop labor campaign against Nike. This analysis shows that activist networks using branded communication strategies can sustain long-term political initiatives even in the absence of the strong central coordination and the organizational resources that seem to be required for success in more conventional advocacy politics. At the same time, there may be political disadvantages in loosely networked consumer activist campaigns that lack the decision-making capacity and strategic coherence of more conventional campaigns run by NGO advocacy organizations. Yet both the Nike and Microsoft cases make clear that the branding of political messages is a powerful networking tool. Moreover, branded political communication helps activists gain access to the mass media on terms far more favorable to activist messages than if those messages were packaged in more conventional ideological terms.

Globalization and the Rise of New Citizen Identities

Underlying the new global political consumerism are a myriad of social and economic changes associated with globalization: transformations of jobs, careers, and labor markets; proliferation of new family models with working parents and more independent children; dislocation of civil society organizations such as unions, churches and civic groups; and the collapse of broad opposition ideologies to the reigning neo-liberal faith in market democracies. These changes vary greatly from nation to nation, yet one common individual-level result seems to be the rise of what has been termed variously a postmodern politics (Inglehart 1997), a politics of the self or a life politics (Giddens 1991), or what I have termed lifestyle politics (Bennett 1998). In this view, individuals increasingly organize social and political meaning around their lifestyle values and the personal narratives that express them. For increasing numbers of citizens—particularly younger generations who have been born into the global experience (roughly, since 1970) —politics in conventional (collective, government-centered, electoral) forms has become less salient (Putnam 2000). Insofar as politics matters at all to many younger citizens, it makes sense within the personal life considerations of job, recreation, shopping, entertainment, fashion, sports, self-improvement, family, friends, and the community involvements that can be scheduled around these things.

Across a whole range of relations with the state, citizens now take a more explicitly consumerist stance, expecting more direct benefits and fewer collective goods, and demanding more choice in education, health care, and other areas of state services. This trend is now so pronounced that Christiansen and Laegreid propose a new model of the state as "the supermarket state," which they see "primarily as a provider of services responding to the demands of consumers or users" (Christiansen & Laegreid 2000). Compounding this triumph of market democracy, many left-of-center parties have embraced globalization and the neo-liberal trade economics that drive it. Witness, for example, Tony Blair's reinvention of the Labour party in Britain, the centrist-business shift of the Social Democrat-Green coalition forged by Gerhard Schröder in Germany, and Bill Clinton's "rebranding" the Democratic Party around a host of Republican positions, including welfare reform.

The market relations between citizens and their representatives have introduced interesting dynamics into contemporary politics, ranging from weaker political identifications with parties and nations, to a greater ease of adopting cosmopolitan lifestyles and global political identities (Castells 1996; Inglehart 1997). In addition, as individuals are dislocated from traditional social and political institutions and placed increasingly in market competition, they are less likely to see governments as supportive or effective in addressing their personal needs. From that point, it is a short identity shift to detach from the activities of traditional citizenship, and embrace, instead, the public identities and stances of critical, independent-minded consumers.

This shift in citizen identities also implies a shift in the political power of individuals in *late modern* societies that are organized increasingly around the social networks of the self. For many in the ranks of the consuming majority, power involves more than just disciplining representatives and candidates to address their lifestyle concerns; it also extends directly to the centers of corporate power in the economic realm. As Margaret Scammell has observed, the global economy has created an ironic exchange of worker power for consumer power:

> As workers, most of us have less power now for all the familiar reasons: technological revolution and economic globalization, abetted by the deregulating governments of the 1980s and 1990s that systematically dismantled many of the legal rights of labor unions. As consumers, though, we at least in the developed North, have more power than ever. We have more money and more choice.... We are better informed shoppers.... Consumer rights and interest groups...are now daily in our mass media. Environmental lobbyists and activists...have a clear and central place in public debate and have demonstrated their ability to score direct hits against the multinationals: Shell and dumping of waste in the oceans, Monsanto and genetically modified foods, Nike and pay and working conditions in its Third World suppliers' factories. (Scammell 2000, 351f)

In some cases, citizens' consumer choices are knowingly—even radically—political, aimed at powerful corporations that embody globalization. In other instances, the citizen consumer may be a lifestyle libertarian inclined toward avoiding politics in step with the sweeping trend of political disaffection in the post-industrial democracies (Eliasoph 1998; Mutz 2000). Yet, even for those who adopt a stance of political avoidance, their fashion statements and product choices may matter in social image terms.

Whether or not they are avowedly political, the behaviors of citizen consumers tend to be centered less around state institutions than most other kinds of political action. As Rose puts it, "Citizenship is no longer primarily realized in a relation with the state, or in a single public sphere, but in a variety of private, corporate and quasi-public practices from working to shopping." (Rose 1999, 166) While the bases of this shift from citizen to consumer may be clear, it is not at all clear how the organization of political consumerism on such a large scale can be made effective, particularly in cases where the scope of that activism is more global than national, and, in either case, less mediated by government regulation and enforcement.

Challenging Global Economic Power through Activist Communication Networks

As noted in several chapters in this volume, many forms of political consumerism fit fairly easily into conventional national politics, from boycotts organized by unions or churches, to product labeling schemes regulated by governments. However, the rise of a new global activism against corporations and other economic organizations presents new political challenges on several fronts. Many activists perceive that global economic arrangements, from trade regimes, to the restructuring of manufacturing, to deregulated labor and capital markets, have empowered corporations to escape the regulatory systems of nations. Indeed, Ulrich Beck (2000) has identified the defining political feature of globalization as the capacity of corporations to engage in *sub-politics*—that is, using the new freedoms offered by global labor, manufacturing, finance and tax options as levers against governments. The dilemma for activists is how to challenge corporate sub-politics when governments themselves are directly implicated, as with participation in trade regimes such as the World Trade Organization, and generally unwilling to challenge the new gospel of neo-liberal economics. How can a sustainable political opposition be organized that crosses borders and cultures? How can larger publics be created and educated in matters of labor, environmental or human rights standards, when most cosmopolitan national publics generally favor the consumer and lifestyle indulgences of globalization? And, perhaps most importantly, how can sustainable accountability mechanisms be implemented to protect social and environmental standards in cases where governments seem unwilling to take a regulatory role?

Many global activists have discovered creative communication-based strategies that address the above dilemmas. Above all, activists have learned that the same electronic communication revolution that facilitated the development of global economic networks (enhancing the sub-politics of the corporate players in those networks) can be used to build global activist networks (enhancing the sub-politics of advocates seeking greater corporate accountability for the social costs of the global economy). As Smith and Smythe argue in their analysis of the WTO protests in Seattle:

> The very processes and means of communicating that made globalization possible, we argue, are making globalization contestable. Information and communication technologies (ICTs), primarily the Internet, have facilitated new forms of expression and connection among groups, the growth of new public spaces which are not easily controlled by states and ruling elites. No longer can nation states assume national sovereignty over publicity and political activity. (Smith & Smythe 2001, 1)

Many different sorts of messages travel easily across the frontiers of cyberspace, since the Web enables receivers of information to find the formats and languages that most appeal to them. One communication format that seems particularly effective in reaching both committed activists and complacent consumers, alike, is the symbolic logic of culture jamming: from marching in turtle costumes at WTO protests, to Jonah Peretti's attempt (described in this volume) to attach the term "sweatshop" to a pair of custom Nikes. A core element of culture jamming is the use of emotionally cultivated brands and logos of corporations and their products to direct attention to the realities of human rights, labor abuses, and environmental degradation that are associated with the production of food, fashion, forest products, and other basic lifestyle ingredients (Klein 1999).

Combining the low cost and global reach of the Internet with the public salience of logo campaigns (that often begin on the Internet and end up in the mass media), sustainable activist networks have developed successful political strategies based on targeting companies and their brands. Unlike boycotts or buycotts, which generally require politically committed consumers to avoid or embrace the products of a company, the logic of logo campaigns may assign a more symbolic role to the consumer as a witness to bad corporate conduct. In many campaigns, the aim is to take the corporation's most precious product—its brand image—hostage in the mass media and connect it to unpleasant images that threaten the fragile, emotional purity of advertising fantasies. Reports of corporate abuses in the news, business, sports, fashion, and celebrity features introduce political messages into the same meaning contexts in which pure consumerist fantasies have been created through advertising. Such messages about often distant political problems would be hard to communicate otherwise to general publics who may be more sensitive to their fashion statements than they are interested in the brute political logic of global economics.

The goals of this sustained anti-corporate warfare generally include: (1) inducing corporate compliance with social or environmental standards regimes, and (2) inserting otherwise hard to communicate political messages into the closely held personal or lifestyle meaning systems of media publics. The networking capacity of the Internet, when combined with logo-logics that cross different cultures and lifestyles, have resulted in surprising political victories—often by surprisingly small numbers of seemingly resource-poor activists. As Alan Cowell observed in the *New York Times* business section:

> Increasingly, with multinational corporations gathering unparalleled power as the standard-bearers of freewheeling capitalism—in many countries, more powerful than the governments themselves—they are being held to account by shoestring advocacy groups like Global Witness that have filled the vacuum created by the end of the ideological contest between East and West, between capitalism and socialism. (Cowell 2000)

Four Patterns of Global Activist Communication

A closer examination of the new global issue activism reveals at least four communication-related principles that explain how activists have organized a sustainable politics that moves easily inside and outside of personal, national, and governmental contexts. A brief review of these four patterns is followed by an analysis of two different international logo campaigns. The Nike sweatshop labor campaign is an ongoing fifteen-year effort by a shifting network of activists to use communication power to force Nike to adopt more responsible labor standards, after the company pioneered a winning global business model using foreign contract suppliers to evade governmental labor regulations. The Microsoft consumer protection campaign involves a fluid network of business competitors, consumer advocacy organizations, computer policy associations and hackers, who have employed various attacks on corporate image to create a public relations context for governmental regulatory politics in North America, Japan, and the European Union. The four communication patterns that characterize global activism in these and other cases are outlined briefly below, followed by illustrations from the Microsoft and Nike logo campaigns.

The Development of Permanent Campaigns

It is often said that we have entered the age of permanent political campaigns, whether waged by elected leaders in order to govern after they win office, or by interest groups to maintain publics to promote their policy agendas. The campaign as a permanent basis of political organization can be traced directly to the changing social conditions of late modern—globalizing—societies and their weakened group, party, and ideological bases of political organization and mobilization. Campaigns in such social contexts thus serve more than just the purpose of communicating political messages aimed at achieving political goals. They also become mobilizing and organizing devices in contexts that lack more fundamental organizing mechanisms such as strong parties, formal interest groups, or ideologically defined social movements.

The origins of the consumerist symbolic logic that runs through many of these campaigns can be traced to "corporate" campaigns pioneered largely by American labor unions in the early 1980s. Searching for winning political strategies to compensate for steep membership declines, labor ended up supplementing traditional organizing and strike tactics with communication strategies aimed at threatening the precious images of corporations in the eyes of consumers, investors, journalists, social interest groups, and other publics (Manheim 2001). These corporate campaigns have now spread throughout activist and advocacy circles, being adopted by environmental, health, human rights, as well as by anti-globalization and sustainable development groups and coalitions. For example, Greenpeace waged a successful campaign against the Starkist label to stop the harvesting of tuna with methods that endangered other species. And the relatively small human rights organization Global Witness successfully targeted the diamond giant De Beers, which ultimately agreed to limit the market for the bloody "conflict" diamonds that motivated mercenary armies to establish regimes of terror in crumbling African states (Cowell 2000).

Some of these campaigns resemble more traditional boycotts in the sense that they are run by relatively centralized organizations or coalitions, and they can be turned off when specified goals are accomplished. However, an increasingly common pattern is for whole activist networks to latch onto particularly ripe targets, such as Nike or Microsoft, because their heavily advertised and ubiquitous logos stick easily to lifestyle meaning systems. This stickiness of logos helps activists get political messages through to audiences whose attention is limited in matters of politics. Such fruitful communication channels also may induce some players to continue running campaigns even when others leave a network, having declared their goals met. This rise of fluid networks, in contrast to more centralized organizations or coalitions, marks a second distinctive feature of the new, global consumer issue activism.

Global Consumer Activists are Networked, Not Centrally Organized

As globalization touches larger numbers of people in different societies, the sheer numbers of organizations and individual players with different points of view also grow. Networking is the ultimate mode of organizing diverse interests (or common interests that have been imbedded in different lifestyle communities and cultures). Beyond its role as a producer of globalization, the Internet also represents a more empowering and personalized communication alternative to mass media, particularly for those who are more comfortable associating in networks than in more conventional interest organizations. For those who have crossed the digital divide, the Internet makes joining campaign networks relatively easy (i.e., at low cost) at the level of individual choice, while adding the collective cost of making campaigns less centrally controllable. Sprawling and often unwieldy networks of organizations and activists are the hallmark of the lifestyle politics and global activism networks that characterize late modern societies.

As campaign membership grows and diversifies, networked node and hub organizations adapt more easily than old-style interest organizations and coalitions to the multiple goals and messages of different players. The Internet not only facilitates communication across intellectually and geographically disparate network elements, but it also provides an organizational structure, as the number of nodes, geographic distances, and value differences in a network increase.

The Internet Becomes an Organizational Structure

The organizational impact of the Internet may be limited to extending or amplifying existing organizational routines, when e-communication is adapted to conventional organizations such as unions or political parties, or to established political processes such as election campaigns. By contrast, the fluid campaign networks of global issue activism make the Internet itself an organizational structure, as activist networks resemble the fluid nodes and hubs of Internet information flows themselves. The Internet is implicated in the new global activism far beyond reducing the costs of communication, or transcending the geographical and temporal barriers found in other communication media. Most importantly, as noted above, the Internet uniquely facilitates the loosely structured networks and affinity ties of this brand of late modern politics. In other words, the Internet is not only a communication medium among networked groups, but the fluid patterns of communication—from the branded messages that cross ideological divides to the difficulties of centrally controlling actions—reflect the loosely linked properties of the new networked politics.

An organizational model of the Internet in global issue activism suggests that its centrality to the relations among players, and its importance as a means of mobilizing action, increase with the number of actors and organizations in a network, the diversity of issues and goals, the geographical (e.g., global) reach, and the length of run time for a campaign. Another prediction is that the stability, effectiveness, and strength of member identification with complex (multi-issue, multi-goal campaigns) increases with the emergence of network coordinating hub organizations that use email and web news to keep dynamic networks in communication over time.

Many activist hub organizations have developed to coordinate campaigns across traditional issue and geographical boundaries. For example, the Nike sweatshop campaign has been networked at various times by Global Exchange (www.globalexchange.org) in the United States and by the Clean Clothes coalition based in the Netherlands (www.cleanclothes.org). The WTO protests in Seattle were facilitated by networking organizations such as One World, Public Citizen and Global Exchange, as well as by web consortia that co-sponsored information hubs and clearing sites. According to a study of organization web sites that were most often linked to by other organization sites at the time of the Seattle protests, the WTO site was the link leader (2,129 recorded links), but several protest hubs followed with impressive network links: One World (348); Institute for Global Communications (111), Seattlewto.org, the sponsored site of the NGO coalition (92); and Corporate Watch (74), among others

(Smith and Smythe, 2001). Such Internet-work was key to WTO in Seattle, and as Lichbach and Almeida discovered, it was also crucial to the co-production of at least eighty-two simultaneous demonstrations in other cities (Lichbach & Almeida 2001). Only twenty-seven of those were in the United States, and the others were in far-flung locations such as France, Spain, Holland, Israel, Mexico, Sri Lanka, India, Pakistan, and the Philippines.

New Media Influence the Mass Media: How Activist Messages Reach Broader Publics

The growing conventional wisdom among communication scholars is that the Internet is changing the way in which news is made. In the early stages of an event or a campaign, the new media provide alternative communication spaces in which information can develop and circulate widely with few of the filters, conventions, and editorial standards of the mainstream (and even the alternative) press. An important feature of this new electronic public sphere is that activists are increasingly in control of their own news reports, and can issue them with technologies (e.g., streamed digital voice and video) that in many cases parallel those used by, or even run ahead of, those employed by conventional journalism. Perhaps the most important development for the future of information on the Internet is this rise of activist information organizations that offer radical alternatives to mainstream news both for activists and for anyone else (e.g., mainstream journalists) who may find them in an information search. See, for example, the Independent Media network (www.indymedia.org), which has pioneered live, streamed video coverage of global action events, a sort of digital CNN for the new global citizen movement.

It is important to understand that the public spheres created by the Internet and the web are more than just parallel information universes that exist independently of the traditional mass media. To the contrary, the gate-keeping capacity of the traditional press is weakened when information appears on the Internet, often in breathless fashion, with fewer official sources, and less time for journalists to decide on its news status before competitive pressures to publicize it in mainstream channels become intense. A spectacular example of micro-to-mass media crossover in global activism occurred in the culture-jamming episode involving Jonah Peretti and Nike, reported in this volume. As Peretti observed, based on the flood of responses he received, this message first circulated on the Internet among sweatshop activists, culture-jammers and their broader networks of friends through the micromedia of E-mail. Then it made its way to "middle media" sites such as weblogs and webzines. From there, in Peretti's words, "...something interesting happened. The micromedia message worked its way into the mass media..."

The flow from middle-to-mass media involves the passage of information through networks of differently situated culture producers. For example, when the story hit prominent (middle media) weblogs such as Slashdot (www.slashdot.com) and Plastic (www.plastic.com), it reached the attention of web-based journalists at more prominent middle media sites such as *Salon*, a U.S. on-line magazine that also published the story (www.salon.com). Many mass media journalists look to sites such as Salon and other trend-setting web locations for new ideas. From there it was a short journalistic step to publish Peretti's Nike sweatshop message in *USA Today*, *Wall Street Journal*, NBC's *Today Show*, *The Times of London,* and other mainstream news outlets. Canadian media consultant Doug Miller was quoted in the *Financial Times* as saying, "I visit 75 boardrooms a year and I can tell you the members of the boards are living in fear of getting their corporate reputations blown away in two months on the Internet" (Macken, 2000).

The New Branded Activism: The Cases of Nike and Microsoft

The above communication patterns are illustrated here in two necessarily brief case studies: the Nike sweatshop labor campaign, and the campaign against Microsoft's alleged restraint of consumer choice and technological innovation. These two campaigns provide useful contrasts between an attempt by one activist network (the Nike campaign) to pressure a company to join standards monitoring systems independently of government brokering, and the other (the anti-Microsoft network) to use logo communication tactics to create a climate of public support for tougher legal and governmental standards. The Nike case reflects the perception of many activists that international labor standards regimes have largely slipped governmental regulation, and that organizations such as the International Labor Organization are ineffective advocates. As a result, many sweatshop activists seek to create labor standards monitoring systems that must be sustained and enforced through consumer pressure. Microsoft, by contrast, is an example of a network of players seeking various kinds of standards (consumer protection, business competition, personal privacy, and labor protections) with governmental enforcement.

The examples used in this analysis are based on extensive data gathered by the author and various colleagues[1] on activist campaign networks, the communication strategies used to frame political messages in terms of corporate images, and the media coverage generated by those message framing strategies. The period reported here for the Microsoft campaign spans the years from 1996 to 1999, a time in which an identifiable activist network emerged connecting diverse organizations with common information links, jointly sponsored conferences and press events, overlapping board of director memberships, and coordinated efforts to introduce negative publicity about Microsoft business and consumer practices into the mass media and government policy circles in the United States, Japan, and Europe. The examples from the Nike campaign reported here reflect network activity as described in activist accounts and (in the more recent period) documented in Internet searches between 1987 and 2000. An empirical assessment of network communication strategies is based on a content analysis of Nike coverage in two leading American newspapers (*Washington Post* and *New York Times*) between 1991 and 1999. The discussion of these cases is organized in terms of the four patterns of global activist communication identified above.

Permanent Campaigns

Both the Microsoft and the Nike campaigns are longstanding efforts that have become more or less permanent campaigns. The Nike effort originated in the late 1980s and gained some public attention in the early 1990s, largely through the efforts of Jeff Ballinger, a labor activist who began trying to place news stories based on his studies of conditions in the Indonesian factories that contracted to produce shoes for the Nike label. The campaign took an important turn in the mid-1990s with the entry of Global Exchange, an activist networking organization that coordinates and runs campaigns in various areas of environmental, human rights, and labor politics. As Ballinger noted, "Global Exchange turned my rundown, VW bus of a campaign into an 18-wheeler" (Bullert 2000, 7). Global Exchange contributed resources, public relations skills, and an activist network that resulted in sustained mainstream media coverage of Nike labor practices abroad and profit margins at home. When the company perceived its logo being threatened with critical news coverage, it made the first steps toward independent monitoring of labor conditions in the factories.

Global Exchange left the campaign after "Nike blinked" and acknowledged responsibility for its labor standards (Herbert 1998). Typical of networked campaigns, new organizations such as the student-led Workers' Rights Consortium soon entered the network to push Nike to the next level of accountability—the acceptance of an independent standards monitoring system. The chronology and development of these and other aspects of this long-running campaign both in America and other nations can be found in Bullert (2000), and in the chronologies by Ballinger on the web site of the Center for Communication and Civic Engagement (www.engagedcitizen.org).

The Microsoft campaign is also more than a decade old, beginning with large-scale hacker attacks on Microsoft products, and active web networks aimed at branding the company as a predatory threat to openness and innovation in software development and a free Internet environment. Business competitors and workers filed various lawsuits dating from the early 1990s, and those suits increased in number and legal coordination until the United States Department of Justice (DOJ) and nineteen states filed a federal antitrust action against the company. The business opponents—dubbed N.O.I.S.E., for Netscape, Oracle, IBM, Sun, and Everyone Else in the insider accounts of the campaign—provided major funding, core elements of the DOJ legal brief, as well as sharing board members, information, and legal strategy with many of the organizations in the campaign.

It would be a mistake to overestimate the role of the business competitors and underestimate the legitimizing and authoritative importance of consumer groups, unions, computer professionals, and prominent intellectuals such as then Harvard Law professor Lawrence Lessig, an outspoken critic of Microsoft, who served as an expert for the judge in the initial federal trial. Among the key players were various consumer and policy groups, several of which were affiliated with consumer activist Ralph Nader. This wing of the campaign added an important "high ground" consumer justice theme that deflected claims that the government lawsuit, and the campaign in general, were solely the creatures of Microsoft business opponents. Like the Nike campaign, the diverse players in the Microsoft network show no signs of letting go of a logo that offered such a great publicity vehicle for communicating a host of messages. The barrage of legal challenges from consumer groups and business competitors has more recently been joined by privacy groups and labor unions attacking Microsoft on various new fronts. The flexibility of logo politics enables campaigns to be joined by diverse interests, all sharing the common belief that a company is a threat to their various causes. A chronicle of the early years of the campaign is found in Bennett and Manheim (2001).

Networked Activism

The Microsoft campaign is a classic example of a large and multipurposed coalition of players, including business competitors, consumer groups, labor, and computer professionals, with hackers playing more shadowy and less coordinated roles in the background. A partial look at the Microsoft campaign network is provided in figure 1.[2] This represents only a partial look at the players in the campaign, and just the part of the network (circa 1998) aimed at subjecting Miscosoft to business and consumer protection standards imposed by the courts and advocated by the U.S. Justice Department.

The links shown in figure 1 represent overlapping board memberships, funding relationships, keynote addresses at conferences, links on web sites, or authorship and web site locations of expert white papers containing the bases for allegations against Microsoft. The full network of all organizations, web rings, and related information and news would include thousands of players and connections in inordinately complex network patterns. Although the international network of organizations is far less developed than the American network, the domestic partners have created international variants of the campaign aimed at government regulatory bodies and the press in Europe and Asia.

The Nike network also contains many organizations, some of which exist largely as Internet presences to exchange information, coordinate actions, and specify political goals. A quick search in May 2001 of Internet sites with either an exclusive or a partial Nike focus (along with themes about international labor, human rights, and environ-

Figure 1
A Small Portion of The Microsoft Network, circa 1997-1998
(Developed with Jarol Manheim)

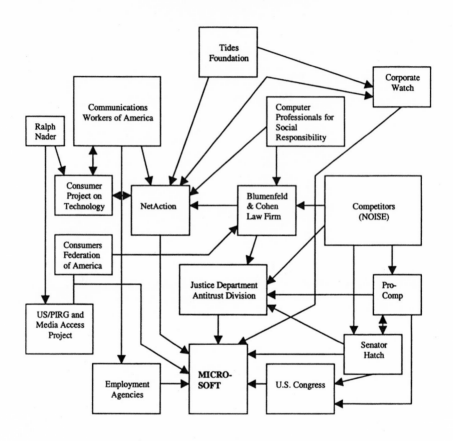

mental abuses, and the need for standards) yielded fifty-eight sites. The sites were more often based in the United States (32), but they were also located in Asia (3), Canada (3), and in Europe (18 sites in five different nations).[3] As is typical of consumerist campaign networks, there were different messages and goals, ranging from "clean clothes" certification, to demands for independent procedures for accountability on labor standards in Nike factories. (For an on-line sample of these sites, go to <www.engagedcitizen.org> and click on research, global citizen issue campaigns, Nike).

The Internet and Political Organization

Both Nike and Microsoft campaigns are characteristic of net-worked politics in that they require, or at least prosper, with the en-try of network coordinating organizations. What is interesting about the new global activism is that a network may contain many of these hub organizations, and they are often not particularly large, resource-rich, or long-established. In many cases, they are relatively small and Internet focused, and they are often created precisely to coordi-nate action and communication among activists. Many of these net-work hubs organizations move from campaign to campaign. As noted earlier, Global Exchange (www.globalexchange.org) played an im-portant role in coordinating the Nike campaign. After it decided that it had moved Nike in the direction of adopting some labor standards and monitoring, it moved on to other consumerist issues such as fair trade coffee.

In the Microsoft campaign, several network coordinating organi-zations emerged, including Netaction (www.netaction.org), which was created initially as the Internet hub for this campaign. Netaction later moved on to other consumerist Internet causes (such as pri-vacy) after playing an information archiving, publicity and activist outreach role, similar to Global Exchange in the Nike campaign. When some members of the network became divided over a weaker set of regulatory standards proposed by the U.S. government in 2002, Netaction returned to an active information and strategy-coordinat-ing role in the campaign once again. Other key organizations in the network included the Consumer Project on Technology, a Nader organization, and Computer Professionals for Social Responsibility, which hosted an important speech by legal expert Lawrence Lessig at a national meeting, and whose members provided legitimizing endorsements for various goals of the campaign. Operating at the fringes of the network were the players less likely to be credible sources of consumer rhetoric such as the large Silicon Valley soft-ware companies.

Perhaps the most important organizational feature of the Internet in new consumerist activism is that it enables diverse wings of a campaign network to maintain contact in ways that allow different issues and political perspectives to co-exist without threatening or-ganizational coherence as directly as differences might threaten more centralized, face-to-face coalitions. On most days, conservative Senator Orrin Hatch and consumer activist Ralph Nader would not find themselves in the same political universe. Yet they have been comfortably occupying network space together for years in the Microsoft campaign, with only a few degrees of separation between them.

Micro, Middle, and Mass Media: Information Pathways to Broader Publics

The Jonah Peretti Nike culture-jamming example noted earlier illustrates a key property of new forms of consumer activist, Internet-based politics: an "under the radar" quality. Electronically driven stories contain the potential to scandalize a campaign target with a swarm of electronic information that rises from an activist information chain, to more general electronic sites (blogs and webzines), to the mainstream press that monitors, and may even own, such web sites. Many news stories now begin on the Internet as catch phrases and anecdotes that take on a life of their own when thousands and even millions of networked citizens hit their send or forward keys. For example, the brilliant stroke of naming Monsanto's sterile seed "The Terminator" elevated anti-Monsanto campaign messages into mainstream news around the globe.

In the Microsoft campaign, the underground (Internet) terminology for Microsoft and its embodiment in Bill Gates easily crossed over into mainstream reporting. Derogatory terms and comparisons leaked out of Internet chats, networked campaign sites, and partisan webzines, and surfaced in mainstream news accounts reporting what opponents were saying about Microsoft: that the goal of the company was to "crush competition," that it was known by opponents as "the Seattle Slasher," and that Bill Gates was the latter-day incarnation of Robber Baron icon, John D. Rockefeller.

A more elaborate case of information moving from new media to traditional news organizations comes from the Nike campaign. Countless stories of worker abuse and bad conditions in Nike factories had long circulated across the Internet, providing an authenticating context for publicity organized by Global Exchange, after it entered the campaign in 1996. The communication strategy combined Internet mobilization (turning out crowds for touring Indonesian factory workers at Niketown locations) with traditional public relations techniques, such as press background briefings, press conferences, well-produced rallies, and other pseudo-events designed to fit news values. The result was to connect Indonesian workers with journalists around America in ways that produced dozens of repetitions of a detailed story about heroic workers battling a mean-spirited company. The result was a huge boost in national press coverage of the Nike scandal on terms dictated largely by the activists and the workers themselves (Bullert 2000).

After the entry of Global Exchange in the campaign network, coverage of Nike in the leading American papers (*Washington Post* and *New York Times*) shifted from a business section story about contract factories as the brilliant new model for business success in the fashion industry, to reporting on damaging consumer and sweatshop labor messages in the main news, sports, and opinion sections of the papers. Figure 2 provides an overview of ten years of Nike coverage in the *New York Times* and *Washington Post*, showing the evolution of the major and minor news themes in the articles. The data are based on a LexisNexis search of the *Post* and the *Times* for items containing the terms *Nike* and *Indonesia* between 1991 and 2000. The general themes in these stories were coded by graduate research assistants according to how they fit into the following news frames: *business frames* describing production, sales, marketing, and profit issues; *consumer frames* describing popular responses to Nike brands, styles, and product endorsers like Michael Jordan and Tiger Woods; and *sweatshop frames* describing bad labor conditions in Nike factories (corruption, pay, child labor, abuses against workers, reprisals against union efforts), along with various protest activities involving these problems. Each story was coded for a major frame and a minor frame, thus making it possible for a sweatshop story to have a business angle, or a business story to have a consumer angle.[4]

The "Niketown worker tour" communication strategy employed by Global Exchange resulted in the dominance of sweatshop framing both as the main focus of stories, and as the most common minor theme in stories with either a consumer or a business focus. A quick look at figure 2 also shows that before the entry of Global Exchange and its logo campaign strategy, most previous stories about Nike in Indonesia were more likely to be single theme reports on business trends, consumer behavior, or (occasionally) a labor problem in contract factories. The predominant Nike story of the early 1990s was a business success tale in which consumers liked the brand, and the company reaped huge profits by contracting its production out to cheap labor suppliers. By the end of the decade, however, after Global Exchange took on the central coordinating role in the campaign, the Nike story became dramatically different: a tale of dubious business morality in which consumers were gouged for expensive shoes produced by exploited workers in corrupt global export and free trade zones.

As figure 2 indicates, Global Exchange communication strategies succeeded in making "sweatshop" the major news theme in coverage of Nike in the two leading U.S. papers. Moreover, the sweatshop theme also became the most common subtext or minor theme in coverage that focused primarily on business or consumer aspects of the Nike story. It was this systematic linking of the Nike image with the unpleasant business of sweatshop labor that led Nike CEO Phil Knight to "blink," and admit that the company had some responsibility for its labor standards.

Perhaps the most remarkable feature of both the Microsoft and Nike campaigns is that they challenge the conventional wisdom that activist messages have trouble getting through the news gates in positive form without first being legitimated by government officials or high status news sources (Bennett 2003; Gamson 1992). Part of the explanation for this success is that logos are already big news. Media organizations are increasingly tuned to the consumer interests of their audiences, with celebrity titillation and so-called "news you can use" increasingly filling the news space with health, fashion trends, new products, investment tips, celebrity gossip, glamorous lives of the CEOs, and other lifestyle features. Thus, "trouble in logo-land" becomes an irresistible spin on corporate stories that are already followed by consumers, investors, and other attentive publics. Packaging politically challenging messages in the context of these consumer values seems to provide positive media access for radical messages that might not even have been admitted through the news gates in an earlier era (or, if they were let into the news, they were more likely to be linked to leftists, radicals, environmentalists, or other more easily stereotyped political sources).

Conclusions about the Future of Global Consumer Activism

These cases illustrate the potential of consumerist politics in globalizing societies. The consumer coding of political action becomes an effective means of telling distant and often complex political stories about labor exploitation, human rights, environmental issues,

Figure 2
Frequencies of Nike News Themes in *New York Times* & *Washington Post* 1991-2000

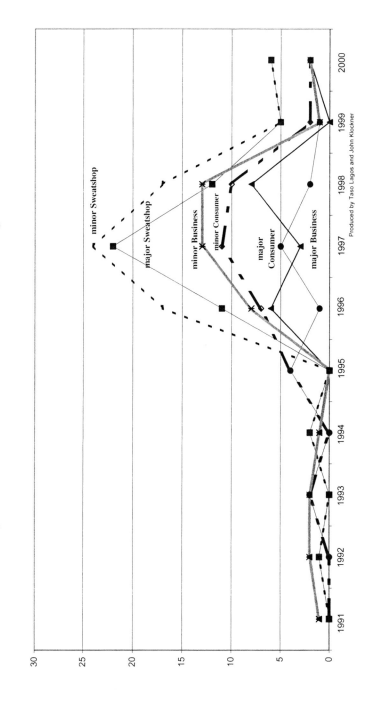

Produced by Taso Lagos and John Klockner

and bad business practices. Branding these messages helps get them through the lifestyle meaning screens of many ardent consumers. This communication strategy may also help make consumers aware of the larger political story of branding itself: that the brand, and more generally the branded consumer, has become the product in the contemporary economy. That is, the new global economy of cheaply produced products becomes hugely profitable through the process of branding consumers to pay a premium to express their identities through attractive fashion and lifestyle images (Klein 1999; Turow 1997; <www.adbusters.org>).

Logo campaigns and the larger cause networks from which they derive turn local sites of consumption (protests at shopping locations), politics (hearings by legislative and regulatory agencies), media (news and sports reporting about Nike offenses), and education (high school economics curricula on globalization of production, sports brands, and profits) into venues for exposing corporate practices and making new democratic accountability demands to regulate those practices. It is important to understand that these campaigns need not create large shifts in public opinion or consumer behavior in order to be successful. The main objective of many communication campaigns based on consumer symbolism is to create a symbolic public as a backdrop against which to target much smaller but more decisive political audiences: government regulators, members of Congress, journalists, or the stakeholders in a company, such as board members or stockholders. Creating dramatic news images of a once powerful, but now troubled, company or its brand may focus the attention of these strategic audiences and motivate them to take various kinds of actions such as holding hearings, bringing lawsuits, or selling shares. The threat of possible brand damage or corporate image problems may be enough to force the target company to modify its behavior, or even join a standards monitoring regime that may transform an entire industry.

Despite their successes, corporate campaigns run by large activist networks, also illustrate how the new consumerist politics may suffer unwieldy coordination problems among diverse coalition partners with different agendas. For example, the influx of large networks of activists running through political territories, once occupied in a more orderly fashion by a small number of rights, environmental, consumer protection, labor and development NGOs, presents an interesting strategic dilemma for movement organizing. In some ways, the goals of these global networks may continue to build upon traditional international NGO activist aims: instilling human rights norms in rogue nations, promoting sustainable national economic development and democratic institutions, or winning concessions from multinational corporations or corrupt governments on behalf of exploited workers. At the same time, the appeal of those earlier global campaigns was often that they were managed centrally by one or a small coalition of NGOs, and pressure was strategically applied to campaign targets until specified goals were reached (Keck & Sikkink, 1998). The ability to stop campaigns not only reinforced the credibility of activist organizations, but it also rewarded the compliance of targeted companies. The recent entry of large numbers of less commonly purposed, networked players increases the prospects for unstable coalitions, greater communication noise, lack of clarity about goals, and poor movement idea-framing.

In short, the new global consumer activism may be a sign of changes in definitions of citizenship and democracy, but it also presents a dilemma for traditional organizations that were more able to control consumer actions—turning them on and off—in the process of attaining specific political goals. Key questions about the future stability of this movement include: who is in charge of campaigns, how are campaign goals defined, what constitutes success, and how to stop others from targeting the same corporation (beating a dead logo) after it has satisfied particular demands. The capacity of networked campaigns to resolve these issues will determine the future of an historic moment in the evolution of democracy and citizenship.

Notes

1. The author acknowledges the important contributions of B. J. Bullert, Taso Lagos, Jarol Manheim, Jay Sellers and the many students who have been involved in these studies.
2. This figure was produced collaboratively with, and used with the permission of, Jarol B. Manheim. See *The Death of a Thousand Cuts* (2001), p. 154.
3. Google searches were run on the terms Nike and sweatshop, with sales and sports sites excluded. English, German, and Swedish searches were run. Other languages would have likely generated more hits.
4. Coder reliabilities for major and minor versions of the three basic story frames were all in the 80 percent range.

References

Beck, Ulrich. 2000. *What Is Globalization?* Cambridge: Cambridge Polity Press.
Bennett, W. Lance. 1998. "The UnCivic Culture: Communication, Identity, and the Rise of Lifestyle Politics." Ithiel de Sola Pool Lecture, American Political Science Association, published in *P.S.: Political Science and Politics* 31 (December): 41-61.
___. 2003. *News: The Politics of Illusion.* 5th edition. New York: Longman.
___, & Robert M. Entman, eds. 2001. *Mediated Politics: Communication in the Future of Democracy.* New York: Cambridge University Press.
___, & Jarol B. Manheim. 2001. "The Big Spin: Strategic Communication and the Transformation of Pluralist Democracy," in W. Lance Bennett and Robert M. Entman, eds., *Mediated Politics: Communication in the Future of Democracy.* New York: Cambridge University Press.
Blumler, Jay, & Denis Kavanagh. 1999. "The Third Age of Political Communication: Influences and Features." *Political Communication* 16: 209-30.
Bullert, B. J. 2000. "Strategic Public Relations, Sweatshops, and the Making of a Global Movement." Working Paper # 2000-14. Cambridge, MA: Joan Shorenstein Center on the Press, Politics, and Public Policy at Harvard University.
Castells, Manuel. 1996. *The Rise of the Network Society.* Oxford: Blackwell.
Christensen, Tom, & Per Laegreid. 2000. "New Public Management: Puzzles of Democracy and the Influence of Citizens." Paper presented at the World Congress of the International Political Science Association. Quebec, 1 August. Aldershot: Ashgate.
Cowell, Alan. 2000. "Advocates Gain Ground in a Globalized Era." *New York Times,* International Business Section. Electronic Edition, 18 December.
Eliasoph, Nina. 1998. *Avoiding Politics: How Americans Produce Apathy in Everyday Life.* New York: Cambridge University Press.
Frank, Thomas. 2000. *One Market Under God: Extreme Capitalism, Market Populism, and the End of Market Democracy.* New York: Doubleday.
Gamson, William. 1992. *Talking Politics.* New York: Cambridge University Press.
Giddens, Anthony. 1991. *Modernity and Self-Identity: Self and Society in the Late Modern Age.* Stanford, CA: Stanford University Press.
Herbert, Bob. 1998. "Nike Blinks." *New York Times.* Editorial page, 21 May.
Inglehart, Ronald. 1997. *Modernization and Post-modernization: Cultural, Economic and Political Change in 43 Societies.* Princeton, NJ: Princeton University Press.
Keck, Margaret E., & Kathryn Sikkink. 1998. *Activists Beyond Borders: Advocacy Networks in International Politics.* Ithaca, NY: Cornell University Press.
Klein, Naomi. 1999. *No Logo: Taking Aim at the Brand Bullies.* New York: St. Martins/ Picador.
Lemann, Nicholas. 2001. "Bush's Trillions: How to Buy the Republican Party of Tomorrow." *The New Yorker,* 19 & 26 February, 72ff.
Lichbach, Mark I., & Paul Almeida. 2001. "Global Order and Local Resistance: The Neoliberal Institutional Trilemma and the Battle of Seattle." Riverside: University of California Riverside Center for Global Order and Resistance.
Macken, Diedre. 2001. "Chain Reaction." *Australian Financial Review* (21 April). (forwarded on-line).
Manheim, Jarol. 2001. *The Death of a Thousand Cuts: Corporate Campaigns and the Attack on the Corporation.* Mahwah, NJ: Lawrence Erlbaum.
Mutz, Diana. 2000. "Implications of the Information Environment for Political Participation." Paper presented at the conference *Communicating Civic Engagement in Europe and the United States.* Seattle, WA: Center for Communication and Civic Engagement, University of Washington. 19-20 May. <http://www.engagedcitizen.org>.

Nolan, James L. 1998. *The Therapeutic State: Justifying Government at Century's End.* New York: New York University Press.

Putnam, Robert D. 2000. *Bowling Alone: The Collapse and Revival of American Community.* New York: Simon & Schuster.

Rose, Nikolas. 1999. *Powers of Freedom.* New York: Cambridge University Press.

Scammell, Margaret. 1995. *Designer Politics: How Elections Are Won.* New York: St. Martin's Press.

___. 2000. "The Internet and Civic Engagement: The Age of the Citizen Consumer." *Political Communication* 17: 351-55.

Smith, Peter J., & Elizabeth Smythe. 2001. "Sleepless in Seattle: Challenging the WTO in a Globalizing World." Paper presented at the meeting of the International Political Science Association, Quebec City, 1 August. Aldershot: Ashgate.

Tarrow, Sidney. 1998. "Fishnets, Internets, and Catnets: Globalization and Transnational Collective Action," in Michael P. Hanagan, Leslie Page Moch, & Wayne Brake, eds., *Challenging Authority: The Historical Study of Contentious Politics.* Minneapolis: University of Minnesota Press.

Turow, Joseph. 1997. *Breaking Up America: Advertisers and the New Media World.* Chicago: University of Chicago Press.

The Nike Sweatshop Email: Political Consumerism, Internet, and Culture Jamming

Jonah Peretti (with Michele Micheletti)

Introduction

Consumption becomes political when consumers assess products through the eyes of citizens. Historically, clothing has been an important political consumerist good. One of the first labeling schemes, the White Label, involved an evaluation of American factories that manufactured cotton underwear (Sklar 1998). The politics of clothing manufacturing continues to engage and mobilize concerned citizens. The issues are basically the same as in the past: working conditions, wages, and child labor. An important difference is that today's efforts are global in orientation. They concern how workers worldwide manufacture the clothing that we purchase from brand name companies. Transnational political consumerist networks, such as the European Clean Clothes Campaign and the North American anti-sweatshop (No Sweat) movement, have developed to create a better working situation for the global garment industry (Ross 2001). Their ultimate goal is the improvement of corporate policy and practices in the global garment industry. The tactics used to reach this goal range from traditional techniques such as contact with politicians, corporate directors, media makers, and international diplomacy, to less conventional ones like using culture jamming, hactivism, and guerrilla media stunts. These unconventional approaches challenge the expensive corporate image-making process by making the politics of products visible for the global consumer.

Political consumerist activists have been especially provoked by Nike's dealings in Third World countries. Nike is seen as a high profile example of a company that cares more about its brand image than the human rights of its workers in the Third World. The ubiquitous nature and global recognition of the Nike logo, the swoosh, made it a perfect target for media-based political consumer actions against sweatshop conditions (Ross 1997; Fung, O'Rourke, & Sabel 2001).

This chapter recounts Jonah Peretti's contribution to the transnational effort to improve working conditions in the global garment industry. His participation consisted of subverting an offer by Nike to create a pair of individualized shoes. Peretti explains how he attempted to challenge the Nike corporate image by ordering a pair of customized shoes. The ensuing email correspondence with Nike became a global anti-sweatshop event, which made national news in large consuming societies. The chapter addresses the role of different kinds of media in the Nike email exchange, the subsequent mobilization of the anti-sweatshop campaign and its network, and ends with a short assessment of the impact of media-oriented transnational political consumerism on corporate policy.

Ordering a Pair of Customized Nike Shoes

The story begins in 2000 when Nike gave its customers the on-line opportunity to order a pair of customized shoes. Nike framed this opportunity to sell shoes via its website as an exercise of freedom of choice and freedom to express one's own lifestyle identity. This corporate celebration of freedom seemed particularly offensive to me, given Nike's long history of labor abuses. Wealthy consumers were being invited to express themselves by designing shoes, but all they were really doing was sending instructions to cheap labor in developing countries. I decided to use this irony to make a political statement challenging Nike's corporate image and labor policies.

On January 5, 2001, I ordered a pair of Nike shoes customized with the word "sweatshop." My request was laced with irony. I was asking Nike to help me protest its own labor practices. My goal was to redirect Nike's publicity machine against itself, by using the same on-line service that Nike was offering to associate itself with personal freedom, to raise awareness about the limited freedom enjoyed by Nike sweatshop workers. This ironic approach is a form of political practice called "culture jamming," which is a strategy that turns corporate power against itself by co-opting, hacking, mocking, and re-contextualizing meanings. I was excited to see how Nike would respond to my challenge.

Shortly afterwards, Nike sent me an email in which they informed me that they refused my order. This was the beginning of my email correspondence with the Nike Corporation, an email exchange that is reproduced in its entirety in box 1. Nike customer service wrote in its automated reply that its refusal could have to do with the fact that my personal iD contained another party's trademark or other intellectual property, the name of an athlete or team we do not have the legal right to use, profanity or inappropriate slang, or that I had left the box blank. They encouraged me to submit a new order. It was clear from my request that I was making a statement about Nike's labor practices, but the automated responses avoided addressing this issue directly. I pushed the issue further by explaining in an email response that my personal iD did not violate any of the criteria outlined in their message, that "I chose the iD because I wanted to remember the toil and labor of the children that made my shoes." Continuing to avoid the issue at hand, Nike responded that my order contained inappropriate slang. They encouraged me again to submit a new order, but I continued to argue my case, explaining that Webster's Dictionary dated the word "sweatshop" to the 1890s, so it could not possibly be considered "inappropriate slang." I also continued to press the labor issue, stating sarcastically, "I was thrilled to be able to build my own shoes, and my personal iD was offered as a small token of appreciation for the sweatshop workers, poised to help me realize my vision." But Nike clearly did not want to address this issue, stating instead that an iD may "contain material that we consider inappropriate or simply do not want to place on our products." It was clear that I would never get my Nike "sweatshop" shoes, but I still delivered a parting shot: "Could you please send me a color snapshot of the ten-year-old Vietnamese girl who makes my shoes?" Nike did not respond.

When my dialogue with Nike was complete, I decided to send the completed transcript to a few friends. Initially, I did this because I thought that the exchange was humorous. Although I liked the way it challenged Nike politically, I did not expect that the dialogue would have a political impact. I never expected that my little culture-jamming project would reach such a broad audience. But my friends passed the email on to their friends, and their friends began to pass it on to still more people. The email then began to race around the world like a virus. I was astonished that something I decided to share with a few close friends could replicate literally millions of times.

Box 1

My Email Correspondence with Customer Service Representatives at Nike

From: "Personalize, NIKE iD" <nikeid_personalize@nike.com>
To: "'Jonah H. Peretti'" <peretti@media.mit.edu>
Subject: RE: Your NIKE iD order o16468000
Your NIKE iD order was cancelled for one or more of the following reasons.
  1) Your Personal iD contains another party's trademark or other intellectual property.
  2) Your Personal iD contains the name of an athlete or team we do not have the legal right to use.
  3) Your Personal iD was left blank. Did you not want any personalization?
  4) Your Personal iD contains profanity or inappropriate slang, and besides, your mother would slap us.
If you wish to reorder your NIKE iD product with a new personalization please visit us again at www.nike.com
Thank you,
NIKE iD

From: "Jonah H. Peretti" <peretti@media.mit.edu>
To: "Personalize, NIKE iD" <nikeid_personalize@nike.com>
Subject: RE: Your NIKE iD order o16468000
Greetings,
My order was canceled but my personal NIKE iD does not violate any of the criteria outlined in your message. The Personal iD on my custom ZOOM XC USA running shoes was the word "sweatshop." Sweatshop is not: (1) another party's trademark, (2) the name of an athlete, (3) blank, or (4) profanity. I chose the iD because I wanted to remember the toil and labor of the children that made my shoes. Could you please ship them to me immediately.
Thanks and Happy New Year,
Jonah Peretti

From: "Personalize, NIKE iD" <nikeid_personalize@nike.com>
To: "'Jonah H. Peretti'" <peretti@media.mit.edu>
Subject: RE: Your NIKE iD order o16468000
Dear NIKE iD Customer,
Your NIKE iD order was cancelled because the iD you have chosen contains, as stated in the previous email correspondence, "inappropriate slang."
If you wish to reorder your NIKE iD product with a new personalization please visit us again at www.nike.com
Thank you,
NIKE iD

From: "Jonah H. Peretti" <peretti@media.mit.edu>
To: "Personalize, NIKE iD" <nikeid_personalize@nike.com>
Subject: RE: Your NIKE iD order o16468000
Dear NIKE iD,
Thank you for your quick response to my inquiry about my custom ZOOM XC USA running shoes. Although I commend you for your prompt customer service, I disagree

with the claim that my personal iD was inappropriate slang. After consulting Webster's Dictionary, I discovered that "sweatshop" is in fact part of standard English, and not slang. The word means: "a shop or factory in which workers are employed for long hours at low wages and under unhealthy conditions" and its origin dates from 1892. So my personal iD does meet the criteria detailed in your first email.

Your web site advertises that the NIKE iD program is "about freedom to choose and freedom to express who you are." I share Nike's love of freedom and personal expression. The site also says that "If you want it done right...build it yourself." I was thrilled to be able to build my own shoes, and my personal iD was offered as a small token of appreciation for the sweatshop workers poised to help me realize my vision. I hope that you will value my freedom of expression and reconsider your decision to reject my order.

Thank you,
Jonah Peretti

From: "Personalize, NIKE iD" <nikeid_personalize@nike.com>
To: "'Jonah H. Peretti'" <peretti@media.mit.edu>
Subject: RE: Your NIKE iD order o16468000

Dear NIKE iD Customer,

Regarding the rules for personalization it also states on the NIKE iD web site that "Nike reserves the right to cancel any Personal iD up to 24 hours after it has been submitted."

In addition it further explains:

"While we honor most personal iDs, we cannot honor every one. Some may be (or contain) others' trademarks, or the names of certain professional sports teams, athletes or celebrities that Nike does not have the right to use. Others may contain material that we consider inappropriate or simply do not want to place on our products.

Unfortunately, at times this obliges us to decline personal iDs that may otherwise seem unobjectionable. In any event, we will let you know if we decline your personal iD, and we will offer you the chance to submit another."

With these rules in mind we cannot accept your order as submitted.

If you wish to reorder your NIKE iD product with a new personalization please visit us again at www.nike.com

Thank you, NIKE iD

From: "Jonah H. Peretti" <peretti@media.mit.edu>
To: "Personalize, NIKE iD" <nikeid_personalize@nike.com>
Subject: RE: Your NIKE iD order o16468000

Dear NIKE iD,

Thank you for the time and energy you have spent on my request. I have decided to order the shoes with a different iD, but I would like to make one small request. Could you please send me a color snapshot of the ten-year-old Vietnamese girl who makes my shoes?

Thanks,
Jonah Peretti
{no response}

* Nike iD is an on-line service that lets people buy personalized Nike shoes. The dialogue began when Nike cancelled an order for a pair of shoes customized with the word "sweatshop." For more recent information on this story see <shey.net>.

Nike Sweatshop Email Makes a Global Impact

People began to contact me, as the Nike sweatshop email spread globally from Inbox to Inbox. Over a three-month period, I received 3,655 inquiries, as shown in figure 1, and it has been estimated that 11.4 million people received the Nike Sweatshop Email (Macken 2001). Initially, I was surprised that sending one email to a few friends could launch a global campaign. I tried to understand how this could have happened. The rapid rate at which my story spread is explained by the dynamics of exponential growth. Consider this hypothetical scenario. You send an email to ten friends, and each friend forwards the email to ten of his/her friends. If this process continues just six steps the message will reach a million people. After ten steps the message would hypothetically reach more people than the total population of the earth. This dynamic explains how the Nike email could spread to so many people in so little time. Australian journalist Deidre Macken (2001) entitled this "the fin chain reaction."

Figure 1
Email Communications to Peretti about the Nike Sweatshop Email

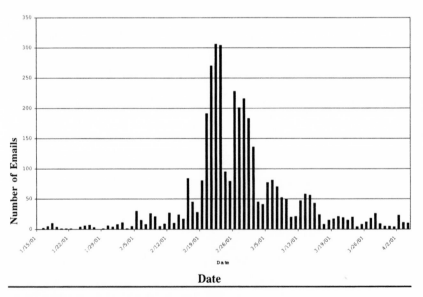

The figure shows a total of 3,655 email responses between January 15 and April 5, 2001. Fewer emails were received during the weekend, which explains the gap in the middle of the figure and the more subtle ripple of the entire figure.

The inquiries contained a variety of responses. Box 2 offers a sample of the kinds of email responses that were sent as a response to my Nike sweatshop exchange. Some were from old friends, long lost classmates, or former professional colleagues. It is not surprising that the Nike email would reach these people—we have mutual friends and share an extended social network. The Nike Sweatshop email started to spread among the informal network of people interested in sharing examples of successful culture jams. By sharing the Nike email, they could participate in a larger movement that is advanced by such networks as Adbusters, who popularized the concept of culture jamming, rtmark, and the Billboard Liberation Front (adbusters.org/, billboardliberation.com/, rtmark.com/). I believe that the campaign thrived because it allowed people to participate in a larger cultural transformation and to do it without the expenditure of much effort. It gave these people another opportunity to participate in a larger social movement. This hunger for participation on the part of the likeminded political consumerist community formed the basis for the first phase of the chain reaction.

Sometimes I felt like I was just along for the ride, because my email correspondence with Nike began to take on a life of its own. This is the second phase of the chain reaction that began to take place. Eventually, as the email exchange jumped across social networks, I began receiving messages from total strangers and from people highly critical to my anti-sweatshop statement. These people were from all walks of life and every demographic group—schoolchildren and retirees, conservatives and liberals, reasonable, and crazy. It was clear that the message had spread far beyond my own network, when I began getting hateful email. Not surprisingly, people began then to wonder whether the story was a hoax, spam, and an urban legend. This led Snopes, a website that tracks down urban legends, to contact me to confirm that the Nike emails did, in fact, take place.

Soon afterwards, the third phase of the chain reaction occurred when the mass media began to pick up on it. Probably the first traditional media outlet to report on the story was the *San Jose Mercury News* (30 January 2001), which served as the network node for other journalists to find the story. Articles appeared soon thereafter on various websites, including Plastic.com, and in the paper and electronic versions of *Time*, *The Village Voice*, and *Wall Street Journal*. Frequently, it was possible for readers to send the story from the

---

Box 2
Kinds of Email Responses Sent on the Nike Sweatshop Exchange

Elemantary School Classmate:
Hi Jonah,
I think I may have gone to grammar school with you. My name is X. Did you go to Chabot Elementary in Oakland, CA? Did you go to X's Daycare? Your name sounded familiar when I got the Nike email, and then I remembered I went to school with somebody with your name so I thought I would find out if it's the same person. Anyway, just to satisfy my curiosity, if you could email me back I would sure appreciate it. Thanks, X

An Old Friend:
Hey Jonah!
I received the entire Nike/Jonah correspondence via a forward from a friend of mine who graduated from UC Santa Cruz a couple years after you. Ironic, huh? I think I could have guessed that it was you without seeing the name on the text. I could almost hear you as I read it. I hope you are doing well in... Boston? I am not sure if you are still there. I am still here in New Orleans, getting ready for Carnival, and graduating from Tulane soon. Please write back when you get a moment. Much Love, X

Professional Colleague:
Jonah—
[Part of message omitted]
Anyhow, the reason for this mail is that a very funny thing happened today. I'm reading my email, when some spam/joke/chain thing comes in, but it's from a friend, so I read it. Very interesting bit about some guy's back-and-forth with Nike about some customized shoes. It wasn't 'til later that I noticed the domain, and said "ah, those boys at the Media Lab, right on!" and then got curious about the name to the left of the @. Checked it against your biz card, and marveled at the small worldness of it all... Best Regards, X

Hate Mail:
Hey, Joe Peretti... I'm kind of an old guy, so I've developed this 'thing' about saying whatever the hell it is I want. Bear with me. I got the below email about you wanting NIKE to screw themselves by submitting to your sophomoric demand to "make a statement" —all for your daddy's $50. Do you think you've got enough 'world-smarts' to Out-Smart NIKE? (Pffftttt...!!!) I grew up in Portland, Oregon. I met Phil Knight quite a few years ago and had a few laughs. Really bright men have a great sense of humor, you know (well, you might be too young). Being a "Media" student or 'whatever' at MIT tells me you probably had not been out of your protected childhood neighborhood until it was time to go to MIT, courtesy of daddy's money. It also tells me you haven't been to South East Asia, or China, or Thailand, or Hong Kong, or Indonesia, Sumatra, the Philippines, Malaysia, or even the Ukraine. I've been to those dunghole 'countries' and more. So let me tell you... the people who are trading their labor for NIKE dollars are living like princes and princesses compared to their non-NIKE peers. The NIKE factories are as close as possible in environment and safety as U.S. standards. MY only gripe with NIKE is that they aren't doing something meaningful for

the desperately poor people in Eastern Europe—where poverty is compounded by brutal winter weather and the young women being kidnapped and put into prostitution by the Israelis. Instead of screwing with NIKE—a company that provides desperately needed jobs to people who would otherwise be planting rice or opium—why don't you just get your name (or "Annoying") on the shoes and wear them to classes—where you should be learning something? I know you're not an example of most of the other fine students at MIT. — X

Listen Buddy,
What are you, some kind of damn communist? You should be grateful you live in a country so wonderful as to give foreigners something constructive to do with their time. A little jerk like you wouldn't even be able to afford a pair of Nike shoes if their executives paid American wages. Sweatshops? Where did you think that little Vietnamese girl was working BEFORE Nike saved her? In a freaking rice paddy, that's where. You go over to Vietnam and try to take away her means of supporting her family. Go ahead punk, just try it. By the time they get done with your ass you'll look like two quarts of MOO GOO GAI PAN in a pint container............catch my drift?
I really hope Nike sends you some shoes with your true handle: "Ingrate"
Grow up, you dimwit. —The Exalted Wint

This email is intended for the person or persons responsible for sending the Nike slang email around the world. I recently saw your email about NIKE and the sweatshops. I just want to tell you this: It is people like you that do the Internet harm. People like you are just morons. Yuu [sic] are a waste of human flesh. The air we breathe us working masses breath should not be wasted on you. GROW UP..... Oh, this was sent through a remailer, so don't bother replying.....jerk... — X

Fan Mail:
I was just forwarded your correspondence with Nike iD Customer Service. (I'm sure you've gotten lots of mail on this by now). After reading it, I have only one question: Will you marry me? —X

Dear Jonah,
Having read your Nike correspondence, forwarded to me by Mario, I have fallen in love with you. My dear, deceased father and I made a sport of such correspondence and I have files of similar sarcastic banter. Who are you? Where are you? We must have been separated at birth.
—X

Dear Jonah,
I recently received an email detailing your absurd yet hilarious interactions with the bastards at Nike and I would hereby like to ask you for your hand in marriage. I am a board-certified physician at a large University Hospital and could keep you in the manner in which you have become accustomed. If not, then please keep up your personal quest for justice and humor. Perhaps Nike would be willing to embroider a picture of Kathy Lee Gifford on your shoes as a sort of consolation prize. Very truly yours, X, M.D.

* The names of the senders have been replaced with an X to protect their privacy.

media websites by email to others. The story continued to have a snowball effect on media actors. *The NBC Today Show* invited me to discuss on national television corporate social responsibility with a representative from Nike. *USA Today* and several European papers, including *The Independent* and *The Guardian* (both British*), La Republica* (Italian), *Jungle World* (German), *Liberation* (French), *Svenska Dagbladet* and *Dagens Nyheter* (both Swedish) ran the story. Later, other national American, European, and Asian dailies would publicize the Nike encounter. The website <shey.net/niked.html> offers more information on this media coverage.

I was amazed by the mass media coverage received by this story. For a few weeks after the email went public, I was interrupted several times each day by telephone calls from reporters soliciting interviews and producers requesting radio and TV appearances. I even conducted interviews with international journalists over email and was invited to speak at international and American political consumerist events and write in well-known journals such as *The Nation* (Peretti 2001a). It is still somewhat astonishing to me that my email exchange transformed itself so quickly from an email forward to a spectacular event that warranted spots on live national television in the United States and globally. Although the email exchange was translated into several different languages, the dominance of English as a second language made the story more accessible globally.

Culture Jamming as Political Participation in Contemporary Political Consumerism

Culture jamming differs considerably from conventional modes of political participation, which focus on change through the political system, for example, in the form of policy regulation. The problem with this kind of participation for global issues is that there is not a political system with the legislative power to regulate multinational global industry like the transnational garment business. Efforts at change demand other forms of engagement and other arenas for this engagement. Culture jamming promotes change by making citizens aware of the contradictions in corporate policy and practice, as well as the contradictions in their own consumer choices. It does so in a humorous way, with the aim of provoking a positive, reflective response rather than a hostile negative reaction. It targets market actors on their home turf—the market—and uses their own language—logos, corporate image-making, and marketing—to do it. When successful, culture jamming creates a new spin on things or spectacular events that alters the information, perceptions, and priorities that powerful actors use to make decisions. These spectacular events are part of a struggle over meaning, which can be used by transnational advocacy networks, such as the Clean Clothes Campaign and No Sweat movement to push for the modification of value context in which the behavior takes place (Kech & Sikkink 1999, 95). In the case of the global garment industry, culture jamming encourages both producers and consumers to make clothing take on a new meaning.

Culture Jamming should also be seen as part of a larger movement to protect the public sphere from being dominated by corporate advertising and commercial speech (Klein 1999; cf. Supreme Court of California 2002). Philosophically, therefore, it is based in a conviction that the public sphere should only be open for free, noncommercial speech (cf. Habermas 1989). Culture jamming even provides a new type of free speech tailored to a media-saturated environment. It allows citizens to reach millions of people without spending millions of dollars producing and purchasing advertisements. Nike pays close to a billion dollars each year to promote its brand image. This makes it difficult for an individual activist or citizen to challenge Nike's view of the world. But culture jamming and tactical media campaigns provide a new alternative, an alternative that broadens the impact and relevance of free speech.

Media and the Nike Sweatshop Email Exchange

Without modern communication technologies, the Nike Sweatshop email exchange would never have existed. Email, personal websites, and filtering websites enable the digital equivalent of word of mouth. The Internet is revolutionary, because it provides a technical distribution network which overlays social networks. This makes news spread faster, and this information makes social networks and transnational advocacy networks more powerful (on this see also Bennett in this volume). Research shows that the Internet played an important role in citizen struggles against the use of landmines globally (Price 1998) and the ratification of the Multilateral Agreement on Investment (MAI) (Ayres 1999; Deibert 2000). Without quick Internet contact it would have been difficult for these activists to use their limited budgets to mobilize support for their causes and coordinate their actions. My Nike experience is another example of the potential of the Internet as a force in democracy. As the Nike Sweatshop email spread, I gained new insight into the structure of the contemporary media ecology. This led me to distinguish between three kinds of communication that are important for citizen engagement in political consumerism and other political activities. They are: micromedia, middle media, and mass media.

Micromedia includes all personal communications technologies, including email, telephones, personal web sites, and even the ancient technology of face-to-face human speech. Although micromedia is intended to support personal communication between a small number of people, the Nike Sweatshop email is an example of a story spreading to a much larger audience through personal communication channels. As people forwarded the story to their friends, they often prefaced it by adding a personal note such as "John, I thought you would appreciate this," or "Check this out, Sarah." Even though the story went to millions of people, the personal quality of the communication remained intact. People got the message only if it was recommended by a personal acquaintance. Forwarding the Nike email linked up individual activists and armchair activists across the globe. The Nike emails helped focus attention on the goals of the global ethical trading movement and the politics of the clothes we wear daily. It created a virtual community of citizens concerned with the power of logos and political consumerism.

A word of caution is necessary here. An email message forwarded by a friend is not an assurance of its accuracy. Irresponsible communication via email has led scholars to question whether this cyber form of political participation promotes democracy. They caution against the risk of the Internet turning into a scandal pit, and use the metaphor of uncontrollable forest fires to explain the harm that inaccurate email information can cause public figures, public causes, and public space (Di Maio 2001; Ayres 1999; Deibert 2000).

Other kinds of media communication are necessary to establish the accuracy of news stories and petitions that call on the public to support causes by forwarding messages. A micromedia technique, that has the benefits of a personal feel but avoids the unruliness and unaccountability of email, is the *blog*, which is short for web log. It helps ordinary people publish their personal musings on the Web. Blogs allow people to become personal web curators by compiling annotated links to web sites that they find interesting. These personal web sites tend to aggregate small audiences of friends and like-minded individuals, who form into a network community. The blog audiences can also help transform an obscure web page into a full-blown public mini-sphere. This occurred when the Nike Sweatshop email was posted on a Blog site called Shey.net (see Peretti 2001b). Once again, micromedia's personal touch expanded to reach a larger audience that was able to critically evaluate the veracity of news accounts by engaging in debate of the merits of events, information, and actions.

Middle media describes emerging publishing technologies that help communities filter and aggregate the messy jumble of content produced by micromedia. Middle media are institutions, because they develop norms and rules to regulate social contacts and communications via the Internet. Compared to more traditional forms of communication, they are more up-to-date and quicker in getting news to the public. With varying degrees of editorial oversight, these sites present fresh links hourly. Examples are slashdot.org, metafilter.com, and plastic.com. More importantly, middle media sites provide opportunities for a larger community of people to engage in discussion about the posted links, for instance the Nike Sweatshop encounter. Within minutes of each post, on-line political consumerist activists engaged in discussions about ways to circumvent Nike's censors, the economics of shoe production, and the politics of the anti-sweatshop movement. Middle media transforms such moments into a globally accessible public sphere. At best, the public space that is created by middle media functions democratically. The middle media users or community define the topics that are of interest to communicate to the public. In so doing, they can avoid problems with mass media gatekeepers who consider themselves the judges of newsworthiness and the public interest. This is exactly what happed in the case of the Nike Sweatshop story. Middle media helped a humorous email forward become a topic of public debate by transforming micromedia buzz into a newsworthy social issue.

Cyberactivism has been criticized for building on global inequalities such as the need for computer equipment, education, and English-language proficiency, and for creating isolated citizens and virtual, rather than real, communities based on face-to-face social interaction (Deibert 2000). There is some truth in these accusations. Nevertheless, activists and concerned citizens turn to the Internet because there is not any transnational political consumerist network in existence that has the resources to compete with multinational corporations in the traditional media marketplace. This is why Internet campaigns are so appealing. Better yet, a successful Internet campaign can result in free mass media coverage in the form of news stories. This is my experience from the Nike Sweatshop story. The use of culture jamming created an authentic event that aroused the interest of many email users and was put on many Blog sites. Journalists, searching, individually, for newsworthy items, discovered the Nike story as an email forwarded to them or while surfing the World Wide Web or reading their email. It was clear in the tones of their voices when speaking with me that they were excited by this process of discovery. I encouraged this journalistic enthusiasm by response comments such as, "it would be awesome if you did a story," or "it is so cool you found the Nike email on the Internet." A few days later the Nike email would be covered by another mass media outlet.

Media-Oriented Transnational Political Consumerism and Change in Corporate Policy

Activists and citizens are increasingly using media-oriented strategies to promote political consumerism and corporate responsibility. This is shown in Monroe Friedman's chapter, which reports that media-oriented boycotts are becoming more prevalent than marketplace-oriented ones. Other political consumer activists, like culture jammers and supporters of the anti-corporate movement, focus on designing campaigns that can challenge corporate advertising by reaching a broad audience nationally and globally. They use the media to change our view of consumer society. Culture jamming as a form of political consumerism has many historical precedents, with the Nestlé campaign as its most notable example (see Keck & Sikkink 1999; Bromberg Bar Yam 1995; see also Friedman's chapter). Frequently culture jamming successfully turns a low-key political consumerist campaign into a media spectacle. This is shown clearly in the Nike email exchange discussed in this chapter.

Media-oriented political consumerist activism that uses culture jamming is not just fun. It is not just a way to blow off steam. This kind of activism has had some strategic successes, and it can be seen as one of the important agents of change that is forcing consumers in industrialized nations to reflect on their relationship with brand name consumer goods. This reflection is gradually changing both consumer and corporate discourse on the goods produced by new-age corporations. The chain reaction of the Nike email exchange and corporate reaction to it, as pointed out in Bennett's chapter, are one example here. Such culture jamming events, together with other more conventional political interventions as litigation, demonstrations, lobbying, dialogue with corporate executives as well as student movement and union activity are motivating both political and corporate actors to give more consideration to the politics behind the clothes products we purchase for ourselves and our families.

It may be argued that these campaigns are not effective because the outcomes of corporate activity have not changed much. Basic workers' rights are still not ensured in the subcontracted factories in the Third World; workers are not receiving a living wage, and Nike is still blacklisted by the anti-sweatshop movement. Another view breaks up effectiveness into a number of steps and offers a somewhat different view of the role of culture jamming and political consumerist transnational networks in this area. It shows that discursive changes are often an initial step towards change in government and corporate policy (Keck & Sikkink 1999). Discursive changes signal, therefore, the inklings of a changing global corporate mentality. To be successful they need nurturing by all involved stakeholders. They need to be embedded in an institutional framework that presses for policy changes and that monitors corporate mission statements to ensure that policy changes are turned into outcomes.

References

Ayres, Jeffrey M. 1999. "From the Streets to the Internet: The Cyber-Diffusion of Contention." *Annals*, AAPSS, No. 566, (November): 132-43.

Bromberg BarYam, Naomi. 1995. "The Nestlé Boycott: The Story of the Who/UNICEF Code for Marketing Breastmilk Substitutes." *Mothering* (Winter): 56-63.

Deibert, Ronald J. 2000. "International Plug 'n Play? Citizen Activism, the Internet, and Global Public Policy." *International Studies Perspectives* 1: 255-72.

Di Maio, Paola. 2002. "Online Media: Micro vs. Macromedia, The Power of Now." *Content-wire*, 30 April. See <content-wire.com/Home/Index.cfm?ccs= 86&cs=253>.

Fung, Archon, Dara O'Rourke, & Charles Sabel, eds. 2001. *Can We Put An End to Sweatshops?* Boston: Beacon Press.

Habermas, Jürgen. 1989. *The Structural Transformation of the Public Sphere: An Inquiry into a Category of Bourgeois Society.* Cambridge, MA: MIT Press.

Keck, Margaret E., & Kathryn Sikkink. 1999. "Transnational Advocacy Networks in International and Regional Politics." *International Social Science Journal*, No. 159 (March): 89-101.

Klein, Naomi. 1999. *No Logo: Taking Aim at the Brand Bullies*. New York: St. Martin's/ Picador.

Macken, Deidre. 2001. "The Fin Chain Reaction." *Australian Financial Review*, 21 April.

Peretti, Jonah. 2001a. "My Nike Media Adventure." *The Nation* (Feature Story) 9 April. Available on-line at <thenation.com/doc.mhtml?i=20010409&s=peretti>.

___. 2001b. "Culture Jamming, Memes, Social Networks, and the Emerging Media Ecology: The 'Nike Sweatshop Email' as Object-To-Think-With."

Price, Richard. 1998. "Reversing the Gun Sights: Transnational Civil Society Targets Land Mines." *International Organizations* 52, No. 3: 613-44.

Ross, Andrew, ed. 1999. *No Sweat: Fashion, Free Trade, and the Rights of Garment Workers*. New York: Verso.

Sklar, Kathryn Kish. 1998. "The Consumers' White Label Campaign of the National Consumers' league 1889-1919," in Susan Strasser, Charles McGovern, & Mattias Judt, eds., *Getting and Spending: European and American Consumer Societies in the 20th Century*. Cambridge: Cambridge University Press.

Supreme Court of California. 2002. *Marc Kasky v. Nike, INC., et al.* S087859.

Part III

Building Responsible Institutions for Multi-Risk Global Society

The Industrial Roots of Contemporary Political Consumerism: The Case of the French Standardization Movement[1]

Franck Cochoy

Introducing the Evolution of Standardization

The official standardization process may be defined as "technological diplomacy," that aims at producing an agreement—a standard—through the building of a consensus gathering of all the involved stakeholders (Olshan 1993). This definition reveals the inherently political character of standardization. Indeed, by linking the setting of standards to an open discussion between a wide range of actors (engineers, state officials, and consumer organizations), standard institutions appear as ancestors of modern "hybrid forums."[2] At its very beginning, standardization had no clear connection with consumer or political issues, and even less with consumer advocates. Yet strangely enough, industrial and technical standardization played an important role in setting some key conditions for the development of consumer awareness about industrial risks and the political aspects of products. The role of standardization in this process is the topic of this chapter. I will show how the interest of standardizers for market matters and consumer issues emerged indirectly through pure industrial preoccupations and efforts. Rather ironically, both industrials and standardizers paved the way for consumers' participation and action in the standardization process. Industrialists took consumer protection as a means to prevent unfair competition, and standardizers promoted the consumer standpoint as a way to "exist" in discussions with their industrial partners.

I discuss how consumer advocates took these kinds of discourse seriously and played an important role in promoting consumer interests in the standardization process. This led to real improvements in the field of product certification, product labeling, and consumer tests. The role of the state in helping consumers alter the balance of power between themselves and the standardizers (even if consumer activists often remained on the periphery of the standardizing process) is my third focus. Finally, I will show to what extent the history of industrial quality standards is strongly connected to the most recent issues of political consumerism, such as the current calls for the traceability of products, social standardization, and fair trade. The claims for new definitions of products under consumer pressure shift the meaning of standards. New technical and social rules governing products move us from an industrial to a risk society, where quality, safety, and ethical issues bring politics directly into the market.

From Industrial Fear of Unfair Competition to Consumer Awareness of the Ambiguities of Standardization

As its name suggests, industrial standardization was originally a matter of production, a question of technique, a source of concern for engineers. The founders of standardization in France used three verbs to define their activity: unify, simplify, and specify (Maily 1946). Unifying the definition of objects—for instance the definition of bolts and nuts—helped to increase the "interoperability" and the "interchangeability" of items that were made in different places. Simplifying the number of models led to gains in terms of stocks and economies of scale. Specifying dimensions and productive operations offered the required conditions for a stabilization of industrial processes and thus for better control of engineering and production. It did not take long for standardization actors to discover the potentialities of their art in terms of market control and risk management. How did this process take place? How did consumer advocates enter the standardization game?

In France, industrial concerns and initiatives preceded and prepared the rise of consumer activist preoccupations and actions. The gas industry played a key role here. In 1930, gas producers feared that home accidents, due to hazardous manufacturers, would jeopardize this type of energy in favor of electricity, its main competitor. In order to assess and counter the disastrous effects of quality uncertainty in the gas market, gas producers wanted to develop a minimal standardization for gas appliances. Moreover, they asked for the certification of technical safety standards and for the display of a certificate that showed consumers that products on sale actually met the standard requirements. This endeavor led to the birth of the "NF-GAS" brand in 1946. It was the first application of "NF," the French national brand of product conformity with French standards. Thanks to the invention of the certification process, standardization was now able to move from industrial work and become a commercial weapon. From this moment on, one would no longer compete on prices only, but also on the quality/safety of products.

The adoption of product certification changed standardization itself. By putting emphasis on a brand displayed on the product body rather than its technical hidden design, certification raised questions about the relevant product characteristics from the market rather than from the engineering perspective. The certificate linked the NF symbol together with the reputation of all the stakeholders of the standardization process. NF served as much to advertise the certified products as to promote the NF brand to the consuming public.

The link between quality and certification was, however, very fragile and questionable. The underlying standards—for example, dimensional specifications—often lacked any reference to issues of technical quality. The first NF certifications were more connected with safety issues (as the gas example shows) than with their technical efficiency. In the postwar period, it was almost impossible for individual consumers to receive information on the technical requirements behind the "NF" label. It is important to emphasize that product certification was launched in the absence of any market pressure or consumer awareness of the issues at stake. The NF label was a pure initiative of industrials who were more preoccupied with the dangers of unfair competition than with the firm's responsibility for consumer protection. In this way, it was thought necessary to hide the "safety motive" in the certification process behind a more pleasant notion of "product quality." As a consequence, consumers took the "NF brand" at its face value. They took it as a sign of product quality, while it was often a guarantee of basic product safety.

Of course, this situation was not tenable. The history of the NF brand was characterized by a series of sometimes heated controversies about the real correspondence of certificates with their public objectives. By introducing the consumer viewpoint in the standardizing process and by focusing on standardizers' claims regarding quality, the NF brand opened itself to public discussion. A forum for its evaluation emerged; certification settled the conditions for strict product review and a negotiated transformation of standardization choices, procedures, and commitments. Thus, certification clearly prepared and helped the shift of industrial standardization towards the market use of standards, and thus favored the entry of consumer advocates in the game.

What is noteworthy is that the consumer occupies a central position in standardization, because standardizers first saw consumer protection as a means to defend themselves, to justify their place and existence as equals in discussions with their industrial partners. Indeed, they knew by experience that manufacturers were prone to standardize in spite of standardizers.

To avoid the risk of being bypassed, or rather short-circuited, French standardizers such as Raymond Frontard, a former director of the French Standards Institute (AFNOR), understood that it was in their interest to view consumers as a new ally and to become their spokespersons. "For many long years, the French Standards Institute has been compelled to substitute itself for the consumer in the difficult dialogue with the producer, to take on the role of the guardian angel of the missing consumer" (Frontard 1969, 90). Yet standard professionals had an ambivalent interest in involving consumers in the standardizing process. On the one hand, dwelling on the consumer's viewpoint helped them to promote another perspective and thus play the role of consensus makers. On the other hand, standardizers wished to control the intrusion of consumers. They wanted to limit their presence to a discursive dimension, rather than leaving the door wide open for their unpredictable participation. Standardizers thus tried to portray consumer identity in a way that served their purposes: they described consumers as incompetent, deaf-mute, and completely deprived of the capacity to act. As another AFNOR representative puts it: "The consumer is a defenseless creature: his technical knowledge is limited, his control means are null, his defense and appeal means are so weak that he needs protection" (Thiard 1969, 605).

Even consumer activists held this negative view of consumers. Thus, standardizers and consumer activists discovered that they had common interests. They also sought to reduce the power of the people that they were commissioned to represent and protect, because they wanted to increase their own power. The consumer advocates' and standardizers' visions became even more similar, as they both embraced the consumer's cause and initially believed that they would be able to support each other. Consumer advocates saw standards as a good way to "equip" consumers with an economic cognition, and standardizers invited consumer representatives to joint standardizing discussions to improve their own expertise and mediation (Cochoy 2002a). However, the promotion of a similar discourse of consumer protection by actors, who had, in fact, very different interests created two problems. It hindered the effective participation of consumer advocates in the standardizing work and led to competition between the two types of representatives (consumer advocates and standardizers).

Standardization and the Fostering of Consumer Knowledge, Skills, and Responsibility

Once consumers were introduced in the "standardizing loop" (even as a pure rhetorical device), it became very difficult to refuse their presence, once they happened to push the door that had been widely opened to them discursively. So standardization was trapped by its own participative discourse. Taking advantage of the modernist argumentation of French standardizers, consumer advocates quickly began to "poke their nose" into the standardization process and, in so doing, they ended up in assessing not only its potentialities but also its biases, faults, risks, and ambiguities. André Romieu, one of the leaders of the French consumer movement at the time, is very clear on this point:

> A standard is first conceived to simplify professional operations and to facilitate transactions: method codification, simplification and interchangeability of models, reduction of stock, handling and marketing costs. . . .Nevertheless if final consumers do their job properly they should not only benefit from the earned productivity gains, but also force the standard to deal with what is of primary interest for them: the calibration of containers, the measurement of filling capacities, the match between content and container, the usability and reliability of products. . . .As a last resort consumers will have the standardization they will contribute to elaborate. Standardization works neither for nor against them, but with them. They would be wrong to become too confident in a standard, because random and unpredictable events will make the standard of tomorrow. (Romieu 1973, 62f)

If standardization taught little to consumers, consumers learned much from standardization. They discovered the social and political dimension of standards negotiation (beneath its apparent technical innocence), realized how close the link was between the meaning of a standard and the underlying social groups, and, consequently, consumer activists understood that it was urgent for them to take the standardizers' discourse on participation seriously as a way to influence the overall process as much as possible.

Their action stemmed from the creation of a technical committee within the International Standards Organization, the ISO TC 73 "Brands of product conformity with standards." This committee was a laboratory favoring a dialogue between consumer activists and professional standardizers. However, it took a long time for the dialogue to start, and it was only in the early 1960s that the International Standards Organization and the consumer unions developed their relationship. The result of these exchanges was the enlargement of the committee's mission as evident in its modified title and constituencies. In 1966, the committee's name was changed from "Brands of product conformity to standards" to the broader "Consumption matters." At the same time, the committee was divided in three subcommittees: the first committee (SC 1) adopted the early title and objective of "brands of product conformity with standards," while the two new arenas (SC 2 and SC 3), "Information labeling and consumer tests" and "Documentation," respectively, brought additional skills in the realm of standard setting. The latter were clearly taking into account consumer concerns for better information about product quality and safety (Lavialle 1968, 70). In this institutional arrangement, the work of the ISO TC 73 led to the development of three different devices designed to help consumer product cognition: the brands of product conformity with standards, information labeling, and consumer tests. These three tools have contributed to unite consumer and industrial visions and therefore to construct the modern view of the consumer as sensitive to quality, information, and an overall comparison of products.

The first tool—brands labels on product conformity as consumer information—is the basis of the committee itself. The first contribution of the ISO TC 73 was to establish the basic principles for the development of certification brands. For the young consumer movement, the emergence of such brands was considered highly positive, since it seemed to link the quality of products with an objective, stable, and relatively transparent definition of their inner properties. This explains why, in the beginning, consumer activists took standardization seriously, as it legitimated their still fragile discourse of consumer protection. In short, standardization seemed to promote both the quality of products and the consumer's interests.

However, the expanding exchanges between standardizers and consumerists taught consumer advocates about the limited influence of standardizers. They discovered that if labels were obviously providing information about the quality of products, it did not say much about the nature of this quality; the reference standards remained black boxes. Consumer advocates also wondered if the requirements written in the standard sheets were sufficient, or whether they should ask for better information about characteristics of the certified product that were ignored by the standard. These two concerns were at the origin of the other two consumer-oriented standardization tools: information labeling and consumer tests. In 1965, under the pressure of consumer advocate partners whose information improved constantly and after a long period of hesitation, the ISO TC 73 adopted a standard, setting up some principles for information labeling. And it was only in 1973 that ISO adopted a Guide for consumer tests, named Standard Methods for Measuring Performances (SMMP). So from the 1960s to the 1970s, consumer organizations struggled not only to obtain some additional devices that could help clarify the use of labels but also to convince the state to pass laws that forced standardizers to give consumer advocates what they refused to grant them, namely product traceability.

Consumer devices (information labeling and consumer tests) and standardization processes were interdependent of each other. They were simultaneously creating rational consumers and the tools necessary for them to put their rationality into practice. Information labels became all the more informative since labels (the names of components and ingredients) and their means of measurement were standardized. Reliable consumer tests demanded the use of special standards that could turn information labeling and consumer tests into possible markets for the standard setting activity. The new devices and standardization processes were also complementary: the practice of the former implicitly led to criticism of the latter, because it brought to the fore the characteristics and quality levels relevant for the design and use of products. Information labeling and consumer tests were in a certain way turning standardization against itself, since they used the collection of metrological tools to examine critically the relevance of standards and the quality of standardized objects.

With their newly gained knowledge on standards and standardization, consumer advocates began to wonder whether they should continue to participate in the standardization process or move out and confront standardizers from the outside. While some of them continued to work with, or close to, official standardizing institutions (e.g., AFNOR and ISO), others (for instance the Federal Union of Consumers, Union Fédérale des Consommateurs) tried to develop a similar, but competitive, technique, the comparative testing of products. The publication of the magazine *Que choisir* and consumer tests completed the construction of a market for guarantees, by enlarging the competition between products to the competition between the criteria for their critical evaluation (Mallard 2000). The development of this rival methodology reinforced the construction of consumers as standardization saw them, that is, as rational and calculating agents, oriented towards product quality and careful examination of its characteristics, and finally as agents deprived of fantasy or casualness.

Standard methods for measuring performances and information labeling succeeded in increasing consumer influence over industrial issues. The certifying logic and standards for consumer tests moved standardization away from the rigid specification of each part of the products, and it promoted the synthetic logic of performance standards. The consumers' synthetic view replaced the engineers' analytical approach. The concern for product use became the starting point of the standardizing process. Reasoning in terms of product performances rather than product specifications gave much freedom in the choice of the technical solutions necessary to meet the demands in terms of product use. Information labeling called consumer attention to identifying relevant characteristics and performances (Cochoy 2000).

State Help in Reversing the Power Balance between Standardizers and Consumers

The ISO TC 73 committee was clearly designed to develop the relationship between standardization and consumers. Whereas the early design of the committee was more a means to address consumer information issues without direct consumer participation, the new "consumption matters" committee was designed to organize real exchanges between consumers and standardizing bodies. Moreover, in 1968, the committee felt the need to distance itself from the influence of other technical committees and related industrial interests. To ensure its independence, the ISO created an international standardization committee for consumer affairs (ISCA). This new body included representatives from the ISO TC 73, the International Electrotechnical Commission (CEI), and consumer organizations. It worked to promote the standardization of consumer goods, and set up priorities to supervise the progress of the work (Thiard 1973). These new institutional arrangements did not, however, mean that consumers took part directly in the standardizing process. Consumers were involved in the setting of priorities, but remained outside the technical work. Consumers were, therefore, more "trustees" than "executives" in the standardization process.

This situation displeased French consumer advocates, who found a way with government's help to counter the asymmetry in power relations. In 1960, the French government created a national committee for consumer affairs (CNC). Its mission was to ensure "the permanent exchange between state and consumer representatives in all consumption matters." The CNC included an equal number of state and consumer representatives and was placed under the presidency of the Minister for Economic Affairs. To conduct its work, the CNC commissioned professional and technical experts. As its official statute clearly states, the Committee followed "the definition of a [state] policy regarding the quality of products" (Romieu 1969, 597). With the active support of the state and the creation of the CNC as an institution independent from standardizing bodies, consumers were able to reverse the balance between consumer and industrial interests. As André Romieu, the first CNC secretary, noted: "from its inception, the French Standards Institute took active part in the work of the CNC's specialized groups even before its chief executive was asked to become one of its members" (Romieu 1969, 598). Thus, the balance between standardizers and consumers was completely reversed: consumers were no longer coming from the outside in order to influence the standardization process. Rather, standardizers came from the outside in order to visit consumer institutions and provide them with technical assistance. It was the AFNOR representatives who went to CNC's workgroup for "consumer information," rather than the CNC members who went to AFNOR's standardizing committees. For the first time, the government and the consumers took the initiative on product quality. Standardizers, thus, were forced to react to consumer initiatives and use the early consumer advocate strategy of active participation rather than passive observation or opposition.

The new balance between consumer and standardization interests was supported both by the state and the consumer movement. As far as the state was concerned, the 1963 law on quality labels required that "certified products must match with standards" and thus linked consumer information with standardization. On the consumer side, the rapid development of consumer tests, thanks to the role played by consumer organizations, strengthened the demand for standards for measuring performances. As a result, the efforts of standardizers and consumers changed places with each other. In 1966, the state representative for standardization asked for the direct participation of consumers in standardization works and commissioned reports about housing and home equipment, textile items, agricultural and food products, and services. These reports, presented in 1967, favored the convergence of consumer action and standardization. For instance, a report on housing conditions and home equipment, authored by the national secretary of a national confederation of popular family associations, asked for a standardized terminology for the evaluation of housing comfort and quality. This request was partly fulfilled in the following years, when the AFNOR standardized water taps, revised all safety standards for electric home appliances, and forwarded to the CNC a list of fifteen committees considered to be of some interest for the consumers. However, the "revision" issue clearly shows that standardizers' efforts were perhaps nothing more than an extension of their usual business. Similarly, the invitation to participate in key committees for consumption matters was no more than the repetition of the standardizers' classical claim for consumer participation—a claim they knew by experience to be often without real consequences.

However, this does not mean that nothing had changed. Standardizers were now obliged to cope with consumer initiatives conducted both inside and outside the standardizing realm. Once introduced into standardization, the "standardized consumer" soon became a "consumer of quality," that is, both a consumer eager to receive the best information and products to purchase quality goods, and a consumer whom industrial quality managers created by their quality control activities.

"A Consumer of Quality": From Industrial Quality to Contemporary Political Consumers

Just as in the industrial standardization history, consumer issues and market matters were at first completely absent in the history of quality. The first concerns about quality were expressed by production engineers, who used sampling and statistical techniques to control the quality of industrial products at the end of the production line (Bayart 1996; Dragomir & Halais 1995). The interests of their clients were at stake in this endeavor. Industrial buyers were eager to find efficient and cheap means to evaluate the quality of what they bought from their subcontractors. After World War II, the first specialists of quality management discovered that the control of products at the end of the production line was not sufficient. The American consultant W. Edwards Deming claimed that quality involved not only machines and workers operating them, but also the whole organization framing production (Gogue 1990). With the rise of "total quality management," the quality of products was for the first time subordinated to the quality of organization itself.

The rise of worldwide subcontracting relationships and of international standardization completed this shift in emphasis. International buyers wanted to make sure that their subcontractors were reliable before they received their products, and they wanted to do so without enduring inspection costs and procedures that were increasingly difficult to put into practice. Standard organizations possessed both the skills and the tools necessary to establish the rules and the certificates necessary to standardize quality. Standardizers were also interested in applying their expertise to new fields so that they could enlarge the "market for standards." The interests of both groups met, and the outcome of this convergence was the elaboration and publication of the famous ISO 9000 series in 1979 (Tamm Hallström 1996). These standards define some of the production, organization, and management rules that aim at stabilizing the quality of products through the quality of the organization itself. This is important because it was the first attempt to supplement the move of industrial standardization towards market issues with a complementary move of standardization and certification processes towards human organizations. With the birth of the ISO 9000 series, the standardization of technical objects is extended to the standardization of social matters (Cochoy & de Terssac 1999).

However, "the standardization of organizational and social matters" did not yet correspond with consumer issues. To take the final consumer into account, international standardization had to take advantage of another story: the story of the growing need for the traceability of products that coincided with the globalization of exchanges. Traceability relies on the written record of elements allowing the reader to go back from consumption to production, from the defective product to the entities or actors responsible for its failure (Fraenkel 1995; Cochoy & De Terssac 2000). From the beginning, traceability was a mere managerial device (included for instance in the ISO 9000 standards) aiming at spotting and correcting "non-conformities" in order to meet the continuous improvement principle of quality management policies. But the claim for product traceability quickly moved out of the walls of factories to become a true "technique for the governance of men and things" (Torny 1998). In France, this movement of traceability from the micro-management of industrial sites to the macro-governance of society was the result of the combined action of the state and the consumers. Consumers saw product traceability as a means to deal with risk society issues and sanitary crises, such as the contaminated blood affair or the mad cow crisis (Torny 1998).

The success of traceability rests on a double advantage. On the one hand, traceability allows consumers to go "from the plate back to the cow"; it helps them to manage and also to anticipate sanitary problems. On the other hand, traceability favors the control of commodities without hindering their circulation. National governments think of traceability as the means to reconcile the globalization of exchanges with political control of products. The spotting and signaling of commodities help to solve the old dilemma between free trade (i.e., let the products circulate at the risk of importing hazardous commodities) and protectionism (i.e., set up custom and sanitary barriers at the risk of weakening the economy).

But the most important issue lies elsewhere: traceability problematizes the relationship between the public and commodities. Before traceability, it was easy for Marx to denounce the fetishism of commodities and to show how the shams of exchange value were hiding the scandalous reality of production relationships. Traceability turns everything upside down. It is precisely the production relationships—the way commodities are produced—that are commoditized. Organization fetishism replaces commodity fetishism. Consumer preference can be based not only on the product but also on the way it is made. This can, thus, direct consumer preferences to working conditions, business ethics, child labor, etc. (Cochoy 2001). Here we see the amazing convergence between standardization, consumer issues, and globalization (Cochoy 2002b). Relevant examples are consumers' calls for "ethics on labels" and the development of "social standards" (Swinnerton & Schoepfle 1994) and ethical business (Maignan et al. 1999). Such developments illustrate both the current move towards a "politicization" of products and the shift of our society from material/industrial references towards new values of consumer responsibility-taking, risk management, and safety issues.

Lessons from the History of Standardization

These short stories of standardization, quality, and traceability teach us four lessons. First, they show the shift of the modern economy towards what Lucien Karpik (1989) calls "the economics of quality," implying that competition entails not only price competition but also the management of product design, the building of trust, and the setting of "judgment devices" (Karpik 1996, 2000). Second, the stories show the global consequence of this shift. Today competition between products depends on a further competition between labels and certificates, and the scale of this competition largely exceeds national labels, as is evidenced by the rise of the European safety standards brand certificate "CE label" that is found on many European consumer products and the worldwide extension of management standards like ISO 9000 and ISO 14000. Standardization promotes common circulation spaces for products that "fit" with the required standards, and it erects "qualitative barriers to entry" for all the products that remain "out of the standards." Third, our short stories teach us that, while the international economics of quality is inevitable, it can be controlled and modified. It is very important for everyone to be aware of this opportunity, to join standardizing agencies, and to take part in the decision process.

As we have seen, standardization institutions are, could, or should be true "hybrid forums," that is, arenas for discussion and dialogue where professionals and lay people work together in formulating collective solutions to complex problems. All standardization committees have as a founding principle the participation of all the stakeholders. The common history of standardization and consumer advocacy teaches us that this principle, even if partly applied, should be taken seriously, and that the building of worldwide standards can be modified to the needs of interests other than those of industry. The importance of this opportunity is best understood when brought together with the fourth lesson, which comes from the history of quality and traceability. Here we see the possibility for consumers to bring political issues into the industrial and technical realm—in other words to fix politics directly into the products. This type of endeavor is particularly important in a context of globalization, where the market seems to be the most efficient—and perhaps the only?—way to carry political interest at the worldwide level. Standardization of products is clearly one of the major modes of the "work of globalization" aiming at building and generalizing common standards, ideals, and values. Since this work of globalization is not inaccessible and immaterial (like the theoretical market) but precisely situated and empirical, it is important to trace its places, its actors, and to do one's best to take part in the process. Thus, it is crucial to reveal/build the political side of these industrial products and consumer goods that have been considered as pure material and technical matters for too long.

Notes

1. This research is part of a larger project in the field of economic sociology on standardization history and its role in market economy. The paper relies, among other sources, on the systematic study of AFNOR journals: *Courrier de la normalisation* (1932-1979) and *Enjeux* (1980-2000).
2. Hybrid forums, as defined by Michel Callon and his colleagues (Callon et al., 2001), are assemblies dealing with problems such as the mad cow crisis or the OGM threat. Because such problems involve conditions of radical uncertainty about the future, science alone can no longer "calculate" the forthcoming state of the world and provide reliable solutions to political authorities. Thus, it appears necessary to invent a collective and political process where experts and laymen have no other choice but talk to each other on an equal basis in order to set up the acceptable decisions, mixing scientific and political viewpoints.

References

Bayart, Denis. 1996. "Savoir organisationnel, savoir théorique et situation: le contrôle statistique sur les échantillons." *Entreprises et histoire*, vol. 13: 67-81.
Callon, Michel, Pierre Lascoumes, & Yannick Barthe. 2001. *Agir dans un monde incertain*. Paris: Seuil.
Cochoy, Franck. 2000. "De l' 'AFNOR' à 'NF'," ou la progressive marchandisation de la normalisation industrielle." *Réseaux*, vol. 18, no. 102: 63-89.
___. 2001. "Les effets d'un trop-plein de traçabilité," in *La Recherche*, special edition, *Le risque alimentaire*, no. 339 (février): 66-68.
___. 2002a. *Une sociologie du packaging ou l'âne de Buridan face au marché*. Paris: Presses Universitaires de France.
___. 2002b."The Work of Globalization: How Standardization May Impact the Globalization of Work," in Jean-Claude Barbier & Elize Van Zyl, eds., *Globalization and the World of Work: A French South African Perspective*. Paris: L'Harmattan, 4: 83-96.

Cochoy, Franck, & De Terssac. 1999. "Les enjeux organisationnels de la qualité: une mise en perspective," in *Sciences de la société*, numéro special, *Organisation et qualité*, no. 46 (février): 3-18 (en collaboration avec Gilbert de Terssac).

____. 2000. "Au-delà de la traçabilité: la mappabilité: Deux notions connexes mais distinctes pour penser les normes de management," in Évelyne Serverin & Arnaud Berthoud, eds., *La production des normes entre état et société civile*. Paris: L'Harmattan, 239-49.

Courrier de la normalisation. 1969. "Le consommateur était au centre de la journée normalisation organisée par l'AFNOR [au salon des arts ménagers 1969]." no. 206 (mars-avril): 190-92.

Dragomir, Radu, & Bernard Halais. 1995. *Petite histoire de la qualité*. Paris: Ministère de l'Industrie, Direction générale des stratégies industrielles, Sous-direction de la Qualité pour l'Industrie et de la Normalisation.

Fraenkel, Béatrice. 1995. "La traçabilité, une fonction caractéristique des écrits au travail." *Connexions*, no. 65: 60-75.

Frontard, Raymond. 1953. "La marque nationale NF": Conférence prononcée le 11 février 1953 au Centre de Perfectionnement Technique. In *Courrier de la normalisation*, no. 113 (septembre-octobre): 315-30.

____. 1969. "Salon des artes mènagers 1969. Points de vue." *Courrier de la normalisation*, no. 106 (mars-avril): 189-92.

Gogue, Jean-Marie. 1990. *Les six samouraïs de la qualité: Les hommes qui ont fondé le management moderne*. Paris: Economica.

Karpik, Lucien. 1989. "L'économie de la qualité." *Revue Française de Sociologie*, vol. 30, no. 2 (avril-juin): 187-210.

____. 1996. "Dispositifs de confiance et engagements crédibles." *Sociologie du travail*, vol. 38, no. 4: 527-50.

____. 2000. "Le guide rouge Michelin." *Sociologie du travail*, vol. 42, no. 3: 369-89.

Latour, Bruno. 1999. *Pandora's Hope: Essays on the Reality of Science Studies*. Cambridge, MA: Harvard University Press.

Lavialle, G. 1968. "Recommandation ISO/R 526: Signification pour les acheteurs des marques de conformité aux norms." *Courrier de la normalisation*, no. 199 (janvier-février): 69-70.

Maignan, Isabelle, O. C. Ferrell, G. Hult, & M. Thomas. 1999. "Corporate Citizenship: Cultural Antecedents and Business Benefits." *Journal of the Academy of Marketing Science*, vol. 27, no. 4: 455-69.

Maily, Jacques. 1946. *La normalization*. Paris: Dunod.

Mallard, Alexandre. 2000. "La presse de consommation et le marché: Enquête sur le tiers consumériste." *Sociologie du travail*, vol. 42, no. 3: 391-409.

Olshan, M. A. 1993. "Standards Making Organizations and the Rationalization of American Life: Science, Rationality, Race, and the Law." *Sociological Quarterly*, vol. 34, no. 2: 319-35.

Publicis. 1965. "Publicis ouvre le débat…sur les unions de consommateurs dans le monde." *Publicis*, supplément au no. 91.

Romieu, André. 1969. "La normalisation est-elle un humanisme?" *Courrier de la normalisation*, no. 210 (novembre-décembre): 597-603.

____. 1973. "La norme, référence de base pour l'information et le service des consommateurs." *Courrier de la normalisation*, no. 229 (janvier-février): 61-3.

Swinnerton, Kenneth A., & Gregory K. Schoepfle. 1994. "Labor Standards in the Context of a Global Economy." *Monthly Labor Review*, vol. 117, no. 9 (September): 52-9.

Tamm Hallström, Kristina. 1996. "The Production of Management Standards." *Revue d'économie industrielle*, no. 75, 1er trimester: 61-76.

Thiard, Antoine. 1969. "Les normes obligatoires et leur rôle dans la protection du consommateur." *Courrier de la normalisation*, no. 210 (novembre-décembre): 609-13.

___. 1973. "La qualité des produits et la satisfaction du consommateur: le problème inter-national." *Courrier de la normalisation,* no. 234 (novembre-décembre): 550-53.

Torny, Didier. 1998. "La traçabilité comme technique de gouvernement des hommes et des choses." *Politix*, no. 44, 4ème trimester: 51-75.

Consumer Responsibility-Taking and Eco-Labeling Schemes in Europe[1]

Andrew Jordan, Rüdiger K. W. Wurzel, Anthony R. Zito,
and Lars Brückner

Introduction

The importance of political consumerism and consumer responsibility-taking has increased in recent years, as the focus of environmental policy in Europe has shifted from industrial pollution control
towards bringing about more sustainable consumption patterns. The
German Federal Environmental Agency (Umweltbundesamt, UBA)
estimates that at least 30 to 40 percent of all environmental problems
are directly or indirectly the result of existing consumption patterns
(UBA 1997, 1). The rise of green consumerism is a response to recognition that current consumption patterns are unsustainable. It has
been encouraged by national multi-issue eco-label schemes, whose
criteria are evaluated by independent third parties (type I schemes
according to the International Standards Organization, ISO), and has
triggered a proliferation of self-declaratory company schemes (ISO
type II schemes).

The first national eco-label was set up in Germany in 1978, and
by the early 1990s more than a dozen national and multinational
eco-label schemes were established around the globe (Kern et al.
2000, 2001; OECD 1999; UBA 1998b). The increasing number of
eco-labeling schemes has led to confusion among consumers, and
attempts have been made to bring about better coordination of competing eco-label schemes. In 1992, the European Union's eco-label
scheme was established, although member state eco-labels have
continued to coexist. Two years earlier, the Nordic Council created
the Nordic Swan multinational eco-label. In the 1990s, a Global
Ecolabeling Network (GEN) was formed, and the ISO issued guide-

lines on minimum standards for eco-labels. The establishment of eco-labeling schemes in several countries attracted the attention of the Organization for Economic Co-operation and Development (OECD) and the World Trade Organization (WTO), which began to consider their implications for free trade (OECD 1997, 1999).

The global diffusion of national and multinational eco-labeling schemes is well documented (Kern et al. 2001). There are also good case studies, which assess a particular eco-label scheme (Eiderström 1998; Schwar 1999; UBA 1991, 1998a), compare different eco-labels concerning various products (Erskine & Lyndhurst 1996; Nadai 1999), or analyze the trade implications of eco-labels (Herrup 1999; OECD 1999; Vogel 1998). However, there are very few cross-country studies, which focus on issues of consumer responsibility-taking.

This chapter focuses on type I multi-issue eco-label schemes rather than unverified type II self-declaratory eco-labels, which have a poor reputation in most EU member states. It also ignores single-issue (type III) schemes, which are evaluated by an independent party (see the chapter by Cashore et al. in this book). This chapter assesses national and supranational eco-label schemes in Austria, Britain, Germany, and the Netherlands as well as the EU. The first section explains why eco-labels should be seen as forming part of a range of "new" environmental policy instruments (NEPIs). The following sections analyze the main institutional features of the national schemes, their relationship with the EU-label, the role of consumers in them, and finally market impact and trade implications. This allows for a comparative assessment of the various eco-label schemes in the conclusion, which explains why, despite similar institutional and procedural features, considerable variations exist as regards the role and function attributed to the schemes.

Eco-Labels as "New" Environmental Policy Instruments

Traditionally, environmental policymakers have relied heavily on "command-and-control" environmental regulations, which stipulate mandatory product or process standards. However, the use of NEPIs— namely eco-labels, voluntary agreements, eco-taxes and tradable permits—has grown significantly in Europe in recent years (Andersen & Sprenger, 2000; Golub 1998; Jordan et al. 2001; Jordan, Wurzel, & Zito 2003; Wicke & Huckestein 1991). NEPIs are usually seen as market-based, cost-effective, flexible, and consumer driven policy instruments (Andersen & Sprenger 2000, 6). Eco-labels largely fit this characterization as they are voluntary informational devices, which can have a significant impact on the market.

Eco-labels are relatively soft policy instruments when compared with traditional regulation, but also in comparison to other market-based instruments such as tradable permits and eco-taxes. They rely mainly on moral suasion, by providing consumers with information about the environmental impact of certain products and services. However, eco-label schemes are largely ineffective in markets that are characterized by a low degree of environmental awareness, although they can help to raise the level of consumer awareness about environmental issues. Widely recognized and supported eco-labels may influence producers in a similar manner to traditional regulatory standards (especially if they stipulate the best available technology, BAT) in markets that are characterized by a high level of green consumerism (OECD 1999). Producers and service providers, which cater to such markets (or market segments), will have a strong incentive to apply for eco-labels to avoid possible competitive disadvantage vis-à-vis eco-labeled products/services from competitors.

German Blue Angel Scheme

As the first nationwide eco-label scheme, the German eco-label acted from 1978 as a reference point or model for many countries (EWWE 1997, 5f; OECD 1999; Schwar 1999). The symbol of the German eco-label is made up of the United Nations environmental logo and has therefore been nicknamed the "Blue Angel" by the public. There are different assessments of the significance of the label. The German environmental minister, Jürgen Tritten (Greens), considers it "worldwide the most successful label for an ecological product policy" (UBA 2001). An OECD report (EWWE 1997) offers a more cautious evaluation: "While the Blue Angel is generally considered one of the success stories of eco-labeling in Europe, its environmental effectiveness may lie more in its impact on business and government procurement practices, and on the setting of environmental standards for certain product groups, than its influence on consumer behavior." This assessment fits the view of Germany as a "high regulatory state," which has relied heavily on BAT-derived environmental product standards (Héritier et al. 1996; Weale 1992; Wurzel 1996, 2002).

In terms of institutional features, the Blue Angel is a voluntary third-party scheme, licensed by the German Institute for Quality Assurance and Labeling (Deutsches Institut für Gütesicherung und Kennzeichnung e.V., RAL). RAL is a self-financing agency set up under private law, with the task of preparing and signing the contracts and undertaking the testing. RAL charges a one-off evaluation fee and a license fee, which depends on the product's annual turnover. The fees are relatively low. Applicants from developing countries are offered reduced rates and technical support to ensure that German business cannot use the eco-label for protectionist purposes. The other main institutional actors involved are the UBA and the Eco-Label Jury. The Eco-Label Jury consists of a wide range of stakeholders, including consumer and environmental NGOs, industry, churches, and scientists. It selects the products and services that are granted the label. This institutional arrangement is crucial for the Blue Angel's credibility and its success, as it guarantees that the scheme is independent and can resist undue industry influence (OECD 1997, 50). The UBA collects and comments on suggestions for new product and service groups. Anyone, including foreign non-EU companies, can put forward suggestions.

The Blue Angel is awarded only to products and services that are "characterized by a particularly high degree of environmental soundness" compared to other products/services fulfilling the same function (UBA 2001). It is not awarded to product/service groups, which as a whole are seen as environmentally friendly (e.g., bicycles). Nor will it be granted to products that "are the source of environmental damage during the production process" (OECD 1997, 6). So far the jury has refused to produce eco-label criteria for private cars, because it considers them inherently more damaging to the environment than public transport. However, the eco-label has recently been awarded to car sharing schemes. Products and services are usually licensed for a three-year period. The time period may be shortened, where more rapid technological progress is expected. The evaluation process takes into account all aspects of environmental protection, including the use of raw materials (UBA 2001). The Blue Angel utilizes a simplified life-cycle analysis (LCA), which relies primarily on an assessment of the product/service's most important environmental characteristics (OECD 1997; UBA 2001).

The scheme's institutional structure has remained remarkably stable since the 1970s. One important difference, however, is the broader composition of the Eco-Label Jury. Environmental and consumer NGOs play a more direct role as participants in the expert hearings. The procedures now include a greater number of assessment criteria, and LCA considerations are given greater prominence (OECD 1999, 49-59). Since the 1990s, the UBA wants to integrate the Blue Angel scheme into a broader, integrated product policy (IPP) and combine it with the EU's Environmental Management and Audit Scheme (EMAS) widely used by German companies. The aim is to achieve a more integrated approach and better coordination among competing voluntary schemes, which aim to raise environmental standards for products and services.

The wide recognition and legitimacy of the Blue Label Scheme has made it difficult for the EU eco-label to establish itself in Germany. The EU eco-label scheme is not widely known among consumers and producers (IÖW 1999; UBA 1996, 1998a). Many consumers who are aware of the EU eco-label consider it inferior, though this is not actually the case for some product groups. Only two German companies had applied for the EU eco-label by early 2002. The "first mover disadvantage" explains the low application rate for the EU eco-label (CEC 2001; Ökopol 2000, 27). The first successful companies would have to make the EU eco-label known to German consumers, while convincing them that it is not inferior to the Blue Angel. Yet the majority of Germany's export-oriented companies support the harmonization of eco-labels, as the multiplicity of national schemes makes it difficult for them to coordinate their export market. However, the EU eco-label scheme is seen as too costly, cumbersome, lacking in transparency, and suffering from low consumer awareness (IÖW 1999).

The success of any eco-labeling scheme depends to a large degree on the level of consumer awareness and consumer use. The media (especially the specialized and local press), and consumer NGOs have played an important role in making the Blue Angel known among consumers. The government has spent only moderate resources on promotion campaigns. The Blue Angel's transparency and independence from business, as well as its governmental approval, have convinced consumers and NGOs, who were initially skeptical, of the scheme's benefits. A survey from 1996 shows that 80 percent of West Germans and 56 percent of East Germans were aware of the national eco-label, and 51 and 30 percent of West and East Germans, respectively, claimed that they always, or at least often, paid attention to the Blue Angel when shopping (OECD 1997, 57; Schwar 1999, 125; UBA 1998a, 18; 2001). Public awareness has changed little over the years. However, between 1992 and 1996 the willingness to pay a premium for eco-labeled products decreased from 59 to 35 percent among West Germans and from 24 to 17 percent among East Germans (OECD 1997, 56-8; Schwar 1999, 125-6; UBA 2001). This is in line with a moderate decline in environmental awareness in Germany in the 1990s (Eurobarometer 1995, 1999). A survey in 2000 showed that the decline in public environmental awareness seems to have bottomed out, although only 12 percent of Germans were "very prepared," while 59 percent were "more prepared" to pay a premium for environmentally friendly products (BMU 2002).

Market impact and trade implications are other important aspects for assessing the success of eco-label schemes. During its heyday in the 1990s, Blue Angels could be found on more than 4,000 products (UBA 1998a, 9). By 2001, the number of Blue-Angel-labeled products declined to 3,355. Consumer awareness of the Blue Angel scheme influences company marketing strategies in Germany. However, the fact that the market penetration of the Blue Angel varies considerably among different product groups cannot be explained by consumer awareness. For example, the uptake of the Blue Angel is very high for low-solvent paints, recycled paper, and office equipment, but very low for televisions, white goods (i.e., large household appliances), and tires. For sanitary paper products (such as toilet paper) the market share of the Blue Angel rose from 32 to 64 percent between 1986 and 1993 (OECD 1997, 50).

Competition among companies for the same market can trigger a high uptake of the eco-label for a particular market segment. According to a survey, 92 percent of companies awarded the Blue Angel face an equivalent product from a competitor, which has also been awarded the label (UBA 1998a, 14). Medium-sized and large companies are substantially driven by concerns about losing market shares to competitors carrying the Blue Angel, rather than by the hope that the eco-label increases their market share. However, the sales figures of small companies seem to have benefited from the Blue Angel (UBA 1998a, 36).

Foreign companies competing on the German market have shown a strong interest in having their products labeled with the Blue Angel. The share of Blue Angels for products by foreign companies amounted to 16 percent in 2001. However, in practice the figure amounts to approximately one-third of all eco-labeled products, because it is often the importer or retailer who applies for the Blue Angel on behalf of a foreign company. This development is best explained by the large size of the German market and the Blue Angel's wide recognition among consumers. The institutional design of the Blue Angel (i.e., its voluntary nature, placement under private law, and simplified LCA requirements, which does not consider products/services that are highly damaging to the environment) means that it cannot be challenged under GATT/WTO rules on free trade.

Austrian Eco-Label

The Austrian eco-label was set up in 1991. The belated establishment of an eco-label scheme fits the assertion that Austria has "a need for catching up" with the environmental forerunners as regards the use of NEPIs (Mol et al. 2000). Its adoption was due to an initiative by the Environmental Minister, an upsurge in public environmental awareness, and the entry of the Green Party into Parliament in the 1980s (Schwar 1999). The German Blue Angel acted as a model for the Austrian eco-label scheme. However, the Austrian scheme exhibits significant differences and "tried not to repeat some of the shortcomings of the Blue Angel" (interview with BMLFUW official 2002).

Unlike the German scheme, a government ministry, the Minister for Agriculture, Forestry, Environment, and Water Management (BMLFUW), awards the Austrian eco-label. A greater number of institutions are also involved in the scheme. They include the Economics Ministry, Association for Consumer Information (VKI), which is a private technical institute, the Eco-label Committee (Beirat Umweltzeichen), and various technical working groups. The central actors are the BMLFUW and the VKI, although the Economics Ministry plays an important role for the eco-label in the tourism sector. The Eco-label Committee, which defines the product/service groups and issues general guidelines, consists of a wide range of stakeholders, although governmental actors play a dominant role. Special working groups are set up under the auspices of the VKI to establish the award criteria, which remain valid for three years. Unlike the Blue Angel, the Austrian eco-label is usually awarded for one year only. Like the German system, anyone can submit proposals for product/service groups, though foreign companies can apply only if they have an office in the EU or a European Free Trade Agreement country (Schwar 1999). Austria has pioneered an eco-label for tourism (BMLFUW 2000, 13; Schwar 1999). This reflects the high dependency of the Austrian economy on tourism and the ecological vulnerability of the Alpine regions.

The Austrian eco-label is based on an LCA. Product criteria must comply with existing health and safety requirements and environmental regulations. The Austrian government claims, that "eco-labeling represents one of the most important modern instruments of product-oriented environmental policy" (BMLFUW 2001). However, officials admit that the eco-label "is not considered as a milestone of Austrian environmental policy," but merely "a step in the right direction" (interview with Austrian Environment Ministry official, 2001). The Environment Ministry views the eco-label as an important supplementary policy measure within a broader product policy.

Just as in the German case, the EU eco-label is not widely known in Austria, and there is a widespread belief that EU eco-label standards are inferior to the national scheme. However, Austria has transposed the more ambitious EU eco-label criteria for light bulbs into her national scheme. There is growing recognition among Austrian NGOs that the EU eco-label is more stringent for some products, but this has not led to significant NGO support or increased consumer recognition. As of early 2002 not a single Austrian company had applied for the EU eco-label. At the same time export-oriented companies, as well as ministry officials, recognize that better cooperation and coordination is needed between national and EU eco-labels. The government's stated aim is "to integrate national experiences in the most constructive manner...Austria supports all attempts to develop the European scheme in a direction which allows for achieving maximum environmental benefit" (BMLFUW 2001). The government has not, however, provided additional resources for this effort.

The Austrian eco-label scheme's basic aim is to provide consumers with more product transparency (BMLFUW 2000, 2). However, it is a relatively stringent scheme, which has not been designed to become a mass label used widely by "green" political consumers. The Austrian eco-label suffers from relatively low recognition among consumers and is therefore not widely sought after by producers. The government tried to remedy this situation in the 1990s by promoting public awareness of the national scheme. More recently, it has adopted a more strategic approach by promoting certain products that have been awarded the eco-label. The government has also shifted its promotional activities from focusing mainly on tourism service providers to targeting environmentally aware tourists (i.e., consumers), in the hope that this will increase the attractiveness of the eco-label (BMFLUW n.d.). It therefore aims to change the behavior of producers by changing first the attitudes of consumers.

The Austrian eco-label has much less market impact when compared to its German counterpart. By 2001, award criteria existed for forty-five product groups (BMLFUW 2001). The highest number of eco-labels is for paper products, household products, refillable beverage containers, and timber products (EWWE 1997, 8). However, despite "individual success stories...the Austrian label has yet to gain widespread industry and consumer acceptance" (EWWE 1997, 9). By 2001, only 152 eco-labels had been awarded for tourism, although there was a 50 percent increase in uptake in 2000 (BMLFUW n.d.). The trade implications of the Austrian eco-label scheme have therefore remained overall only marginal. The number of foreign companies applying is low, which is explained by the small size of the Austrian market. Even Austrian companies have shown little enthusiasm for the national eco-label scheme and instead prefer to demonstrate their environmental credentials by adopting self-declaratory eco-labels or by participating in the EU's EMAS.

Dutch Eco-Label

Like Germany and Austria, the Netherlands is often portrayed as an environmental leader state (Liefferink 1996; Andersen & Liefferink 1997; Zito 2000). It has made wide use of a broad range of NEPIs (Jordan et al. 2001; Mol et al. 2000). However, the Netherlands is a latecomer regarding the national eco-label scheme, which was set up as late as in 1992. Party politics and personalities explain this. Unlike the other two cases already discussed, Dutch environmental groups were a driving force behind the establishment of the national eco-label (interview with Environment Ministry official in 2001).

The core institutional features of the Dutch eco-label scheme are reminiscent of the German and Austrian schemes. The Dutch eco-label scheme is a third-party, voluntary scheme, organized under private law. The main institutional actors involved are the Environmental Ministry (VROM) and the Eco-label Foundation (Stichting Milieukeur), which includes representatives of all relevant stakeholders (environmental and consumer NGOs, industry, and government officials). All stakeholders have the same voting rights within the Stichting Milieukeur. NGOs also participate within the Stichting Milieukeur's Board of Experts, which plays a central role in defining the criteria for the product and service groups.

The Dutch eco-label places considerably more emphasis on LCA when compared to the German Blue Angel. Like the German scheme, its application fee is relatively low, and the license fee depends on the product's annual turnover. In 1995, the Dutch eco-label scheme was the first scheme within the EU to develop criteria for foodstuffs, due largely to the importance of food and flower exports for the Dutch economy. However, the uptake of the national eco-label in the foodstuffs sector has remained considerably lower, compared to the non-food sector (interview with VROM official in 2002). The Dutch eco-label scheme has so far failed to become widely known among consumers and producers. In the late 1990s, the government therefore began a public relations campaign to promote the national and EU eco-labels (EWWE 1997, 7).

The EU's eco-label scheme was adopted in the same year as the Dutch scheme. However, the parallel launch of the EU eco-label had no real impact on the main features of the national scheme. Although Dutch companies are strongly export oriented, they have displayed little interest in the EU eco-label. In 2002, there were only two EU eco-label award holders in the Netherlands. This is the case even though the Dutch government supports the strengthening of the EU eco-label (including the creation of an independent European Eco-label Agency), and suggests combining eco-label schemes with other types of NEPIs. However, the Dutch government has not provided significant funds for the promotion of the EU eco-label. More recently, the Dutch government has tried to facilitate closer coordination between the national and EU eco-label, because the latter has adopted relatively stringent criteria for products such as refrigerators and light bulbs.

As Dutch environmental groups were a driving force behind the eco-label's adoption, it is not surprising that the scheme "is meant to address especially the Dutch consumer...and [aims] to create a 'green' consciousness. It focuses less on producers and retailers" (interview with VROM official 2001). For the VROM the main advantage of a national scheme is that it can be applied to the "specific national context in terms of consumer education, influencing industry [and] the promotion of eco-friendly products. Even those industries not participating in the national scheme read the product criteria carefully and might respond accordingly, as they expect consumers to continue developing an increasingly 'green' consciousness" (interview with VROM official in 2001).

The Dutch eco-label has failed to achieve a major market impact or significant trade implications. Because of low consumer awareness, there has not been a virtuous "demand-supply-demand" circle. Most large Dutch companies favor brand marketing over eco-labels, which are awarded for a specific product or service. Many Dutch companies prefer different NEPIs while others choose to use their own company labeling schemes. However, Dutch companies that export to Germany have applied for the Blue Angel label for fear of losing market shares. Moreover, the number of products awarded the national eco-label rose from 76 to 93 between 1997 and 1998 (EWWE 1997; UBA 1998a). The mad cow disease and foot-and-mouth crises have shattered consumer confidence in agricultural products in Europe and increased interest in the Dutch foodstuffs eco-label scheme.

Eco-Label Debate in Britain

The British debate about a national eco-label started in earnest in the 1990s after a wave of green consumerism swept through Britain in the late 1980s (Jordan 2002; Weale et al. 2000; Wurzel 2002). The Department of the Environment (DoE) and the Department of Trade and Industry (DTI) published a joint discussion paper on eco-labeling in 1989. However, while the DoE and DTI favored the establishment of an EU-wide scheme, the House of Commons Environmental Committee suggested the setting up of a national scheme in addition to the EU eco-label (Haigh 1999). Following a consultation exercise, the government indicated that it was prepared to consider the creation of a national scheme, which would be based on a LCA approach. However, because of the launch of the EU eco-label "it was evident that details of the UK's scheme would wait until the EC Regulation was agreed" (Haigh 1999, chap. 11.7). The British government set up an Eco-labeling Board, which became the Competent Body for the EU's eco-label scheme. However, its functions were taken over by the Department of the Environment, Transport and the Regions (DETR) in 1998 (Haigh 1999, chap. 11.7) which has formed part of the Department for the Environment, Food and Rural Affairs (DEFRA) since 2001 (DEFRA 2002).

In general, the British government has taken the position that no additional benefit would be gained from establishing a national eco-label in addition to an EU scheme. Initially, it played a very active role in the creation and the management of the EU eco-label scheme. But it scaled down its promotional efforts after a review from 1998 found that "people were not taking up the EU eco-label" (interview with DEFRA official in 2002). A few years later, DEFRA (2002) concluded that "developments since 1992 [i.e., when the EU label was established] show that eco-labeling cannot by itself transform the environmental behavior of industry and consumers, or meet their needs, in the way that was hoped when the [EU] scheme was set up." The British government offers advice for business and consumers about green claims and labels, but it no longer focuses primarily on eco-labels to encourage green consumerism (DEFRA 2002). Instead it strongly supports EMAS and IPP as new regulatory tools (Zito & Egan 1998). This fits the needs of British industry well, as many large producers in Britain are opposed to government and EU supported eco-labels and prefer self-declaratory labels. Large retailers (e.g., Sainsbury) often argue that their brand name is already a sign of quality, which should not be compromised by competing labels. It is therefore unsurprising that British companies have largely failed to promote the EU eco-label. British consumers are largely oblivious to the EU eco-label despite the fact that there is no competing national scheme.

Overall, the British approach to eco-labeling fits with the national environmental regulatory style, which has often been characterized as a pragmatic ("trial-and-error" driven) and consensual search process for the most cost-efficient environmental options (Jordan 2002; Vogel 1986; Weale et al. 2000; Wurzel 2002). The British government's stance on eco-labels has been devoid of a grand strategy and characterized by a multitude of relatively small-scale initiatives (DEFRA 2002).

The EU Eco-Label Scheme

The EU eco-label was established in 1992. In terms of institutional features, it is a voluntary scheme, which promotes products/services that are less damaging to the environment compared to functionally equivalent products/services (CEC 2000a; Eiderström 1998; Erskine & Lyndhurst 1996). It can be awarded for a period of up to three years, according to criteria, which are based on an LCA. Applications for the EU eco-label must be put to the national Competent Body. An Advisory Committee, made up of officials from the Competent Bodies and chaired by the Commission, then considers the applications. The decision is left to the Council of Ministers, if the Advisory Committee fails to agree on the product criteria by qualified majority voting, although great efforts are made to achieve consensus. There is also a Consultation Forum, which grants access to stakeholders (such as industry and NGOs). NGOs are of the opinion that this body has been circumvented by industry groups that directly lobbied the Commission (Eiderström 1998; EEB 1998).

The Commission's original proposal (CEC 1991) suggested placing an EU Jury in charge of establishing the criteria for the EU eco-labels. However, member governments opposed this and insisted instead on a scheme that was "more based on mutual recognition of the decisions of national competent bodies" (Haigh 1999, chap. 11.7). The Advisory Committee works out the product groups and criteria for which one member state is assigned "lead country" status. The lead country forms an ad hoc working group in order to draft the product group criteria. At first, the member states were the driving force, but the Commission has gradually expanded its influence over the eco-labeling system (EEB 1998).

The 1992 EU eco-label scheme was strongly criticized (Eiderström 1998; Erskine & Lyndhurst 1996; Herrup 1999; Karl & Orwat 1999; Nadai 1999). It suffered from a cumbersome and non-transparent decision-making process and competition with national eco-label schemes. Its fees were relatively high, and importers complained that it was in breach of the WTO rules (Herrup 1999; Vogel 1998). The revision of the scheme was due in 1997, although it was finally completed in 2000. The slow progress on restructuring the scheme is explained by disagreement among the members of the Commission, EU member states, and the European Parliament (EP), who have found it difficult to agree on the institutional design of the labeling scheme (ENDS Daily, 3 July 2000; Wurzel 2000). The revision introduced the following major changes: (1) establishment of the EU Eco-Labeling Board (EUEB), composed of the Competent Bodies from the member states; (2) expanded scope of the label to cover services; (3) establishment of an Eco-label Management Committee within the Commission to improve the transparency of the scheme; (4) more involvement of consumer and environmental groups, and (5) a set ceiling for the license fees which allows small businesses that use EMAS to be eligible for a discount.

European consumers have remained largely oblivious to the EU eco-label scheme. This is particularly so in member states with their own national eco-label. Member governments have done little to promote the EU eco-label. However, the revised EU eco-label has gained greater acceptance from NGOs, but this has not been transformed into consumer awareness. The EU's recent emphasis on soft policy instruments and voluntary agreements (Mol et al. 2000; Jordan et al. 2001; 2003) may provide a life-line for the embattled EU eco-label, as it could form part of a wider IPP strategy which draws on a wide range of NEPIs (CEC 2001). It can be concluded that without stakeholder support, the EU eco-label is unlikely to become a successful NEPI that helps to bring about more sustainable consumption patterns.

Given this, the market impact and trade implications are, not surprisingly, rather meager. During its first four years, the EU eco-label developed criteria for only six product groups. By 2000, the number had risen to eighteen. However, by then only 41 products carried the EU eco-label. The market share of EU eco-labeled products remains low, even in member states without their own national eco-label or without labels for certain product and/or service categories. EU eco-labeled paints and varnishes have achieved less than 0.1 percent of the market share, although some national eco-labels have a very high market penetration within these market segments. By early 2002, the number of EU eco-labeled products had risen to 103, but they still make up only a small fraction of the products/ services on the market. Yet, even though companies do not apply for it, the EU eco-label is used as a benchmark by some companies. There is considerable interest in the EU eco-label among large retailers and export-driven producers, although some of them would prefer a global eco-label. However, the Commission has an uphill struggle if it wants to convince producers and service providers about the benefits of the EU eco-label. Currently, there is little danger that the EU eco-label will be challenged under WTO rules, as it has very little market impact (OECD 1999; Vogel 1995, 1998).

Conclusion

Multi-issue third party (type I) eco-labels are the most trusted schemes among consumers in Europe where they are used relatively widely. Germany, Austria, and the Netherlands have all adopted national schemes, while Britain has relied on the EU eco-label, which competes with the national eco-labels in the other three member states. The main features of the institutional structures of the eco-label schemes assessed in this chapter are similar. They are all voluntary schemes, which involve stakeholder consultation and rely on third party verification. With the exception of the EU eco-label, they have all been set up under private law. All four eco-label schemes have moved towards cradle-to-grave LCA considerations, although this is arguably least the case for the German Blue Angel, which instead has strongly emphasized simplicity and transparency. The different schemes all try to encourage environmental responsibility-taking among consumers, by providing information about products and services, which are less damaging to the environment than functionally equivalent products/services. The schemes all aim to raise environmental awareness while promoting more sustainable consumption and production patterns.

However, despite considerable institutional similarities this chapter also shows that the role and function played by the different eco-label schemes within their respective markets vary. Of the eco-label schemes assessed, the German Blue Angel is the only one that has achieved wide consumer recognition and considerable market penetration, although its heyday may have passed already. The number of applications for the Blue Angel scheme has declined in recent years. In 2002, the German government therefore supported a re-launch of the scheme in order to prevent its decline. The Austrian and Dutch environmental labels, and especially the EU scheme, have a much lower profile among consumers and a lower uptake from producers. In 2001, there were more than 3,500 Blue Angel labeled products/services, while only 103 products/services carried the EU eco-label. However, the product/service criteria for the EU eco-label are increasingly being used as a benchmark by large companies, in particular by those companies that have not actually applied for the label.

Many product/service groups eligible for eco-labels reflect national market priorities. For example, Austria has pioneered eco-labels for tourism while the Netherlands was the first country to award eco-labels for food. Some of the criteria adopted are closely related to the wider national environmental regulatory style (Vogel 1986; Wurzel 2002). For example, the German Blue Angel puts emphasis on the BAT, while the Dutch eco-label emphasizes LCA. Britain, on the other hand, has failed to adopt a national eco-label and instead relies mainly on the EU eco-label and on self-declaratory labels.

The degree to which business finds eco-label schemes attractive depends most of all on the level of public environmental awareness in general and consumer awareness of the eco-label in particular. However, whether businesses apply for the eco-label or not often also depends on whether competitors make use of the eco-label for functionally equivalent products. In general, producers and service providers are more driven by fears about a loss of market shares rather than the hope of increasing their market share due to an eco-label award. However, this is less the case for small companies, while many large companies (especially in Britain) want to make sure that their brand name will not be negatively affected by the eco-label. Once a critical mass of businesses has successfully applied for an eco-label within a certain market segment, the remaining companies find themselves under considerable market pressure to seek the label for their competing product(s). Market dynamics therefore explain why the eco-label has a very high uptake in certain market segments and why it fails to gain hold in other markets. The chapter in this volume by Cashore et al. on forest stewardship certification also underscores the significance of market characteristics as an important factor explaining the development of labeling schemes for forestry products.

Our chapter shows, that eco-labels can play an important role in fostering environmental responsibility-taking among political consumers. An active role on the part of the government is a necessary, but not sufficient, condition for the establishment of successful national eco-label schemes. The Austrian and Dutch governments both have set up national eco-labels, which have so far failed to achieve widespread consumer recognition or a significant market impact. The same is true for the EU eco-label.

The success of national and supranational eco-label schemes depends heavily on environmentally aware citizens who consider everyday consumer choices as forming part of environmental sustainability. Moreover, business needs to take seriously sustainable development or at least consider whether ignoring national and/or supranational eco-label schemes may lead to a loss in market share of its products/ services. Thus, a complex relationship between government and citizen/NGO activity, as well as consumer demand and business supply, is at work, which affects the legitimization and uptake of eco-label schemes.

The voluntary nature of eco-label schemes (and other legally non-binding NEPIs) allows stakeholders to determine their scope and uptake as they can choose between competing voluntary environmental policy tools. In some cases, this may threaten the existence of more stringent (national) eco-labeling schemes and lead to a lowering of environmental requirements.

Eco-labels are only one among several NEPIs available to policymakers who want to encourage more sustainable consumption and production patterns. Policymakers in Austria, Britain, Germany, the Netherlands, and the EU increasingly consider eco-labels as forming part of a wider sustainable development strategy that includes a range of different voluntary policy tools (such as EMAS and IPP). However, despite the increased importance of (national and supranational) eco-label schemes in Europe they have so far largely remained supplementary tools for more traditional (command and control) regulation.

Note

1.   The research underpinning this chapter was funded by the Economic and Social Research Council's (ESRC) Future Governance Programme (project number: L216252013). It forms part of a larger project entitled "Environmental Governance: The Use of 'New' Environmental Policy Instruments (NEPIs)." More information about the project can be found at: <www.uea.ac.uk/env/cserge/research/ fut_governance/Home.htm>.

The authors would like to thank the participants at the conference on political consumerism in Stockholm as well as the editors and Michele Micheletti, in particular, for helpful comments on an earlier draft.

References

Andersen, Mikael Skou, & Duncan Liefferink, eds. 1997. *European Environmental Policy: The Pioneers*. Manchester: Manchester University Press.

Andersen, Mikael Skou, & Rolf-Ulrich Sprenger, eds. 2000. *Market-Based Instruments for Environmental Management*. Cheltenham: Edward Elgar.

BMLFUW. 2000. *Das Österreichische Umweltzeichen*. Vienna: Ministry for Agriculture, Forestry, Environment, and Water Management. See <www.bmu.gv.at/ u_kennzeichen_auszeich/oe_umweltzeichen/>.

BMLFUW. 2001. *Das Österreichische Umweltzeichen. The Austrian Eco Label*. Vienna: Ministry for Agriculture, Forestry, Environment, and Water Management. See <www.bmu.gv.at/u_kennzeichen_auszeich/oe_umweltzeichen/>.

BMLFUW. n. d. *SIGNatur: Umweltinformationsblatt für Produzenten, Beschaffer, Tourismusbetriebe und Umweltengagierte*. Vienna: Ministry for Agriculture, Forestry, Environment, and Water Management.

BMU. 2002. *The Blue Angel*. See <http://bmu.de>.

CEC. 1991. *Proposal for a Council Regulation (EEC) on a Community Award Scheme for an Eco-Label*. Brussels: Commission of the European Communities [COM(91) 37 final, 11 February].

CEC. 1996. *Proposal for a Council Regulation Establishing a Revised Community Eco-label Award Scheme*. Brussels: Commission of the European Communities [COM(96)603].

CEC. 2000a. "Regulation (EC) No 1980/2000 of the European Parliament and of the Council of 17 July 2000 on a Revised Community Eco-Label Award Scheme." *Official Journal*, L 237 of 21 September 1-12.

CEC. 2000b. *Study on Different Types of Environmental Labelling (ISO Type II and III Labels): Proposal for an Environmental Labelling Strategy*. Brussels: Commission of the European Communities [Report prepared by Environmental Resources Management].

CEC. 2001. *The European Union Eco-label*. See <www.europa.eu.int/comm/environment/ecolabel/>.

DEFRA. 2002. *Finding out about the Ecolabel and Other Environmental Labels, UK-Ecolabel Guidance Note 3*. London: Department of the Environment, Food, and Rural Affairs.

DETR. 1998. *Prior Options Review of the UK Ecolabeling Board*. London: Department of the Environment, Transport, and the Regions.

EEB. 1998. *EEB's Contribution to the EU Eco-Label Scheme*. Brussels: European Environmental Bureau.

Eiderström, Eva. 1998. "Ecolabels in EU Environmental Policy," in J. Golub, ed., *New Instruments for Environmental Policy in the EU*. London: Routledge.

ENDS Daily. (various years). Daily e-mail service, Environmental Data Services, 40 Bowling Green Lane, London, EC1R ONE, e-mail: envdaily@ends.co.uk; Homepage: <www.ends.co.uk/envdaily>.

EWWE. 1997. *Environmental Watch: Western Europe, Special Issue, Eco-Labels*. Arlington: Cutter Information.

Erskine, Camilla, & Lyndhurst Collins. 1996. "Eco-Labelling in the EU: A Comparative Study of the Pulp and Paper Industry in the UK and Sweden." *European Environment* 6: 40-7.

Eurobarometer. 1995. *Europeans and the Environment in 1995. Survey Conducted in the Context of the Eurobarometer 43*. Brussels: 1 BIS. Report, produced for the European Commission, Directorate General Environment, Nuclear Safety and Civil Protection.

Eurobarometer. 1999. *Les Européens et l'environnement 1999*. Brussels: Directorate General Environment, Nuclear Safety, and Civil Protection.

Golub, Jonathan, ed. 1998. *New Instruments for Environmental Policy in the EU*. London: Routledge.

Haigh, Nigel, ed. 1999. *Manual of Environmental Policy: The EC and Britain*. Harlow: Cartermill Publishing (looseleaf manual with bi-annual updates by the Institute for European Environmental Policy in London).

HC. 1990. *Environment Committee: Eighth Report*. London: Her Majesty's Stationary Office [HC 474-1].

Héritier, Adrienne, Christoph Knill, & Susanne Mingers. 1996. *Ringing the Changes in Europe. Regulatory Competition and the Redefinition of the State. Britain, France, and Germany.* Berlin and New York: de Gruyter.

Herrup, Andrew. 1999. "Eco-Label: Benefits Uncertain, Impacts Unclear." *European Environmental Law Review*: 144-53.

IÖW. 1999. *The European Eco-Label in Germany: Development of Recommendations for Action to Increase Acceptance; Commissioned by the Federal Environmental Agency.* Wuppertal: Institut für ökologische Wirtschaftsforschung GmbH.

Jordan, Andrew. 2002. *The Europeanization of British Environmental Policy: A Departmental Perspective.* London: Palgrave.

Jordan, Andrew, Rüdiger K. W. Wurzel, Anthony R. Zito, & Lars Brückner. 2001. "The Innovation and Diffusion of 'New' Environmental Policy Instruments (NEPIs) in the European Union and its Member States." Paper for the "Human Dimensions of Global Environmental Change and the Nation State," organized by the Potsdam Climate Change Institute in Berlin on 8-9 December.

___, Rüdiger K. W. Wurzel, & Anthony R. Zito, eds. 2003. *New Instruments of Environmental Governance. National Experiences and Prospects.* London: Frank Cass.

Karl, Helmut, & Carsten Orwat. 1999. "Environmental Labelling in Europe: European and National Tasks." *European Environment* 9: 212-20.

Kern, Kristine, Helge Jörgens, & Martin Jänicke. 2000. Die Diffusion umweltpolitischer Innovationen: Ein Beitrag zur Globalisierung von Umweltpolitik." *Zeitschrift für Umweltpolitik* 23: 507-46.

Kern, Kristine, Ingrid Kisslin-Näf, Ute Landmann, & Corine Mauch. 2001. "Ecolabelling and Forest Certification as New Environmental Policy Instruments. Factors Which Impede and Support Diffusion." Paper prepared for the ECPR Workshop on The Politics of New Environmental Policy Instruments, Grenoble.

Köhler, Helmut. 1990. "Der gerupfte Umweltengel oder Die wettbewerbsrechtlichen Grenzen der umweltbezogenen Produktwerbung." *Jahrbuch des Umwelt-und Technikrechts* 12: 344-63.

Lauber, Volker. 1997. "A Latecomer Which Became a Pioneer," in M. S. Andersen & D. Liefferink, eds., *Environmental policy: The Pioneers.* Manchester: Manchester University Press.

Liefferink, Duncan. 1996. *Environmental Policy and the Nation State: The Netherlands, the EU and Acid Rain.* Manchester: Manchester University Press.

Mittendorfer, Cornelia, ed. 1994. *Umweltzeichen und Öko-Audit: Was können die sanften Instrumente?* Vienna: Bundesarbeiterkammer.

Mol, Arthur, Volkmar Lauber, & Duncan Liefferink, eds. 2000. *The Voluntary Approach to Environmental Policy-making in Europe.* Oxford: Oxford University Press.

Nadai, Alain. 1999. "Conditions for the Development of a Product Ecolabel. *European Environment* 9: 202-11.

OECD. 1991. *Environmental Labelling in OECD Countries.* Paris: Organization for Economic Co-operation and Development.

OECD. 1997. *Eco-labelling: Actual effects of Selected Programmes.* Paris: Organization for Economic Co-operation and Development.

OECD. 1999. *Working Party on Pollution Prevention and Control: Conclusions and Papers Presented at the International Conference: Green Goods v Eco-Labelling For a Sustainable Future* (Berlin, 26-28 October 1998). Paris: Organization for Economic Co-operation and Development.

Ökopol. 2000. *Promotion and Marketing the European Eco-label in Germany and Austria: Report Compiled for the Directorate General Environment of the Commission of the European Communities.* Hamburg: Institut für Ökologie und Politik GmbH.

Schuster, Gerhard, ed. n.d. *Das österreichische Umweltzeichen*. Vienna: Verlag Österreich.
Schwar, Beatrix. 1999. *Umweltzeichen und betrieblicher Umweltschutz*. Vienna: Verlag Österreich.
UBA. 1991. *The Environmental Label Introduces Itself*. Berlin: Umweltbundesamt.
UBA. 1996. *Das Europäische Umweltzeichen: Wege zum produktbezogenen Umweltschutz in Europa*. Berlin: Umweltbundesamt (Texte 62/96).
UBA. 1997. *Nachhaltige Konsummuster und postmaterielle Lebensstile, Vorstudien*. Berlin: Umweltbundesamt (Text 30/97).
UBA. 1998a. *Erfolgskontrolle Umweltzeichen/Assessing the Success of the German Eco Label*. Berlin: Umweltbundesamt.
UBA. 1998b. *Logo? Ökologisch ausgerichtete Kennzeichen für Produkte und Dienstleistungen*. Berlin: Umweltbundesamt.
UBA. (2001), see <www.umweltbundesamt.de/umweltzeichen>.
Ungerer, Brigitte, & Franz Waarden, eds. 1995. *Convergence and Divergence? Internationalisation and Economic Policy Response*. Aldershot: Avesbury.
Vogel, David. 1986. *National Styles of Regulation: Environmental Policy in Great Britain and the United States*. Ithaca, NY: Cornell University Press.
___. 1995. *Trading Up: Consumer and Environmental Regulation in a Global Economy*. Cambridge: Harvard University Press.
___. 1998. "EU Environmental Policy and the GATT/WTO," in J. Golub, ed., *Global Competition and EU Environmental Policy*. London: Routledge.
Weale, Albert. 1992. *The New Politics of Pollution*. Manchester: Manchester University Press.
___, Geoffrey Pridham, Michelle Cini, Dimitrios Konstadadkopulos, Martin Porter, & Brendan Flynn. 2000. *Environmental Governance in Europe: An Even Closer Ecological Union?* Oxford: Oxford University Press.
Wicke, Lutz, & Burkhard Huckestein. 1991. *Umwelt Europa: Der Ausbau zur ökologischen Marktwirtschaft*. Gütersloh: Verlag Bertelsmann Stiftung.
Wurzel, Rüdiger K. W. 1996. "The Role of the EU Presidency in the Environmental Field: Does It Make a Difference Which Member State Runs the Presidency?" *Journal of European Public Policy* 3, 2: 272-91.
___. 2000. "Flying into Unexpected Turbulence: The German EU Presidency in the Environmental Field." *German Politics* 9, 3: 23-43.
___. 2002. *Environmental Policy-making in Britain, Germany and the European Union*. Manchester: Manchester University Press.
Zito, Anthony. 2000. *Creating Environmental Policy in the European Union*. London: Macmillan.
___, & M. Egan. 1998. "Environmental Management Standards, Corporate Strategies and Policy Networks." *Environmental Politics* 7, 3: 94-117.

Legitimizing Political Consumerism: The Case of Forest Certification in North America and Europe

Benjamin Cashore, Graeme Auld, and Deanna Newsom

Introduction

As international and domestic public policy processes made limited efforts in the 1980s and early 1990s to address the problem of ecological deterioration of the world's forests, environmental groups and their allies turned to the marketplace in the hopes of creating more efficient and effective institutions to govern forest management. The market's supply chain is the key arena in this political struggle over forest resource use. Institutional consumers, such as business and government as well as individual consumers along the supply chain, are encouraged and coerced by environmental groups to demand that the wood products they purchase come from sustainably managed sources. This chapter explores forest certification, which can be defined as a non-state market driven (NSMD) governance system (Cashore 2002) that is dependent on choices made by customers of forest products.

We analyze the institutional development of forest certification as a tool for improving the condition of the world's forests, and examine the difficulties and obstacles in legitimizing NSMD political consumerism in the marketplace. This is done in four steps. First, we trace the development of the origins of the global forest certification system, the Forest Stewardship Council (FSC), and the forest certification programs created by industry and landowner associations designed to compete with the FSC for rulemaking authority. Second, we locate forest certification as the most dominant form of NSMD governance in this area and identify the key features and the role of institutional consumers and global civil society in shaping its development. Third, we conceptualize how the competing NSMD forest certification systems achieve three distinct types of legitimacy.

We conclude by discussing the case study results more generally and what they tell us about: the types of legitimacy that create strong institutionalization and the role of consumers and non-governmental organizations in influencing support for NSMD forest certification along the supply chain.

Emergence of Forest Certification: The FSC and Its Competitors

The FSC's origins can be traced to two related events. First, following widespread scrutiny of tropical deforestation, timber retailers and distributors (themselves often the targets of traditional consumer boycott campaigns) began looking for credible sources of sustainably managed forest products (Meidinger 1999, 4). Second, the failure of the Earth Summit in 1993 to create a global forest convention (Bernstein & Cashore 2000, 2001) led many environmental groups to feel, that they were expending significant effort and resources on state-sanctioned international forums with no discernible policy gains. As a result of these two related events, the World Wide Fund for Nature (WWF) and other transnational groups decided to use market-based mechanisms to influence forest landowners and forest companies to certify their products as coming from sustainable forests. In doing so, they expanded the repertoire of political consumerism from the traditional negative approach that involved boycotts (as discussed in Friedman's chapter) with positive political consumerism in the form of a certification or labeling scheme, a topic taken up in the chapter by Wurzel et al. in this volume.

The FSC was created in 1993 and was legally registered in 1994. It sees forest certification as forcing upward worldwide standards governing sustainable forest management. Its NSMD governance approach diverges considerably from traditional clientelist public policy processes. It institutionalized a tripartite decision-making process that limits business dominance in policy deliberations (Meidinger 1997, 1999). The FSC also forbids direct government involvement in rulemaking and has a wide-ranging policy scope that encompasses environmental and social rules.

Sustainable development forms the basis of the FSC principles.[1] The principles are performance-based and broad in scope. Included among the criteria for certification are principles involving tenure and user rights, community relations, workers' rights, environmental impact, management plans, and monitoring and preservation of old growth forests (Moffat 1998, 44; FSC 1999). The FSC program also requires the creation of regional or national working groups, which are responsible for developing specific indicators and verifiers to apply the principles and criteria more locally.

As support for the FSC certification program increased among forest producers and consumers, industry and forest landowner associations responded with their own versions of forest certification (Cashore et al. 2001). In the United States, the FSC competitor is the American Forest and Paper Associations' (AF&PA) Sustainable Forestry Initiative (SFI) program. In Canada, it is the Canadian Standards Association (CSA) program, initiated by the Canadian Pulp and Paper Association (now the Canadian Forest Products Association). In Europe, there were a number of national FSC competitor programs that developed early in the 1990s. By the late 1990s, the Pan European Forest Certification (PEFC) system, created by landowner associations that felt especially excluded from the FSC process, emerged as the key competitor program. These FSC competitors are now attempting to create an umbrella program to coordinate their programs so that they can develop a better international presence that only the FSC enjoys currently.

The SFI, CSA, and PEFC programs differ from the FSC in that they apply a narrower view of sustainable development and take forest owners' concerns as their point of departure. Their performance requirements follow existing voluntary best management practices (BMPs) programs, legal obligations, and regeneration requirements. Thus, procedurally AF & PA member companies are required to file a report with the SFI regarding their forest management plans and the objectives they are addressing, but specific company data are not reported. Instead, information is aggregated and given to a panel of experts for review. The CPPA turned to the reputed Canadian Standards Association (CSA)[2] to develop a certification governance program. Similar to the SFI, the focus began as "a systems based approach to sustainable forest management" (Hansen & Juslin 1999, 20) where individual companies are required to establish internal "environmental management systems (EMS)" (Moffat 1998, 39). The SFI now permits voluntary third party audits.

The PEFC was created in 1999 and was based on criteria identified at the Helsinki and Lisbon Forest Ministers Conferences in 1993 and 1998 (PEFC International 2001). From the start, the program was explicitly designed to address forest managers' criticisms of the

FSC, which was perceived as not taking private landowners' opinions into account, and as putting unrealistic requirements on individual landowners. Landowners have the majority vote on all decisions made by the PEFC. The PEFC national initiatives developed procedures for certifying entire regions, and leaves the development of certification rules and procedures to the discretion of national initiatives. A European Secretariat, which is dominated by landowner and industry representatives, decides whether to accept national initiatives as part of the PEFC recognition scheme (Hansen & Juslin 1999). However, national initiatives are not required to address the agreed upon criteria and indicators (Ozinga 2001). Overall, the program offers few prescriptive requirements and leaves forest landowners and forest companies in control of the rulemaking process.

As explained in figure 1, the FSC competitor programs operate under a different conception of NSMD governance (Cashore 2002). They believe that business should dominate rulemaking, and nongovernmental and governmental organizations should only be involved in advisory, consultative capacities. Underlying these programs is a strongly held view that there is incongruence between existing forest practices and civil society's perception of these practices. Under the SFI, CSA, and PEFC, procedural approaches are ends in themselves, and individual firms retain greater discretion over implementation of program goals and objectives. This conception of governance draws on environmental management systems approaches that have developed at the international regulatory level (Clapp 1998; Cutler, Haufler, & Porter 1999; Prakash 1999; Kollman & Prakash 2001).

Key Features of NSMD Governance[3]

As can be seen in figure 2, Cashore (2002), using the case of forest certification, has identified four key features that distinguish NSMD governance from other forms of shared governance and private-sector firm level initiatives. They are the role of governments, markets, organized interests (business along the supply chain, and individuals as consumers and value holders), and compliance incentives. Arguably, the most important feature of NSMD governance is that there is no use of state sovereignty to force businesses to comply with transnational standards. There are no popular elections under NSMD governance systems, and no one can be incarcerated

Figure 1
Comparison of FSC and Key FSC Competitor Forest Certification Schemes

PROGRAM	FSC	PEFC	SFI	CSA
Origination	Environmental groups, socially concerned retailers	Landowner	Industry	Industry
Performance or Systems based	Performance	Combination	Combination	Combination
Territorial focus	International	Europe Origin, now International	United States North America	Canada
Verification Options	Third party	Third Party	First, second or third	Third Party
Chain of custody	Yes	Yes	No	Limited
Eco-label or logo	Label and Logo	Logo and label	Logo, label emerging	Logo

Source: Adapted from Moffat (1998, 152), Rickenbach, Fletcher, & Hansen (2000)

Terms: *Performance or systems based* characteristics distinguish programs from whether they focus primarily in the creation of mandatory on the ground rules, governing forest management, or in the development of more flexible and often non-mandatory procedures that address environmental concerns. *Third Party* means an outside organization verifies performance; *Second Party* means that a trade association or other industry group verifies performance; *First Party* means that the company verifies its own record of compliance. *Chain of Custody* refers to whether the programs track the wood from certified forests all the way to the individual consumer. A *logo* is the symbol that certification programs used to advertise their programs. It can be used by companies making claims about their forest practices. An *eco-label* is used along the supply chain to give institutional consumers the ability to discern whether a specific product comes from a certified source.

or fined for failing to comply. This point is important because it means that since the state does not require adherence to its rules, organizations, companies, and landowners must undertake *evaluations* to decide whether they want to comply or not.

This does not mean that governments are not important actors in NSMD governance. They can act as traditional interest groups attempting to influence NSMD policymaking processes by means ranging from offering advice to asking to help write specific rules. They

Figure 2
Key Features of NSMD Governance

Role of the market	Products being regulated are demanded by purchasers further down the supply chain
Role of the state	State does not use its sovereign authority to directly require adherence to rules
Role of stakeholders and broader civil society	Authority is granted through an internal evaluative process
Enforcement	Compliance must be verified

Source: Cashore 2002

are not, however, a source of authority, an important difference when compared to the eco-labeling schemes discussed in this book. Governments can also act as any large organization by making procurement policies and taking other kinds of economic actions that may influence market driven dynamics. In the case of forest certification, governments can act as landowners. Indeed, in many countries public land ownership is a key part of forest policy and, to the extent that governments are persuaded to attempt to adopt certification on their lands, they are drawn into an NSMD system as landowners. Governments may also use their policy authority to influence a particular key target audience of an NSMD governance program, thus creating a hybrid effect in which NSMD logics apply to some audiences but not to others. In such a case, it is crucial to understand whether compliance of a key audience is a result of NSMD dynamics or state authority. For example, a government law requiring that all forestland owners become certified according to the FSC would negate any need to understand landowner evaluations of the FSC, as they are complying as a matter of law rather than of individual calculations.

A second key feature of NSMD governance is that authority is granted to NSMD governance systems by "external audiences" who must undertake their own evaluative decisions about compliance. These evaluations are crucial for understanding whether and how NSMD governance may gain legitimacy to create the rules. External audiences include forest companies and landowners, who are the ultimate target of forest certification as well as environmental and social groups, purchasers of wood products along the supply chain, and individual consumers. These audiences are affected or empowered by the third key feature of NSMD governance, authority granted through the market's supply chain. Much of FSC's efforts to promote and encourage forest owners and managers to apply sustainable forest management (SFM) occur further down the supply and demand chain, that is, toward those value-added industries that demand the raw products, and ultimately to the retailer and its customers (Bruce 1998, chap. 2; Moffat 1998, 42f). To satisfy this demand, the FSC grants not only forestland management certification but also *chain of custody* certification for those companies wishing to purchase and sell FSC products.[4]

The fourth key feature of NSMD governance is the presence of a verification procedure to ensure that the regulated entity actually meets the stated standards. Verification is important, because it provides a validation necessary for legitimacy to occur, and to distinguish products to be consumed along the supply chain. In the case of the FSC and CSA, external auditing companies conduct the mandatory auditing process. The SFI originally developed looser verification procedures, but voluntary independent third party auditing is now the method of choice for most companies operating under SFI. The desire to be seen as a good corporate citizen is linked to a market advantage.

Forest Certification and Legitimacy

To analyze whether forest certification does or does not gain legitimacy from its relevant audiences, we (Cashore 2002; Cashore, Auld, & Newsom 2002; Auld 2001; Newsom 2001; Lawson & Cashore 2002) have used Suchman's seminal work in organizational sociology, in which he identifies three different types of legitimacy that audiences may grant an organization. The motivations of those seeking legitimacy and the durability of the legitimacy granted to the organization are key characteristics. Suchman identifies three different types of legitimacy achievement strategies that organizations may pursue in their efforts to obtain legitimacy, which are important for understanding the interactive process between the external audiences and the NSMD governance system. In this section, we review these categories and then use them to present and analyze the competition among NSMD governance systems (see Cashore

2002). Suchman (1995, 574) defines legitimacy as "a generalized perception or assumption that the actions of an entity are desirable, proper, or appropriate within some socially constructed system of norms, values, beliefs and definitions." He identifies three types of legitimacy that are central to understanding support for forest certification as an NSMD governance system: (1) *pragmatic legitimacy* rests on the "self-interested calculations of an organization's most immediate audiences," where the material "well-being" of the legitimacy grantor is enhanced (Suchman 1995, 589); (2) *moral legitimacy* reflects a "positive, normative evaluation of the organization and its activities and rests not on judgments about whether a given activity promotes the goals of the evaluator, but rather on judgments about whether the activity is 'the right thing to do'" (Suchman 1995, 579); and (3) *cognitive legitimacy,* which is based on neither interests nor moral motivations, but rather on "comprehensibility" or "taken for grantedness." In the former case, legitimacy is given because the actions of an organization are understandable, in the latter case, legitimacy is given because "for things to be otherwise is literally unthinkable" (Suchman 1995, 583). Suchman implies that pragmatic legitimacy may be the least durable. Our case studies show that the pragmatic legitimacy can be durable, but it varies and depends on the external audience that grants it. Moreover, as Suchman predicted, cognitive legitimacy is probably the most durable, though we cannot draw this conclusion because forest certification has not been in existence long enough for us to make this assessment.

Suchman noted that organizations seeking legitimacy are rarely passive. They actively employ *legitimacy achievement strategies.* This assumption is confirmed in our research on forest certification. The battle for legitimacy was actively fought by the FSC and its competitors on different fronts. They also used a variety of techniques. Suchman identified three types of achievement strategies, which are important for our review.

Manipulation achievement strategies refer to those cases in which organizations actively seek to change preferences of those from which it wants legitimacy. Thus, the FSC and its core supporters, such as the WWF, have been actively involved in the creation of new interests by organizing buyers groups (Rametsteiner et al. 1998; Hansen 1998) as institutional consumers now operating in Europe (Mirbach 1997; WWF UK 2001), North America (Certified Forest

Products Council 1999), and globally through the recent creation of a global forest and trade network (The Global Forest and Trade Network 2000). Manipulation strategies are important because, if successful, they grant legitimacy to forest certification programs and allow them to stay closer to the core conception of certification for which they initially were created.

In addition, forest certification programs can attempt to achieve legitimacy by using *conforming strategies* on external audiences. For example, our cases show that the FSC has changed its rules governing harvesting in old growth forests, added a new rule on forest plantations, and developed small landowner initiatives, all in an attempt to gain pragmatic legitimacy from supply-side interests. Likewise, FSC competitor programs are constantly adding new rules and including new stakeholders in an effort to appeal to retailers, who are currently demanding only FSC wood. Conforming strategies are seen as less desirable by certification programs and stand in contrast to manipulation strategies because they alter certification programs. They often move the program slightly away from its original conception. Indeed, part of the question is how far FSC, and FSC competitor programs, can go in conforming to gain legitimacy from non-core interests without risking disapproval from their core audiences. Conforming strategies are often undertaken when manipulation strategies have failed to alter significant degrees of support.

Finally, certification programs may attempt to achieve legitimacy by using active *informing strategies* that focus on those audiences likely to grant legitimacy, if they were simply aware of the program. Informing strategies include advertising campaigns or information targeted to like-minded, organized interests. Our research found that informing was used as a strategy in the case of forest certification, though less so than the other two legitimacy achievement strategies. Identifying whether a program uses conforming, manipulating, or informing strategies is important because it directly addresses whether certification programs remain close to their original goals, or whether they must weaken their approach to forest sustainability in an effort to become accepted in the marketplace. Because conforming strategies are less preferred than manipulation ones, identification of conforming strategies helps us establish when a certification program is having difficulty gaining support.

Differences in Legitimacy Granting in Forest Certification

We applied the legitimacy types and legitimacy achievement strategies to our cases and found key differences in terms of support and the ability of FSC to pursue manipulation versus conforming strategies (for a detailed analysis, see Cashore, Auld, & Newsom 2002). FSC gained moral legitimacy from its core audience of environmental and social organizations and from key retailers. It gained scant legitimacy from forest companies and landowners, who granted pragmatic and moral legitimacy instead to FSC competitor programs created by their own associations. In British Columbia, Canada, the FSC made significant inroads through active legitimacy achievement strategies, with the result that initial forest company rejections of the FSC gave way to a situation in which seven of the ten largest companies in the province indicated some support for it (Cashore, Auld, & Newsom 2002). However, in the United States, most large forest companies continue to reject the FSC and have instead strongly supported the AF&PA's Sustainable Forestry Initiative. In the United Kingdom, state forest owners reluctantly supported the FSC, while small, private landowners initially turned to the PEFC (a stance that has proven highly volatile with landowner associations recently shifting to a position of greater neutrality). The PEFC has gained the support of most state and private forest landowners in Germany. The FSC is supported by a minority of state forest landowners whose German political masters support an environmental agenda (Auld 2001; Newsom 2001). In Sweden, large industrial forest companies support the FSC, while small landowners reject it (Cashore, Auld, & Newson 2002).

Why Different Legitimacy Achievement Patterns?

Five interrelated factors help explain divergence in legitimacy achievement (Cashore, Auld, & Newsom 2002). They are regional dependence on foreign markets, priority given to forest management issues on the political agenda, character of forest sector ownership, associational systems of forest companies and landowners, and nature and structure of FSC's competitor programs. Each factor is discussed in this section.

First, in regard to a region's degree of dependence on foreign markets, our study shows that forest companies and landowners in a region that sells a high proportion of its forest products to foreign markets appear more susceptible to FSC legitimacy manipulation achievement strategies when institutional consumers further down the supply chain are located outside the regional borders. For example, in the case of British Columbia, environmental groups pressured demand-side companies in Europe and the United States to terminate their contracts with companies operating in the region that did not conform to FSC criteria (Stanbury 2000; Vertinsky 1997). We also found that when a region is a net importer of raw materials, domestic FSC legitimacy achievement strategies are enhanced when retailers demand that foreign and domestic supply are subject to the same scrutiny. Thus, the FSC is more able to pursue manipulation strategies when institutional consumers make purchasing commitments that apply to both domestic and foreign products. For instance, the UK case reveals that when the supply-side in a region is small and cannot produce the volume of forest products required to meet local demand it becomes susceptible to competition from FSC imports (Auld 2001). When the British home improvement retailer B & Q issued an ultimatum to it suppliers that, by the end of 1999, it intended to purchase only FSC certified wood, local processors were cast under the same net, even though they were not the source of original concerns (Stanbury 2000; National Home Center News 1998; DIY 1998). In fact, competition from FSC-certified suppliers in Sweden and the fear that countries in the Baltic States would follow suit (Tickel & WWF 2000; Hansen & Juslin 1999) made UK local producers recognize the need to protect their UK market share by conforming to FSC sustainability requirements.

The second key explanatory factor is the extent to which forest management issues are on the domestic public policy agenda or not. When forest management practices are seen as an issue for the public policy agenda, forest companies and landowners will take independent action to avoid potential political controversy. We found that forest companies are more likely to give the FSC pragmatic legitimacy, when forestry practices are perceived as a major problem in need of government action. Pragmatic legitimacy becomes even more important when governmental initiatives fail to remove the issue as a perceived problem. For example, despite a decade of governmental efforts in British Columbia, the deep dissatisfaction that existed among many environmental groups and a significant section of the general public forced forest companies to look at the FSC as a way of avoiding constant scrutiny and ongoing consumer boycott and market-based campaigns. In contrast, in Germany, where there was no discernible societal support or years of direct action campaigns against German landowners, the PEFC was successful in its efforts to gain legitimacy from forest landowners (Newsom 2001).

The third key explanatory factor is the nature of forestland ownership. Our research reveals that forest companies and landowners, in regions where land ownership is fragmented, will be less likely to grant the FSC pragmatic legitimacy because of the high transaction and implementation costs. This is illustrated in the case of the U.S. Southeast where most forestland is owned by non-industrial private forest landowners. Wood processors in the region require a continuous fiber supply in order to feed their highly specialized, capital-intensive mills. Consequently, industrial forest companies consider the logistical problems associated with the FSC chain of custody requirements overwhelming, given their large number of small fiber suppliers. Our research also reveals that many forest landowners in this region are ideologically opposed to FSC-style certification (Newsom et al. 2002; Vlosky 2000), which helped convince many industrial companies to give pragmatic support to the FSC competitor, the SFI (Auld, Cashore, & Newsom 2002). At the same time a small number of large landowners in the region were more easily converted to the FSC because they enjoyed economies of scale in the costs of implementing FSC certification. The United Kingdom is between British Columbia and the U.S. Southeast with 35 percent of its forestland held by the government (Forest Industries Council of Great Britain 2000) and the other by non-industrial private forest landowners. These conditions led the FSC to apply a conforming strategy to meet the actual needs of these companies. It did so by changing the threshold percent requirements for an FSC product to carry a label. The FSC was even able to use successful manipulation strategies by targeting large areas of government lands, which meant that processors had sufficient FSC wood supply even without the certification of any large portion of the private growers. Thus, the presence of one key landowner open to certification has made possible broader acceptance of the FSC in the UK (Auld 2001).

Our fourth factor is the nature of forest company and landowner associational systems. This characteristic is necessary to understand competition for legitimacy and FSC legitimacy achievement strategies. In particular, members of the supply-side in a region, where companies and landowners are well-represented and unified, are less likely, everything else being equal, to grant the FSC pragmatic legitimacy. For instance, in the United States, a highly centralized associational system under the AF & PA (Cashore 1997) allowed the FSC competitor program, the SFI, to undertake highly strategic choices to gain its support among large industrial companies and minimize the influence of the FSC. Once support was granted, the SFI turned its legitimacy achievement strategies to the institutional consumers down the supply chain in the hopes of convincing them to support SFI certification in addition to their FSC commitments. The SFI facilitated these efforts by undertaking a number of conforming strategies (e.g., developing tougher standards and third-party procedures) and expanding its decision-making institutions to include conservation and professional organizations. The Canadian forest sector, by contrast, was represented by a fragmented and regionally focused associational system (Coleman 1987, 1988), which inhibited the adoption of a unified stance on certification issues. This situation explains the pragmatic legitimacy that the supply-side in BC has given to the FSC. When the FSC became a serious issue, no industry association had a clear mandate to develop a response. Once a few companies showed an interest in pursuing FSC, other companies followed suit.

The final key legitimacy mediating factor is the nature and structure of FSC's competitor programs. Our research indicates that, in order for FSC competitor programs to maintain support from companies and landowners (or at least not have to share legitimacy with the FSC), they must develop a program that walks a fine line between being too prescriptive (which means that the costs of FSC do not seem more difficult) and too weak (so that the market will not accept the program). Supply-side members' decisions to support the FSC (or not) are influenced strongly by how well the competitor program balances costs and benefits. In our Canadian cases, the standards of an FSC competitor program were perceived as being too rigorous to be acceptable by the supply side. Canadian forest companies initially endorsed the CSA. However, its costs, level of public scrutiny, and time commitments eventually met, or exceeded, those of the FSC. At the same time, the program could not offer the potential market benefits of the FSC. Consequently, what had been a program that was meant to limit FSC success became one among a number of certification alternatives. In its attempts to gain support from the environmental community by conforming to existing Canadian public policy norms about public consultation, it appears that the program lost some of its pragmatic appeal with the industry.

Legitimacy, Core Audiences, and Durability of NSMD Governance

The emergence of NSMD and legitimacy, it is granted, varies according to the region being studied, the organizations granting legitimacy, and the nature of the competition between the FSC and its competitor programs. General patterns emerge from these complex dynamics that address legitimacy granting and the durability of NSMD institutions. First, both FSC and its competitors have core audiences, whose support is fundamental to the existence of the NSMD governance system. The FSC core audience is composed of environmental groups, likeminded social interests, and a small handful of retailers whose values resonate with the FSC approach. The FSC competitors' core audience is forest companies and/or landowners who strongly support a more flexible, discretionary approach to forest certification for pragmatic and moral reasons. Just how far the FSC and its competitors can go in undertaking conforming strategies in their efforts to woo non-core audience members along the supply chain (forest companies and forest landowners for the FSC and institutional consumers for the FSC competitors), is a very important question in need of further research.

Research in public policy asserts that deep core values held by actors in a policy subsystem are hard to change and provide the key to understanding the potential success of conforming strategies (Sabatier & Jenkins-Smith 1993). Our research indicates that this factor is an important brake on FSC and FSC competitors' efforts to gain legitimacy. For example, as a member of the FSC core audience, the U.S. Sierra Club's opposition to FSC certification on U.S. federal lands (they wish to see all these lands protected from harvesting) has limited FSC efforts to gain an immediate and quick source of sustainably managed timber (MacCleery 1999). Similarly, U.S. forest companies are increasingly concerned that the SFI's new Sustainable Forestry Board and efforts to accommodate moderate conservation groups as The Nature Conservancy and Conservation International, might eventually result in policies that they view as too prescriptive.

For the FSC, there is a clear relationship between maintaining moral legitimacy from its core audience and achieving pragmatic legitimacy from forest companies and landowners. So far, its success has been mixed, with British Columbia and the UK eventually yielding some degree of pragmatic support from key companies and landowners, while efforts to achieve the same support in the United States, the Canadian Maritimes, and Germany have been hampered. Whether forest companies granting pragmatic legitimacy to the FSC results in cognitive legitimacy over time remains arguably the most important question for future research on NSMD governance.

Yet one should be wary about accepting Suchman's assumption that pragmatic legitimacy is always the least durable type. For profit maximizing companies, pragmatic legitimacy seems more durable than moral legitimacy. Pragmatic evaluations will trump moral ones and are thus potentially more durable because companies want to stay in business. But such support is double-edged. While it may mean that companies will support certification when it offers a clear market advantage, the reverse is also true. Companies granting only pragmatic legitimacy will reconsider their support if they view certification as a liability. Indeed, understanding the conditions that produce *both* moral and pragmatic legitimacy appears to be the key to durability.

Conclusion

Forest certification is, first and foremost, about restructuring power relations among competing interests over use and exploitation of the world's forest resources. Environmental groups, dissatisfied with public policy processes, created their own governance systems and used the marketplace to force or encourage compliance. Their governing institutions created corporatist style, tripartite procedures (though redefined to include business, environmental, and social divisions) that explicitly forbade business domination in the policy process. These institutions directly challenged traditional business-government dominated clientelist policy networks that, until recently, have characterized domestic and international forest policy development. In response, business and landowner associations have created their own NSMD governance systems that offer a more traditional approach to forest resource management.

Competition for legitimacy on forest certification appears to legitimize the idea of forest certification among a wide range of audiences. Competition can at the same time eliminate the original FSC conception of NSMD governance, or result in a compromise that may or may not be supported by either set of core audiences. An FSC-style conception of governance (or even a hybrid conception), accepted as legitimate by an array of actors along the supply chain, can conceivably alter the power relations in traditional environmental governance in two ways. It grants more decision-making authority to non-business interests than many traditional public policymaking processes. It also makes it more difficult for environmental organizations to criticize businesses that abide by FSC rules as environmentally unfriendly. This makes it difficult for environmental organizations to demand government action, as the businesses possess the legitimacy granted to them by the NGO-supported NSMD governance system. Government may also refer to NSMD governance systems to explain why it has decided not to take regulatory action on environmental concerns. Thus, NSMD governance systems allow governments to avoid taking political responsibility in areas important for global common well-being.

What is clear is that domestic legitimacy contests are far from predetermined. They are influenced not only by a region's place in the global forest economy, the nature of public policy problem definition, and land ownership patterns and associational systems, but also by the strategic choices made by the FSC and its competitor programs. What remains to be seen is what kind of role final-end-product consumers will play in the emergence of NSMD governance. It is possible that, if one system emerges as appropriate for institutional consumers further down the supply chain, then individual consumer choices may matter very little for understanding the emergence of NSMD governance. If, however, end-product consumers are able to choose among competing certification programs in the marketplace, they could conceivably be very influential in determining which type of NSMD governance system will be seen as legitimate.

As this is an ongoing struggle for legitimacy, it is important that research carefully analyzes the types of evaluations that occur and explores how pragmatic and moral legitimacy granting might eventually lead to the granting of cognitive legitimacy. If NSMD governance gains cognitive legitimacy from an array of external audiences, it could shift rule-making authority from traditional public policy processes and, thus, radically reshape existing power struggles over resource and environmental protection. Thus, political consumers—be they institutional actors as business or government in its procurement function, or individual families just wanting to buy new patio furniture—may play a crucial role in reshaping the parameters of environmental practice globally.

Notes

1. Originally a two-chamber format was created with social and environmental interests together in one chamber with 75 percent of the votes, and an economic chamber with 25 percent of the votes. There are currently three equal chambers among these groups with one-third of the votes each. Each chamber is further divided equally between the North and South.
2. The CSA program actually contains two standards: one explains how to develop an environmental forest management system, and the other focuses on auditing requirements (Hansen & Juslin 1999, 20).
3. This section draws heavily from, and is based on, Cashore (2002).
4. Likewise, in the case of the Marine Stewardship Council (MSC), sustainable fisheries are promoted by offering market demand that can be accessed by companies adhering to their rules through a chain of custody provision (Simpson 2001).

References

Auld, Graeme. 2001. "Explaining Certification Legitimacy: An Examination of Forest Sector Support for Forest Certification Programs in the United States Pacific Coast, the United Kingdom, and British Columbia, Canada." Master's thesis, School of Forestry and Wildlife Sciences, Auburn University.

Auld, Graeme, Benjamin Cashore, & Deanna Newsom. 2002. "Perspectives on Forest Certification: A Survey Examining Differences Among the U.S. Forest Sectors' Views of Their Forest Certification Alternatives," in L. Teeter, B. Cashore, & D. Zhang, eds., *Forest Policy for Private Forestry: Global and Regional Challenges.* Wallingford, UK: CABI Publishing.

Bernstein, Steven. 2001. "Legitimacy in Global Governance: Three Conceptions." Paper presented at the annual meeting of the American Political Science Association, 29 August-1 September, San Francisco, California.

___, & Benjamin Cashore. 2001. "The International-Domestic Nexus: The Effects of International Trade and Environmental Politics on the Canadian Forest Sector," in M. Howlett, ed., *Canadian Forest Policy: Regimes, Policy Dynamics and Institutional Adaptations.* Toronto: University of Toronto Press.

___. 2000. "Globalization. Four Paths of Internationalization and Domestic Policy Change: The Case of Eco-forestry Policy Change in British Columbia, Canada." *Canadian Journal of Political Science* 33 (1): 67-99.

Bruce, Robert A. 1998. "The Comparison of the FSC Forest Certification and ISO Environmental Management Schemes and Their Impact on a Small Retail Business." Master's thesis, University of Edinburgh Management School, UK.

Cashore, Benjamin. 1997. *Governing Forestry: Environmental Group Influence in British Columbia and the U.S. Pacific Northwest.* Toronto: University of Toronto, Department. of Political Science.

___. 2002. "Legitimacy and the Privatization of Environmental Governance: How Non State Market-Driven (NSMD) Governance Systems Gain Rule Making Authority." *Governance Journal* 15 (4) (October).

___, Graeme Auld, & Deanna Newsom. 2002. "Forest Certification (Eco-labeling) Programs and their Policy-Making Authority: Explaining Divergence Among North American and European Case Studies." *Forest Policy and Economics* (forthcoming).

Certified Forest Products Council. 1999. Certified Forest Products Council packet. Beaverton, Oregon.

Clapp, Jennifer. 1998. "The Privatization of Global Environmental Governance: ISO 14000 and the Developing World." *Environmental Governance* 4 (3): 295-316.

Coleman, William D. 1987. "Federalism and Interest Group Organization," in H. Bakvis, & W. M. Chandler, eds., *Federalism and the Role of the State*. Toronto: University of Toronto Press.

___. 1988. *Business and Politics: A Study of Collective Action*. Kingston: McGill-Queen's University Press.

Cutler, Claire, Virginia Haufler, & Tony Porter. 1999. "Private Authority and International Affairs," in C. Cutler, V. Haufler, & T. Porter, eds., *Private Authority in International Politics*.

DIY. 1998. Hodkinson Tells World Bank of B&Q's FSC Plans. DIY, 23 January 1998.

Forest Alliance of British Columbia. 2000. *Forest Alliance Pleased with Provincial Government Commitment to Certification*. Vancouver, BC: Forest Alliance of British Columbia.

Forest Industry Council of Great Britain. 2000. *A Reference for the Forestry Industry*. London: Forest Industry Council of Great Britain.

FSC. 1999. *FSC Principles and Criteria*. Forest Stewardship Council.

Hansen, Eric. 1998. "Chapter 3: Certified Forest Products Market Place." *Forest Products Annual Market Review*, edited by U. N. T. Committee. Geneva, Switzerland: United Nations Timber Committee.

___, & Heikki Juslin. 1999. *The Status of Forest Certification in the ECE Region*. New York and Geneva: United Nations, Timber Section, Trade Division, UN-Economic Commission for Europe.

Kollman, Kelly, & Asseem Prakash. 2001. "Green by Choice: Cross-National Variations in Firms' Responses to EMS-Based Environmental Regimes." *World Politics* 53 (3): 399-430.

Lawson, James, & Benjamin Cashore. 2002. "Firm Choices on Sustainable Forestry Forest Certification: The Case of JD Irving, Ltd," in L. Teeter, B. Cashore, & D. Zhang, eds., *Forest Policy for Private Forestry: Global and Regional Challenges*. Wallingford, UK: CABI Publishing.

MacCleery, Doug. 1999. *NFS Certification Issues*. Washington, DC: USDA Forest Service.

Meidinger, Errol E. 1997. "Look Who's Making the Rules: International Environmental Standard Setting by Non-Governmental Organizations." *Human Ecology Review* 4 (1): 52-54.

___. 1999. "Private Environmental Regulation, Human Rights, and Community." *Buffalo Environmental Law Journal* 7: 123-237.

Mirbach, Martin von. 1997. "Demanding Good Wood." *Alternatives Journal* 23 (summer).

Moffat, Andrea C. 1998. "Forest Certification: An Examination of the Comptability of the Canadian Standards Association and Forest Stewardship Council Systems in the Maritime Region." Halifax, Nova Scotia: Dalhousie University (MES, Environmental Studies).

National Home Center News. 1998. "B&Q Pledges to Work towards Forest Certification." *National Home Center News* 24 (2): 9.

Newsom, Deanna. 2001. "Achieving Legitimacy? Exploring Competing Forest Certification Programs' Actions to Gain Forest Manager Support in the U.S. Southeast, Germany, and British Columbia, Canada." Auburn, AL: Auburn University, School of Forestry and Wildlife Sciences.

___, Benjamin Cashore, Graeme Auld, & Jim Granskog. 2002. "Forest Certification in the Heart of Dixie: A Survey Of Alabama Landowners," in L. Teeter, B. Cashore, & D. Zhang, eds., *Forest Policy for Private Forestry: Global and Regional Challenges.* Wallingford, UK: CABI Publishing.

Ozinga, Saskia. 2001. "Behind the Logo, an Environmental and Social Assessment of Forest Certification Schemes. Moreton-in-Marsh: Fern, based on case studies by WWF France." Taiga Consulting, Taiga Rescue Network, Natural Resource Defense Council (NRDC), Fern, Finish Natural League, and Greenpeace.

PEFC International. 2001. Welcome to PEFC. 2001 [cited 2001]. Available from <www.pefc.org>.

Prakash, Asseem. 1999. "A New-Institutional Perspective on ISO 14000 and Responsible Care." *Business Strategy and the Environment* 8: 322-35.

Rametsteiner, Ewald, Peter Schwarzbauer, Heikki Juslin, Jari Karna, Roger Cooper, John Samuel, Michael Becker, & Tobias Kuhn. 1998. *Potential Markets for Certified Forest Products in Europe.* Joensuu, Finland: European Forest Institute.

Rickenbach, Mark, Rick Fletcher, & Eric Hansen. 2000. *An Introduction to Forest Certification.* Corvallis, OR: Oregon State University Extension Service.

Sabatier, Paul A., & Hank C. Jenkins-Smith. 1993. "The Advocacy Coalition Framework: Assessment, Revisions, and Implications for Scholars and Practitioners," in P. A. Sabatier, & H. C. Jenkins-Smith, eds., *Policy Change and Learning: An Advocacy Coalition Approach.* Boulder, CO: Westview Press.

Simpson, Scott. 2001. "B. C. Salmon Industry Seeks Ecological Certification: Industry's Ability to Meet Global Council's Standards Hangs on Sustainability Question." *Vancouver Sun*, Thursday, April 26. Internet posting.

Stanbury, William T. 2000. *Environmental Groups and the International Conflict Over the Forest of British Columbia 1990 to 2000.* Vancouver, BC: SFU-UBC Centre for the Study of Government and Business.

Suchman, Mark C. 1995. "Managing Legitimacy: Strategic and Institutional Aproaches." *Academy of Management Review* 20 (3): 571-610.

The Global Forest and Trade Network. 2000. The Global Forest and Trade Network: Leaders for responsible forestry: Forest Stewardship Council, WWF.

Tickel, Oliver. *World Wildlife Fund for Nature. 2000. Certification: A Future for the World's Forests.* Godalming, Surrey, UK: WWF Forests for Life Campaign.

Vertinsky, Ilan, & William T. Stanbury. 1997. "Boycotts in Conflicts over Forestry Issues: The Case of Clayoquot Sound." *Commonwealth Forestry Review* 76 (1): 18-24.

Vlosky, Richard P. 2000. "What Do Non-Industrial Private Forest Landowners in Louisiana Think about Third Party Certification." *Forest Landowner* 59 (6): 45-47.

WWF UK. 2001. History of the WWF 95+ Group [Online information]. WWF-UK 2001 [cited March 2, 2001]. Available from <www.wwf-uk.org/95+group/1286History.html#>.

Part IV

Politicizing Consumers and Change in Politics

Who Are These Political Consumers Anyway? Survey Evidence from Denmark

Jørgen Goul Andersen and Mette Tobiasen

Introduction

In recent years, "political consumerism" has increasingly been discussed as a new, independent form of political participation and channel of political influence. A political consumer is usually defined as a person who makes value considerations when buying or refraining from buying certain goods and products, in order to promote a political goal (Micheletti 2000, 3).[1] For example, consumers may be concerned with environmental consequences, or they may wish to punish producers who use child-laborers and countries that violate standards of human rights. Unlike the theoretical textbook consumers, who act as utility-maximizing individuals exclusively in terms of their personal interests without concern for the social (or aggregate) consequences of individual acts of consumption, a political consumer is concerned with exactly such consequences. This breaks a fundamental division of labor between economics and politics, which are supposed to function according to different logics or languages. The same holds for the political consumer's kin: the political investor.

But how significant is this phenomenon? Does it truly deserve to be conceptualized as a genuinely new mode of political participation? Is it really a *political* phenomenon? What macro-level societal and institutional changes explain the emergence of political consumerism? Who are the political consumers? These questions will be addressed below on the basis of a nationwide representative study—the "Danish Citizenship Study"—conducted in 2000 as part of the "Danish Democracy and Power Project."[2] It will be argued that on the macro-level, political consumerism should be interpreted within a framework of globalization, individualization, and changing political opportunity structures; correspondingly, on the individual level, we suggest that political consumerism forms a relatively coherent phenomenon, and that it is a conscious form of political participation rooted in political engagement and belief in its efficiency.

Conceptualization and Hypotheses

Before the concept of political consumerism was coined in the 1990s (Svendsen 1995), such phenomena were mainly analyzed within the lexicon of consumer boycotts. For long, the study of boycott actions has been a specialized field in the study of action groups (Friedman 1999); in Europe, boycotts were considered part of a wider cluster of political participation known as political action at the individual level, and as "New Social Movements" at the aggregate level (Barnes, Kaase et al. 1979). However, political consumerism reaches beyond boycott actions, as illustrated in figure 1.

There are at least four ways in which political consumerism goes beyond the classic boycott action. First, abstaining from buying certain products does not always signify collective mobilization orga-

Figure 1
Delineation between Political and Non-Political Consumption

	Political consumption: Influence other actors/ collective outcome		Non-political consumption: Satisfy personal need or complying with religious/personal norm	
	collective/ organized	individual/ non-organized	normative	utilitarian (ordinary consumption)
Abstaining from buying (negative pol. consumption)	boyott action	political-ethical consumer	e.g. religious prohibition	
Deliberately choosing (positive pol. consumption)	solidarity action	political-ethical consumer	e.g. ethnic solidarity	ordinary consumption

nized by an action group. Second, political consumerism also includes deliberately choosing certain products for political reasons (buycott), referred to as a distinction between negative and positive political consumption. Third, boycott actions are temporary, whereas political consumerism includes routine patterns of behavior. Finally, context matters. Within the framework of globalization, political consumerism takes on a particular significance, sometimes providing the only opportunity to influence outcomes as transnational companies are outside the regulatory powers of national governments.

These are some of the *analytical* reasons for interpreting political consumerism as a new phenomenon, irrespective of how it relates empirically to other forms of political participation at present. But some of the arguments above raise the question of whether political consumerism should be considered political at all. What, if anything, is political about buying organic products? Are there any differences between political consumers and "green consumers?" We suggest that the criterion of a deliberative attempt to influence or change society (Halkier 1994, 24, 29-36) is the only possible way to distinguish between "ordinary" consumption and "political" consumption. Whereas "ordinary" consumers are only concerned with satisfying a purely personal need, a political consumer must, at a minimum, be concerned about aggregate implications; that is, be concerned about the possibility of deliberately using his or her "voting right as a consumer" to affect aggregate outcomes. This is what ultimately blurs the division between politics and economics; this consciousness about collective effects is what provides, in a minimalist version, a sense of "imagined community." Thus, buying organic products only because of taste should not be considered political consumerism. Finally, there are instances of normatively determined acts of consumption that cannot be considered political: first and foremost, compliance with religious or personal norms as found among vegetarians or among people who abstain from buying meat from certain animals. Our operational definitions below correspond directly to the definitions above.

Assuming that political consumerism is an analytically independent phenomenon, we can now address the question of how to explain and interpret it. Although our analysis is based on micro-level survey data, we believe that the most relevant questions belong to the macro level and should be given priority, even though the link to micro-level evidence is less straightforward. In the first place, we assume that political consumerism is a genuine *political* phenomenon. If this is true, it should be at least as strongly linked to political engagement and other forms of political participation; furthermore, people should believe that it has an effect.

Next, we suggest that political consumerism may be interpreted within the context of globalization (Beck 1998; Held et al. 1999; Giddens 1990, 2000). Technological globalization in terms of the revolution in technology and communication across borders has increased the potential for this type of political action. Furthermore, due to the increasing focus on environmental and other global problems, as well as economic globalization in terms of liberalized investments and other capital movements across borders, there are obvious issues around which citizens can mobilize as political consumers. Acting as a political consumer may often be the only opportunity to exert influence, or at least an obvious supplement to other methods. Besides, it may be quite efficient, as transnational companies are perceived as vulnerable to the slightest change in market shares, or damage to their corporate image. Likewise, threats to exports and tourism revenue may cause governments to become more sensitive to certain issues. The hypothesis that political consumerism is linked to globalization cannot be tested directly; but as an indirect test, we will examine whether political consumerism is related to global political orientations.

Thirdly, we suggest that political consumerism is linked to movement towards more individualized forms of political participation, appropriate for a "postmodern" society. Such a society is one in which people have larger political resources, except time; where conflicts are too crosscutting or issues are too short-lived to be represented by parties and associations; and where media and public opinion play an important role (Beck 1998; Held et al. 1999; Giddens 1990, 2000). As an indirect test, we will look for clusters of individualized forms of political participation. Besides, this suggestion contrasts with Beck's (1994, 1997) assumption that people flee the formal political system for other political arenas, because they do not believe that the established system can cope with the new challenges. According to Beck, this manifests itself in distrust in politicians and in the institutions of the political system. An alternative hypothesis suggested here is that political consumerism is instead a supplement, and therefore positively linked to other forms of political participation, and at least not negatively linked to political trust.

These are the chapter's main hypotheses. From our perspective, explaining individual-level variations as such is less theoretically interesting. We limit ourselves to examine, in accordance with theories of postmaterialism (e.g., Inglehart 1990), whether political consumerism is associated with postmaterialist values, and whether political consumerism is linked to income, in accordance with rational choice theory.

Political Consumerism—An Overview

This section provides an overview of political consumerism in Denmark. How widespread is this phenomenon? Has it increased over time? What are the social characteristics of political consumers? As indicated above, we distinguish between two dimensions: (1) boycotting goods and products for political reasons ("negative" consumerism), and (2) buycotting—deliberately choosing certain goods or products over others for political reasons ("positive" consumerism) (Micheletti 2000). The answers are presented in table 1.[3]

Table 1
Boycotting and Deliberately Choosing Products for Political, Ethical, or Environmental Reasons, 2000. Percentages (N=1640)

		Deliberately bought certain products for political, ethical or environmental reasons within last 12 months		total
		yes	no	
Boycotted certain products within last 12 months	yes	19	2	21
	no	26	53	79
Total		45	55	100
Index of political consumerism: 2. both of these: 1. at least one (typically positive only): 0. none:		19 28 53		

Question wording: "There are different ways of attempting to bring about improvements or resist deterioration in society. During the last 12 months, have you done any of the following?"

Table 2
Political Cosumerism by Social Characteristics. Percentages.

	0	1	2	N=(100%)
Men	56	27	17	822
Women	50	29	21	818
18-29 years	46	32	23	329
30-39 years	47	30	23	321
40-49 years	45	33	22	291
50-59 years	54	28	18	289
60-69 years	58	24	18	188
70 years +	75	19	6	224
primary school (7-9 years)	69	18	13	659
primary school (10 years)	49	33	18	586
high school ('gymnasium')	31	39	30	393
no vocational training	64	21	15	539
apprenticeship level	40	24	16	484
short further education	42	36	22	144
college level	35	39	26	276
university level	33	39	28	171
0-149.999 DkK annually	61	24	15	555
150-199.999 DkK	56	26	19	226
200-299.999 DkK	46	32	22	469
300-349.999 DkK	45	32	23	104
350-399.999 DkK	37	41	22	71
400.000 DkK or more	43	33	24	122
mca analysis	eta	beta	beta	beta
Gender	.07	.05	.06	.11
Age	.20	.13	.11	.16
basic education	.28	.17	.17	.08
further education	.23	.14	.13	.11
personal income	.15		.05	
political interest	.28			.26
party choice	.19			.11
R^2		10.5 %	10.5 %	18.1 %

It turns out that 21 percent of those surveyed had boycotted products within the last twelve months before the interview, whereas 45 percent had deliberately chosen certain products for political reasons. The answers were largely cumulative: among the 21 percent who had participated in a boycott, 19 percent had also deliberately chosen certain products. We have thus formed an additive scale from the two questions where 19 percent are both positive and negative political consumers, 28 percent are positive or negative (but almost always positive only), and 53 percent not political consumers at all. Because it is nearly cumulative, we may use the scale both as a classification and as a measure of intensity.

For boycotting, we also have a comparable measure from 1990, albeit with a reference period of three years rather than twelve months. Apparently boycotting has increased, but not very much. In 1990, 22 percent had boycotted certain products. This is almost the same as in 2000, but taking into account the difference in reference period and inferring from its effect on other measures of participation, there seems clearly to have been a minor increase. Boycotting in particular may be subject to considerable fluctuations because of the influence of major campaigns and events that potentially mobilize citizens to act as political consumers. However, in this case, there were no large-scale campaigns such as the "Brent Spar" campaign or any testing of nuclear weapons before any of these measurements, so that the (inferred) small increase seems reliable as a long-term trend.

Turning to social variations, we note in table 2 that political consumerism is slightly more widespread among women than among men, but the difference is only six percentage points (see more on the role of women in political consumerism in Micheletti in this volume). Generational differences are also modest: political consumerism declines slightly from the age of fifty (mainly due to education), and sharply from the age of seventy (a genuine age effect). We might have expected higher participation among the young, but it should be added that in most other areas, young people are significantly less active than the middle aged.

Political consumption is strongly determined by education: among respondents with only seven to nine years of primary school, 31 percent are political consumers, compared to 69 percent among high school graduates. A similar pattern is found when it comes to further (vocational) education. Although there is some overlap, both have

---

Political Investors

We also included two indicators about political investments, one directed to members of occupational pension funds and another directed to shareholders. As most shareholders only hold shares in their bank or their own work place, we have also calculated results for what could be called "genuine investors" in shares, who constitute only 11 percent of the adult population.

The proportion who wants their pension fund to take ethical and political considerations, even at the expense of return to the members, is rather high—at 40 percent, or close to the proportion of political consumers. When we asked about having "considerable ethical or political concerns" when managing their own shares, however, there were not many political investors left. Even if we leave out investors who have little choice as they only hold shares in their own firms or in their bank, only 7 percent remained among those labeled "genuine investors;" on balance, this group is even more biased against political investments. One interpretation is that people are more egoistic about their own money. But an alternative interpretation is that people do not feel that they are in a position to take big personal economic risks just to serve some ethical purpose; clearly, the potential costs are much higher for political investments through pension funds.

Genuine private investors who take significant political considerations only constitute about 1 percent of the adult population. Pension funds, on the other hand, are potentially very powerful, and even though a majority of members favor pure "shareholder value," the funds are unlikely to be entirely unaffected by the minority that embraces broader concerns. From an influence point of view, this is potentially very interesting. From a participation point of view, however, political consumerism remains the most salient.

Source: Goul Andersen & Tobiasen. 2001.

highly significant effects. The bivariate association with income is also positive. We might think that the higher concentration of political consumers among people with higher education is due to higher incomes, and thus the ability to afford the often more expensive products. However, it turns out that the income effect is completely spurious, in that after considering differences in education the causal effect of income is close to zero. Lower income per se, in other words, does not cause individuals to abstain from political consumerism.

Is Political Consumerism Political?

With a participation rate of 47 percent, political consumerism compares quite well as a mode of political participation: the comparable rate of political action (including signatures) is 32 percent; 23 percent are members of a political interest association, and only 50 percent voted in the 1999 European Elections (data not presented). But is political consumerism a truly *political* form of participation? The data presented below suggest that it certainly is. First, political consumerism is strongly related to political interest and to party choice. Among those much interested in politics, 66 percent are political consumers; among those "not very" interested, the figure is just 36 percent; and among the politically apathetic only 20 percent (data not presented).[4] As the MCA analysis in table 2 reveals, this association is genuine and explains most of the effect of basic education, that is, this effect is mainly mediated through political engagement, and not income. Nor is it mediated through postmaterialist values: we found little association with postmaterialism whatsoever (data not presented).[5]

Furthermore, political consumerism is considered a quite efficient form of political participation. Table 3 presents the perceived efficiency of various modes of political participation, measured on a scale from 0 (not efficient at all) to 10 (highly efficient). Voting in elections is considered by far the most efficient, with an average score of 8.20. Gaining media attention, working in associations, and working in political parties are all considered slightly more efficient than political consumption (scores 5.71 and 5.81), which, in turn, is considered slightly more efficient than contacting politicians. Demonstrations, legal or illegal, and the Internet are not considered efficient. The standard deviations illustrate that people are much more divided about the perceived influence of political consumerism thanabout other modes of participation.

One of the dividing lines is people's own behavior as political consumers. This is less trivial than it might seem. One could easily imagine individuals buying certain products mainly for reasons of personal, moral or "political correctness," without considering their actions politically efficient at all. But among those who have both boycotted and bought certain products, average perceived efficiency is 6.95 and 7.25, respectively. Among political consumers, only voting is considered clearly more efficient. Thus, it is obvious that political consumers themselves typically do consider such behavior to be a mode of political influence—and quite an efficient one at that.

In short, we have no reservations characterizing political consumerism as a new and genuine mode of political participation. The next question is how it relates to other forms of political participation, and to political trust. As mentioned, modern political consumerism was born in the context of new social movements in the 1970s, and

Table 3
Perceived Efficiency of Different Acts of Participation
(average scores on 0–10 scale)

	whole population			by political consumerism			
	st.dev.	mean	rank order	0	1	2	eta
Boycotting certain products	2.63	5.71	6	4.94	6.15	6.95	.31
Choosing certain products	2.66	5.81	5	4.64	6.77	7.25	.44
Vote in elections	1.98	8.20	1	8.12	8.28	8.32	.05
Work in associations	1.92	6.50	3	6.31	6.68	6.69	.10
Work in political parties	2.17	6.24	4	5.95	6.54	6.55	.14
Gain media attention	2.53	6.54	2	6.08	7.03	7.00	.19
Contact politician	2.47	5.58	7	5.26	5.99	5.81	.14
Peaceful demonstrations	2.42	4.56	8	4.07	5.01	5.21	.21
Illegal protest	2.45	3.02	10	2.76	3.20	3.45	.12
Influence via the Internet	2.60	3.89	9	3.57	4.03	4.47	.14

there remains a strong correlation between participation in grass-root actions and political consumerism. Among those who have participated in actions (as a minimum by giving a signature), 71 percent are also political consumers—as compared to 38 percent of those who have not. The correlation between the three-point index of political consumerism and a three-point index of political actions is $r = .33$ (data not presented). It therefore comes as no surprise that an explorative factor analysis, including conventional modes of political participation, as well as modes of political action, links political consumerism to political actions (data not presented).[6] More specifically political consumerism loads onto the same factor with signing petitions and donating money, whereas other forms of political action ("actives" and "demonstrations/illegal actions") load on separate factors. This is significant, as signing petitions and donating

Table 4
Correlations between Political Trust, Political Consumerism, Participation in
Voluntary Associations, and Participation in Political Actions
(Pearson correlations)

	membership associations	political actions	political consumerism
1. Local government	.12	.01	.01
2. (National) government	.09	.08	.10
3. Parliament	.11	.08	.14
4. The courts	.15	.08	.18
5. Public administration	.11	.04	.06
6. The police	.08	-.02	.02
7. The political parties	.09	.10	.09
8. Politicians	.09	.09	.12
9. The European Union	.09	.02	.06
10. United Nations	.16	.07	.15
Index (1-8)	.14	.08	.13

Question wording: "I will now read out names of different institutions such as the police, government, civil service, etc. Please tell me how strongly you personally trust each of these institutions?" 0=no trust at all, 10=very strong trust.

money are the most individualized forms of participation. Even if this cluster of individualized forms of political participation across the conventional dividing lines does not constitute hard evidence, it seems plausible to suggest that political consumerism is linked to underlying processes of individualization in society, and patterns of political participation.

This finally brings us to the association with political trust. Like participation in political actions, political consumerism has been theoretically linked to notions of distrust in political institutions and politicians. We may infer from table 3 that this seems implausible, as political consumers actually regard all forms of political participation as *more* efficient than those who are not political consumers. Furthermore, as table 4 shows, political consumerism is also positively linked to trust in established institutions and in politicians. In this sense, political consumerism resembles participation in voluntary associations. Unlike in the 1970s, even participation in political actions has become positively related (although weakly) to political trust (this holds also for Sweden and Norway (cf. Goul Andersen & Hoff 2001, chap. 9).

In short, the distinction between institutionalized and non-institutionalized modes of participation in terms of trust simply does not hold any more, in contrast to what has been suggested by Beck and by most other theoretically oriented researchers in the field. This does not necessarily mean that political consumerism is uncritical of industrial modes of production and the normal political system, but the critique does not seem to imply political distrust—rather to the contrary.

Political Consumerism and Global Political Orientations

Finally, we examine the extent to which political consumerism is related to global political orientations, in accordance with the suggestions above that political consumerism should be interpreted in relation to processes of globalization. While this is essentially a macro-level argument, we should at least expect to find *some* corresponding micro-level indications of more global, political orientations among political consumers. We will focus on three aspects: knowledge, attachment, and solidarity.

The first section in table 5 presents the correlation between political consumption and knowledge about international organizations (EU, NATO, UN, OECD, WTO, and Amnesty International). On average, knowledge about these organizations is rather limited, but it is significantly higher among political consumers. The correlation remains, although slightly weakened, even after controlling for age, gender and school education (eta = .20 to beta = .16).

The next section examines the correlation between political consumerism and an index of feelings of supranational attachments: to the Nordic countries, to Europe, and to the world. In this case, however, the correlation is weak, even before we enter any controls. A possible explanation is that these questions have a low reliability; however, it seems more likely that identity, in the very narrow sense of feeling attached to some region in the world or to the entire world, has very little impact on behavior. A strong issue orientation or a more specific sense of solidarity may have a greater impact.

Table 5
Political Consumerism and Global Political Orientations

Dependent var./index of pol. consumerism	Index 0-10 (simple average)	Index 0-10 (controlled for age, gender & school education)
A. Knowledge about international org.		
0	3.72	3.83
1	4.40	4.27
2	4.66	4.58
eta/beta	.20	.16
B. Attachments above nation-state level		
0	5.91	5.94
1	6.34	6.31
2	6.31	6.28
eta/beta	.10	.09
C. Global solidarity I		
0	7.62	7.65
1	8.24	8.21
2	8.28	8.24
eta/beta	.19	.17
D. Global solidarity II [1]		
0	6.53	6.50
1	7.03	7.05
2	7.53	7.58
eta/beta	.18	.19

[1] Transformed to 0-10 scale. The variable values are reversed in order to comply with the direction in the other scales.

Question wordings: See appendix.

The third section describes an index of relevant questions about what it takes to be a "good citizen": treating immigrants fairly, helping poor people around the world, and supporting human rights. This index correlates nicely with political consumerism (beta = .17 with index as dependent variable). Furthermore, factor analysis of a battery of such "good citizen"-questions reveals not only that these three questions form a common factor; actually, they do so together with a fourth question about political consumerism (data not presented).

Finally, the last section enters yet another index on "global solidarity" based on an item about a more even distribution of the Earth's resources, and two items on human rights; this index is quite strongly correlated with the former (r = .46), and the results, in terms of association with political consumerism, are similar (beta = .19).

Overall, we find quite strong evidence that political consumerism is linked to a sense of global solidarity and to knowledge about international organizations. The correlation with political consumption also suggests that modern "cosmopolitanism" does contain political aspects, despite claims that global identity is purely cultural and not political. We clearly observe elements of a kind of "global citizenship" here. To repeat, this does not constitute any strong test of our macro-level interpretation of political consumerism as rooted partly in the process of globalization; nonetheless, it does add to the plausibility of such an interpretation.

Conclusion

Even though political consumerism has by no means sky-rocketed in the last decade—it has rather fluctuated—our survey data indicate a long-term growth and reveal that it has clearly become one of the standard modes of political participation in Danish society today. We focused on two main dimensions: boycotting, and deliberately choosing certain products. Both may be organized by action groups or be more or less individual, but each is always aimed at influencing other actors, rather than simply satisfying individual needs. Defined this way, nearly one-half of the Danish population qualifies as political consumers.

The analysis reveals that political consumerism is fairly widespread across age groups and gender. It is *not* causally linked to income, but rather to education. The mediating link between education and political consumerism is, first and foremost, political engagement, not income or values. This supports the assumption that it is a genuinely *political* form of behavior, and this is further confirmed by the finding that political consumers see political consumerism as a very (cost-) efficient way to exert influence. In contrast to a number of theories, we found a positive correlation between political consumerism and political trust, which is comparable to the correlation between participation in voluntary associations and political trust.

As to macro-level interpretations, we suggested that political consumerism was related to individualization in political behavior, as well as to new problems and new opportunity structures associated with globalization. Although these propositions could not be tested directly, they are supported by the findings that political consumerism is strongly related to the most individualized forms of participation in voluntary associations and political actions, and to global political orientations, respectively.

Appendix
Question Wordings, Global Orientations

A. Knowledge about International Organizations:

This index is based on six items that made up one battery of questions. The exact wording was:

How much knowledge would you say you have about the following organizations and the issues they work with? If any of the organizations are unknown to you, please tell.

a. EU
b. NATO
c. UN
d. OECD
    (Organization for Economic Co-operation and Development)
e. WTO (World Trade Organization)
f. Amnesty International

Response-categories:
0 = very little knowledge
10 = very much knowledge
Respondents who answered "don't know," "never heard about the organization," or "no answer" are excluded from the index.
Cronbach's Alpha: .93.

B. Attachment to Above Nation-State Level:

This index is based on three items that were asked as part of a question battery about attachment:

Now, I would like to ask you some questions about your attachment to the place you live, for instance to the neighborhood, the town or the country in which you live. On this scale from 0 to 10 where 0 means "no attachment at all" and 10 means a "very strong attachment," how attached are you to...

a. the neighborhood or village in which you live?
b. the municipality or town in which you live?
c. the region in which you live?
d. Denmark as a whole?
e. the Nordic countries?
f. Europe?
g. the world, humanity as a whole?

A factor analysis results in two dimensions, where items (e) the Nordic countries, (f) Europe, and (g) the world, humanity as a whole, falls out on one dimension.

Respondents who answered "don't know" or "no answer" are excluded from the index.

Cronbach's Alpha: .78.

C. Global Solidarity I:

This index is based on three items that were asked as part of a question battery about citizenship duties. The exact wording of the introductory text and the items were:

As you know, there are different opinions as to what it takes to be a good citizen. I would therefore like to ask you to examine the characteristics listed on the card. Looking at what you personally think, how important is it:

l. not to treat immigrants worse than native Danes.
n. to try to help those people in the rest of the world who are worse off than you.
o. to support the observance of human rights in every part of the globe.

Respondents who answered "don't know" or "no answer" are excluded from the index.

Cronbach's Alpha: .75.

D. Global Solidarity II:

This index is based on three items that were asked as part of a question battery about (political) attitudes. The exact wording of the introductory text and the items were:

Now I have some additional questions about viewpoints from the political debate. And I would like to know if you completely agree, partly agree, partly disagree or completely disagree with the following ... [respondents could also answer "neither agree nor disagree" and "don't know"]:

a. Denmark ought to work for a better distribution of the Earth's resources, even if it means that we in countries like Denmark have to adjust to a lower standard of living.

n. The government should be forced to listen more to Amnesty International, also when Denmark is the object of accusation.

p. Denmark should take the lead in the protest against countries that violate human rights, even if it is harmful to Danish export interests.

Respondents who answered "don't know" or "no answer" are excluded from the index.
Cronbach's Alpha: .55.

Notes

1. Others speak of "dollar voting," (Kjeldgaard & Bregengaard 1999, 12) or "purchase voting" (Smith 1989, 10) among political consumers exercising "consumer-sovereignty" through the market (Smith 1989).
2. The "Danish Citizenship Study" is also part of the ESF-network on "Citizenship, Involvement, and Democracy" (CID). For more information about this network, please consult: <www.mzes.uni-mannheim.de/projekte/cid/>.
3. Unless otherwise indicated, all data are weighted by age due to disproportional stratification (under sampling) of people aged seventy or more.
4. As for party choice, the association with political consumerism is only moderate; the proportion is 73 percent among left-wing voters, 62 percent among adherents of the center parties, 47 percent among social democrats, 45 percent among liberals and conservatives, and 39 percent among right-wing populists (Goul Andersen & Tobiasen 2001, 48).
5. Introducing political interest into the equation also reveals that the picture of political consumerism among women and young people changes a little: Participation is not very high, but if we take into account the fact that women and young people are relatively less interested in politics in general, they do reveal a positive bias here.
6. The factor analysis results in seven factors:
    1. *Activist political action:* Worked in a political action group, worn/put up posters/badges, collected money, collected signatures/donations, distributed broadsheets/pamphlets/posters, active to get an action started.
    2. *Voting*: Voted in general election 1998, voted in municipality election 1997, voted in election for European Parliament in 1999.
    3. *Political party activity*: Worked in a political party, participated in political meeting, member of political party/youth organization.
    4. *Personalized contact*: Contacted politician, contacted association/organization, contacted civil servant, contacted lawyer/legal body, contacted or appeared in the media.
    5. *Individualized political action*: Signed a petition, boycotted certain products, deliberately chose certain products, donated money.
    6. *Protest political action:* Participated in public demonstration, participated in a strike, participated in illegal protest activity (signed a petition also loads on this dimension).

7. *Political engagement:* Discussion of politics with others, interest in politics in general.

The factor analysis applied is Oblique Rotation, pattern matrix based on entries from Principal Component Method (PCA). Since all variables are dichotomous the results must be interpreted with care, partly because, ideally, we had used other correlation-coefficients more suitable for dichotomous variables, and partly because of the risk of "difficulty factors" (Rummel 1970, 303-304). Another caveat is that many of the variables are highly skewed—for example, only 0.7 percent have participated in an illegal protest, and only 1.5 percent have worked in a political action group. In these cases, thus, the correlations are based on very few occurrences, which, however, is often a problem across countries when analyzing patterns in political participation. But, even if we exclude variables that have very uneven splits (less than 5 percent in one of the categories, which amounts to 8 variables), the four individualized protest action items still load on one dimension (this also holds true if we exclude all variables with less than 10 percent in one category, which amounts to thirteen variables).

Furthermore, regardless of which experiments we conduct (e.g., if we only include political action items in the factor analysis, or if we introduce one item at the time in the model) the results are robust; the four items, which make up the individualized protest action dimension, still load on the same dimension. This is also reflected in rather high gamma-coefficients among the four variables (between .38 and .89). Finally, even though the factor analysis certainly is explorative, the results are similar to other analyses of patterns in political participation (Petersson et al. 1989: 98; Parry, Moyser, & Day 1992, 51). However, it is remarkable that the individualized political action falls out on one dimension.

References

Barnes, Samuel, Max Kaase et al. 1979. *Political Action: Mass Participation in Five Western Democracies.* Beverly Hills, CA: Sage.

Beck, Ulrich. 1994. "The Reinvention of Politics: Towards a Theory of Reflexive Modernization," in Ulrich Beck, Anthony Giddens, & Scott Lash. *Reflexive Modernization: Politics, Tradition, and Aesthetics in the Modern Social Order.* Oxford: Polity Press.

___. 1997. *The Reinvention of Politics: Rethinking Modernity in the Global Social Order.* Cambridge: Polity Press.

___. 1998 [1997]. *Vad indebär globaliseringen? Missuppfattningar och mögliga politiska svar.* Gothenburg: Bokförlaget Daidalos AB.

Friedman, Monroe. 1999. *Consumer Boycotts: Effecting Change Through the Marketplace and the Media.* London: Routledge.

Giddens, Anthony. 1990. *The Consequences of Modernity.* Cambridge: Polity/Blackwell.

___. 2000. *Runaway World: How Globalization is Reshaping Our Lives.* New York: Routledge.

Goul Andersen, Jørgen, & Jens Hoff. 2001. *Democracy and Citizenship in Scandinavia.* Houndsmills: Palgrave.

Goul Andersen, Jørgen, & Mette Tobiasen. 2001. *Politisk forbrug og politike forbrugere: Globalisering og politik i hverdagslivet.* Århus. Aka-Print A/S (Magtudredningen).

Halkier, Bente. 1994. "Grønt Forbrug—hverdagspolitik?" *GRUS* 44: 22-39.

Held, David, Anthony Mcgrew, David Goldblatt, & Jonathan Perraton. 1999. *Global Transformations: Politics, Economics, and Culture*. Stanford, CA: Stanford University Press.

Inglehart, Ronald. 1990. *Culture Shift in Advanced Industrial Society*. Princeton, NJ: Princeton University Press.

Kjeldgaard, Margit, & Per Bregengaard. 1999. *Den Politiske Forbruger... i den store verden!* Columbus.

Micheletti, Michele. 2000. "Shopping and the Reinvention of Democracy: Green Consumerism and the Accumulation of Social Capital in Sweden." Paper presented for the *ECPR Joint Session*. Workshop: Voluntary Associations, Social Capital and Interest Mediation: Forging the Links. Copenhagen. 14-19 April.

Parry, Geraint, George Moyser, & Neil Day. 1992. *Political Participation and Democracy in Britain*. Cambridge: Cambridge University Press.

Petersson, Olof, Anders Westholm, & Göran Blomberg. 1989. *Medborgarnas makt.* Stockholm: Carlssons Bokförlag.

Rummel, R. T. 1970. *Applied Factor Analysis*. Evanston: North Western University Press.

Smith, N. Craig. 1989. "Consumer Boycotts." *Scientific Business* 27: 9-15.

Svendsen, Steen. 1995. "Den politiske forbruger." *Fremtidsorientering* 4 (September): 9-15. 32-5.

Consumption, Risk, and Civic Engagement: Citizens as Risk-Handlers

Bente Halkier

Introduction

"You are what you eat!" The understanding behind this phrase may help explain why food has been one of the highly contested and politicized areas of consumption in Denmark in the last decade. Recent survey data shows that Danish food consumers express distrust in relation to the safety of a number of ordinary food items. Nearly half examine declarations of goods and are occupied with health and environmental aspects when shopping for food (Halkier & Holm forthcoming). At the same time, public information (e.g., Veterinær- og Fødevare-Direktoratet 1999), as well as policy chapters from the Danish political and administrative institutions (e.g., Miljøstyrelsen 1996), and the public debates in the Danish media (e.g., DR1, TV2, summer 1999), give considerable attention to consumers' handling of different food political issues. In Denmark, there has been an emphasis on informing consumers as part of the governments' shifting strategies for handling food risks. Hence, in the social division of responsibility for food risks, the choices of ordinary consumers are constructed as central—ranging from buying organic milk to demanding the labeling of food containing genetically modified organisms.

The question, however, is whether and how such consumption practices can be categorized as a kind of political participation. I will discuss this question with reference to an empirical study of Danish consumers' handling of environmentally related risks in food. The discussion is organized around three themes that are traditionally debated in analyses of political participation. The three themes are *agency*, *community*, and *influence*, and they can be seen as different dimensions of political participation, as they are often debated in relation to concepts of political participation, social movements, and models of democracy. The dimension of agency deals with the capacity of citizens to act (Giddens 1984; Held 1987). The dimension of community deals with the degree in which citizens experience a belonging to a collectivity related to their actions (Anderson 1983; Eyerman & Jamison 1991; Maffesoli 1996). Finally, the dimension of influence deals with the ways in which citizens are capable of making a difference to societal problems with their actions (Clegg 1989; Hirschman 1970).

I suggest that elements of all three dimensions should be present in order to understand something as constituting political participation. We are constantly active without making a difference to societal problems, so it cannot be distinguished from the rest of everyday life. However, unintentionally contributing to societal problems is also something most of us do, at least at an aggregate level, for example, by using our credit cards, watching television, and taking the train to work. At the same time, contributing to societal problems on one's own, and for private interests, results in some interesting borderline discussions.

This chapter begins by theoretically relating consumption, risk, and political participation. Next, it briefly presents the main results and methods of the empirical research project used for discussing the political character of particular consumption practices—namely environmentally related risk handling in food consumption. Third, the chapter discusses whether the different kinds of risk handling in food consumption should be regarded as political consumption, by relating consumers' risk handling to three dimensions of political participation: agency, community, and influence.

Consumption, Risk, and Political Participation

Consumption is a particular field of practices within everyday life, which combines the satisfaction of needs with expressions of identity (Falk 1994; Gronow 1997b; Warde 1997). Consumption not only includes the activities of buying goods and services, but also social relations connected to the provision, allocation, and use of goods and services. Thus, consumption is part of the social space in which people participate in creating and reproducing meanings about the occurrences of everyday life, by attempting to knit together common experiences and roles (Gullestad 1989; Luckman 1989). Consumers' experiences are the basis and result of their interaction with, or in relation to, important others (Berger & Luckmann 1987, 33-48; Goffman 1959, 245; Lave 1988, 178f; Schütz 1975, 23-41). These experiences of life, however, are intimately related to the dynamics and institutions of society at large in ways that become clear when dealing with food consumption-related risk. Environmental risks, closely related to the institutional dynamics of production, reproduction, consumption, infrastructure, technology, and science, are being placed on the "kitchen table agenda." Trivial practices of individuals and families thereby become weighty issues.

Food consumption practices constitute a particular kind of consumption, since food is literally incorporated into the body—or indeed kept out of it. Analyzing food consumption thus means dealing with people's everyday experiences and practices. Symbolically, these processes are linked to individuals' interpretations of social belonging and distancing (Falk 1994, 24-7, 134-7). Furthermore, food practices as such are characterized by predominantly habitual activities (Warde 1997, 199) in which practices are remembered by the body and routinely carried out (Hastrup 1995, 182-4).

Risk points to "the possibility that an undesirable state of reality may occur" (Renn 1992, 56). Thus, risk represents something threatening that individuals must handle. A distinction is made between risk and danger. Risk covers people's intentional and systematic ways of dealing with threats and insecurities, whereas individuals are exposed to danger irrespective of their own choices. Risks are taken, whereas dangers arise (Beck 1992, 21). When consumers attempt to tackle environmental risks related to their food, risk handling becomes immersed in the social experiences of food consumption, and expert definitions and administrative criteria for risk become mixed into people's everyday experiences. Thus, risk handling is incorporated into practices, interpretations, and relations that may not have anything to do with risk in the first place. Risk becomes part of practices that have to do with entirely different purposes than the handling of risks, such as preparing tasteful meals. Risks get linked into existing interpretations, or else change them, such as interpretations of trust in various societal institutions. Risks are used to express social relations, such as how one's family works. Hence, consumers produce their own ways of understanding and handling risks in food consumption (Sellerberg 1991, 196). This could explain why many studies of public beliefs about different types of risk show that laypeople hold a broader understanding of risk, one that expresses values and relations of social trust and distrust (Simmons 1997, 253; Slovic 1992, 150; Wynne 1992, 281-3).

When consumers attempt to handle risk problems in their food consumption, they act within what is currently a politicized area of societal problems, with a number of food scandals and conflicts of control and regulation occurring across Europe (Berg 2000; Kjærnes 1999). Hence, risk handling in food consumption can be seen as a kind of politicized consumption. Furthermore, politicized consumption can be seen as yet another particular form of political participation in modern representative democratic welfare states, because politicized consumption fits in with the changes in the patterns in such participation (on changing forms of political participation, see also Stolle and Hooghe this volume).

Political participation in Denmark displays a tendency of supplementing traditional with new forms of participation. These are of a more individualized character (as e.g., users and consumers), or occur in micro-local contexts (the school board and the local supermarket co-op), or aim to directly influence concrete policy solutions and implementation (Goul Andersen 1993, 72-4; Goul Andersen et al. 2000). At the same time, concepts are being discussed in order to label the different individual and ad hoc types of political participation. "Life politics" is the well-known concept from Anthony Giddens (1991, 214f), where political participation consists of individual citizens enacting practical choices in their personal lives, an attitude that entails living responsibly in the global society. "The everyday maker" is a Danish concept (Bang & Sørensen 1997), where political participation consists of localized ad hoc involvement against the background of concrete experiences of solving common issues and problems in everyday life.

In order to discuss the degree to which politicized consumption—such as risk handling in food consumption—seems to be political, a series of criteria become necessary. I discuss three dimensions that are often mentioned in the debates about concepts of political participation, social movements, and models of democracy (Eyerman & Jamison 1991, 161; Goul Andersen et al. 2000, 12–5; Held 1987, 290f; Kriesi 1992). The three dimensions are:

- The degree of agency

- The degree and type of community

- The degree and type of influence

All three dimensions reflect important debates within the social sciences, debates concerning structures and actors, sociality and individualization, and the workings of power in modern society. They cannot be discussed thoroughly in a short chapter. Furthermore, parts of these debates are carried out in a general and abstract way, whereas this chapter attempts to discuss the dimensions in one of their many particular contexts. These dimensions will be conceptually clarified and discussed below.

Handling the Risks of Consumption

The empirical study that informs this chapter's discussions is the research project "The Risks of Consumption."[1] It is a qualitative in-depth study of how consumers handle environmental risk in food consumption, using parents with small children as an example of consumers. The data consist of analyses of a number of focus group interviews with Danish parents of small children about food and risk, as well as a text analysis of public texts dealing with food, risk, and environment.[2] In this chapter, focus will be on the first part of the data-material. The study examined six focus groups, with three pairs of parents in each group, during 1999. The focus group participants differed in educational level as well as socioeconomic status. In this section, I will present some of the main empirical results, summarizing the systematic variations of consumer practices across the different focus areas. This is done by presenting a typology of risk handling. Using this method, otherwise complex empirical results are simplified and structured, making it easier to follow the discussion of whether and how such different types of consumption practices constitute political participation. The different types of risk handling are only briefly described, without quotes, in order to save this for the discussion of the political dimensions in the last three sections.[3] The three types of risk handling are called *worried risk handling*, *irritated risk handling*, and *pragmatic risk handling*.

In worried risk handling, consumers follow the public debate on health and environment closely, and they obtain information about the different matters that they see as problematic. Emotionally, they feel intimidated by the risk-communication of mass media, and in their homes and social networks risk in food consumption is a subject of negotiation and conversation. The parents attempt to use food-stuffs that they typify as less risky—for example organic products and bread without straw shortening chemicals—as individual or family ways of managing the existence of this sort of risk in their daily lives. In worried risk handling, consumers typically identify with being societal actors that are capable of acting and making a difference through their role as consumers. However, relations of trust and mistrust are divided. Sometimes great confidence is expressed in, for example, declarations of content and the state-run organic products labeling scheme. Sometimes mistrust is expressed in public authorities, producers, retailers, experts, and the media. In other words, trust is placed in different relations in society, typically institutional relations versus social network relations (Misztal 1995, 101).

In irritated risk handling, risk is primarily associated with risk communication in the media, campaigns, and leaflets as well as interpersonal communication. Consumers experience risk communication as a threat to other relations of everyday life—such as eating what you like. This risk handling occurs within the tension between the two imperatives of modern commodity culture, to release control and to impose self-discipline (Featherstone 1990, 13).[4] Food is enjoyed and is an important part of social relations with others, and consumers talk about food in their social networks. The public debate about the environment, risk, and food is, however, followed from the sidelines. But consumers are frustrated when risk communication creates dilemmas in their everyday lives, dilemmas to which they may not see any solutions. In relation to irritated practices, consumers have difficulty seeing themselves as societal actors through their role as consumers. A diffuse lack of trust is expressed in the accumulated amount of risk-knowledge in society, rather than expressing mistrust in particular actors and institutions. Irritated risk handling is often attempted in varying ways. The issue of risk can be dismissed most of the time. Or, for example, during one week risk related to food and shopping is dismissed and people cook and eat what they want. The next week, media, family, or friends remind consumers about risk, and they might, tentatively, change practices to something perceived as less risky for a short while.

In pragmatic risk handling, risk is understood as a daily life-problem along the lines of all other daily problems. Consumers may not consider environmentally related risks in consumption unless there is, for example, a television program about something that they regard as such. Food in general is not something that is necessarily talked about, but rather something to make and eat together. Hence, risk is a (potential) problem, with which one must have a "sensible

relationship" in a busy everyday life. Within pragmatic risk handling, parents do not want to exaggerate the involvement in risk
issues at the expense of other priorities in their daily family lives.
However, neither do they want to neglect risks that they understand
as truly important, for example, those relating to the health of their
children. They place their trust in risk handling, either with public
authorities or with people they know personally. Either way, pragmatic risk handling requires establishing practical routines, which
absolve parents from reflecting excessively on the issue or bother-
ing themselves emotionally with it (Ilmonen 2001, 13f). Greater
energy is spent making daily life function satisfactorily than in trying to influence society via the consumer role.

A recent survey of Danish consumers suggests something about
the distribution of the three types of risk handling (Halkier & Holm
forthcoming). It is, of course, difficult to transmit insights from quan-
titative to qualitative studies, but with this methodological reserva-
tion in mind, the distribution among Danish consumers can be described as follows. Forty-four percent are characterized by "examining practices," parallel to worried risk handling. Thirty percent are
characterized by "rejecting practices," slightly parallel to irritated
risk handling. And 25 percent are characterized by "routinized practices," parallel to pragmatic risk handling.[5]

This section has presented the variations in food consumption
practices among parents interviewed in a simplified typology of
three different types of consumer risk handling. The three types of
risk handling reflect, in a sense, different strategies that ordinary
consumers develop in their everyday lives when faced with a politicized consumption area such as food. In the remaining three
sections, the political participatory character of these individuals'
risk handling will be discussed by looking at the three types of
risk handling in relation to each of the three dimensions in political participation set up earlier in the chapter: agency, community,
and influence. I am not attempting to create a scheme to link exactly how political each of the three types of risk handling might
be, primarily because I would never claim that it is possible to determine conclusively whether some everyday act is political or not.
Rather, a mixed picture should probably be expected, as suggested
by earlier studies (Eden 1993, Halkier 1999, Læssøe et al. 1995). A
mixed picture regarding degrees of civic engagement and types of
participation also comes out of the analysis of this study.

Agency

The degree of agency involved in the practices of people shows something about whether and how citizens can be seen as active societal actors. Hence, agency separates societally directed actions from all other actions. In principle, individuals' everyday actions create consequences for others and for societal dynamics. In this sense, we are all actors all the time. But most of us do not drive in our car to work for the purpose of contributing to global warming. Nor do we buy conventionally produced fruit in order to support the use of pesticides. Most of our actions carry unintended consequences along with them (Giddens 1984, 27), often at an aggregated, and hence political, level. Thus, one important conceptual part of agency is intentionality: Are citizens' actions carried out with intentions of certain consequences? Another important conceptual part of agency concerns whether the conditions for actions are structured in ways that make it likely for those actions to be carried out. This other part of agency is often discussed under the heading of autonomy in relation to political participation (Held 1987, 290f): Do citizens have resources and maneuverability to carry out their actions with intended consequences?

Some degree of autonomy is usually a criterion for assessing political agency. Intentionality, however, seems to be particularly relevant to political agency in everyday life, due to the organization of everyday life practices in pursuit of purposes that are often apolitical—compared to practices of grassroots participation and other political organizations. As shown in the discussions in political sociology, practices in organizations have other purposes alongside the political ones—often referred to as the socio-symbolic dimension of participation (Olsen 1991, 12)—and organized political participation results in unintended, as well as intended, consequences. But the difference in social context is about the explicit priority of the purposes of the practices. In everyday life, the purposes of practices tend to be implicit, many-fold, and not necessarily intentional.

Looking at the three types of risk handling in food consumption, the main patterns in relation to agency seem to be the following. Worried risk handling contains intentionality with a shifting experience of autonomy. In pragmatic risk handling, a relative degree of autonomy is experienced, but without much intentionality of practices. And in irritated risk handling, consumption practices are not experienced as holding a great deal of autonomy.

In worried risk handling, consumers intentionally choose particular consumption practices that they typify as being less risky, for example, buying organic foods, buying Danish fruit, using goods with as few additives as possible, and a number of other specific choices. This is expressed in the following quote from one of the women in the study:

> I don't know...you know, I think I have a tendency to have ideological taste buds...someone once told me...[laughter]...I simply BELIEVE that organic tomatoes taste better than the traditional ones...so if they have something organic for sale...in the shop today...you know, if they for example have organic cauliflower, that can make me feel like eating cauliflower soup. I don't feel like it all winter, because...I don't know, I AM quite selective, because you know...I just pass by the vegetable shelves cause never mind about the traditional ones, it's about organic things, right...now they had cucumbers, right, so we are going to get tatziki this week...so I go after the organic label a lot in this manner...then now and then we get a tin of non-organic sausages and bad consciousness.

When the parents express worried risk handling, they tend to underline consumption practices as a space for action by ordinary people. In that sense, they express confidence in consumption as a type of agency within society, which is illustrated in the next quote from another woman:

> But...all right, I do believe that you can do something by talking about it, you know...in your workplace or what you do...even though it is...small things, you can do something in that way...get your own vegetable garden.

At the same time, consciousness of limitations to the autonomy of such agency is also expressed, again by one of the women:

> But mostly I get a bit angry, really irritated about it is bloody well too...much that such products are made, that products that are so lousy and bacteria infested are being sold, then this, then that and such things, and sprayed and everything. Mmm, it doesn't give the consumer, as a consumer you don't get real options of choice, I think. Cause it's difficult to choose between the devil and the deep blue sea, right? All right, you can choose organic goods and then...say a quiet prayer that it's okay.

In pragmatic risk handling, food consumption practices mainly work as routines, which are the subject of little reflection or discussion in the social network—unlike worried risk handling. Routine practices draw upon tacit knowledge, and they are often remembered by the body. Thus, it is very difficult to find a degree of intentionality in such practices—other than the rationalizations that informants make of their practices in discussions with each other. Here is an account of one of the women:

> I think about such things as fruit and the like, you can't assess when they say that it's not sprayed, but I don't believe very much in that, you know. I think it's sprayed in some degree all of it, you know. But really, you can't do anything else...you have to buy it and wash it and...eat it.

In irritated risk handling, food consumption practices are experienced as one of the dilemmas of everyday life, related to different structural conditions for choices. This typically results in a perception of the ordinary consumer as a weak kind of agency in society, here illustrated by a quote from one of the men:

> But I am also tired of the way that...something is being taken up, right, and then I actually sit and get worked up about it and say that it's too bad...but my possibilities for doing ANYTHING AT ALL about it are not really there, hmm? You know...the fish doesn't improve because they make such a television show, does it? I have just got yet another problem thrown in my face, right?

On the other hand, it might be argued that since irritated risk handling entails actively acknowledging that reflecting too much about food risks is neither good nor important to one's everyday life, this could also be a kind of position of autonomy to take.

Thus, interpreting risk handling in food consumption as a form of political agency, even at this basic level, is not clear. Whether risk handling is constructed as an autonomous space for action in everyday life, or constructed as a powerless position, this type of consumer agency entails two structural problems. There are things that consumers cannot know, and there are things that consumers cannot choose, even when they do know. This is due to the individual consumer strategy of institutional dependency on expert knowledge and the market mechanisms for the production and selling of food. The dependence on expert knowledge, for example, creates a large amount of insecurity as to when consumers make the right decision, because knowledge about food risks is compound, complicated, and with shifting conclusions being communicated through the media (Wynne 1996). Here is an example from one of the women:

> You just don't know...cause then sometimes I get to think about...bacteria might be something that makes you ill here and now, but you just don't KNOW about the additives, is this in a longer term...and why ARE there more incidences of cancer, or is it just because now it gets discovered, right. Or IS it because something is completely sick in our food, right? But you just can't...if you have to get food on the table every day, you just can't go around and thinking about it every day.

The consumers' dependence on conditions of production, even when they feel they do know what is risky, also frustrates agency.

One of the men put it like this:

> Of course you can deliberately choose something that is healthy, but there are some things that we cannot choose ourselves. Now you talk about the fish being healthy food...but in reality, they have poured DDT and all sorts of things in the sea that the fish are munching upon.

Such ambivalent tendencies surrounding agency in ordinary politicized consumption practices are in accordance with a British study (Macnaghten & Urry 1998, 97-101). It shows that the main ambivalence that arises in relation to everyday risk handling concerns the consumers' feeling of being pulled between, on the one hand, an increased insecurity about how to know what to do, and on the other, an increased awareness of possessing agency—the capacity to do something.

Community

In relation to political participation, community is traditionally addressed in two ways. Firstly, politicized practices are seen as taking place in relation and in reference to the discourses and institutions of a larger political collectivity (Goul Andersen & Tobiasen 2001, 14f; Sørensen 1997, 89-92). Secondly and more narrowly, politicized practices are seen to take place together with others in a community (Eyerman & Jamison 1991; Melucci 1989), be it a concrete organization or movement, or be that an imagined community (Anderson 1983). One of the ways in which political consumption and politicized consumption choices have been problematized as types of political participation, is exactly because they seem to be such individualized acts taking place in the intimate sphere and the marketplace, thus lacking both criteria for community (Gabriel & Lang 1995).

Community, however, is the dimension of political participation that provokes the most disagreement when looking at political consumption (see Micheletti, Goul Andersen & Tobiasen, and Stolle & Hooghe in this volume). The first way of addressing community refers to the discussion about how to define political participation. The question is whether it is important to distinguish between consumers' motives for action, which are either personal or societal. This is a difficult distinction to make since many consumption practices may draw upon mixed motivations. Consumers buy organic butter because it tastes better and because it supports a societal environmental goal. Furthermore, the question when something is considered political is one of socio-cultural definitions. An often-mentioned motive for buying organic food is personal health, and this is not usually considered a societal or political goal. But it might be, if public politics in the health sector places a larger emphasis on prevention. However, if we as researchers do not at least, as a general rule, hold on to criteria for political consumption that refer to societal collectivities, the concept of consumption as political participation risks becoming so broad that it empties out.

With regard to the criteria of politicized practices taking place in relation to the discourses and institutions of a larger, societal political collectivity, the accounts of parents appear rather ambivalent, and this goes across the three types of risk handling. On the one hand, parents express their responsibility as consumers to be dependent on how other societal actors administer their responsibility for food risks and environmental problems. So references to a larger collectivity appear in discussions about the issues of food risk. The following negotiation of societal responsibility among two women and a man illustrates this:

> *K:* But the single family has a lot to say, you know there's lots of politics in how we shop, we do that rather differently you know, right, but there is really politics BEHIND how we do.
>
> *L:* I think so too…we have a big responsibility. But the government we've elected, they also ought to, how to put it, show a kind of educating responsibility in this, in how they piece things together…because I think when we choose…
>
> *Nh* (interrupts): But politically this has become different…we are four people out here[6]…and we are all members of the party Venstre,[7] I won't deny that, and you are definitely NOT. Politically the leftwing started all this, and then I'll admit that we came along, and I think that's good, but we look at it in a slightly different way…cause it's not enough that those who vote leftwing become ecological…it's not enough, it won't be enough people eating…
>
> *L* (interrupts): No, some of the rightwing people have to begin to buy organic too…so get back to the party and do some work, you!

Notice the reference in the last part of the negotiation to the special responsibility of the man with the political party-affiliation, pointing to the potential that the parents see in linking consumption practices with collectively organized activities.

On the other hand, looking at parents' discussions about risk handling in the food area, it is much harder to find expressions that refer explicitly to motivations that have to do with seeing risk handling in consumption as a common societal problem. Rather, the dominating discursive repertoires evolve around using risk handling to solve private family problems of personal safety and health. The parents established consensus around the following three main norms of how to solve food risk problems in one's own, private, everyday life. The norms are:

- Personally known products are best (then we know what's in them).

- You should buy Danish (then we trust our institutions know what's in them).

- You must keep your fear of pollution in check (then we don't let our worries interfere too much with our everyday practices).

These norms can be interpreted as expressing more personal than societal or collective motives for action.

A second way of addressing community as a dimension of political participation in consumer practices is to see consumer actions as part of a concrete or imagined community. Is it sensible to include such a narrow definition of collectivity for such an "individualized collective action?" (Micheletti 2003). Not necessarily, especially if community is understood as something quite unified in terms of identity. Recent studies of political participation in Denmark show that grassroots participation and identities spread in all directions (see Goul Andersen & Tobiasen in this volume). So it depends somewhat on whether community is defined as unifying citizens under a common identity, or whether community allows citizens partial identification across socio-cultural variations. In this sense, it is an open question whether community in this second, narrower version should be included as a claim for considering consumption practices to be political participation.

However, community in this latter sense is referred to among the parents. Especially within worried risk handling, but also within pragmatic risk handling, consumers associate with a diffuse, imagined community of consumers who act upon food risks in their daily lives. This imagined community of active co-consumers helps make their own individual practices useful or meaningful in relation to improving the conditions for food safety and quality and environmental consideration in food. In the following quote, one of the men refers in a typical way to an inclusive "we" about consumers in the end of the quote:

> It's obvious to see what is happening in American farming at the moment, how incredibly many American farmers who have restructured their production to genetically modified products...and now they have found out that the consumers don't want it...and now they try to change production back again, cause it's not profitable for them...to produce genetically modified crops, and that's clearly the pressure from consumers who boycott the products. And I think that this is the strongest weapon we have got, it's simply to boycott things that we say, that we won't touch.

As part of the parents' expressions of worried risk handling, there are usually references to other people whom they know personally who also choose particular consumption practices or uphold particular routines, such as buying organic goods. These people are often from the social network, with which the more worried parents also discuss some of the dilemmas of acting as a conscious consumer. In this sense, the community around the risk handling practices is both imagined *and* concrete.

These kinds of references to imagined or concrete community around risk handling as a part of a societal actor strategy are hard to find among the expressions of irritated risk handling. Here, parents find it difficult to understand themselves as food consumers, who can act together with other consumers. One of the men says:

> Yes maybe exactly because there is so much, that no matter WHAT you buy, it is infested with some sort of risk of one thing or another. Maybe something is added, maybe it's sprayed, growth hormone is added, you can't see through it anyway.

Thus, seeing risk handling in food consumption as community-related, politicized practices trigger a complex conceptual discussion. Empirical results display mixed patterns, just like the relations of such practices to agency. Consumers do not necessarily understand their practices as part of a community of co-consumers—be that concrete and/or imagined. And although consumers draw upon discursive repertoires, related to a larger societal collectivity, when it comes to the participatory form, they do not seem to be doing it when it comes to the motivational substance of their practices.

Influence

In order to discuss the degree of influence that risk handling consumers might obtain, it is necessary to discuss the different types of influence they can exert in their role as consumers. The ordinary consumer strategy for influencing society works directly via two dynamics: An "exit" dynamic (Hirschman 1970) on a globalized market for everyday foodstuff, and a very localized "voice" dynamic in the social networks of consumers. When the influence of ordinary consumers is discussed and assessed, usually the focus is on the exit dynamic, meaning how consumers influence via the market mechanism by moving their purchase power around. However, because consumption is not just the purchasing act, but also the different social and symbolic uses in everyday life (Warde 1997), it is important to include the voice dynamic in the social networks of consumers as well.

The discussion in this section takes place at a slightly different analytical level as it is not primarily based on the interviewed consumers' assessments of their influence. Instead this section discusses the pros and cons of the two types of consumer influence channel: global exit and local voice. Risk handling in food consumption is used as an example. This is also why the focus shifts here from the three types of risk handling. Relating the types of risk handling to the types of consumer influence can be made on the basis of what is already presented in the chapter, and it forms an unsurprising pattern: Worried risk handling uses both exit and local voice, since particular goods are bought intentionally to fight food-risks and it is something that is discussed in the families and networks. Pragmatic risk handling uses exit but not local voice, since particular goods are bought and particular cooking habits are established to fight food-risks, but in routinized and tacit ways. Irritated risk handling does not necessarily use exit; and the use of local voice varies.

When parents as consumers attempt to influence food safety, food quality, and environmental solutions, the market opens up a space for fast and easy action where people are already present. They do not have to enter an organization and devote time to meetings, and they can influence concrete solutions in society directly by supporting or boycotting them, instead of going the long way round through representative political institutions. This pattern of influence seems at least partly to be present in the growth of the Danish market for organic foods (Klint 1996; Michelsen et al. 2001). Furthermore, a recent Danish survey shows that milk, vegetables, and meat/poultry organic products are considered to be the safest, or second safest, type of product for purchase (Halkier & Holm forthcoming).

On the other hand, the only signals sent via the exit dynamic are responses to retailers and producers that there is a demand for specific goods. This results in diffuse political signals for "less foreign fruit" or "more environmental friendliness," whereas consumers do not participate in a public debate about what the content of the alternatives should or could be. They are crucially dependent upon what producers supply (Keat 1994, 27-30), and in many cases alternatives do not exist. If society as a whole is to become capable of forming and choosing such alternatives, it is a prerequisite that the specific problems and alternative solutions are part of a sustained political process in arenas where all relevant interests can participate.

Furthermore, ordinary consumers' demands and activities via the market are scattered and unorganized. Hence, they remain invisible to the public sphere, to organizations, and to the political system. This makes it difficult for consumers' demands to reach a common societal political agenda, where attempts are made to make decisions and implementations binding for all of society. Unless, that is, consumers can establish alliances with organized political actors in order to visualize their activities and demands. Thus, consumer influence via the market is not necessarily very influential. The question is also how democratic that influence may be. As market actors, such as producers and consumers, are not elected, and their contributions to implementations in food and environmental policies cannot easily be controlled, there is a risk of losing democratic accountability (Held 1987, 204).

The other dynamic for ordinary consumer influence is a voice in the social networks where decisions about purchases are discussed, where uses of particular foodstuffs are identified as lifestyle elements, and where norms for what consumers ought to do are negotiated. This dynamic is a more long-term one, which does not necessarily influence short-term policymaking, but rather influences the social and cultural norms and the political legitimacy of different solutions. When consumers handle food risks and talk about it to each other in their everyday lives, they participate in the formation of political experience. Such activity can be seen as part of the normal procedures of a democratic, public sphere (Kaare Nielsen 1991).

In other words, the social network voice dynamic for influence from politicized consumption practices is part and parcel of the larger debates about supplementing a "government" understanding of political processes with a "governance" understanding (Bang, Dyrberg, & Hansen 1997). Here politics is seen as taking place in all societal relations as processes, building among other things on a Foucauldian concept of power as constructive and transformative (Clegg 1989, 153-9). Thus, when consumers negotiate norms for acceptable food consumption practices, they also participate in disciplining each other's body practices as part of the "governmentality" (rationality of government) (Dean 1999; Foucault 1991) of the policy areas.

Finally, one might ask whether there seems to be a pattern of connection between the use of the different types of influence and the other dimensions of political participation, agency and community. Apparently, using both local voice and exit as in worried risk handling is linked with the intentionality dimension of agency, and community. In contrast, using exit only, as in pragmatic risk handling, is linked more with the autonomy dimension of agency and community. This suggests that using local voice reminds consumers of the limitations of consumption as political participation via discussions in their social network. Such discussions and negotiations about one's scope to act is a normal part of other types of political participation, such as voting and interest organizations. Hence, while consumers experience their practices as not necessarily holding a high degree of autonomy, this need not mean that such practices do not constitute political participation.

To sum up, the assessment of risk handling as politicized consumption practices in relation to their political influence is a complex picture—just like regarding agency and community. The ordinary consumer strategy seems to be weaker in direct influence on the substance of policymaking, but perhaps stronger in influence on social and cultural norms, which are the basis for the legitimacy of the substance and processes of policymaking in the areas of food, health and environment.

Conclusion

What kind of political agency is observed when individuals are ascribed with political responsibility in their capacities as consumers? Using the Danish case of risk handling in food consumption as an example of politicized consumption, there seems to be a mixed picture around each of the three dimensions of political participation suggested: Agency, community, and influence. Risk handling can be, but is not necessarily, intentional, and it varies drastically whether consumers view themselves as having enough autonomy to influence society. Some consumers interpret their risk handling practices as part of a community of co-consumers acting together, whether concrete or imagined—but others do not necessarily experience their practices in the same way. And although consumers refer to their responsibility for food risk problems in relation to the co-responsibilities of other societal actors, they primarily refer to solving their own private problems of safety, health, and quality, rather than common societal problems with food and environmental politics. Finally, the ordinary consumer strategy seems to influence only weakly the substance of policymaking (directly), but the same consumer strategy might prove more effective as indirect influence on social and cultural norms.

A comparison made between two views of consumers' roles concerning environmentally related food risks—that of consumers' own narratives and that of the public texts they refer to—confirms the existence of a mixed picture (Halkier 2001a). Ambivalence is the pervasive feature of consumers' constructions of their own roles as risk-handlers, while constructions of the consumer's role in public texts for the most part fail to recognize or represent ambivalence. Rather, the public texts analyzed here are identified as constructing the consumer's role primarily as a weak actor.

Can one speak of a difference between politicized consumption and political consumerism? Maybe we should reserve the term political consumerism for the worried type of risk handling in food, where consumption practices are used intentionally to further some goals both by means of voice and exit. Conversely, the other two types of risk handling, pragmatic and irritated, might be referred to as different appropriations of the discursive repertoire of politicized consumption. The term appropriation is used within media sociology to coin the practices of media users when they make discursive repertoires in the media their own, by fitting these into their everyday life (Thompson 1995, 42)—interpreting messages in their own ways, using messages for their own social purposes, etc.

However, a problem remains even for labeling the strategy of worried risk handling political consumerism. This has to do with the lack of systematic, explicit reference to common societal motivations for risk handling in the accounts of the consumers, which applies to all three types of risk handling. Just like the other dimension of community—whether consumers refer to some kind of belonging to an imagined or concrete community—it should probably be an open question for further research whether we want to demand analytically that consumers must refer to common societal motivations as well as private interests in order to label their practices as political consumerism.

Notes

1. The research project was financed by The Strategic Program for Environmental Research in Denmark and was carried out as a part of the Centre for Social Scientific Environmental Research (CeSam).
2. The types of public texts are those that the participants in the focus groups refer to mostly in their argumentations about what is risky and safe food, and what role consumers can play.
3. More detailed accounts can be found in Halkier 2000 and Halkier 2001a, 2001b.
4. Elsewhere I have described this as the contested space of the body and related all three types of risk handling to this type of tension (Halkier 2001b).
5. The research project is called "Consumption between Everyday Life and Politics." It was financed by the Danish Consumer Agency, and the data consist of a CATI survey with a representative sample of Danish consumers. The reporting of the results is still in the writing stage. "Examining practices" label consumers who study declarations of goods and are occupied with health and environment while shopping for food. "Routinized practices" label consumers who are occupied with health and environment while shopping for food, but do not study declarations. "Rejecting practices" label consumers who are not occupied with health or environment while shopping for food.
6. Who are organic farmers.
7. Right-center political party in Denmark.

References

Alexander, J. C., & B. Giesen. 1987. "From Reduction to Linkage: The Long View of the Micro-Macro Link," in J. C. Alexander et al., eds., *The Micro-Macro Link.* Berkeley: University of California Press.

Anderson, B. 1983. *Imagined Communities.* London: Verso.

Bang, H., & E. Sørensen. 1997. *Fra Græsrødder til Hverdagsmagere.* Copenhagen: Department of Political Science, Copenhagen University (Demokrati fra Neden. Arbejdspapir no. 3).

Bang, H., B. Dyrberg, & A. D. Hansen. 1997. "Elite eller Folkestyre—Demokrati fra Oven og/eller fra Neden?" *Grus* No. 51.

Bauman, Z. 1992. *Intimations of Postmodernity.* London: Routledge.

Beck, U. 1992. *Risk Society.* London: Sage.

Berg, L. 2000. *Trust in Food in Europe.* Oslo: Statens Institutt for Forbrukerforskning, SIFO (Working Chapter no. 17).

Berger, P., & T. Luckmann. 1987. *The Social Construction of Reality.* Harmondsworth: Penguin Books.

Bourdieu, P. 1984. *Distinction: A Social Critique of the Taste.* London: Routledge and Kegan Paul.

Clegg, S. R. 1989. *Frameworks of Power.* London: Sage.

Dean, M. 1999. *Governmentality: Power and Rule in Modern Society.* London: Sage.

DR1. (summer 1999). *News.* 1.6-1.9.

Eden, S. 1993. "Individual Environmental Responsibility and its Role in Public Environmentalism." *Environment and Planning* 25: 1743-58.

Eyerman, R., & A. Jamison. 1991. *Social Movements: A Cognitive Approach.* Cambridge: Polity Press.

Falk, P. 1994. *The Consuming Body.* London: Sage.

Featherstone, M. 1990. "Perspectives on Consumer Culture." *Sociology* 24 (1): 5-22.

Forbrugerrådet. 1997. *Forbrugeren i Centrum*. Copenhagen: Fremad.
Foucault, M. 1991. "Governmentality," in G. Burchell, C. Gordon, & P. Miller, eds.. *The Foucault Effect: Studies in Governmentality with two Lectures by and an Interview with Michel Foucault*. Chicago: Chicago University Press.
Gabriel, Y., & T. Lang. 1995. *The Unmanageable Consumer: Contemporary Consumption and Its Fragmentations*. London: Sage.
Giddens, A. 1984. *The Constitution of Society*. Cambridge: Polity Press.
____. 1991. *Modernity and Self-Identity*. Cambridge: Polity Press.
Goffman, E. 1959. *The Presentation of Self in Everyday Life*. New York: Anchor Books.
Goul Andersen, J., 1993. "Politisk Deltagelse i 1990 sammenlignet med 1979," in J. Goul Andersen et al., eds., *Medborgerskab: Demokrati og Politisk Deltagelse*. Herning: Systime.
Goul Andersen, J., Lars Torpe, & Johannes Andersen. 2000. *Hvad Folket Magter: Demokrati, Magt og Afmagt*. Copenhagen: Jurist-og Økonomforbundets Forlag.
Gronow, J. 1997. *The Sociology of Taste*. London: Routledge.
Gullestad, M. 1989. *Kultur og Hverdagsliv*. Oslo: Universitetsforlaget.
Halkier, B. 1999. "Consequences of the Politicization of Consumption: The Example of Environmentally Friendly Consumption Practices." *Journal of Environmental Policy and Planning* (1): 25-42.
____. 2000. *Kan Man Spise Dårlig Samvittighed? Forbrugeres Håndtering af Risiko ved Fødevarer i Hverdagen*. Roskilde: Institut for Kommunikation, Journalistik og Datalogi/ Roskilde Universitets Center.
____. 2001a. "Consuming Ambivalences: Consumer Handling of Environmentally Related Risks in Food." *Journal of Consumer Culture* 1 (2): 205-24.
____. 2001b. "Risk and Food: Environmental Concerns and Consumer Practices." *International Journal of Food Science and Technology* 36 (8): 801-12.
Halkier, B., & L. Holm (in review). "Tillid til Mad: Forbrug mellem Dagligdag og Politisering." *Dansk Sociologi*.
Hastrup, K. 1995. "The Inarticulate Mind: The Place of Awareness in Social Action," in A. P. Cohen & N. Rapport, eds., *Questions of Consciousness*. London: Routledge.
Held, D. 1987. *Models of Democracy*. Cambridge: Polity Press.
Hirschman, A. O. 1970. *Exit, Voice, and Loyalty*. Cambridge, MA: Harvard University Press.
Ilmonen, K. 2001. "Consumption and Routine." In J. Gronow & A. Wade, eds. *Ordinary Consumption*. London: Routledge.
____. & E. Stø. 1997. "The Consumer in Political Discourse: Consumer Policy in the Nordic Welfare States," in P. Sulkunen et al., ed., *Constructing the New Consumer Society*. London: Macmillan.
Kaare Nielsen, H. 1991. *Demokrati i Bevægelse*. Århus: Århus Universitetsforlag.
Keat, R. 1994. "Scepticism, Authority, and the Market," in R. Keat et al., ed., *The Authority of the Consumer*. London: Routledge.
Kjærnes, U. 1999. "Food Risks and Trust Relations." *Sosiologisk Tidsskrift* 7: 265-84.
Klint, J. 1996. *Er der Salg i Etik?* Copenhagen: CASA.
Kriesi, H. P. 1992. "Support and Mobilisation Potential for New Social Movements," in M. Diani, & R. Eyerman, eds., *Studying Collective Action*. London: Sage.
Læssøe, J. et al. 1995. *Grønne Familier*. Lyngby: Institut for Teknologi og Samfund, Danmarks Tekniske Universitet.
Lave, J. 1988. *Cognition in Practice*. Cambridge: Cambridge University Press.
Luckmann, T. 1989. "On Meaning in Everyday Life and in Sociology." *Current Sociology* 37: 17-30.
Macnagthen, P., & J. Urry. 1998. *Contested Natures*. London: Sage.

Maffesoli, M. 1996. *The Time of the Tribes: The Decline of Individualism in Mass Society.* London: Sage.

Melucci, A. 1989. *Nomads of the Present.* London: Hutchinson Radius.

Micheletti, Michele. 2003. *Political Virtue and Shopping. Individuals, Consumerism, and Collective Action.* New York: Palgrave.

Michelsen, J., K. Lyngaard, S. Padel, & C. Foster. 2001. "Organic Farming Development and Agricultural Institutions in Europe: A Study of Six Countries." *Economics and Policy* No. 9.

Miljøstyrelsen. 1996. *En Styrket Produktorienteret Miljøindsats.* Copenhagen.

Misztal, B. 1995. *Trust in Modern Societies: The Search for the Bases of Social Order.* Cambridge: Polity Press.

Olsen. J. P. 1991. "Individuel Autonomi, Politisk Autoritet og Demokratiske Institutioner." *Nordisk Administrativt Tidsskrift* 72 (1).

Renn, O. 1992. "Concepts of Risk: A Classification," in S. Krimsky, & D. Golding, eds., *Social Theories of Risk.* Westport, CT: Praeger.

Schütz, A. 1975. *Hverdagslivets Sociologi.* Copenhagen: Hans Reitzel.

Sellerberg, A. 1991. "In Food We Trust? Vitally Necessary Confidence—and Unfamiliar Ways of Attaining It," in E. Fürst et al, eds., *Palatable Worlds. Sociocultural Food Studies.* Oslo: Solum Forlag.

Simmons, P. 1997. "The Construction of Environmental Risks: Eco-Labelling in the European Union," in P. Sulkunen et al., eds., *Constructing the New Consumer Society.* London: Macmillan.

Slovic, P. 1992. "Perception of Risk: Reflections on the Psychometric Paradigm," in S. Krimsky, & D. Golding, eds., *Social Theories of Risk.* Westport, CT: Praeger.

Sørensen, E. 1997. "Brugeren og Demokratiet." *Grus* 53: 81-96.

Thompson, J. B. 1995. *The Media and Modernity: A Social Theory of the Media.* Cambridge: Polity Press.

TV2. (summer 1999). *News.* 1.6-1.9.

Vetrinær-og fødevaredirektoratet. 1999. *Kontrol er en Mærkesag.* Copenhagen.

Warde, A. 1997. *Consumption, Food, and Taste.* London: Sage.

Wynne, B. 1996. "May the Sheep Safely Graze? A Reflexive View of the Expert-Lay Knowledge Divide," in S. Lash et al., eds., *Risk, Environment and Modernity.* London: Sage.

___. 1992. "Risk and Social Learning: Reification to Engagement," in . S. Krimsky, & D. Golding, eds., *Social Theories of Risk.* Westport, CT: Praeger.

Why More Women? Issues of Gender and Political Consumerism

Michele Micheletti

Introduction

Attitudinal studies on political consumerism show that women more than men are involved in political consumerist activities. More women participate in boycotts, although studies from Sweden and Denmark indicate that gender differences in boycott activity are still in place, but are decreasing over time (Blomberg, Petersson, & Westholm 1989; Teorell 2001; Goul Andersen & Tobiasen 2001, 21). What is interesting is that women use labeling schemes more than men. Available market studies from Sweden, Denmark, and the United States show that women stand out as users of organic food labels, the Max Havelaar fair trade label, and eco-labels for seafood, respectively (LUI 1999, 3; Klint 1997, 28; Wessells, Donath, & Johnston 1999). LUI, a Swedish survey institute specializing in consumer research for the farming community, finds that women shoppers also stand out on such aspects as whether food is guaranteed free of salmonella, GMOs, growth hormones, medicines, chemical additives, and chemical pesticides (LRF/Ekologiska Lantbrukarna 2001, 21). The authors of the U.S. study on eco-labeled seafood report that the "gender of the respondent has an impact on choice, with women more likely to choose certified products across all species," and that "variables representing age, income, education, and political affiliation are generally insignificant individually and jointly..." (Wessells, Donath, & Johnston 1999, 51f). Consumer political activists confirm the importance of women, and underscore that middle-class women are the focal group for all new consumerist efforts. They are seen as the people with the interest and means for this kind of political involvement (Dobson 2000).

How can we explain women's interest in political consumerism? This chapter attempts to answer this question in five steps. First, it summarizes historical research on political consumerism focusing on women's engagement and then, in its second step, uses the summary to formulate general characterizations on the role of women in it. Third, it discusses whether the same motivations for women's engagement are in place today, or whether other motivations explain the contemporary dominance of women. As current research in the field has not focused on women, results from a Swedish case study of green consumerism, which shows interesting gender differences, are used to answer this question. All research findings are then used in the fourth step taken in this chapter, which involves the formulation of possible explanations for the gender gap in political consumerism. It asks whether there is something special about women that attract them to political consumerism. A different question is posed in the fifth step, which asks whether there is something special about the market that seems relevant for explaining the gender gap in political consumerism.

Women's Historical Involvement in Boycotts and Labeling Schemes

When scholars look for women in political consumerism they find them easily. This section reviews examples of women's involvement in a variety of historical political consumerist settings—from revolutions and struggles for social justice, fair trade, and civil rights, to international politics. Women are clearly present in revolutionary struggles in which consumerism has played an important role. Everyday goods have constitutional significance in these cases, and involvement with consumer goods is an easy way for women to enter the sphere of social concerns and politics. A good illustration is the role of women in the Swadesi movement, which forms a crucial part of the Indian struggle for independence. Another instance is the American Revolution, which embedded such everyday items as tea, clothing, and other imported British goods with political meaning and identity. Women and other groups of people expressed their protest against English rule by organizing and participating in the subscription list movement, which provided information on the purpose of the boycott and requested a written pledge of support. When women were not allowed to play an active role in subscription groups that men had organized, they organized their own groups that were beyond the reach of men (Breen 1999, 113ff). The subscription movement allowed women, who were not full citizens because they lacked the right of suffrage, to become directly involved in the most important political issue of the day. Women found that their everyday routines of providing consumer goods for the family were intimately interlocked with the high politics of diplomacy and the constitutional status of the colonies (Breen 1988).

Women also played a key role in market-based action for social justice, as shown in the food boycotts of the early 1900s. Women consumers in the United States and Europe expressed their dissatisfaction with the supply, quality, and price of groceries in what, at that time, were called meat and milk strikes. A particularly active group was working-class housewives, whose involvement in the strikes has been studied closely by historians. Between the 1920s and 1940s, American urban and rural housewives across the nation voiced public dissatisfaction about the price of food. The revolts by housewives were, in the words of one historian, "far more widespread and sustained, encompassing a far wider range of ethnic and racial groups than any tenant or consumer uprising before it" (Orleck 1993, 156). Women used the civic skills they had at hand. Women union members helped organize housewives as consumers and forged consumer alliances between working women and housewives. Organizers for the Communist Party used motherhood as a parole to unite women, because they realized that "when appealed to as mothers, apolitical women lost their fears about being associated with radicalism in general and the CP in particular" (Orleck 1993, 157). Private concerns for the family gave women courage to voice their complaints publicly. The housewives' neighborhood consumer councils and networks, which were created in the 1930s to fight high food prices, were relatively stable networks. Scholars conclude that the demands that these women raised in their networks "reflected a complex understanding of the marketplace and the potential uses of the growing government bureaucracy" (Orleck 1993, 156). They are examples of how women consumers were able to politicize agricultural products and hold their own against producers who were men (cf. Frank 1985).

Their actions are interesting, because they show how women from different backgrounds could unite on a common concern. Immigrant urban women created networks with rural women to target the actors who profited from high food prices. Local neighborhood women's councils, created to fight food prices, often cut across ethnic and religious lines. The political philosopher, Iris Marion Young, uses the housewives' revolt to explain seriality, that is, how focus on a particular, everyday problem, like chicken prices in the lower East Side of Manhattan, led angry women to mobilize into ad hoc networks and express their dissatisfaction publicly, which, in turn, helped them understand better their roles as wives, mothers, and women in society (Young 1994, 735). Women took pride in their empowerment as political consumers. Work on food issues politicized motherhood, the family, and the home, and it built bonds among women. Not surprisingly, these networks threatened men and led to conflict with the worker's movement, which felt uncomfortable with politically empowered housewives and the attention given to consumption over production in the class struggle. The housewives' revolts in the United States show clearly how the marketplace became a place for women to discuss their concerns and voice them politically at a time when other political space was generally off-limits to them.

Food boycotts in Europe also involved women. The limited and scattered information available shows that their activities and goals were somewhat different than in the United States. A more recent European case that deserves more study is the food revolt in 1972 by Swedish women. It was the first widespread food protest since World War I. Their protest activity is known as "Skärholmen Wives" (*Skärholmsfruarna*, wives from a Stockholm suburb); they organized a boycott against what they considered unjust milk and meat prices. The boycott spread all over Sweden and ended in a demonstration in Stockholm attracting 6,000 protesters. During the protest, retailers and dairies noted a dramatic decrease in milk sales. That women— or protesting ladies, as one journalist called them—politicized food prices in this fashion did not go unnoticed. "Housewives' Milk War Becomes a Political Threat" was one telling newspaper headline. Parliament addressed the group's concerns; Prime Minister Olof Palme met with them to discuss high food prices, and a popular political issues program on national television invited them to debate food prices with the minister of trade and supermarket chain representatives. Their demands fell well in line with popular discontent over high food prices, and shortly thereafter Parliament passed legislation to lower milk prices.

Women have also played a key role in internationally well-known political consumerist actions, but their presence has not been the focus of study. However, an engendered reading shows that the international boycott of Nestlé, for its marketing of infant formula in the Third World, most likely would neither have taken place nor been so successful and effective without the involvement of women health care professionals and women organized in a variety of civic networks (see Bromberg Bar-Yam 1995; Sikkink 1986). The same is true for the role of women in the political consumerist actions that were the backbone of the American civil rights' movement. Women's political consumerism was involved in the struggle long before Rosa Parks instigated the famous Montgomery bus boycott in 1955, a boycott discussed in David Vogel's chapter (King 1999). Women also initiated many of the early efforts later categorized as "Don't Buy Where You Can't Work" campaigns (see Cheryl Goldberg's chapter for more information on this campaign). These women were often politically active and well situated in their communities (Goldberg 1999, 244f). Moreover, the grape boycott in the 1960s, that started in the United States and spread to other countries, would probably not have been successful without women's involvement. The reason, which is discussed in a later section, is women's perception of risks. The boycott really began to have an impact when the United Farm Workers' Union decided to turn its struggle into an issue of shopping for food for the family. When consumers learned that the pesticides used on grapes were also hazardous to their families and not just to the health of the farm workers, they began to boycott grapes in great numbers (Benford & Valadez 1998).

Women also participated in political consumer actions organized by powerful and established social movements, for instance the workers' movement boycott activities that took place in different countries in earlier parts of the twentieth century. Once consumption became a union issue, the labor movement became more interested in women as political actors. Union involvement with consumer issues opened up a public space in labor activities for women because it was important that they, as homemakers, wives, and mothers, understood the cause and applied it in their everyday shopping activities. This erased the clear boundary between the public sphere of work and politics and the private sphere of family and household economics. Thus, when unions "chose to politicize consumption, they also sought to change the way housewives performed their unwaged labors of consumption" (Frank 1994, 6). The class struggle was, therefore, fought on two fronts—publicly in the realm of production and privately as consumer choice. The situation was different in Europe, where the male dominated workers' movement feared that focus on consumption would politicize the home and empower women in the wrong way (cf. Aléx 1994).

Not everyone agreed with this assessment, as we see clearly in one of the first labeling schemes, the White Label Campaign (1898-1919) of the National Consumer's League in the United States (Sklar 1998). The label is an early example of an anti-sweatshop, no-child-labor, fair trade label. Success then, just as today, depended on mobilizing women as political consumers to buy according to the label. The focal group was also the same group as today, middle-class women who had the economic means and ideological reasons to pick and choose among product brands. The chosen product was dear to the mother's heart: women's and children's machine-made white cotton underwear, a product purchased nationally in great number. Florence Kelly, the league's general secretary, was well aware of the powerful role that women could play as political consumers. She said, "No one except the direct employer is so responsible for the fate of these children as the purchasers who buy the product of their toil" (as quoted in Sklar 1998, 27). Scholars conclude that the campaign gave women a tool to exercise moral and political power, in a time when men dominated formal civil society and government settings.

Women and Political Consumerism: Lessons from History

The review of historical cases of women's involvement shows four interesting similarities. First, women became inadvertently involved in political consumerism as a way of working with issues that were close to home and part of their role as wives and mothers. Their worries about serving their families proper food were not at first seen as political in nature, but they became political once the women began to discuss their worries with each other. Food strikes and network creation were the result of this unintentional political mobilization. This kind of involvement was sparked by self-interest and reflects *the private motive for political consumerist activism.* Second, particularly middle-class women saw their role as consumers as an explicit way of working with social and political concerns. They could use the power implicitly embedded in market choice to influence the politics behind products intentionally. We see this clearly in the subscription list movements, "Don't Buy Where You Can't Work" campaign, and the early anti-sweatshop label. This kind of involvement builds on other-regarding interests and is called the *public motive for political consumerist activism* (cf. Burtt 1993). Such motivations result from concern about injustice and unfair treatment of certain groups of the population at home or abroad. At times, and as discussed further in this chapter, the two motives go hand in hand. Third, women became involved with market-based political activity for the simple reason that conventional political venues did not welcome their participation. Gender discrimination forced them to look elsewhere to influence politics. Finally, the historical examples show three important side effects of network creation and day-to-day work on the network's issues: empowerment, consciousness-raising, and identity formation. Women grew as citizens and became conscious of the public implications of their role as mothers and wives.

Are these four similarities a mere characterization of history, or do they also apply to women's involvement in contemporary political consumerism? Do they pertain only to women's attempts at creating a better life for themselves, their families, and others, in a time period before women were granted full civil, political, and economic rights as citizens? Are different characteristics in play today in democratic societies, now that women can participate more fully in politics, society, and economic life?

Swedish Women and Contemporary Green Political Consumerism

Sweden is a good case to use to study whether the four characteristics of women's historic involvement discussed above have any relevance for explaining the current dominance of women as political consumers. Sweden is known for its progressive policies on gender equality and women's rights. Women are integrated in the work force, civil society, and politics to a higher degree than in many other industrialized, Western countries. They are, therefore, highly visible in the public sphere. Such political cultural traits would seem to signal that the characteristics found in the historic setting should not appear in the Swedish case. At the same time, available survey data discussed earlier in this chapter show that Swedish women are more involved with political consumerism than men. How can we explain this? To answer this question we turn to a case study of contemporary green political consumerism in Sweden, which concerns Sweden's largest environmental association, the Swedish Society for Nature Conservation (*Svenska Naturskyddsföreningen*, SNF), which in the 1980s began working with issues of green political consumerism. In 1992, it established an internationally known and highly successful eco-labeling scheme, Good Environmental Choice (*Bra Miljöval*), which sets the standard for many industrial household products marketed in Sweden today (see Micheletti 2003 for details).

Green shopping was first put on the SNF agenda in the 1980s. Professional women working on environmental issues, as well as daily women shoppers, encouraged the shift to green political consumerism. Women members of the SNF expressed concern about pesticides on foods and chemicals in household products that they purchased daily for their families. They urged the SNF to take green consumerism seriously. Gro Harlem Brundtland's report on ecological modernization, *Our Common Future,* helped frame the effort ideologically. As a first step, they called for a green shopping guide, which took the form of a book entitled in translation, "Buy and Act Environmentally: An Everyday Handbook for a Better Environment," published in 1988. The focus on green political consumerism had several positive side effects for women members of the SNF. It opened up new ways for them to participate in their association, led to an increase in women members, and reinforced the importance of the local associational base as an arena for member activity and everyday routines for sustainable development. Women members have been very innovative and spontaneous locally in forging contacts between themselves and consumer market actors through green supermarket evaluations and yearly environmentally-friendly weeks.

The key actors in green political consumerism are middle-aged, middle-class women. This interest led to the establishment of a members' network, the "Act and Buy Environmentally" network, which in the 1990s was the most popular and successful members' network within the SNF. Unlike other networks, it is dominated by women. Analysis of available network name lists shows that about 80 percent of all regional contact people, 75 percent of the contact people for the yearly environmentally-friendly week, and 70 percent of the contact people for the network in the local SNF units are

women. Women members participate in the network because it makes
them feel good and useful. They are reported to be extremely visible, active, and social participants. Social interaction in the network
is an important priority, and they enjoy working together in groups.
My research shows that these women would most likely score high
on tests of such civic skills as organizing meetings and public speaking, and their abilities most likely explain the network's success. It is
rather noteworthy that these active women members with civic skills
that normally lead to a variety of kinds of political participation tend
to be rather disinterested in more established SNF politics like electoral politics and office holding.

The network women are consumer and family oriented, concerned
about the tangible effects of environmental problems on everyday
life, unconcerned about their personal status within the organization, and disinterested in institutional hierarchies. They are active
members of the Buy and Act Environmentally network, because it
gives them influence over their everyday lives and a forum for taking responsibility for future generations. They want this everyday
influence, but not organizational status or power. In this sense, they
question the male priorities that have dominated the SNF, and have
found green political consumerism a natural setting for their private-
public and public-private worries. They can be contrasted with the
typical male member, who tends to be older in age, a loner, oriented
toward the natural sciences, and more concerned with personal organizational status. He may even question whether green political
consumerism is really an environmental concern.

Amusing names for the two member groups are used in the SNF.
The men are called "beetle-bug geezers" (*skalbaggsgubbar*) for their
focus on nature conservation and their fragmented view of environmental life cycle assessments. They are characterized as driving their
cars out to the forest to look at bugs, without reflecting on the environmental effects of driving a vehicle powered by fossil fuels for the
health of the bugs and global warming. The women are called "plas-
tic-cup protesting women" (*plastmuggstanter*) for their intense concentration on very concrete everyday use of products and everyday
issues as important for global sustainability. The differences between
men and women that have come to the surface because of green
political consumerism are mirrored in the character of the Good
Environmental Choice unit itself. Unlike other SNF units, most of
the people on the staff are women, and most people who apply for

positions are women.

The SNF grew in strength in these years. It gained about 135,000 members between 1980 and 1992 and over 12,000 between 1989 and 1991, the year that marks its highest membership number ever (206,274). Unfortunately, organizational policy on not using personal identification numbers makes it impossible to see the growth in membership in gender terms. Yet it is clear from other SNF sources that green consumerism initially attracted 1,000 new members per week, many of whom were women. A member survey from 1990 shows significant findings on gender differences on green political consumerism. Twice as many women as men (52 v. 23 percent) stated that green political consumerism was an important reason for joining the SNF and a very important issue for those members who became members in 1985 or later rather than earlier (42 v. 29 percent). The survey also reports that green political consumerism may be a more important reason for joining the association for members who never have held office than for those who have done so. This seems to apply particularly for women: a greater number of women than men without posts view green consumption as a very important reason for membership (54 v. 27 percent). It is noteworthy, given the survey results reported in Goul Andersen and Tobiasen's chapter, that people lacking university education appear to find it more important. Also members who joined in 1985 or later consider learning about green political consumerism a very important reason for membership, while those who joined earlier see the issue as important but not to the same extent (44 v. 34 percent) (SNF 1990).

A general conclusion from the case study is that green political consumerism appeals to people, and particularly women, who want to work with environmental issues in new ways. Moreover, the characteristics of the members involved in green political consumerism pose puzzles for scholars of political participation, because they do not really fit with their findings on politically involved citizens. Possible explanations for this discrepancy are given in the next chapter section. It also needs to be noted that the general characterizations from history usually apply to this contemporary and very different civil society and political setting. Profiling of green political consumerism encouraged women to join the association, become more active in it, and become active in it in a different way. It gave them an institutional venue for involvement in issues that appealed to them, and created a setting for involvement that allowed them to concentrate on their private concerns over environmental risks for their family and others to practice daily their public dedication to sustainability. Thus, we see both a private and public motive for involvement, which together facilitated everyday environmental activism, as Bente Halkier states it in her chapter. Regarding exclusion from traditional politics, the third historical characteristic, the involved women obviously do not lack empowerment in the traditional sense. Yet they willingly or unwillingly were marginalized in the SNF. Their interest in green political consumerism led to the creation of an organizational network that changed this situation by giving them a place to work on their issues in their own way.

What Explains the Gender Gap in Political Consumerism?

Why are more women interested in political consumerism? What explains the gender gap? Is there something special and different about women? Or can it be that there is something special and different about the market that leads women to it as an arena for political engagement? We see both explanations in the historical examples and case study. The first question is answered with the help of research on women's political participation and focuses on socialization, situational, and structural explanations (cf. Flammang 1997, chap. 4). The second question, discussed in the next section, compares the market with traditional political forums to explain its use by women and other groups.

The *socialization model of women's political participation* focuses on how individuals learn to behave according to sex roles. A sex role characteristic of relevance here is women as family shoppers. Engendered statistics of consumer behavior are difficult to come by, but we know from scattered evidence that women dominate as family shoppers. It is, thus, this traditional sex role that explains their dominance as political consumers. The model predicts that the gender gap will disappear once men assume more responsibility for day-to-day family life. Perhaps this explains the decreases in the gender gap on boycotting found in Denmark and Sweden, two countries with notable gender equality profiles. In sum, the gender gap is only a difference between whether women or men do the family shopping. Both women and men who are family shoppers and who are privately and publicly concerned about the politics behind products have the proclivity to become political consumers. Recent survey results from Denmark might give evidence for this proposition, as the gender gap seems narrower in the 1990s, when more men assumed roles as family caretakers (see Goul Andersen & Tobiasen in this volume). Also Halkier's research in this volume does not seem to distinguish gender differences in reactions in food risk handling behavior.

The situational model of women's political participation argues that there is indeed something special about women. Women are special because of their responsibilities as wives and mothers. These characteristics will always situate women differently than men and form their private and political personal identity. Scholars using this model report that motherhood discourages engagement in instrumental political system-oriented politics (e.g., voting and interest groups) and encourages everyday voluntary community activism involving survival issues and nurturance values like humanitarianism, preservation of life, and risk responsibility-taking (Flammang 1997, 119ff). This model predicts that the gender gap will not disappear because being a wife and mother is an integral part of womanhood.

The term *momism* is used for political participation based on compassion, self-interest, nurturance, and social commitment (High-Pippert 2001; Eliasoph 1998; Goss 2001). How does momism explain the gender gap in political consumerism? It points to research results which show that women participate more because they, as wives and mothers, are concerned about the effects of consumer goods on their families and humankind. Political consumerism can, therefore, be seen as an engendered form of political participation, triggered by an ethic of care (cf. Deveaux 1995). It is an example of the private motive for engagement discussed earlier, and can develop into a public motive if the issues that hit home are contextualized in a larger setting.

Momism is also used in social psychological research on risk perceptions, whose point of departure is risk society (see Kennedy's and Halkier's chapters) and engendered perceptions and behavior. Social psychologists argue that women have a lower risk threshold than men, "not because they know less, but because they care more. In particular, women appear to care more about the potentially serious if often empirically underdetermined threats to the health and safety of their communities and families" (Davidson & Freudenburg 1996, 328). Their research shows that women are more perceptive of environmental risks as threats to people they care for personally.

They call this phenomenon *mother effects* (Flynn, Slovic, & Mertz 1994), which appears to be a reasonable explanation for women's interest in the SNF green political consumerist network. Qualitative interview research from Sweden confirms that lower risk thresholds lead to green political consumerism (Solér 1997). Thus, the gender gap in political consumerism can be explained by the situational role of women as care-providers. The private motive for political consumerism is evident here, but, as discussed in Stolle and Hooghe's chapter, engagement can become public-oriented when women activate themselves to search for safe consumer goods for their family.

Factors such as recruitment networks, issue profiles, and the internal character of conventional channels for political participation are the current focus of the *structural model of women's political participation* (Flammang 1997, 122ff; Verba 2001; Burns, Schlozman, & Verba 2001). Scholars using this model evaluate these structural factors to see whether they function as discriminatory mechanisms or secondary sexism (Pateman 1979, 20), which discourage women's political participation, marginalize them, and place them in the periphery of political and organizational life (Pateman 1983, 110, 1989). This research tradition explains historical and contemporary political consumerism as women's response to exclusion from and problems in traditional institutions of the political system. Thus, women, as those who in subscription list groups during the American Revolution and in the case study, view political consumerism as a way to work on their issues, because traditional channels of political participation are seen as less attractive, not giving them the opportunity to work on issues of importance, and generally discouraging their involvement. This model points to the public motive for political consumerist activity discussed earlier, and predicts that women will continue to use consumer choice as political choice until political institutions become more women-friendly. Thus, there is not really anything special about women that encourage their involvement in political consumerism. Rather, the gender gap is explained by problems with traditional politics that force them to turn to market-based involvement to work on political issues that concern them as citizens.

Most likely all three models contribute to an explanation of the dominance of women in political consumerism, and their explanatory power is dependent on the individuals and political consumerist context understudy. It appears that the sex role model applies more to historical instances of women's involvement in political consumerism in countries now characterized by relatively good gender equality. Yet it is interesting that women in Sweden, a country with high levels of gender equality, are more engaged in political consumerism than men. The case study discussed in the chapter shows that both the situational and structural models are relevant here. But it is important to keep in mind that the case study covers only one instance of political consumerism under a short period of time. Perhaps there are different explanations for why women become involved in political consumerism and stay involved in it. A longitudinal study of women's involvement in a particular instance of political consumerism is, therefore, necessary to establish the explanatory power of the different models.

Characteristics of the Market and Women's Involvement in Political Consumerism

The chapters by Monroe Friedman, Cheryl Greenberg, and David Vogel show how marginalized groups historically used the market as a venue for working on political issues ignored by traditional politics or outside its control. Other research emphasizes how market-based involvement liberates and empowers women. Goul Andersen and Tobiasen's research reveals that young people are more interested in political consumerism than one would expect, given other characteristics relevant for studying levels and kinds of political participation. This volume also shows that political consumerist involvement is characterized by local sites of action, horizontal networks, flexibility, individualized and serial participation, intense communication among the participants, crisscrossing of the private and public spheres, and transnational institution-building. Is there something special about the market that encourages this kind of political involvement? The preliminary answer developed in this section considers its everyday nature, which facilitates low-cost political involvement, individualized engagement as well as its character as a new frontier for political experimentation.

Low-cost political involvement means that people do not need to invest many physical, social, or human capital resources to participate in politics. Involvement does not call for a change in daily routines or life philosophies. They do not need to become members of an association, learn how to participate in it, set off time to attend meetings, and engage in activities different than those of everyday life. Issue engagement that is low cost does not require acquaintance with new structures, settings, and procedures. In other words, the threshold for participation is easy to cross. For many political consumerists, shopping is low-cost political involvement. It is comfortable because it involves familiar routines, people, choices, issues, and places. All that is required as a first step is that they use non-economic values when making consumer choices. The attractiveness of the market as a site for ethics and political action is, thus, its character as a low-cost form of involvement, a simple and easy way of expressing one's point of view. People can engage in political consumerism simultaneously as they attend to their daily chores, and they can do so on the basis of private or public motives for involvement.

This characteristic implies that the market is special because it allows people to act politically in their private lives by combining public and private involvement in one single action. The market is, therefore, quite different from traditional political forums that are based on a clear dichotomy between the public and private spheres, which require that people behave in particular ways and perform special tasks. The act of voting is probably the best example here. Women find less dichotomous involvements attractive, as shown in feminist research on political participation, momism, and general theoretical work captured in the slogan "the personal is political" (Jaquette 1976). This explains the attractiveness of the market for women. It helps them to make politics part of their everyday lives. Because the market is open for engagement based on life politics, as discussed in Halkier's chapter in this volume, it is thus perceived by women and other groups as a low-cost form of political participation. This is not to say, however, that a low-cost form of political participation does not take considerable effort and time, as indicated earlier in this chapter. It is just that this kind of engagement comes more naturally than participation in traditional forums for politics, which tend to be physically and psychologically located at a greater distance from the home.

Scholarship on everyday-making underscores the importance of low physical and psychological thresholds for civic involvement, which is based on a blurring of public and private lines of reasoning. This research chronicles how citizens take the initiative to create settings that transgress the public/private divide by working on issues in a hands-on way, for instance to keep local post offices open and to improve local schools (Bang & Bech Dyrberg 1999). They develop their own ways of understanding and tackling political problems that are based more on a private motive for engagement. Everyday-makers are street-level political entrepreneurs seeking solutions for very concrete problems and street-level auditors of institutional performance. This implies that they *individualize political engagement*. Political consumers can also be characterized in this way.

Thus, from research in women's studies, and on everyday-making as well as political consumerism, we can develop the following explanation for the attractiveness of the market as a site for politics. It allows citizens to define and work with political issues in their own way, in their own time frame, and in a very local and specific way. The market is, thus, attractive to marginalized groups because it does not force them to socialize themselves into public and political roles that have been stipulated by dominant groups in society. Women can engage in politics in a women-friendly way, young people according to their perceptions of life styles, and ethnic and non-white racial groups with multicultural sensitivity. In other words, these groups can do their own political thing. For many scholars, this is the essence of individualization and the proper role of self-interest in politics (Beck 1997; Burtt 1993).

Why does the market as an arena for ethics and action allow for this kind of political diversity and pluralism? The answer seems to be its character as a new frontier for politics. Although the market has been used as a site of politics for centuries, it has still an unregulated political character, most likely because conventional political actors and institutions have not really attempted to establish themselves in it. Market-based activism is not really molded by the presence and agendas of established political players who socialize citizens to participate in politics in certain ways. Neither is the consumer market a site for politics framed by governmental regulation. Unlike strikes and demonstrations, boycotts and buycotts can be conducted without government permits and corporate permission. Even with corporate advertising and when political mechanisms are in place for economic steering, government and corporate powers cannot completely control how people spend their money in the marketplace. This makes market-based political activism attractive for marginalized groups, as it at times is the only or last resort available for them.

The market, as shown in several chapters, is also a fertile ground for political experimentation by citizens wanting to influence politics in new ways. They can try out new political issues, tools, and tactics that are disallowed and uncommon in established political forums. We see the use of new tactics and tools clearly in Jonah Peretti's Nike Sweatshop Email Exchange. Finally, as the world becomes more economically global, with the consequence that nation-states lose control over multinational corporations, and human rights and environmental problems become more transnational, as shown in Andreas Follesdal's chapter, market-based tools are at times the only immediate way to regulate the market behavior of multinational corporations. Here organized consumer action sets up normative standards for producer accountability and consumer responsibility in multi-risk global society. These watchdog institutions, as illustrated in the chapters by Jordan et al. and Cashore et al., supplement the codification, standard-setting, and monitoring by nation-states, the UN, ILO, and other regional and international organizations.

Conclusion

The cases discussed in this chapter, as well as the proposed explanations of the gender gap, force us to consider "the productivity, creativity, autonomy, rebelliousness and even the 'authority' of the consumer" (Slater 1997, 51). Political consumers have agency, and they are full of citizen creativity (cf. Nava 1991, 165; Yúdice 1995). Political consumer activism has played and can play an important part in transforming society, economics, and politics. When compared to public decision-making arenas, the market is less distanced from our daily lives, and it allows women and other groups to use their creativity in a multitude of more individualized ways. This is the case because the looseness and indeterminacy of consumption appeals to people who tend to find themselves marginalized in formal, institutional political-system settings. The market is, therefore, a site for women to participate in politics, a site for them to legitimate their concerns, and a site for their struggle for public recognition. In this and other ways, consumer activism reinvented, and is still reinventing, citizenship (cf. Stevens 1994).

This chapter also shows how political consumerism gives tangibility to politics (cf. Sørensen 1997). This occurs when women and other groups put political demands on goods and the institutions

responsible for producing them. They insist on more product transparency and a more caring attitude on the part of producers. In doing so, political consumers are calling implicitly or explicitly for
new decision-making rules and institutions that reflect global
sustainability and justice. Political consumers are political entrepreneurs, and market goods are a good site to penetrate the importance
of daily life for democratic development. At best, political consumerism is characterized by self-government, governance, responsibility-taking, globalization, personal ethics, and individual reflexivity
(cf. Bang 2000). Can shopping be more political?

References

Aléx, Peter. 1994. *Den rationella konsumenten: KF som folkuppfostare 1899-1939.* Stockholm: Brutus Östlings Bokförlag Symposion.
Bang, Henrik. 2000. *Excellent Ordinarity: Connecting Elites with a Politics of the Ordinary.* Copenhagen: Copenhagen University, Demokratiprojektet (Working paper No. 22).
___, & Torben Bech Dyrberg. 1999. *Governance, Self-Representation, and Democratic Imagination.* Copenhagen: University of Copenhagen (COS-Report No. 6).
Beck, Ulrich. 1997. "The Reinvention of Politics: Towards a Theory of Reflexive Modern-ization," in Ulrich Beck, Anthony Giddens, & Scott Lash, *Reflexive Modernization: Politics, Tradition and Aesthetics in the Modern Social Order.* Cambridge: Polity Press.
Benford, Robert D., & Danny L. Valadez. 1998. "From Blood on the Grapes to Poison on the Grapes: Strategic Frame Changes and Resource Mobilization in the Farm Worker Movement." Paper for the Annual Meeting of the American Sociological Association, San Francisco, 21 August.
Blomberg, Göran, Olof Petersson, & Anders Westholm. 1989. *Medborgarundersökning. Råtabeller.* Stockholm: Maktutredningen.
Breen, T. H. 1988. "'Baubles of Britain': The American and Consumer Revolutions of the Eighteenth Century." *Past & Present* 199 (May): 73-104.
___. 1999. "Narrative of Commercial Life: Consumption, Ideology, and Community on the Eve of the American Revolution," in Lawrence B. Glickman, ed., *Consumer Society in American History: A Reader.* Ithaca, NY: Cornell University Press.
Bromberg Bar Yam, Naomi. 1995. "The Nestlé Boycott: The Story of the WHO/UNICEF Code for Marketing Breastmilk Substitutes." *Mothering* (winter): 56-63.
Burns, Nancy, Key Lehman Schlozman, & Sidney Verba. 2001. *The Private Roots of Public Action: Gender, Equality, and Political Participation.* Cambridge, MA: Harvard University Press.
Burtt, Shelley. 1993. "The Politics of Virtue Today: A Critique and a Proposal." *American Political Science Review* 87: 360-68.
Davidson, Debra J., & William R. Freudenburg. 1996. "Gender and Environmental Risk Concerns: A Review and Analysis of Available Research." *Environment and Behavior* 28 (3): 302-39.
Deveaux, Monique. 1995. "Shifting Paradigms: Theorizing Care and Justice." *Hypatia* 10 (2): 115-19.
Dobson, Chad. 2000. Head of Consumer Choice Council. Interview. Washington D.C., 22 February.

Eliasoph, Nina. 1998. *Avoiding Politics: How Americans Produce Apathy in Everyday Life*. Cambridge: Cambridge University Press.

Flammang, Janet A. 1997. *Women's Political Voice: How Women are Transforming the Practice and Study of Politics*. Philadelphia: Temple University Press.

Flynn, James, Paul Slovic, & C.K. Mertz. 1994, "Gender, Race, and Perception of Health Risks." *Risk Analysis* 14 (6): 1101-08.

Frank, Dana. 1994. *Purchasing Power: Consumer Organizing, Gender, and the Seattle Labor Movement 1919-1929*. Cambridge: Cambridge University Press.

____. 1985. "Housewives, Socialists, and the Politics of Food: The 1917 New York Cost-of-Living Protests." *Feminist Studies* 11: 255-86.

Goldberg, Cheryl. 1999. "Don't Buy Where You Can't Work," in Lawrence B. Glickman, ed., *Consumer Society in American History: A Reader*. Ithaca, NY: Cornell University Press.

Goss, Kristin A. 2001. "Let's Make an Issue of It: The Forgotten Role of Emotion and Cognition in Political Participation." Paper for the American Political Science Association, San Francisco. 30 August-2 September.

Goul Andersen, Jørgen, & Mette Tobiasen. 2001. *Politisk forbrug og politiske forbrugere. Globalisering og politik i hverdagslivet*. Aarhus: Magtudredningen, Aarhus Universitet.

Gustafson, Per E. 1998. "Gender Differences in Risk Perception: Theoretical and Methodological Perspectives." *Risk Analysis* 18 (6): 805-11.

High-Pippert, Angela. 2001. "A Million Moms, MADD Mothers, and Feminists: Media Coverage of Women Activists." Paper for the American Political Science Association's Special Session on Women and Politics, San Francisco. 29 August.

Hyman, Paula. 1989. "Immigrant Women and Consumer Protest: The New York Kosher Meat Boycott of 1902." *American Jewish History* 70 (1): 91-105.

Jaquette, Jane S. 1976. "Political Science." *Signs* 2 (1): 147-64.

King, Mary. 1999. *Mahatma Gandhi and Martin Luther King Jr.: The Power of Nonviolent Action*. Paris: UNESCO Publishing.

Klint, Jakob. 1997. *Max Havelaar-mærkede produkter: en undersøgelse af forbrugeren og storkunden*. Copenhagen: CASA.

LRF and Ekologiska Lantbrukarna. 2001. Vägen till marknaden: Ekologiska produkter: Ett underlag för kommunikation om ekologiska produkter med konsumenternas önskemål och kunskaper som grund. Stockholm: LRF, unpublished report.

LUI Marknadsinformation AB. 1999. Konsumentundersökning om ekologiska produkter/KRAV. Stockholm: LUI, unpublished report.

Micheletti, Michele. (2003). *Political Virtue and Shopping. Individuals, Consumerism, and Collective Action*. New York: Palgrave.

Nava, Mica. 1991. "Consumerism Reconsidered. Buying and Power." *Cultural Studies* 5 (2): 157-73.

Orleck, Annelise. 1993. "'We are That Mythical Thing Called the Public': Militant Housewives during the Great Depression." *Feminist Studies* 19: 147-72.

Pateman, Carole. 1979. "Hierarchical Organizations and Democratic Participation: The Problem of Sex." *Resources for Feminist Research* 8: 19-22.

____. 1983. "Some Reflection on Participation and Democratic Theory." *International Yearbook of Organizational Democracy* 1: 107-20.

____. 1989. "Feminist Critiques of the Public/Private Dichotomy," in Carole Pateman, *The Disorder of Women: Democracy, Feminism and Political Theory*. Oxford: Polity Press.

Petersson, Olof, Anders Westholm & Göran Blomberg. 1987. *Medborgarnas makt*. Stockholm: Carlssons.

Petersson, Olof, Jörgen Hermansson, Michele Micheletti, Jan Teorell & Anders Westholm. 1998. *Demokrati och medborgarskap: Demokratirådets rapport 1998*. Stockholm: SNS förlag.

264   Politics, Products, and Markets

Sikkink, Kathryn. 1986. "Codes of Conduct for Transnational Corporations: the Case of the WHO/UNICEF Code." *International Organization* 40: 815-40.

Sklar, Kathryn Kish. 1998. "The Consumers' White Label Campaign of the National Consumers' League 1898-1919," in Strasser, McGovern, & Judt eds., *Getting and Spending. European and American Consumer Societies in the 20th Century.* Cambridge: Cambridge University Press.

Slater, Don. 1997. "Consumer Culture and the Politics of Need," in Mica Nava, Andrew Blake, Iain MacRury, & Barry Richards, eds., *Buy This Book: Studies in Advertising and Consumption.* London: Routledge.

SNF. 1990. Statistics from a survey of members conducted by SIFO. Unpublished material.

Solér, Cecilia. 1997. *Att köpa miljövänliga dagligvaror.* Stockholm: Nerenius & Santérus Förlag.

Sørensen, Eva. 1997. "Brugeren og demokratiet." *Grus* 53: 81-96.

Stevens, Georgia L. 1994. "Linking Consumer Rights with Citizen Roles: An Opportunity for Consumer Educators." *Journal of Consumer Education* 12: 1-8.

Teorell, Jan. 2001. *Political Participation and the Theories of Democracy. A Research Agenda.* Paper for American Political Science Association, San Francisco, California.

Verba, Sidney. 2001. "Culture, Calculation, and Being a Pretty Good Citizen: Alternative Interpretations of Civil Engagement." Irvine, CA: Center for the Study of Democracy, University of California at Irvine. Unpublished paper accessible at <www.democ.uic.edu/democ/papers/verba.htm>.

Wessells, Cathy, Holger Donath, & Robert J. Johnston. 1999. "U.S. Consumer Preferences for Ecolabeled Seafood: Results of a Consumer Survey." Kingston: University of Rhode Island, Department of Environmental and Natural Resource Economics. Unpublished report.

Young, Iris Marion. 1994. "Gender as Seriality: Thinking about Women as a Social Collective." *Signs: Journal of Women in Culture and Society* 19: 713-38.

Yúdice, George. 1995. "Civil Society, Consumption, and Governamentality in an Age of Global Restructuring." *Social Text* 45 (4) (winter): 1-25.

Consumers as Political Participants? Shifts in Political Action Repertoires in Western Societies

Dietlind Stolle and Marc Hooghe

Introduction

In recent years, a number of studies have lamented the decline of social cohesion and civic engagement in Western societies. The claim is that not only political trust, but also generalized trust and civic engagement of various forms are steadily plunging. Some authors even portray this phenomenon as a symptom of a pervasive democratic crisis in Western societies (Bellah et al. 1985; Etzioni 1993; Putnam 1995, 2000; Lane 2000). These studies, which document the loss of social cohesion and a decline in social interaction, have received considerable criticism, which, in turn, has led to a continuing and vigorous debate (Portes 1998; Paxton 1999). One might even state that the cultural conflict between modernists and postmodernists, which is well known in the humanities, has now spread into sociology and political science. We see a clear opposition between, on the one hand, authors decrying the loss of traditional institutions and forms of participation, and on the other hand, authors stressing the opportunities created by the rise of new, more fluid forms of interaction and participation, of which political consumerism is one good example. Explicitly or implicitly, most of the authors focusing on the decline of traditional participation mechanisms are at least partly influenced by communitarian insights on the importance of vibrant community, and therefore we think it is safe to refer to this literature as a representation of communitarian pessimism.

There are three main arguments that evolved as a response to the pessimistic claim regarding the decline of social and political participation. The first one states that the observations of the decline of civic engagement and social cohesion are empirically inaccurate

(Klingemann & Fuchs 1995; Schudson 1996; Paxton 1999; Ladd 1996). The second argument accepts the validity of the presented data and acknowledges that they represent a real social trend. These authors, however, claim that the communitarian description is one-sided because it fails to pay attention to the rise of new forms of commitment, participation, and interaction, which are seen as potential equivalents to traditional participation and integration mechanisms (Beck 1993; Lichterman 1996; Castells 1997; Eliasoph 1998; Wuthnow 1998). The third argument is closely related to the second, but it goes a step further by arguing that the existing political institutions are inadequate to address citizens' new concerns and their new styles of involvement. In this account, these changes represent the developmental trajectory of advanced post-industrial societies, and they do not cause any worries for the future of democratic governance (Inglehart 1997; Inglehart & Baker 2000; Norris 1999, 2002). In fact, phenomena such as political consumerism might potentially substitute for conventional forms of political participation that are increasingly perceived as less efficient and less suitable for the global nature of political problems.

However, neither the defendants of traditional forms of participation nor those praising the possibilities of new ones have shown enough evidence for the political and social consequences of these new developments. For example, does web-surfing, the occasional petition e-mail, or political consumerism lead to the development of collective identity, generalized trust, or political efficacy? Are these new forms in any way related to fostering the strength of democracy? If not, how can the role of associational, party, and union membership be compensated for in the modern world of individualized political action?

In this chapter we examine these questions theoretically. First, we explore the three arguments against the communitarian worries and critically assess their validity. It will become obvious that we do not have enough insight from research to draw a final conclusion in the battle between communitarians and their critics. Furthermore, we explore the extent to which these suggested, new forms of social and political participation are indeed connected to a strong and vital democracy. Finally, we investigate the potential role of political consumerism, specifically as a new form of political participation, while reflecting on ways to adequately measure and study this new phenomenon.

Communitarian Worries

Concerns about the erosion of traditional social ties and institutions have always been the center of attention in the social sciences. Already in the nineteenth century, authors like Tönnies, Durkheim, and Weber wondered how social order and cohesion could be maintained given the political and economic modernization of most Western societies. Since the 1980s, philosophical debates between liberals and communitarians seem to have fostered a revived interest in this theme among political and social scientists. If vibrant communities are indeed essential for individual and collective development and well-being as communitarian theory proclaims (Etzioni 1993; Walzer 1990), it becomes all the more crucial to know whether such communities actually still exist in Western societies. Responding to this communitarian agenda, social scientists have increasingly turned their attention to the study of all kinds of aspects of social cohesion and interaction.

One of the first and most seminal books in this respect is that of Robert Bellah et al., *Habits of the Heart* (1985), documenting how the rise of a new, more utilitarian kind of individualism is destroying traditional patterns of interaction in the United States, which were based on cooperation and close-knit social ties within small communities. These old "habits of the heart" are rapidly being replaced by more fluent interaction patterns, based on self-interest, unique preferences, and individualistic solutions, Bellah and his associates argue. In subsequent publications, the erosion of at least some traditional institutions has indeed been well documented.

For example, since the 1960s Americans have been losing trust in their government and in government institutions, a trend that has been shown for most liberal democracies (Nye, Zelikow, & King 1997; Pharr & Putnam 2000). Not only political trust seems to be declining but also various forms of political and social participation. Political parties traditionally have served as a connection between citizens and the political system, but in a number of countries these parties are confronted with a rapid decline of party identification. Not only are membership figures going down, but citizens seem to rely less on ideological clues provided by political parties to establish their own political and world views, and as a consequence voter volatility seems to be on the rise (Wattenberg 1996; Schmitt & Holmberg 1995; Dalton & Wattenberg 2000). Partly as a result of

the decline of trust in government and the weakening of party identification, voter turnout has also steadily declined since the 1970s, a
phenomenon which is not limited to the United States, but is also
prevalent in other Western societies (Nie, Verba, & Petrocik 1979;
Teixeira 1992; Jackman & Miller 1995; Lijphart 1997; Hooghe &
Pelleriaux 1998; McDonald & Popkin 2001).

The most systematic account of the potential erosion of social
and civic life can be found in the work of Harvard political scientist
Robert Putnam (1995, 2000). According to Putnam, the loss of confidence and social ties does not remain limited to the political sphere but
pervades all aspects of society. Americans not only refrain from joining
political parties, they also tend to participate less actively in all kinds of
voluntary associations. Drawing on commercial lifestyle surveys, Putnam
demonstrates that it is not only associative participation that has been
going down in American society; the same trend can be observed for
various forms of informal interaction, including the traditional common meal at the family dinner table, visits to friends and neighbors,
card games with friends, and social dinners at restaurants.

Putnam (2000) argues that the loss of civic engagement is not
only troublesome with regard to social cohesion but also in terms of
their political consequences. Since Almond & Verba (1963), it is
generally assumed that a thriving civic culture contributes to the
stability of democratic political systems (Harrison & Huntington
2000). In an earlier publication on civic culture in Italy, Putnam
(1993) demonstrated that the regions with the highest density of
voluntary associations are also the regions with highly performing
regional governments and institutions. Putnam's conclusion that civic
engagement is declining in the United States, therefore implies that
this downward trend could threaten the long-term stability of American democracy. The underlying message is quite clear: the loss of
community in American society eventually destabilizes a democratic
civic culture, which, in turn, would have negative consequences for
the viability of democracy as such.

More specifically, voluntary associations and other forms of social bonds have become the standard indicators of healthy democracies. Authors inspired by the communitarian philosophy consider
them important for two main reasons. First, they matter because of
their socialization function, which means that they socialize members to become more civic-minded and more oriented toward cooperation, trust, and reciprocity. Second, associations matter because

of the external link they provide between citizens and the state—they offer a way for citizens to influence state and governmental affairs. Intermediary organizations aggregate individual interests and thus contribute to processes of complexity reduction and gatekeeping, which are necessary for a political system to function effectively. Or, as Verba, Schlozman, and Brady (1995, 37) summarize it: "Political participation affords citizens in a democracy an opportunity to communicate information to government officials about their concerns and preferences and to put pressure on them to respond." A decline in associational life implies that both of these functions are being threatened.

In sum, we observe that not only do the pessimistic studies describe a decline of traditional integration mechanisms, they also state that this decline poses a fundamental threat for the survival of healthy communities and democratic political systems. This kind of literature has met fierce opposition, leading to a kind of trench warfare. Three kinds of arguments are being invoked to criticize the pessimistic literature. These three defense lines will be presented in the following sections. Although this division into three separate arguments is to some degree arbitrary as some authors deploy several of these arguments simultaneously, the division allows us to summarize the main points of this criticism, while enabling the development of a coherent research agenda for the study of new and old forms of participation and social capital.

Empirical Criticism

The first argument against communitarian pessimism is largely empirical: it is stated that the available data simply do not support the conclusion that engagement and cohesion are on the decline. This argument applies mostly to the situation in the United States. A number of authors question the validity of the data being used by Putnam and other communitarian authors (Schudson 1996; Paxton 1999). A rather famous example involves the way Putnam uses declining membership figures of PTA's (Parents Teachers Associations) to support his claim that parental involvement in the school education of their children is on the decline. Ladd (1999, 31-43) and Crawford and Levitt (1999) draw attention to the fact that a large number of local PTA chapters are no longer affiliated with the national umbrella organization, which would explain the decline of national membership figures. Furthermore, criticism has been voiced that Putnam's decline figures appear to be dramatic, because they are founded on the assumption that rising education levels should automatically lead to more participation. However, with his latest research effort, *Bowling Alone* (2000), Putnam has probably silenced most aspects of these critiques as he lists an abundance of indicators showing the decline of various forms of social interactions, with or without controls for education. With regard to the United States, the decline of at least some traditional participation mechanisms seems by now a well-established fact.

A variation of this first argument is that the erosion of civic life may indeed be taking place in the United States, but this observation should not be generalized to other Western societies. At least for the moment, we do not have any conclusive evidence that participation levels are also declining in Western Europe. However, we do know that, as in the case of their American counterparts, European political parties and trade unions seem to be losing members. Results are less clear with regard to other forms of participation, and they do not warrant the conclusion that overall participation levels are declining in Europe (Topf 1995; Renooy 1996; Dekker & Van den Broek 1998; Putnam 2002; Hooghe 2003a). At least the enormous amount of evidence that was assembled for the *Beliefs in Government* project does not support pessimistic assumptions (Klingemann & Fuchs 1995). This does not imply that there would not be any reason for concern in Western European societies. It is very well possible that Europe will be confronted with the same structural processes as the United States, but with a certain time lag. In the Netherlands, for example, a decline in participation levels has been observed among younger and well-educated cohorts (Dekker & De Hart 2000; Thomassen, Aarts, & van der Kolk 2000). Most blatantly perhaps is the strong evidence for systematic decline of political trust in most European countries, with the exception of the Netherlands (Inglehart 1997; Listhaug 1995; Norris 1999). However, future empirical evidence will have to determine whether the effects we currently observe are period or cohort effects.

In sum, we have to conclude that this first line of argument adds some useful information to the general picture: not all forms of participation seem to be in decline, nor is the existence of this trend firmly established in all Western societies. The pessimistic literature, therefore, needs to be qualified in these aspects. However, we cannot deny that European societies also show signs of erosion of political trust and of some types of participation.

Not Less, But Different

The second argument against communitarian pessimism does not question the figures and trends described in the erosion literature. These authors seem to acknowledge the fact that traditional participation and integration mechanisms, like parties and trade unions, are indeed in decline in Western societies. The fundamental line of critique here is that the communitarian authors put forward a one-sided description of social trends because they exclusively focus on traditional mechanisms while neglecting the new participation styles and methods which are rapidly replacing the old ones (Gundelach 1984). The willingness to participate in politics and societal affairs is still as strong as it was a few decades ago, these authors argue, but this willingness will no longer translate into membership in traditional political organizations (Eliasoph 1998; Lichterman 1996). Rather, citizens today and especially younger generations will prefer participation in loose, less hierarchical, informal networks and all kinds of lifestyle-related sporadic mobilization efforts. Membership in informal local parental groups, political consumerism, membership in advocacy networks, the regular signing and forwarding of e-mail petitions, and the spontaneous organization of protests and rallies are just a few examples of this phenomenon.

Although we are witnessing a great diversity in these new participation mechanisms, we identify here at least four common characteristics in relation to them: (1) structure; (2) substantive issues; (3) regularity; and (4) style of these new involvements. First, these new forms of participation abandon the traditional, formal, and bureaucratic organization model in favor of new, horizontal, and more network-like models. Loose connections are rapidly replacing static bureaucracies (Wuthnow 1998). Furthermore, these new forms of participation rely much more on elite challenging action repertoires than on the traditional elite directed repertoires (Hellemans & Hooghe 1995; Inglehart 1999; Stolle & Welzel 2000). Instead of collaborating in formal umbrella structures, these new initiatives, according to Castells (1997), are better adapted to the needs of the current information society by developing horizontal network structures. Second, in general these new initiatives are also less concerned with institutional affairs, such as party politics, contrary to more traditional political organizations. Lifestyle elements are being politicized and, although the actors no longer label their action explicitly as being "political," these preoccupations do lead to political mobilization (Bennett 1998; Eliasoph 1998). The new forms of participation clearly break the traditional boundaries between the classic public and private divide. Michele Micheletti's chapter in this volume describes how women started to fight food prices, triggered by seemingly private motivations, and became increasingly involved in political discussions and further political protests. In other words, previously perceived private spheres, such as food consumption, become a platform for political mobilization.

Third, new forms of participation seem more spontaneous and somewhat more irregular than traditional forms of participation. Even though traditional political acts such as voting do not happen at frequent intervals either, the participation in petitions, protests, and consumer boycotts, for example, emphasize the importance of spontaneity, irregularity, easy exit, and the possibility of shifting-in and shifting-out as a form of involvement. Finally, new forms of participation are certainly less collective and group-oriented in character, even though they might be triggered by larger societal concerns (e.g., global injustice) and might also have aggregate consequences (e.g., change of corporate practices). Yet the actual act of participation is often individualized in character, whether we take the decision to forward a selected e-mail as did Jonah Peretti, when he triggered among other reactions a worldwide response to Nike's production practices (in this volume) or whether we make the decision to purchase a certain product. Such individualized acts do not necessarily lead to group interaction, such as those in unions, voluntary groups, regular council meetings, etc. In short, new forms of participation seemingly exhibit new qualities compared to conventional forms of participation.

A typical example of this new phenomenon is the protest movement that developed in Belgium as a reaction against the murder of several young children. Although the movement clearly presented itself as being non-political, it constantly phrased demands and requests towards the political system and in doing so met with considerable success (Deneckere & Hooghe 2003). The mobilization success of these and similar movements demonstrates at least that, under certain circumstances, the horizontal networks can be just as effective as the more traditional bureaucratic organizations. Further examples are e-mail campaigns to protest the election fiasco in the U.S. presidential elections 2000. Thousands of voters repeatedly sent their electronic signatures to demand the correct counting of votes in Florida. A spontaneous e-mail cascade caused even the powerful Chinese government to make concessions in an incident of an explosion in a local school, apparently a result of fireworks production by children.

Loose, non-bureaucratic, individualized action is also a good description for political consumerism. As previous chapters demonstrate, political consumers attach great importance to non-economic values (e.g., political and ethical values and social attitudes) when they choose between products, producers, and services. This means that they consider the market as an arena for politics and ethical action, and that they consider market actors to be responsible for political and social development. Although political consumerism might be steered and influenced by existing horizontal and global consumer associations, the actual act of what is called the political consumer choice is practiced in an individualized, most likely sporadic, and spontaneous manner.

Finally, the doubts regarding the obsessive focus on formal memberships and organizations have been echoed by scholars who work on gender relations, who argue that the research on formal and informal socializing is misguided because it looks in the wrong places. By focusing exclusively on the decline of formal organizations, the communitarian authors fail to acknowledge the fact that women's participation in political and social life has risen constantly during the past [few?] decades.[1] In many Western societies women have caught up with men in terms of education levels and participation in the labor market, and since we know that both education and paid labor have positive "spill-over" effects on voluntary participation and political interest (Andersen & Cook 1985; Verba, Schlozman, & Brady 1995), we have every reason to believe that women's participation has risen since World War II, despite the limited time budget that is available to working women. This fact is seldom acknowledged in the communitarian literature because of a one-sided orientation towards formal participation structures.

In view of these critics, true networks and forms of social engagement can be found in daily social interactions (Dekker & Uslaner 2001), namely at the workplace (Mutz & Mondak 1998), in schools and neighborhoods (Newton 1997), and in caring networks such as baby-sitting circles and other child-care networks (Lowndes 2000). In particular, women tend to prefer more egalitarian networks, which is reflected in some examples of "feminist organizations" (Ferree & Martin 1995). Lowndes' point in particular urges us to reconsider how informal and small-scale care networks actually contribute to the maintenance of social cohesion within a society. A typical example would be that young mothers in the suburbs jointly bring their children to, and pick them up from, school. These kinds of arrangements are mostly informal and ad hoc and therefore not usually registered in survey research on participation. But nevertheless, they are likely to contribute significantly to the maintenance of social cohesion and the advancement of quality of life within these suburbs.

In short, this second camp of critics urges us to broaden our view of what is relevant political and social participation. The critique maintains that we might have missed recent developments in forms of participation that are not as easy to observe, count, and measure. These forms of participation are more fluid, sporadic, and less organized. In addition, we might have looked in the wrong places all along, particularly because women have been regularly involved in social interactions that might have wider societal consequences.

Less and Obsolete

The third argument against communitarian pessimism is the most fundamental and, from a theoretical point of view, also the most interesting. These authors go a step further in that they claim that the observed decline does not necessarily have negative effects for social or political stability. Their argument is that maybe formal participation mechanisms and traditional political organizations have been necessary during the development phase of mass democracies, but that in contemporary societies they have lost much of their relevance. These authors argue that the decline of trust in government and politics should not be seen as a threat to political stability, but rather as an indication of the fact that these systems have reached adulthood and therefore have learned to live with the scrutiny of critical citizens (Inglehart 1997; Welzel & Inglehart 1999; Norris 1999, 2002).

The data indeed show that the younger age cohorts, who are identified by Putnam as responsible for the decline of civic participation, are also among the groups most strongly attached to democratic values. Especially in the work of Inglehart, the decline of traditional political integration is conceptualized as being part of a global and structural transformation of value patterns in Western societies, moving away from survival values such as obedience, trust in hierarchies, and work commitment, towards more self-expressive and postmaterialist values such as tolerance, freedom, and individual fulfillment. A more critical attitude toward the political system should not be seen as a threat to the stability of democratic regimes.

Although political institutions will face a challenge because of the rise of these new generations of critical citizens, these younger age cohorts are firmly in favor of democracy, and therefore the spread of their value pattern does not threaten the stability of democracy as we know it. In fact, the attitudinal changes we observe in younger age cohorts also lead to behavioral changes. Younger cohorts are not just more critical toward existing mainstream political institutions, they are also more inclined to participate in non-hierarchical groups, such as the Green party. The openness of Green party meetings and the horizontal decision-making process in Green parties (which is not always to their political advantage) stands in particular contrast to the well-organized and hierarchical decision-making patterns in other well-established parties and organizations.[2]

In sum, in Inglehart's view, younger cohorts develop distrust in these existing, traditional political institutions, but with their deep belief in democracy and the importance of democratic rules they influence the political system through new types of protest actions, initiatives, and new organizations. Even though Goul Andersen and Tobiasen, in this volume, show that political consumers are overall not necessarily less trusting in political institutions than members of traditional associations, their results also reveal that political consumers are less in favor of hierarchical institutions, such as the police and public administration. With the claim that traditional groups and organizations are now obsolete and should make room for these newer institutions and organizations, Inglehart has opened a Pandora's box of social and political participation and social capital research.

New Challenges for Social and Political Participation Research

The critics of the communitarian school have provided us with important insights into potential changes of political action repertoires utilized by citizens in advanced industrialized societies. The question emerges about what exactly is the link between these forms of participation and democracy. Do new forms of participation take over the functions provided by voluntary associations[3] or do they fulfill new functions? We first consider the socialization function (Hooghe 2003b). Political scientists and sociologists have not studied the effects of such networks and new forms of participation systematically. For example, with alternative forms of social participation such as child-care circles, we do not know exactly which societal and political consequences these activities have. Do parents engaged in these networks of exchange learn generalized values such as trust and norms of reciprocity? If not, what exactly are the socializing consequences of such networks? How exactly is the development of generalized values and trust influenced in interactions that involve less face-to-face contact and less personal commitment and delegation of tasks? In other words, the actual potential of various social interactions to socialize trust and cooperation or other democratic attitudes remains insufficiently tested by both the communitarians and their critics. As a first step, Inglehart's research demonstrates that citizens who use new flexible tools of political participation are more democratic in their value orientations. This suggests, perhaps, that such values are produced elsewhere in our societies, for example through affluence in childhood (Inglehart), through education and schooling (Lipset), or through a fair and egalitarian social and judicial system (Rothstein & Stolle 2003). In this account, social and political forms of participation might, however, at most contribute to the perpetuation and maintenance of certain values—they will not radically alter them (Hooghe 2003c). In sum, it is possible that the socialization function, which is traditionally ascribed to voluntary associations, has now been taken over by other institutions, but research has to produce more evidence for this thesis.

Second, we consider the external function of some forms of participation. We have described the character of new forms of social and political participation as more short-lived, more spontaneous, less organized, and more fluid. Under these conditions, do these new forms of political participation provide sufficient links between the citizens and the political system? One of the problems is that decision-making within parliamentary democracies inevitably will be a long-term process, respecting procedures and consultations. If mobilization campaigns become short-lived events, the impact of such campaigns and their resulting political actions will automatically become more limited. How can long-term institutionalized decision-making processes be systematically influenced without an ingrained organizational structure that aggregates citizens' opinion?

Third, the weakness of activities like checkbook activism and political consumerism may not necessarily be its low promise for socialization effects (even though this too is an unsolved issue) but rather its lack of legitimacy as final barriers inhibit inclusive participation by all citizens. While we know that active involvement in social and political organizations is spread unequally within society, this inequality nevertheless remains somewhat limited because of the fact that even the privileged classes are confronted with an upper limit of time availability. Such an upper limit does not exist for the availability of financial resources or knowledge and education (Verba, Schlozman, & Brady 1995, 288-303). A major shift from voluntary participation towards financial or knowledge-based participation would, therefore, lead to a drastic sharpening of political inequalities, giving even more political leverage to the financially and educationally privileged, the former of which is already the case with regard to campaign contributions in the United States (Dworkin 2000, 351-85). This trend might also apply to political consumerism. In order to be able to choose among a variety of products, one needs education and knowledge about various products and the luxury of financial resources. In other words, even though political consumerism is an activity that certainly draws in various groups of the population, such as women in general and housewives in particular, the problem is that this activity might be a privilege only of those who have education, knowledge, and information, and those who possess financial resources. Goul Andersen and Tobiasen's chapter delivers interesting empirical insights here. Whereas, on the one hand, they find that education, global identity, and knowledge largely influence the use of political consumerist acts, the effect of income per se, on the other hand, was negligible at similar levels of education. This suggests that education is the decisive resource for this form of participation.

Finally, for new forms of political participation such as e-mail petitioning and political consumerism, it is not really clear what is the meaning of such engagements in an individual's life, and whether this meaning is necessarily political. It could very well be that private motivations dominate a certain act that seems political or at least other-regarding to us. Where is the demarcation line between truly private and truly public acts, and when do we see a connection and blurring of lines between the two? For instance, in the past decades a flourishing, commercially organized, gay subculture has come into existence in some metropolitan areas like San Francisco, London, or Amsterdam. Gay and lesbian magazines, shops, and travel agencies are an important constitutive element of this culture. However, while some authors consider this kind of commercial venture as a public and even politically inspired manifestation of gay and lesbian identity, for others it is just a form of individual consumer preference without any political consequences (Adam, Duyvendak, & Krouwel 1999). The preference to travel with a gay travel agency might be a matter of convenience or taste and might not trigger further political action or influence on political identities.

Can any such engagements be interpreted as political participation? Take the example of e-mail petitions. How can we distinguish between someone who regularly visits political websites, participates in chat-room discussions, and signs e-mail petitions of a political nature from someone who sends the petition along as it comes from a friend that he trusts, even though he is not very aware of the actual political problem for which he gave the signature? Or how do we establish the difference between someone who doesn't visit McDonald's because she doesn't like hamburgers and someone who boycotts the golden arches because they are seen as a symbol for economic globalization? And what if this second person goes out to a McDonald's once a year? The distinctions are important because, if these activities are not sufficiently political, the link between citizens and the political system might not be successfully guaranteed through these forms of participation.

A related problem is that it seems very difficult to actually measure these activities with conventional survey questions or other methods of data collection. Previously important memberships were clearly defined and attached to an organizational unit. Informal participation, however—and that is almost definitional—is no longer attached to an organizational unit in obvious ways. It is clear that new questions and new approaches for acquiring information from citizens about the variety of these forms of engagement have to be designed for this purpose. Any new survey that examines the new forms of political participation should take these concerns into account.

Until we have addressed these above issues, we cannot be certain about the full role of the new forms of participation and their ability to substitute for the decline of traditional forms of engagement both quantitatively and qualitatively. In the last section below, we demonstrate how some of these specific concerns apply to the concept of political consumerism.

Political Consumerism—A Form of Modern Political Participation?

Like many new forms of political and social participation, political consumerism has not been systematically researched in the social sciences. This lack of research makes it more difficult to solve the battle between communitarians and their critics. In the following, we apply our list of cautions with new forms of social and political participation to the concept of political consumerism and suggest some conceptual solutions as well as further research to advance knowledge on this phenomenon. However, little is known about its socialization effects and so we mostly limit ourselves to a discussion about measuring and conceptualizing political consumerism, and conclude with some thoughts about the inclusiveness of political consumerism and how it might link citizens to the political system.

How can the act of political consumerism provide the context for the socialization of civic values and attitudes? This question has not been examined thoroughly, yet from the empirical chapters in this volume we know that mostly value predispositions, such as global identities, are potential prerequisites for political consumerist acts. Another example is offered in Greenberg's chapter, where she shows that under conditions of threat, group identities, for example, blacks in urban neighborhoods in the period around World War II, might cause boycott behavior against other groups. Again, previously attained identities become mobilized under certain circumstances to trigger forms of political involvement. However, Micheletti in this volume shows how originally private concerns, such as food prices and the related outrage, can lead to the development and shaping of political identities and further political action for women and particularly housewives. Yet, given the short-term character of these campaigns, we do not know how lasting the resulting political attitudes and values are. This issue is open for further research.

A second issue arises. How can we define political consumerism, and how are we able to distinguish citizens who act as political consumers from those who do not? We propose two criteria that need to be fulfilled in order for shopping behavior and economic decisions to be considered as forms of "political consumerism." The first criterion might be labeled "awareness": the actor involved has to have sufficient knowledge and a politically or socially inspired motivation for his/her consumer decisions. The second criterion would be the regularity of the action: the actor must take decisions on a regular basis; a one-time decision is not sufficient to be considered as a form of "political consumerism."

We have already alluded to the difficulties involved in defining when consumerism is truly political. When measuring political consumerism, we propose here to think of the concept in several dimensions. The first step is to distinguish citizens who are aware of labeling schemes and various ethical dimensions of products and services from those who do not even know that such consumer choices, beyond price and conventional quality concerns, are available. The latter group is composed of individuals who have not even thought about differences in products or services based on any kind of labeling (whether it be an environmental scheme or socially responsible investing in ethical funds or concern issues as discrimination, labor exploitation, etc.). This seems like a simple distinction. Even if the latter group would buy the "right" products, because of a purely individual or economic motivation, this hardly can be considered as a form of political consumerism.

We like to use simple scenarios to elucidate our points and, thus, introduce Eva, Paul, and Lisa. When Eva goes shopping, she regularly looks for labeling schemes and certain company names. Paul is not aware of these distinctions; he buys whatever is cheapest. Clearly, Eva is what we call a conscientious consumer, whereas Paul is not. Lisa, on the other hand, once saw a sign in the supermarket that indicated that the coffee sold there was produced without any child labor. She thought of her children and was inspired by the moment to buy this coffee. The point is that this was a one-time act. Is Lisa a conscientious consumer? We think not. In sum, we have identified two important aspects that distinguish conscientious consumers from those who are not: awareness of labeling schemes and frequency of buying these kinds of products and services. Let's see how these dimensions of conscientious shopping can be graphed in figure 1.

Figure 1
Identifying the *Conscientious* Consumer

Awareness → Frequency of conscientious Purchases ↓	Yes	No
Yes	Conscientious consumers Eva	
No	*Lisa*	*Paul*

The figure clearly indicates that only consumers who are aware of labeling schemes and those who buy labeled products regularly, like Eva, can be called political consumers. Are all conscientious consumers also political consumers? Not quite. There is Anna, and Anna's daughter has an allergy against peanuts. For any food item Anna buys for the family, she has to check the ingredients carefully. Very soon in her shopping trips Anna discovers that certain companies label their food products better than others, in fact, some candy producers label their products as "peanut-free." She finds this convenient and develops the regular habit of buying the food products of this company. Even though Anna is certainly a *conscientious* consumer, she does not seem to be a *political* consumer, because her motivation is purely private, in this case the health of her daughter. She can be distinguished from someone who buys certain types of chocolate that have been labeled as "fair trade" products. In other words, motivation plays a role. Consumers who are politically, socially, and environmentally motivated to make certain product decisions are clearly what we would label *political* consumers. Consumers with private motivations, such as Anna, are not. However, what happens after a while if Anna's daughter has a terrible experience with chocolate that was badly labeled, which led to her being hospitalized? Anna gets so upset about bad labeling that she joins a citizen consumer group, regularly participates in their meetings, and even contributes articles to their website. It seems that Anna, even though inspired by private experiences, eventually becomes a politically active consumer.

It is apparent that we need to make further distinctions, namely among the different motivations of conscientious consumers and consumers' potential for political action. Both our dimensions (public awareness and regularity) are important for the identification of *political* consumers. Active political consumers are either publicly motivated (or have transformed their private concerns into public action), and they link political consumerism to a form of political action, such as joining consumer groups, signing petitions, writing letters to newspapers or companies, contacting politicians, journalists, and civil servants, using the Internet to keep informed on political consumerism, etc. *Public* motivations for labeled products may possibly be related to concerns for the environment, equality in society, and global social justice. Such public motivations could be accompanied by forms of *political action*, such as membership in citizens' and consumer groups and persuading others to make consistent and frequent political consumerist market choices, etc., or they could be *passive* like Eva who regularly buys labeled products, among them environmentally safe products, but is not a member of a consumer group, or does not visit the Web to read consumer news, etc. Private motivations for a purchase based on labeling schemes are related to health concerns, allergies, diet, etc. However, we can only consider citizens with private motivations *political* consumers if they link their private concerns to some other forms of political action or to group or society related goals. Citizens who purchase labeled products based purely on private motivations, for example lifestyle issues or even diseases/allergies (as in the case of Anna before the daughter had the incident), are not considered political consumers. Figure 2 clarifies our distinctions regarding political consumer behavior and what we may possibly call apolitical consumer behavior.

In figure 2 we distinguish between the motivational and political activity dimension. Only one of the cells yields a category that we consider to be political consumer behavior. Private motivation combined with no political action on behalf of consumer issues does not typify political consumerism, even though the consumers involved can rightly be called conscientious consumers.

In sum, as is true with various new forms of political participation, political consumerism is a complicated concept to define operationally, which makes it difficult to measure correctly. However, good measurements of the concept are important in order to be able

Figure 2
Identifying *Political* Consumers
(from the group of conscientious consumers)

Motivation →↓ Potential for political action	Public	Private
Active	Active political consumers *"Ideal" political consumer*	*Anna after incident*
Passive	Passive political consumers *Eva*	Conscientious But not political consumerism *Anna before Incident*

to respond to the worries of communitarians. Without good measurements we cannot clearly say whether, quantitatively, political consumerism has a place as a common political action repertoire and whether, qualitatively, it has the effects that are desirable for democracy. Therefore, our suggestion is that we apply the concept only to those consumer decisions that are taken on the basis of public motivation and awareness as well as taken on a regular basis by the actor.

Finally, there are two other considerations that need to be included in future discussions about political consumerism. Setting the socialization function aside, the worry of communitarians about the importance of intermediary groups, because of their external links between citizens and the political system, deserves further attention. Even though other political activities on behalf of consumer issues enter at least in part our proposed definition of political consumerism, the problem is that most political consumerist actions are directed at companies and large corporate organizations and not at governments or specific governmental policies. Does political consumerism really provide the link between citizens and the political system, as most political scientists argue that voluntary associations do? What is the extent to which governments are truly influenced by this type of citizen involvement? Surely, governments are also producers of products, governments provide services, and they even receive the signals from consumers regarding their values and preferences. However, governments cannot be directly held accountable and responsible for consumer actions unless these actions are also directed at it. In these cases, consumerism might even have the opposite effect because it allows citizens to seek individual solutions (e.g., buying organic and thus "healthy" food) instead of pressing for government action for generally applicable rules on, for instance, food safety.

Furthermore, political consumerism like many other forms of participation is not all-inclusive. Education, certain values, and predominantly the purse might determine the extent to which it is an accessible and accepted political tool. This has truly worrisome democratic implications. However, there is no ideal form of political or even social participation that does not depend on socioeconomic resources. Given the fact that fair-trade and environmentally friendly products still are substantially more expensive than regular brands, we have to consider the possibility that political consumerism might be even more strongly biased than other forms of political participation. In sum, political consumerism might be only within reach for those groups of the population who (because of their cognitive, financial, and other resources) already are highly active in social and political life. Consumer activities, therefore, might have limits in the way they can directly substitute for traditional channels of political participation. However, there is a catch 22. The more citizens shop for eco-labeled products or products that guarantee safety and respect for workers who produce the products, the greater their market share and the more we would find such products to be affordable and in reach for larger groups of the population. From this perspective, political consumerism has the potential of becoming an inclusive form of involvement that should not be forgotten in the debate about our current state of civicness.

Notes

1. However, see evidence about a continued and, in fact, increased gender gap in political interest at least in the context of the Netherlands in van Deth 2000.
2. Some recent and not-yet published research, however, points to the fact that, now that Green parties have entered government coalitions in a number of European countries, they quickly abandon their open internal structures in favor of more traditional party organizing, cfr. Conference on "Green parties in Government," Free University of Brussels, 7 December 2001.
3. However, there is strong disagreement about whether voluntary associations fulfill the socialization function in the first place. For some aspects of the debate, see Hooghe & Stolle (2003).

References

Adam, Barry D., J. W. Duyvendak, & A. Krouwel, eds. 1999. *The Global Emergence of Gay and Lesbian Politics.* Philadelphia: Temple University Press.

Almond, Gabriel, & Sidney Verba. 1963. *The Civic Culture.* Princeton, NJ: Princeton University Press.

Andersen, Kristi, & Elizabeth A. Cook. 1985. "Women, Work, and Political Attitudes." *American Journal of Political Science* 29(3): 606-25.

Baumgartner, Frank, & Beth Leech. 1998. *Basic Interests.* Princeton, NJ: Princeton University Press.

Beck, Ulrich. 1993. *Die Erfindung des Politischen.* Frankfurt: Suhrkamp.

Bellah, Robert et al. 1985. *Habits of the Heart.* Berkeley: University of California Press.

Bennett, W. Lance. 1998. "The UnCivic Culture: Communication, Identity, and the Rise of Lifestyle Politics." *Political Science & Politics* 31(4): 741-61.

Brady, Henry, Key Lehman Schlozman, & Sidney Verba. 1999. "Prospecting for Participants." *American Political Science Review* 93(1): 153-68.

Castells, Manuel. 1997. *The Rise of the Network Society.* Oxford: Blackwell.

Crawford, Susan, & Peggy Levitt. 1999. "Social Change and Civic Engagement: The Case of the PTA," in Theda Skocpol & Fiorina Morris, eds., *Civic Engagement in American Democracy.* Washington D. C.: Brookings Institution.

Dalton, Russel, & Martin Wattenberg, eds. 2000. *Parties without Partizans.* Oxford: Oxford University Press.

Dekker, Paul. 2000. "Social Participation and Political Involvement." Paper presented at the 18th World Congress of the International Political Science Association, Québec. 1-5 August.

___, & R. Uslaner, eds. 2001. *Social Capital and Everyday Life.* New York: Routledge.

___, R. Uslaner, & Andries van den Broek. 1998. "Civil Society in Comparative Perspective: Involvement in Voluntary Associations in North America and Western Europe." *Voluntas* 9 (1): 11-38.

___, & Joep de Hart. 2000. "Het sociaal kapitaal van de Nederlandse kiezer," in Marc Hooghe, ed. *Sociaal kapitaal en demokratie.* Leuven: Acco, pp. 83-112.

Deneckere, Gita, & Marc Hooghe. 2003. "La Marche Blanche en Belgique (octobre 1996), une mouvement de masse spectaculaire mais éphémère." *Le Mouvement Social* (202: 153-64).

van Deth, Jan. 2000. "Interesting but Irrelevant: Social Capital and the Saliency of Politics in Western Europe." *European Journal of Political Research* 37 (2): 115-47.

Dworkin, Ronald. 2000. *Sovereign Virtue: The Theory and Practice of Equality.* Cambridge, MA: Harvard University Press.

Eliasoph, Nina. 1998. *Avoiding Politics.* Cambridge: Cambridge University Press.

Etzioni, Amitai. 1993. *The Spirit of Community.* New York: Crown.

Ferree, Myra Marx, & Patricia Martin, eds. 1995. *Feminist Organizations.* Philadelphia: Temple University Press.

Gundelach, Peter. 1984. "Social Transformation and New Forms of Voluntary Associations." *Social Science Information* 23 (6): 1049-81.

Hall, Peter. 1999. "Social Capital in Britain." *British Journal of Political Science* 29 (3): 417-61.

Harrison, Lawrence, & Samuel Huntington, eds. 2000. *Culture Matters: How Values Shape Human Progress.* New York: Basic Books.

Hellemans, Staf. 1990. *Strijd om de moderniteit.* Leuven: Universitaire Pers.

___, & Marc Hooghe, red. 1995. *Van mei '68 tot Hand in Hand: Nieuwe sociale bewegingen in België.* Leuven: Garant.

Hooghe, Marc, ed. 2000. *Sociaal kapitaal en democratie.* Leuven: Acco.

___. 2003a. "Why Should We Be Bowling Alone? Results from a Belgian Survey on Civic Participation." *Voluntas* 14 (1): 41-59.

___. 2003b. "Participation in Voluntary Associations and Value Indicators." *Nonprofit and Voluntary Sector Quarterly* 32 (1): 47-69.

___. 2003c. "Value Congruence in Voluntary Associations." In Marc Hooghe & Dietlind Stolle, eds. *Generating Social Capital: Voluntary Associations and Institutions in Comparative Perspective.* New York: Palgrave.

___, & Dietlind Stolle, eds. 2003. *Generating Social Capital: Voluntary Associations and Institutions in Comparative Perspective.* New York: Palgrave.

___, & Koen Pelleriaux. 1998. "Compulsory Voting in Belgium: An Application of the Lijphart Thesis." *Electoral Studies* 17 (4): 419-24.

Inglehart, Ronald. 1997. *Modernization and Postmodernization.* Princeton, NJ: Princeton University Press.

___. 1999. "Postmodernization Erodes Respect for Authority, But Increases Support for Democracy," in Pippa Norris, ed., *Critical Citizens.* Oxford: Oxford University Press.

Inglehart, Ronald, & Wayne Baker. 2000. "Modernization, Cultural Change, and the Persistence of Traditional Values." *American Sociological Review* 65 (1): 19-51.

Jackman, Robert, & Ross Miller. 1995. "Voter Turnout in the Industrial Democracies during the 1980s." *Comparative Political Studies* 27: 467-92.

Klingemann, Hans-Dieter. 1999. "Mapping Political Support in the 1990s," in Pippa Norris, ed., *Critical Citizens.* Oxford: Oxford University Press.

Klingemann, Hans-Dieter, & Dieter Fuchs, eds. 1995. *Citizens and the State.* Oxford: Oxford University Press.

Ladd, Everett. 1996. "The Data Just Don't Show Erosion of America's 'Social Capital'." *The Public Perspective* (June): 5-22.

___. 1999. *The Ladd Report.* New York: Free Press.

Lane, Robert. 2000. *The Loss of Happiness in Market Democracies.* New Haven, CT: Yale University Press.

Lichterman, Paul. 1996. *The Search for Political Community.* Cambridge: Cambridge University Press.

Lijphart, Arend. 1997. "Unequal Participation: Democracy's Unresolved Dilemma." *American Political Science Review* 91(1): 1-14.

Listhaug, O. 1995. "The Dynamics of Trust in Politicians," in Klingemann, H. D., & Fuchs, D., eds., *Citizens and the State.* Oxford: Oxford University Press.

Lowndes, Vivien. 2000. "Women and Social Capital: A Comment on Hall's 'Social Capital in Britain'." *British Journal of Political Science* 30 (3): 533-7.

McDonald, M., & S. Popkin. 2001. "The Myth of the Vanishing Voter." *American Political Science Review* 95 (4): 963-74.

Merton, Robert, & Alice Kitt. 1950. "Contributions to the Theory of Reference Group Behavior," in Robert Merton & Paul Lazarsfeld, eds., *Continuities in Social Research.* Glencoe: Free Press.

Mutz, Diana, & J. Mondak. 1998. "Democracy at Work: Contributions of the Workplace Toward a Public Sphere." Paper presented at the Annual Meeting of the Midwest Political Science Association Meeting, Chicago. 23-25April.

Nie, Norman, Jane Junn, & Kenneth Stehlik-Barry. 1996. *Education and Democratic Citizenship in America.* Chicago: University of Chicago Press.

___, Sidney Verba, & John Petrocik. 1979. *The Changing American Voter.* Cambridge: Harvard University Press.

Norris, Pippa, ed. 1999. *Critical Citizens: Global Support for Democratic Government.* Oxford: Oxford University Press.

___. 2002. *Democratic Phoenix. Reinventing Political Activism.* Cambridge: Cambridge University Press.

Nye, Joseph, Philip Zelikow, & David King, eds. 1997. *Why People Don't Trust Government.* Cambridge, MA: Harvard University Press.

Paxton, Pamela. 1999. "Is Social Capital Declining in the U.S.?" *American Journal of Sociology* 105 (1): 88-127.

Pharr, Susan, & Robert Putnam, eds. 2000. *Disaffected Democracies.* Princeton, NJ: Princeton University Press.

Portes, Alejandro. 1998. "Social Capital: Its Origins and Applications in Modern Sociology." *Annual Review of Sociology* 24: 1-24.

Putnam, Robert. 1993. *Making Democracy Work: Civic Traditions in Modern Italy.* Princeton, NJ: Princeton University Press.

___. 1995. "Bowling Alone: America's Declining Social Capital." *Journal of Democracy* 6 (1): 65-78.

___. 2000. *Bowling Alone: The Collapse and Revival of American Community.* New York: Simon & Schuster.

Renooy, Piet. 1996. "De wonderbaarlijke continuïteit van het vrijwillig initiatief binnen de verzorgingsstaat," in Mark Bovens & Anton Hemerijck, eds., *Het verhaal van de moraal.* Amsterdam: Boom Meppel.

Rothstein, Bo, & Dietlind Stolle. 2003. "Social Capital, Impartiality, and the Welfare State: An Institutional Approach," in M. Hooghe & D. Stolle, eds., *Generating Social Capital: Voluntary Associations and Institutions in Comparative Perspective.* New York: Palgrave.

Sandel, Michael. 1996. *Democracy's Discontent.* Cambridge: Harvard University Press.

Schmitt, Hermann, & Sören Holmberg. 1995. "Political Parties in Decline?" in Hans-Dieter Klingemann & Dieter Fuchs, eds., *Citizens and the State.* Oxford: Oxford University Press.

Schudson, Michael. 1996. "What If Civic Life Didn't Die?" *The American Prospect* (March): 17-28.

Skocpol, Theda, & Fiorina Morris, eds. 1999. *Civic Engagement in American Democracy.* Washington, DC: Brookings Institution.

Stolle, Dietlind. 2000. "Onderzoek naar sociaal kapitaal," in Marc Hooghe, ed., *Sociaal kapitaal en democratie.* Leuven: Acco.

___, & Christian Welzel. 2000. "Social Capital, Communitarianism and Human Development." Paper presented at the Annual Meeting of the American Political Science Association, Washington, D.C. 31 August-3 September.

Tarrow, Sidney. 1994. *Power in Movement.* Cambridge: Cambridge University Press.

Teixeira, Ruy. 1992. *The Disappearing American Voter.* Washington, D.C.: Brookings Institution.

Thomassen, Jacques, Cees Aarts, & Henk van der Kolk, eds. 2000. *Politieke veranderingen in Nederland, 1971-1998.* Den Haag: SDU.

Topf, Richard. 1995. "Beyond Electoral Participation," in Hans-Dieter Klingemann & Dieter Fuchs, eds., *Citizens and the State.* Oxford: Oxford University Press.

Verba, Sidney, Kay Lehman Schlozman, & Henry Brady. 1995. *Voice and Equality.* Cambridge, MA: Harvard University Press.

Walzer, Michael. 1990. "The Communitarian Critique of Liberalism." *Political Theory* 18 (1): 6-23.

Wattenberg, Martin. 1996. *The Decline of American Political Parties.* Cambridge, MA: Harvard University Press.

Welzel, Christian, & Ronald Inglehart. 1999. *Analyzing Democratic Change and Stability.* Berlin: Wissenschaftszentrum Berlin.

Wuthnow, Robert. 1998. *Loose Connections: Joining Together in America's Fragmented Communities.* Cambridge, MA: Harvard University Press.

Conclusion

Andreas Follesdal, Michele Micheletti, Dietlind Stolle

Good political consumerism gives citizens the opportunity to revel in material goods while practicing good moral conduct. It allows citizens to express themselves as self-oriented, lifestyle social actors and simultaneously express their other-regarding political commitments about global mutual respect and personal integrity. It represents a win-win situation for workers, consumers, producers, and the environment in a world often characterized by win-lose and lose-lose choices. Consumers can be seen as key actors in the merging, marrying, navigating, and bridging of morality with markets.

Our volume shows the importance of the phenomenon of political consumerism for political history and for politics in the world today. For scholars, political consumerism is an emerging significant area for academic study. For activists, the market is a site for contentious politics, and consumer choice a tool for political progress. For policymakers, political consumerism is an interesting development, which combines government regulation and voluntary compliance to form new regulatory tools. This concluding chapter brings together themes regarding political consumerism as a site for ethics and action. The chapter offers answers to central questions on the differences between historical and contemporary forms of political consumerism, the role that consumers individually and collectively can play in crafting unregulated global economic space into a moral framework for action and choice, and the kinds of demands that both scholars and practitioners should consider placing on political consumerist actors and institutions. This chapter also elucidates how the study of political consumerism challenges current concepts in the social sciences, particularly political participation.

Consumer Choice as Political Action—Then and Now

Consumers have used, and use, their consumer choice to vent their political frustrations and exhibit their political values. In so doing, political consumerism sets and shapes the agenda of politics. At times, agenda-setting happens quite explicitly and intentionally. Media and political actors respond directly to the outrage expressed in political consumerist actions. In other cases, political consumerism plays a more subtle agenda-setting role, by encouraging citizens to give thought to the broader implications of their purchasing choices. Citizens are urged to consider the consumer choices that they previously have taken for granted in a more reflective way. When this happens, political consumerism raises consciousness by putting previously invisible or neglected issues on the individual consumer's cognitive agenda. More research is necessary to distinguish the differences between consumer choice as an agenda-setting political action and purchases that take place in an unreflective manner. Some of the previous chapters concluded that we need to understand the motivations and interests behind the choice for or against a certain product to establish when consumerism is political and when it is not.

Although there are important exceptions in both history and the present, it appears that political consumerism is motivated, at least partially, by the identities citizens hold and by their interests in others' living conditions. Historically, mobilization of racial, religious, and ethnic identities played a role in influencing consumer choices. Today's political consumerism in democracies is more oriented towards the plight of other people and common resources, than the plight of oneself or one's own group. Contemporary political consumerism is more transnational and global than many of its historical relatives. The issue of global human rights and global ecology, which are the focus of several of our chapters, are two good examples.

In recent decades political consumerism has been used as a strategy to put issues of human rights, democracy, and sustainability on the global political agenda. Political consumers aim at sensitizing people to the role that transnational corporations play in these policy regimes. Among the issues targeted are corporate practices regarding workers' rights, the human rights violations committed by their subcontractors, environmental problems caused by their manufacturing practices, the effect of their presence on local communities, as well as the lax enforcement of human rights by governments in the countries that have granted multinational corporations permission to operate within their state boundaries. Citizens have even come to use political consumerism to demand enforcement of existing international human rights norms and environmental standards in the absence of global instruments of formal governance. Thus, the contemporary aims of political consumerism are tied to ambitions regarding the emergence of a new global political order.

Political Consumerism: A New Form of Political Participation?

One of the important questions that arise in the context of political consumerism is whether it is a political phenomenon and a potentially new form of political participation. An answer to this question takes its point of departure in the strength of economic globalization and the weakness of political globalization. Citizens mobilize against corporations as well as financial institutions, which have reacted swiftly to the new and unregulated opportunities that have opened up for them. They are voicing their dissatisfaction against what they consider the negative aspects of business practices in the global marketplace. Unlike the past, their criticism does not concern only the effects of business in a particular country. Rather it is general criticism of what they believe are global corporate wrongdoings. Citizens' expressions of concern are also swifter and more coordinated than previously, because the development of information technology puts political anger directly online globally. Such immediate information flows can instantly mobilize large groups of the population for political purposes.

The study of political consumerism, as well as its interpretation as a political phenomenon, both challenge and question how we conventionally conceive of political participation in three important ways. First, political consumers focus on new targets of their political actions; second, mobilization for political consumerism blurs the public and private divide, and finally, a related consequence is that political consumerism constitutes a truly individualized form of participation. We discuss each of these challenges in turn.

Regular acts of voting, membership in political and economic organizations, and explicit political discussion have long been seen as good measurements of citizens' involvement in politics. These involvements directly target governmental institutions and policies and the political process *from within* the political system. Political consumerism is different. Although political consumers may target government institutions and policies, they use market-based tools as boycotts to communicate their dissatisfaction. Examples are the boycott of South Africa and French wines. In other cases and more frequently, their target lies outside the conventional political realm, is not directed at national or supra-national governments, and instead focuses its criticisms and efforts most prominently on market institutions and the market as a site of politics. The reason is that citizens perceive their governments as powerless regarding, for example, international labor regulations and the setting of environmental standards. The potential solutions are sought through corporations that are expected to take initiatives, and ideally through international institutions and supranational governmental regulations that observe, monitor, and sanction labor, environmental, and product standards. These new, political targets are a challenge to conventional conceptions of political participation.

Second, political consumerism is, unlike other forms of political participation, a very private political act. Shopping and choosing products is part of our everyday lives and has usually been considered an activity of the private sphere. That such a private act can have political motivations or political consequences challenges conventional views about political participation, as most other forms of participation exhibit a certain public dimension. Even though voting is a private act itself, it is a public phenomenon and is publicly organized. Joining a public rally or meeting takes place in a sphere conventionally described as public. Even signing a petition brings one in contact with political activists. Yet, shopping for certain products lacks many of these public dimensions and therefore blurs the public and private divide in politics.

Finally, and this is closely related to the previous point, political consumerism is an individualized act of involvement. Only very few citizens, who care about political consumer issues, also see it as an explicit collective political tool. Moreover, the modalities of political consumerism are extremely flexible as consumers can, completely freely, determine how, when, and where they act as political consumers or as just consumers concerned about taste, material quality, and price. Whereas voting and joining political meetings are determined to take place on a certain day and time, and the signing of petitions is restricted to a certain format, political consumerism is different as it is fairly independent of time, space, and type of consumer choice. It can easily fit into many people's lifestyle and can be easily adapted. This level of individualization is an entirely new aspect of political participation, and therefore challenges it as a concept. In short, since political consumerism occurs outside the classic governmental-citizen relationship, breaks through public-private divides, and captures a very individualized political type of involvement, it will play an important role in shaping the concept of political participation.

Securing Risk Society through Political Consumerism

Consumers are also key actors in designing institutions for handling repercussions from the developments of industrialization, globalization, and individualization. These processes have created problems with governability that make many single nation-states flounder with insufficient problem-solving ability. Citizens individually and collectively find themselves obliged to step forth as active participants. Widespread environmental and human rights threats make consumers consider how to demand safer economic and political systems, and to take greater responsibility for their own protection. They see no other choice.

Consumers can be privately oriented risk-handlers as mothers, or increasingly fathers, who seek to protect their family by shopping only for ecological products. They can also seek to create publicly oriented institutions to establish criteria for ensuring a safer or less risky world. Political consumerist institutions, such as forest stewardship certification, eco-labeling schemes, as well as fair trade and organic food labels, are foremost examples here. The studies included in this volume show that labeling schemes enhance political participation in three important ways. First, they put issues of postmodern risks on the global political economic agenda and, thereby, create public opinion, which is a key to collective and individualized political participation. Second, they give consumers information to enable them to make conscious choices about the kinds of global risks wrought by consumer products. Third, they can monitor the performance of global industry on a number of postmodern risk factors and, thereby, carry out an increasingly important function of output performance evaluation. Thus, labeling schemes help to influence and shape the quality and style of the production process as firms with successful schemes encourage their utilization by other corporations. In sum, political consumerist institutions can be said to enhance the informational bases for action and accountability.

The institutions have not been in place a sufficient amount of time to evaluate whether they, in fact, have developed into a new, political economic global order. Neither can an assessment of their value for global democratic development be undertaken at this time. Yet, it is clear that the use of information technology by these schemes, through newsletters and informative home pages, facilitates communication and contacts among geographically dispersed consumers. The newly established political consumerist institutions are, in an important sense, watchdogs for sustainable development, human rights, and social dumping. Due to their presence, it is becoming more difficult for multinational corporations to hide questionable practices in less powerful parts of the world. The international efforts of standard-setting regarding human rights, development, and workers' rights are having important impacts, even in the absence of formal mechanisms of enforcement. They offer ethical citizens and consumers alternatives to industry-based, lax standards regarding the environment and citizen rights globally. And as our chapters show, they are having an effect on global business. Businesses have responded in three ways. They have explicitly fought against the establishment of political consumerist institutions, developed their own schemes when challenged by the bite of consumer-initiated ones, and sometimes sought certification by consumer-initiated schemes.

We draw three conclusions here. First, political consumerism shows how market-based, new regulatory forms (i.e., soft law) can be a constructive force in our ever more risky world, but its impact is yet to be determined. Second, political consumerism is developing into an international regime in its own right. Third, given the growing significance of political consumerism globally, and particularly the growth of its institutions, it is becoming increasingly more urgent for scholars to evaluate its legitimacy, democratic and otherwise. We must give serious consideration to the kinds of legitimacy requirements and criteria that should be used for assessing political consumerist actions and institutions. We need to distinguish constructive from unconstructive, and even illegitimate forms of political consumerism, so that activists, concerned citizens, and general consumers have guidelines for assessing the politics behind products in a broader, contextual fashion. What may appear, at first glance, to be a good consumer deed, may upon further reflection show itself to be reeking with xenophobia and causing negative side effects. Our chapters offer poignant examples of how political consumerism can go wrong.

Lessons for Scholars and Practitioners Evaluating Political Consumerism

The knowledge gathered in this first anthology on political consumerism indicates that, while the phenomenon is hardly new, it is not yet well understood as an instrument of change. Systematic study of when and why political consumerism works, and when it does not, is beyond the present volume. Nevertheless, our chapters teach lessons about the phenomenon of political consumerism. We venture that political consumerism is more legitimate and effective, that it commands compliance and better achieves its stated final objectives when:

- political consumerist action is focused on clear targets and that its general aim can be realized by the company targeted by the action. This means that the targeted company must be able to respond constructively to credible threats of political consumerism. If companies suspect that they cannot avoid criticism, no matter how they change their policies or practices, threats may have little impact. Clear demands, standards, and thresholds are required on the part of political, consumerist actors;

- the demands placed by political consumers are likely to alleviate the problem on which they focus. The credibility of any political consumerist action will suffer, if the demands put on the targeted company are unlikely to achieve a more desired state of affairs;

- the threat of consumer action is credible. Such credibility is enhanced, if action is easy for the consumers to participate in with little self-sacrifice. This occurs when consumers can participate in a political, consumerist action by replacing one brand with a good substitute at little extra cost;

- the costs to the target company are sufficiently high in terms of sales, image, or other important values. If a drop in sales is the most important value, this will require the mobilization of a critical mass of consumers and, thus, skillful political consumerist leadership. If reputation or image is the targeted value, media messages, showing how the targeted company violates broadly shared values, need to be formulated carefully. Vulnerable companies are those whose leadership or mission statements clearly share political consumerist values, who are well-known to mass consumers, and whose marketing strategies portray the company as possessing benevolent values or as carrying messages that can easily be used against them in a political, consumerist fashion;

- the organizations involved in the action have credibility even under scrutiny. The standard-setting and monitoring bodies should not be easily accused of mixed motives or flawed data. Concerned consumers and citizens must not be misled by competing, fraudulent standards and misinformation on business practice on the part of political consumerist institutions. They must therefore have transparent processes, clearly stated criteria for certification, and mechanisms of accountability. Calls for boycotts must be based on facts that are not easily disputed, and judgments that are considered reasonable. Thus, there should be clear symbolic links between the objectionable practice and the target for action, to foster compliance by consumers. Also, political consumer activity must safeguard against unauthorized actions by individual consumers likely to detract from the agreed-upon cause. Most importantly, once a boycott action or media campaign has reached its desired goals of change in production practices, it is important that it is stopped and that participating consumers "reward" the pro-active company for implementing better standards for its products or production processes. This requires, firstly, that information about the constructive change of a company's production practice be publicized as widely as possible and, secondly, that the organizations engaged in political consumerist activism can convince their followers to reward the pro-active company by ending their actions against it;

- the action must not render any vulnerable party worse off. The demands of political consumerism must be put in a broader political and social context that considers the needs and rights of all stakeholders. Protests should preferably not lead companies to leave a country that violates human, labor, and environmental rights if the result is likely to lead to further unemployment or abuse.

In sum, it is obvious from the lessons learned in this first book that influential political consumerist action requires a combination of various factors. Successful efforts need consumer support and loyalty. This requires considerable leadership skills on the part of the action organizers. Efforts are effective when they have tangible outcomes, that is, contribute to solving the problems focused upon in the actions. Here it is important that both leaders of actions, as well as consumers, understand the capability sphere of the targets of political consumerism. Criticism of corporate policy must include suggestions for change that offer constructive ideas about outcome effects. Criticism must be put in the geographical, political, social, and cultural context of the problem. Otherwise outcries against child labor, insufficient workers' rights, and weak environmental protection may be criticized for reflecting our Western penchants, and for lacking sensitivity for the needs and wants of the people who need protection. This problem seems particularly acute, as political consumerism has become more transnational and is used to affect the conditions of people in far away countries.

Political Consumerism's Potential for Global Change

The lessons have clarified some of the crucial issues in assessing the legitimacy and strength of political consumerist actions and institutions. It is now time to assess the limits of political consumerism as a market-based political tool for global change. A basic issue is the breadth and strength of political consumerism as a means of change. We point out in our introduction to this volume that some scholars view consumerism as the answer, or a partial answer, to the woes of the world, while others hold a more skeptical view. The chapters offer sound advice for an initial assessment of the potentials of political consumerism globally.

First, they show that political consumerism is reformist rather than revolutionary in character. Although more research is necessary, it appears that most political consumers accept globalization and consumer society as a fact of life. They accept the structural foundation of global capitalism and the enticements of material consumer society. What they want to do is modify their negative side effects. This makes political consumerism less satisfactory as a political tool for many anti-globalists and people highly critical of market capitalism in general.

Second, many political consumerist actions target specific problems and specific market actors. Political consumerism's strength is the opportunity it provides for citizens to work with central political problems of global magnitude in a hands-on, everyday way. This is part of its attractiveness for people, who do not want to or cannot put much effort into political participation. Yet, a weakness here is that successful political consumerism does not necessarily imply successful solution to problems. As we indicated earlier, successful actions may lead business to bring their own problematic practice to an end, but this does not necessarily improve the plight of those previously suffering from bad business practice. Ending child labor does not ensure that the children, formally working in factories, are now attending schools and living a good life. In fact, it has been shown on many occasions that the alternative to bad business practice is a worsened standard of living for workers and their families. We conclude that political consumerism can be understood, at best, as a temporary cure for deep problems that require the help of international law, civil society, and the state for their solution.

Third, it is important to distinguish negative political consumerism (boycotts) from positive political consumerism (buycotts, labeling schemes, monitoring institutions) when assessing its strengths and weaknesses as a force for global change. As our chapters point out, boycotts tend to be contentious in nature and somewhat instable as tools for long-term change. This characteristic can preclude cooperative solutions and constructive dialogue among all stakeholders, and particularly between consumers and producers. Also, boycotts tend to be one-shot actions that have difficulty in auditing performance over time. They are weapons that are difficult to wield, in the sense that boycott leaders find it hard to exercise authoritative leadership over their dispersed followers. Yet we also know that boycotts can be a first step for more long-term political consumerist involvements. For instance, they can function as a trial balloon to survey consumer interest for other kinds of political consumerism as represented by labeling schemes.

Some of the negative effects of boycotts are avoided in buycotts, which seek to build institutions that gain legitimacy from all the stakeholders, monitor practice over time, and have as their goal incremental, progressive improvement. In fact, an important change in the phenomenon of political consumerism over the years is the increase in positive political consumerism. It appears that concerned citizens and consumers now realize that boycotts are defective as tools for change. They are seeking the development of more stable institutions engaged in fact finding, standard setting, and coordinating sanctions through a variety of labeling schemes.

The conclusion is that positive political consumerism is a sign of our postmodern times (cf. Bauman 1995). It might serve as part of the solution to the dilemmas implicit in globalization, individualization, and the postmaterialization of industrial society. It represents the creativity of consumers and citizens, individually and collectively, in confronting new situations and establishing normative control of global life. Yet, this postmodern reflexivity is problematic in itself. It opens up opportunities for centralized rule-makers as the state and international governmental organizations to avoid taking responsibility for our common well-being and encourages governmental responsibility-floating. This occurs when national, regional, and international governments can excuse themselves, or rationalize their non-action, by pointing to the initiatives taken by market-based individuals and institutions in solving problems. The problem is that these individuals and institutions presently lack the kind of genuine political foundation necessary for good structural governance. They are based on "beyond compliance" strategies that only work when actors are encouraged to participate in them. An important measure of performance, which needs more study, is whether they can be successful and effective even though they lack teeth in the form of hard laws and "command and control" politics, which not only set up normative practices through regulatory politics but also have legal power to enforce policies and sanction their offenders. The question is whether new, transnational, market-based regulatory policy tools, building upon agreement among all shareholders, can become a moral framework of the global market. Can they, as argued by Adam Smith in his insistence on government regulation of the market, instill moral sentiments in globalized market capitalism?

Reference

Bauman, Zymunt. 1995. *Life in Fragments: Essays in Postmodern Morality*. Oxford: Blackwell Publishers.

Contributors

Graeme Auld, Ph.D. student, Yale University School of Forestry and Environmental Studies, New Haven, Connecticut.

W. Lance Bennett, professor of political science and Ruddick C. Lawrence Professor of Communication, and director, Center for Communication and Civic Engagement, University of Washington, Seattle.

Lars Brückner was a research associate in the Department of Politics and International Studies at the University of Hull, UK. He currently works as an advisor in environmental affairs in Brussels.

Benjamin Cashore, assistant professor, Sustainable Forest Policy chair and director, Program on Forest Certification, Global Institute of Sustainable Forestry, Yale School of Forestry and Environmental Studies, New Haven, Connecticut.

Franck Cochoy, professor of sociology, University of Toulouse II/ CERTOP-CNRS, France.

Andreas Follesdal, professor of philosophy at the Centre for Human Rights, University of Oslo, and research professor at ARENA, Norway.

Monroe Friedman, professor of psychology at Eastern Michigan University.

Jørgen Goul Andersen, professor of political sociology, Department of Economics, Politics and Public Administration, Aalborg University, Denmark.

Cheryl Greenberg, professor of history at Trinity College, Hartford, Connecticut.

Bente Halkier, sociologist and political scientist, associate professor in Communication at Roskilde University, Denmark.

Marc Hooghe, assistant professor, Department of Political Science, Free University of Brussels, Belgium.

Andrew Jordan, Centre for Social and Economic Research on the Global Environment, University of East Anglia, Norwich, UK.

Paul Kennedy, reader in sociology and global studies, Manchester Metropolitan University, UK.

Michele Micheletti, associate professor of political science, Stockholm University, Sweden.

Deanna Newsom, program associate, TREES Program, Rainforest Alliance, Richmond, Vermont.

Jonah Peretti, director of R&D at Eyebeam and assistant adjunct professor at New York University.

Dietlind Stolle, assistant professor of political science at McGill University, Quebec, Montreal, Canada.

Mette Tobiasen, assistant professor of political sociology, Department of Economics, Politics and Public Administration, Aalborg University, Denmark.

David Vogel, professor, Haas School of Business, Department of Political Science, University of California, Berkeley.

Rüdiger K. W. Wurzel, lecturer, Department of Politics and International Studies, University of Hull, UK.

Anthony R. Zito, lecturer, Department of Politics, University of Newcastle, Newcastle, UK.

Index